CONTENTS

4

INTRODUCTION

Grilling is a great way to cook delicious and healthy meals as well as enjoy the outdoors. For many people, grilling food is also very beneficial as it can help lower calorie intake thus may help with weight loss. While grilling does not necessarily remove all fats from meat, it allows extra fat to melt and drip off and not get absorbed. Moreover, grilling also helps seal in vitamins and minerals, unlike other cooking methods. However, many people opt not to use this cooking method because of the misnomer that the food that they are going to cook will be limited to charred meats. Fortunately, grilling will never restrict you to cooking meat alone. With the right griller, you will also be able to bake, broil, and even make casseroles. This is where the Pit Boss Wood Pellet Grill comes in.

Why Pit Boss Wood Pellet Grill?

The Pit Boss Wood Pellet Grill is the latest buzz in the BBQ world and it uses wood pellets to grill your food thus adding extra kick, flavor, and dimension to your food. Unlike conventional charcoal grills, this particular grill requires you to use compressed pellets and feed them into the grill's fire pot to heat the grill to the desired temperature. Having said this, wood pellet grills allow you more control over the temperature settings of your grill. This prevents you from charring or overcooking your good. Plus, you don't need to babysit your grill at all times compared to your usual charcoal grill. Since you don't need to watch over the grill at all times, you now have more time for entertaining. Isn't this what grilling is all about?

Benefits Of Pit Boss Wood Pellet Grill

If you are contemplating on replacing your old charcoal grill, then now is the time to do it. The Pit Boss Wood Pellet Grill comes with a lot of benefits that you will never enjoy with your conventional charcoal grill.

Effortless ignition: To light your wood pellet grill, you don't need accelerants like lighter fluid to start a fire. Simply prime the fire pot and ignite the grill with a mere touch of a button. The intuitive controller of the grill will take care of everything for you.

Even heat: Wood pellet grills provide generally even heat throughout every nook and cranny of the grill. This means that you can place your food anywhere in the grill and everything will cook at the same time. It comes with a PID (Proportional, Integral, Derivative) Controller that adds complexity to the temperature control method. With this controller, you will not only have a better control temperature range, but you also have the capacity to monitor the smoke produced, track your pellet consumption, and monitor your meat without the need to open the grill.

Wireless connectivity: The Pit Boss Wood Pellet Grill is a smart kitchen device that will make your life so much easier! It comes with a phone app that you can control via Wi-Fi or Bluetooth so that you can control the grill from your smartphone even if you are out on a grocery run.

Great smoke flavor: Wood BBQ pellets come in a myriad of flavors from hickory, pecan, maple, cherry, and many others. You also have the freedom to mix different flavors to make your food more interesting. These wood pellets are not only great in adding another layer of flavor to your meats but they will definitely make your baked goods more interesting.

Comes with pre-programmed cooking cycles: To make your grilling easier, the Pit Boss Wood Pellet Grill comes with pre-programmed smoking cycles. This removes the guesswork when cooking different kinds of foods.

Cooks all kinds of foods: Wood pellet grills are capable of cooking just about all kinds of foods. You can grill, BBQ, smoke, bake, broil, and even sear. It is one of the few kitchen devices that you can truly call an all-in-one cooking machine.

Why The Pit Boss Wood Pellet Grill Is Your Better Option

First introduced in the market in 1999, the Pit Boss Wood Pellet Grill has been around for more than tw decades to make grilling easier and more convenient to many people. While it is still a fairly new bra compared to its older counterparts, this brand of wood pellet grill is very dependable. Although reviews onli would put the Pit Boss Wood Pellet Grill second to its biggest competitor, Traeger Grill, in terms of size a portability, it is my firm belief that there are still so many benefits that make the Pit Boss Wood Pellet G worthy of your time and bucks.

- **More affordable:** If you are looking for a line of wood pellet grills that are affordable, the Pit Boss Wo Pellet Grill comes with affordable options. You don't need to shell out a lot of money to buy this kitch appliance. Their wood pellet grills have a price range of $390 to $2499 depending on the capacity of the gr This is an extremely cheaper option compared to other wood pellet grills that start at $500 and above.
- **Simpler interface and parts:** The manufacturer of the Pit Boss Wood Pellet Grill banks on simplicity its main selling point. It comes with an intuitive user interface that makes it so easy to control. Moreover, it al comes with fewer parts that make it very easy to assemble.
- **Uses relevant technologies:** Modern Pit Boss Wood Pellet Grills come with relevant technology. The include remote settings using Bluetooth and Wi-Fi specifically on its Platinum line of grills.
- **Built-in working station:** The Pit Boss Pellet Grill comes with a built-in working station including bu in tool hooks and a solid side shelf. This makes it a perfect kitchen appliance that you can put in any part of yo outdoor space. When it comes to movability, it may not be as portable as other brands of wood pellet grills bu comes with locking caster wheels that will allow you to push the grill anywhere and keep it in place. reinforced leg design makes it a sturdy wood grill for heavy-duty cooking.

Using the Pit Boss Wood Pellet Grill
Wood Pellet Guide For Grilling

Understanding your many options for wood pellets for grilling is crucial for you to maximize your cooki experience with our Pit Boss Wood Pellet Grill. In fact, choosing the right wood pellet is the heart and soul cooking with your wood pellet grill. Wood pellets are basically the main fuel source of the grill. They are ma from 100% natural hardwood that is dried, grounds, and manipulated to equally sized pellets using extrer heat and pressure. There are two types of wood pellets that are available in the market: heating pellets and foc grade pellets. Heating pellets are made from wood that is not meant for smoking your meats and they are ma together with glue and other additives that are not good for your food. Examples of heating pellets include the made from spruce and pine.

Thus, when buying wood pellets for your Pit Boss Wood Pellet Grill, make sure to look for the food-grade pell as they do not contain binders and additives. Moreover, they also impart interesting flavor to your food maki them more interesting and delicious. Food-grade pellets include mesquite, hickory, cherry, pecan, apple, o and alder. And so, the proverbial question *which food-grade pellet goes well with what food?"*

- **Competition blend:** Comes with a smoky and sweet aromatic tang. It is made from a blend of hicko maple, and cherry thus it comes with a soft fruity undertone. This is perfect for beef, pork, chicken, fish, veggi fruits, and desserts.
- **Hickory:** Comes with a rich bacon-like flavor and is great for roasts and smoking meats.
- **Mesquite:** This wood pellet comes with a strong aroma with a hint of tangy and spicy flavor. This i great wood pellet for those who enjoy Tex-Mex cuisines.
- **Apple:** This comes with a mildly sweet and smoky flavor and is great for pork and baking desserts.

Classic: Comes with a bold blend of mesquite, hickory, and pecan that imparts a full-bodied flavor that 1 bring out the best in any chicken, pork, veggies, and seafood.

Fruit: This blend of wood pellets imparts an all-natural fruity undertone thus making it great for pork 1 baking. Surprisingly, it also works well with poultry and seafood.

Charcoal blend: Comes with a bold aroma of oak and a smoky hint of charcoal. This is a great blend for ef, pork, game, and poultry.

1en it comes to choosing the right wood pellet for your grill, make sure that you opt for quality brand pellets. tting a cheaply made brand will not only ruin your food but can also damage the inner workings of your pellet ll. Fortunately, the Pit Boss Wood Pellet Grill has its own brand of wood pellets to choose from.

illing Tips For Beginners

lling and smoking your food using the Pit Boss Wood Pellet Grill is no rocket science. However, if it is your st time using a wood pellet grill, below are great tips that you can help as a beginner.

Know your meat: Different kinds of meats require different grilling settings. When choosing meat for lling, you need to know the composition (fat to muscle ratio, cartilage, bones) of your meat, color, and texture. ferent cuts of meats need to be treated in different ways. For instance, lean cuts such as chicken breasts dry t easily compared with red meat.

Always brine your meat: To impart flavor and moisture to your meat, you can brine your meat in vance prior to grilling or smoking.

Do not flip your meat all the time: The Pit Boss Wood Pellet Grill is unlike your open charcoal grill. pping the meat means that you need to open the grill and this will reduce the internal temperature inside the oking chamber. Only flip the meat once. In fact, you don't even need to do it since all sides can cook evenly.

Get the right accessories: The Pit Boss Wood Pellet Grill comes with many types of accessories that you 1 use to maximize your grilling and smoking experience. You can get skillet pans, side shelf, iron griddle, iron aster, meat hooks.

arting Up Your Grill

rting up the Pit Boss Wood Pellet Grill is as simple as plugging it in and turning your temperature dial. While ounds as easy as it seems, there are some things that you need to take note of.

Place fuel in the hopper: The fuel of your grill is the wood pellet. Make sure that you have at least 2 unds of pellets for every hour of smoking. If you are going to grill, you need 4 pounds for every hour of fast lling.

Set the grill to smoke and open the lid: Open the hood of the grill and set it to smoke. This is an portant step as it gives the igniter the chance to light before feeding more wood pellets. Oxygen is needed for igniter to light. If the lid is closed, it will not line up and the pellets will merely line up in the pot and may intually spill over the cooking chamber. This usually takes about three minutes to light up.

Watch out for thick smoke: When you notice that there is thick smoke billowing out of the grill, this ans that your pot has caught and that your pellets are burning. Fortunately, the Pit Boss Wood Pellet Grill can this problem on its own. Allow the smoke to billow out from the grill for 4 minutes and it will eventually sipate.

Crank up and start grilling: Once the pot catches, the convection fan will start blowing on the flame ide the grill. You can then crank up the temperature so that you can start grilling. You can close the lid so that heat will climb to the desired temperature.

BAKING RECIPES

Mexican Cornbread Casserole

Servings: 6
Cooking Time: 30 Minutes
Ingredients:
- 1 Lb Beef, Ground
- 1 15Oz Drained Black Beans, Can
- 1 Box Corn Muffin Mix
- 1 15Oz Enchilada Sauce, Can
- 1 Onion, Chopped
- 1 15Oz Drained Pinto Beans, Can

Directions:
1. Start Grill at 300 degrees with flame broiler open.
2. Mix corn muffin mix according to directions.
3. Place cast iron skillet over flame broiler and heat for a few minutes, leaving Grill lid open.
4. Add onion and ground beef/sausage to skillet and break up
5. Cook until meat is done about 5 to 10 minutes.
6. Add both cans of beans, and enchilada sauce, stir to combine.
7. Bring mixture to a simmer.
8. Carefully close flame broiler and turn Grill up to 400 degrees.
9. Spread prepared corn muffin mix over top of meat and bean mixture and bake for 15 minutes until cornbread mixture is lightly browned.
10. Let sit 15 minutes before serving.

Whole Roasted Duck

Servings: 5
Cooking Time: 150 Minutes
Ingredients:
- 2 Tbsp Baking Soda
- 1 Tbsp Chinese Five Spice
- 1 Whole Thawed Duck
- 1 Granny Smith Apple, Peel, Core And Dice
- 1 Quartered Orange, Slice
- 2 Tbsp Pit Boss Champion Chicken Seasoning, Divided

Directions:
1. Wash the duck under cold running water, inside and out, then pat dry with paper towel.
2. Mix Champion Chicken seasoning and Chinese Five Spice together. Mix with baking soda for extra crispy skin. Season the duck, inside and out.
3. Tuck the orange and apple slices in the cavity.
4. When you're ready to cook, turn your Pit Boss grill to smoke mode, let the fire catch and then set to 300 degrees F (149 degrees C) to preheat.
5. Add duck to a roasting pan or directly onto the grill grate.
6. Roast for 2 – 2 ½ hours or until the skin is brown and crispy and the internal temperature of the thigh is 160 degrees F (71 degrees C).
7. Add foil loosely over the duck and let rest for 15 minutes.

Smoked Lemon Sweet Tea

Servings: 6 - 8
Cooking Time: 60 Minutes
Ingredients:
- 8 Black Tea Bags
- 4 Cups Boiling Water
- 2 Cups Ice
- 8 Lemons
- 2 Cups Sugar
- 2 Cups Water

Directions:
1. Place the tea bags in a heat-safe pitcher. Bring 4 Cups o water to a boil and pour over tea bags. Let steep for 5-10 minutes. Remove tea bags and set pitcher aside to cool.
2. Turn on your Pit Boss and set to smoke mode. Combine cups of sugar and 2 cups water in a small aluminum pan. Smoke for about 45 minutes, stirring occasionally, or until t mixture reduces to a thick, simple syrup. Remove from the g and let it cool.
3. Fire up your Pit Boss to 450°F and open the flame broil If using a charcoal or gas grill, set heat to high.
4. Cut the lemons in half and sear over the flame broiler until charred, about 7 minutes. Remove from grill and set as to cool.
5. Juice the lemons into a medium bowl. Pour lemon juice through a metal strainer into the tea pitcher to remove seed and pulp.
6. Pour the cooled simple syrup into pitcher and stir until fully incorporated with tea and lemons. Add 2 cups of ice an refrigerate until serving.

Cornbread Stuffing

Servings: 6 - 8
Cooking Time: 95 Minutes
Ingredients:
- 2 Tbsp Butter
- 1 Cup Chicken Stock
- 6 Cups Cornbread, Cubed
- ½ Cup Dried Cranberries
- 1 Egg
- ½ Cup Heavy Whipping Cream
- 1 Lb. Italian Sausage
- 1 Diced Onion
- 1 ½ Tsp Pit Boss Pulled Pork Rub
- 2 Tbsp Sage, Fresh
- ½ Tsp Fresh Thyme

Directions:
1. Fire up your Pit Boss and preheat to 250°F. If using a g or charcoal grill, set the temp to low heat.
2. Portion sausage into quarter-size pieces and place on mesh grate. Place grate on the grill and cook for 1 hour. Sausage pieces will have a smoky deep brown color. Move t mesh tray of sausage to the side of the grill with indirect he
3. Open the Flame Broiler Plate and increase the temperature to 350°F. Place a large cast iron skillet on the g over direct flame. Add butter and onions and cook until the onions caramelize lightly, stirring often. Add the sage and thyme and stir to combine.
4. Gently fold in the dried cranberries and cubed cornbre then add sausage directly from mesh grate.
5. In a small mixing bowl, whisk together the heavy crean chicken stock, egg, and Pulled Pork Rub. Pour mixture over cornbread stuffing mix.
6. Cover grill and cook 30 minutes or until heated throug and crispy on top.

Cranberry Apple Sage Stuffing

Servings: 7
Cooking Time: 45 Minutes
Ingredients:

- 10 Cups Day Old Diced Bread, Sliced Loaf
- 2 1/2 Cups Broth, Chicken
- 1 Cup Butter, Unsalted
- 1 Cup Diced Celery, Cut
- 1 1/2 Cups Fresh Cranberries
- 1 Beaten Egg
- 1 Medium Granny Smith Apple, Peel, Core And Dice
- 2 Tbsp Minced Parsley, Fresh
- 1 Tbsp Minced Rosemary, Fresh
- 2 Tbsp Roughly Chopped Sage
- Salt And Pepper
- 1 Tbsp Minced Thyme
- 2 Cups Diced Yellow Onion, Sliced

Directions:

Turn your Pit Boss Pellet Grill to smoke mode, let the fire catch and then set to 350°F to preheat.

Melt butter over medium heat. Add onions then celery and cook until onions start to become translucent.

In a large bowl, mix together bread, apples, cranberries, cooked onion and celery mixture, and fresh herbs.

Add half of the chicken broth to the mixture and stir.

Beat together eggs and the rest of the chicken broth in a small bowl. Pour into the bread mixture and stir until completely combined.

Add salt and pepper to taste.

Pour stuffing into a cast iron pan or baking dish. Cover with foil and bake on the grill for 30 minutes. Remove the foil and cook for an additional 15 minutes.

Serve immediately and enjoy!

Monster Cookies

Servings: 20
Cooking Time: 35 Minutes
Ingredients:

- 2 Packages Candy Eyeballs
- Green, Blue And Purple Food Coloring
- 1 Box Of Yellow Gluten Free Cake Mix
- 1/2 Cup (Optional) Granulated Sugar
- 2 Large Eggs
- 1/3 Cup Powdered Sugar
- 1 Teaspoon Pure Vanilla Extract
- 6 Tablespoon Melted Vegan Butter (Unsalted)

Directions:

Preheat your grill to 350°F. Close the flame broiler.

Line two large baking sheets with parchment paper. In a large bowl, combine cake mix, melted butter, eggs (or egg substitute), powdered sugar, sugar (optional), and vanilla and stir until combined. (substitute 2 flax eggs for Vegan – 1 tbsp flaxseed meal and 5 tbsp water per egg).

Divide dough between 3 bowls and dye each bowl a different color.(We used green, blue and purple).

Roll dough into tablespoon-sized balls.

Place about 2" apart on the baking sheet and grill until cookies have cracked and the tops look set, 8 to 10 minutes. – Turn half way through baking, after 4-5 minutes.

6. Immediately, while the cookies are still warm, stick candy eyeballs all over the cookies.

7. Let cool completely before serving.

Carrot Cake

Servings: 10
Cooking Time: 35 Minutes
Ingredients:

- 1/2 Cup Apple Sauce, Unsweetened
- 2 Tsp Baking Powder
- 1 Tsp Baking Soda
- 1 1/2 Cups Brown Sugar
- 1/2 Cup Butter, Room Temp
- 3/4 Cup Canola Oil
- 3 Cups Carrot, Grated
- 1 1/2 Tsp Cinnamon, Ground
- 2 (8-Ounce) Packages Cream Cheese, Room Temperature
- 4 Egg
- 2 Cups Flour, All-Purpose
- 1/2 Tsp Ginger, Ground
- 1/4 Tsp Nutmeg, Ground
- 1/2 Tsp Salt
- 1/2 Cup Sugar
- 3 Cups Sugar, Icing

Directions:

1. Preheat your Grill to 350F.

2. Line the bottom of 2 9-inch cake pans with parchment paper and spray the sides with cooking spray. Set aside.

3. In a large bowl, combine flour, baking powder and soda, spices and salt.

4. In a smaller bowl, combine oil, eggs, sugars, and applesauce and whisk together. Add carrots and stir until well combined.

5. Pour the wet ingredients into the dry. Stir until combined but take care not to over mix. Pour the batter evenly between the two cake pans. Bake for about 35 minutes in your Grill, rotating the cake pans halfway between the cook. Remove once a toothpick is inserted in the middle of the cake and comes out clean.

6. While the cake is cooling, prepare the frosting. Beat the cream cheese until smooth with a hand mixer. Add the butter and icing sugar and mix until fully combined.

7. On a clean plate or cake stand, place one half of the cake and top with a good layer of cream cheese frosting. Place the second half on top and cover with the remaining frosting. Icing tip: try not to lift your knife while icing. Instead make long, smooth strokes. Lifting the knife often make cause crumbs to get into your icing. Top with pecans if desired.

Smoked Beer Cheese Dip

Servings: 6
Cooking Time: 20 Minutes
Ingredients:

- 6 Oz Beer, Can
- 8 Oz Cream Cheese
- 1 Tsp Onion Powder
- ½ Tsp Pepper
- ½ Tsp Salt
- 2 Cups Shredded Cheese

Directions:

1. Fire up your Pit Boss Grill and set the temperature to 350°F. If you're using a gas or charcoal grill, set it up for medium high heat. Preheat with lid closed for 10-15 minutes.
2. In the cast iron pan add cream cheese, shredded cheese, beer, onion powder, salt and pepper. Once grill is at 350°F place cast iron skillet onto the grill and cook for about 10 minutes, stir and cook for another 5-10 minutes.
3. Top with more shredded cheese and fresh parsley. Serve with fresh baked pretzels as well.

Bbq Chicken Pizza On The Grill

Servings: 4
Cooking Time: 10 Minutes
Ingredients:
- 3 Boneless, Skinless Chicken Breast
- 5 Cups Flour, Strong
- 3 Cups Georgia Style Bbq Sauce
- 3 Cups Mozzarella Cheese, Shredded
- 1 Tsp Olive Oil
- 3 Cups Pit Boss Georgia Style Bbq Sauce
- 1 1/2 Cups Red Bell Peppers, Diced
- 1 1/2 Cups Red Onion, Diced
- 1 Tsp Sugar
- 1/2 Cup Water, Hot
- 1 1/4 Cup Water, Warm
- 2 Tsb Active Yeast, Instant

Directions:
1. Roll your pizza dough so it forms a base about a 1/2 inch thick. To impress your friends and family, you'll want to aim for a nice, pizza like shape. HINT: use a sprinkle of cornmeal on the countertop to aid in moving the dough.
2. Now for the toppings! Start by spreading 1 cup of Georgia Style BBQ sauce onto each base. Make sure to leave a small portion for the crust! Next, load up with sliced, cooked chicken breasts, diced red onions and red bell peppers before finishing off with a two cups of shredded mozzarella cheese.
3. Place the pizza stone in your grill and preheat to 500°F. Pick up your pizza using a flat surface like a chopping board and slide the pizza carefully onto the hot stone. Close the lid and let your homemade wood-fired pizza bake for 10 - 12 minutes. Remove once your pizza has a golden crust and the cheese is bubbling. Cut and serve for pizza you'll hardly want to share.

Spiced Cherry Pie

Servings: 6-8
Cooking Time: 60 Minutes
Ingredients:
- 1/2 Teaspoon Cinnamon, Ground
- 1/2 Teaspoon Cloves, Ground
- 1/2 Cup Cornstarch
- 1 Pound Frozen Sweet Dark Cherries, Thawed
- 1 Teaspoon Water (Beaten With Egg) 1 Egg
- 1 Lemon, Juice
- 1 Lemon, Zest
- 2 Prepared Store Bought Or Homemade Pie Crust
- 1 Teaspoon Pit Boss Hickory Honey Sea Salt Seasoning
- 1 Cup Sugar, Granulated
- 1 Teaspoon Vanilla Extract

Directions:

1. In a large bowl, mix together the thawed cherries and their juices, sugar, cornstarch, lemon zest, lemon juice, cinnamon, clove, vanilla extract and Hickory Honey Sea Salt. Allow to sit for 30 minutes.
2. Flour a work surface and roll out one of the prepared pie crusts so that it fits a 9 inch pie tin. Fill with the cherry pie filling and refrigerate. When the pie is chilled, roll out the second pie crust, brush the edge of the first pie crust with the egg mixture, top with the second pie crust, crimp the edge with a fork, and chill. Alternatively, cut the second pie crust into strips and form a lattice pattern, attaching the strips with the egg mixture. Chill the pie for 15-30 minutes, or until the dough is very cold and firm. Brush the top of the pie with the remaining egg mixture.
3. Turn your Pit Boss Grill to 350F and grill for 45 minutes to 1 hour, or until the pie crust is golden and firm and the filling is bubbly. Remove from the grill and allow to cool at room temperature for at least 4 hours to set the filling, then serve and enjoy!>

How To Make Sourdough Bread

Servings: 4
Cooking Time: 45 Minutes
Ingredients:
- 200 G All-Purpose Flour
- 200 G Bread Flour
- 10 G Kosher Salt
- 80 G Sourdough Starter
- 350 G Water, Bottled, Room Temp
- 50 G Whole Wheat Flour

Directions:
1. Day 1: Use a kitchen scale to weigh out 25 grams whole wheat flour, 25 grams all-purpose flour, and 50 grams of bottled water. Place flour in a glass jar with a lid, then pour water on top. Stir with a fork to combine. The mixture should resemble thick paste. Cover the jar and place it in a warm location, ideally 70°F, for 24 hours.
2. Day 2: Use a kitchen scale to weigh out 25 grams whole wheat flour, 25 grams all-purpose flour, and 50 grams of bottled water. Discard half of the starter and add the weighed ingredients to the jar. Stir with a fork to combine. Cover the jar and place it in a warm location for 24 hours.
3. Day 3: You will likely see a few more bubbles today. Use kitchen scale to weigh out 25 grams whole wheat flour, 25 grams all-purpose flour, and 50 grams of bottled water. Discard half of the starter and add the weighed ingredients to the jar. Stir with a fork to combine. Cover the jar and place it in a warm location for 24 hours.
4. Day 4: You should see a lot more bubbles and the starter should increase in volume. Use a kitchen scale to weigh out 25 grams whole wheat flour, 25 grams all-purpose flour, and 50 grams of bottled water. Stir with a fork to combine. Cover the jar and place it in a warm location for 24 hours.
5. Day 5: The starter will be very bubbly and double in volume. This starter is now ready to use! Use the starter or refrigerate for up to 4 days, then feed again.

Lemon Pepper Chicken Wings

Servings: 4
Cooking Time: 30 Minutes
Ingredients:

1/4 Cup Black Peppercorns, Ground
4 Pounds Chicken, Wing
2 Tsp Coriander, Ground
2 Tsp Garlic Powder
2-3 Tbsp Lemon, Zest
1 Tsp Salt, Kosher
3 Tsp Dried Thyme, Fresh Sprigs

ections:

Start your Grill on "smoke" with the lid open until a fire is
ablished in the burn pot (3-7 minutes). Preheat to 400F.

In a bowl, begin to mix the ground pepper and zest of the
on together, then add the rest of the ingredients.

Place the wings in a bowl and toss with a little olive oil,
a few tablespoons of the seasoning, toss with your hands,
n repeat until the wings are well seasoned to your liking.

Place the wings on the grill, and cook them for about 15
utes, then flip and grill for another 15 minutes.

Continue to flip the wings, until they are done and crispy.
nove the wings from the grill, and serve.

Margherita Pizza

vings: 6
king Time: 25 Minutes
redients:

Basil, Chopped
2 Cups Flour, All-Purpose
Mozzarella Cheese, Sliced Rounds
1 Cup Pizza Sauce
1 Teaspoon Salt
1 Teaspoon Sugar
1 Tomato, Sliced
1 Cup Water, Warm
1 Teaspoon Yeast, Instant

ections:

Combine the water, yeast, and sugar in a small bowl and
sit for about 5 minutes.

In a large bowl, stir together the flour and salt. Pour in the
st mixture and mix until a soft dough forms. Knead for
ut 2 minutes. Place in an oiled bowl and cover with a cloth.
the dough sit and rise for about 45 minutes or until the
gh has doubled in size.

Roll out on a flat, floured surface (or on a pizza stone)
il you've reached your desired shape and thickness.
Preheat your Grill to 350 degrees F.

On the rolled out dough, pour on the pizza sauce, cheese,
then tomatoes and basil. Place in your Grill and bake for
ut 25 minutes, or until the cheese is melted and slightly
len brown.

Mint Chocolate Chip Cookies

vings: 24
king Time: 12 Minutes
redients:

1/2 Cup Butter, Melted
1 Package Chocolate Chip Cookie Mix
8-10 Drop Food Coloring
1/2 Tsp Mint, Extract

ections:

Preheat your Grill at 350F.

2. Follow the directions on the back of the Chocolate Chip
Cookie mix and also add the mint extract and green food
coloring. Mix until combined.
3. On a baking sheet lined with parchment paper, drop balls
of dough about 2 tbsp in size onto the pan.
4. Place in your Grill and bake for 10-12 minutes. Let cool
for a couple minutes before removing from the pan. Enjoy!

Smoked Bourbon Pecan Pie

Servings: 6
Cooking Time: 45 Minutes
Ingredients:
- 2 Tbsp Bourbon
- 1/2 Cup Brown Sugar
- 1/3 Cup Unsalted Butter, Melted
- 1/2 Cup Light, 1/2 Cup Dark Corn Syrup
- 3 Egg
- 1/4 Tsp Hickory Honey Smoked Salt
- Decoration Pecan
- 1 1/4 Cup Chopped Pecans, Coarsely Broken
- 1 Prepared Or Homemade Pie Shell, Deep
- 1/2 Cup Sugar
- 1 Tsp Vanilla Extract

Directions:
1. Heat your Pit Boss Grill to 375F. Meanwhile, prepare your
pie crust in a 9 cast iron skillet or heat proof pie plate.
2. In a large bowl, beat the eggs until smooth. Add the brown
sugar and white sugar and mix until smooth. Add the light corn
syrup, dark corn syrup, vanilla, bourbon, melted butter, and
Hickory Honey Salt. Mix until smooth. Stir in your chopped
pecans and pour into the pie crust. Top with the whole pecans,
if desired.
3. Grill covered for 35-45 minutes, until the pie is just set
around the edges but still has a slight jiggle in the center.
4. Allow the pie to cool completely before slicing. Enjoy!

Basic Crescent Rolls

Servings: 8
Cooking Time: 12 Minutes
Ingredients:
- 1 Crescent Dough, Can

Directions:
1. Preheat your Grill to 375F.
2. Unroll the dough and separate into triangles. Roll up the
triangles and place on an ungreased nonstick cookie sheet.
Bake for 10 -12 minutes on your Grill. You will know that they
are finished when the rolls are golden brown.

Thanksgiving Smoked Turkey

Servings: 6 - 8
Cooking Time: 300 Minutes
Ingredients:
- 1 Turkey Brining Kits
- 12 – 14 Lbs Turkey
- 1 Gallon Water, Cold
- 4 Cups + 1 Gallon Water, Warm

Directions:
1. Start by defrosting the turkey overnight in the
refrigerator.

2. Once turkey has been defrosted begin to make the brine by adding 4 cups of water and the brine mixture to a large stockpot.
3. Bring the mixture to a boil and add 1 gallon of cold water.
4. Place the turkey in the brine bag and pour the brine mixture over the turkey and refrigerate 1 hour per pound.
5. Once turkey has been brined rinse the turkey with cold water and set on a pan.
6. Using the seasoning in the brine box, season the turkey. Once turkey has been seasoned start your Pit Boss smoker by turning it to 275 degrees.
7. Place your turkey in the smoker and place the temperature probe in the deepest part of the breast. Cook at 275 until the breast and thigh meat internal temperature has reached 165°F to 170°F.
8. Remove the turkey from the smoker, let cool, and cut the turkey into your desired pieces. Enjoy!

Pancake Casserole

Servings: 6
Cooking Time: 60 Minutes
Ingredients:
- 2 Tbsp Butter
- 1/2 Cup Chocolate Chips
- 4 Egg
- Maple Syrup
- 12 - 14 Pancakes
- Powdered Sugar
- 1/4 Cup Sugar, Granulated
- 1 Tsp Vanilla Extract
- 1 1/2 Cup Whole Milk

Directions:
1. In a mixing bowl, whisk together flour, baking powder, sugar, and salt. Then pour in the milk, egg and melted butter; mix until smooth.
2. Fire up your Pit Boss Platinum Series KC Combo and preheat the griddle to medium-low flame. If using a gas or charcoal grill, preheat a large cast iron skillet over medium-low heat.
3. Lightly oil the griddle, then scoop the batter onto the griddle, using approximately ¼ cup for each pancake. Cook 1 to 2 minutes per side, until golden brown. Set aside to cool for 15 minutes, then assemble the casserole.

Homemade Blueberry Pancakes

Servings: 4
Cooking Time: 10 Minutes
Ingredients:
- 2 Cups Blueberries, Fresh
- 1 Cup Pancake Mix
- 1/2 Cup Sugar
- 3/4 Cup Water, Warm

Directions:
1. Preheat your Grill to 350°F. Place the cast iron griddle on the grates of your grill.
2. In a large bowl, pour water, pancake mix and 1/2 cup of the blueberries and mix until combined.
3. Pour the batter onto the griddle in 4 equal parts. Cook with the lid closed for about 6 minutes, or until the edges of the pancakes are slightly cooked. Flip each pancake and continue cooking for another 4 minutes.

4. Pour the hot blueberry sauce over your freshly cooked pancakes and enjoy!

Double Chocolate Cake

Servings: 12
Cooking Time: 40 Minutes
Ingredients:
- 1 1/2 Tsp Baking Soda
- 1/2 Cup Butter, Melted
- 1 Cup Buttermilk, Low Fat
- 1 Jar Chocolate Icing, Prepared
- 3/4 Cup Cocoa, Powder
- 1 Cup Coffee, Hot
- 2 Large Egg
- 1 3/4 Cups Flour, All-Purpose
- 3/4 Tsp Salt
- 2 Cups Sugar
- 1 Tbsp Vanilla

Directions:
1. Preheat your to 350 degrees F.
2. Stir together flour, sugar, cocoa, baking soda and salt in large bowl. Combine eggs, buttermilk, butter and coffee and mix until smooth. Add in hot coffee and stir until combined and the dough is runny.
3. Pour the batter into two prepared baking pans and bake on the top rack of your for 40 minutes, turning the pans 180 degrees halfway through.
4. Allow to cool and then frost with chocolate icing.

Sweet And Spicy Baked Beans

Servings: 20
Cooking Time: 120 Minutes
Ingredients:
- 1 - 21 Oz Apple Pie Filling, Can
- 1 Gallon Baked Beans
- 1 Tbs Chilli, Powder
- 1 Green Bell Pepper, Diced
- 1 10 Oz Drained Jalapeno, Can Diced
- 1 Cup Maple Syrup
- 1 Onion, Diced
- 1 Lb Pork, Pulled

Directions:
1. Start Grill at 350 degrees.
2. Place all ingredients in mixing bowl and mix well.
3. Pour bean mixture into foil pans.
4. Bake in grill till bubbling throughout – about 2 hours.
5. Rest at least 15 minutes before serving.

Homemade Corn Tortillas

Servings: 11 - 22
Cooking Time: 10 Minutes
Ingredients:
- Cooking Spray
- 10 Oz Masa Harina
- 1 Tbsp Vegetable Oil
- 9 Oz Water, Hot
- 3 Oz Water, Room Temperature

Directions:

In a large mixing bowl, mix together masa and hot water. ~ with a wooden spoon or by hand. Cover with plastic wrap ⌐ allow to sit at room temperature for 1 hour.

Turn out the dough. Dough will be crumbly. Incorporate 1 ⌐lespoon of water at a time, while kneading and pressing ⌐ether, until a soft, smooth texture is reached. If too sticky, ⌐ a dusting of Masa.

Divide dough into 1 ounce balls, then spray with cooking ⌐ay.

Place a piece of parchment paper on a tortilla press. Set a ⌐gh ball in the center, then top with another piece of ⌐chment paper. Flatten dough ball with the press, then ⌐nsfer to a sheet tray. Separate each layer with plastic wrap ⌐ spray with cooking spray. Repeat until all dough balls are ⌐ssed.

Loaded Portobello Mushrooms

⌐vings: 4
⌐oking Time: 20 Minutes
⌐redients:
- 8 Bacon, Strip
- 1 Cup Cheddar Cheese, Shredded
- 3 Cloves Garlic, Minced
- Green Onion
- 4 Large Portobello Mushrooms
⌐ections:
Preheat your Grill to 350 degrees F.
Core the mushrooms and remove the gills completely.
Sprinkle garlic in each mushroom, followed by bacon, 1/4 ⌐ cheese, more bacon and lastly green onions.
Place on the grates of your Grill and cook for about 20 ⌐nutes.
Serve hot. Be careful taking the first bite - they"re very ⌐cy! Enjoy!

Bossin' Nachos

⌐vings: 6
⌐oking Time: 10 Minutes
⌐redients:
- 1 Pound Beef, Ground
- 3 Cups Cheddar Cheese, Shredded
- 1 Green Bell Pepper, Diced
- 1/2 Cup Green Onion
- 1/2 Cup Red Onion, Diced
- 1 Large Bag Tortilla Chip
⌐ections:
Start your Grill on "smoke" with the lid open until a fire is ⌐ablished in the burn pot (3-4 minutes). Preheat to 350°F.
While you're waiting, empty a large bag of nacho chips ⌐nly onto a cast iron pan. Start loading up with toppings - ⌐ked ground beef, red onion, red pepper, cheese, green ⌐ons. These are just the toppings we had on hand, so feel ⌐e to add anything you like! Make sure you do a couple layers ⌐ chips so everyone gets a good serving of nachos. And don't ⌐ skimpy with the cheese - lay it on heavy!
Place your loaded nachos on the grill and let the hot ⌐oke melt your toppings into one cheesy creation. Heat at ⌐)°F for 10 minutes or until the cheese has fully melted. ⌐move and serve with sour-cream and salsa.

Strawberry Rhubarb Pie

Servings: 8
Cooking Time: 30 Minutes
Ingredients:
- 1/3 Cup Flour
- 1 Tbsp Lemon, Zest
- 1 Prepard Pie Shell, Deep
- 3 Stalks Rhubarb
- 2 1/2 Cups Strawberry
- 1 Cup Sugar

Directions:
1. Summer baking never has to stop when you can use your Wood Pellet Grill to bake anything from cookies to pie! In this recipe, we will show you how to bake a delicious barbecued strawberry rhubarb pie without turning your kitchen into an oven.
2. Preheat grill to 400°F.
3. Slice rhubarb and strawberries into bite sized pieces. Combine sugar, flour and lemon zest with rhubarb and strawberries. Pour into prepared pie crust. Cover with top crust.
4. Bake in Grill for 1 hour or until crust is crispy.
5. Serve hot.

Chili Fries

Servings: 6
Cooking Time: 10 Minutes
Ingredients:
- 1 Cup Cheddar Cheese, Shredded
- 1 Cup Chili Con Carne, Prepared
- 1 Bag French Fries
- 1 Tablespoon Olive Oil
- 1 Tablespoon Sweet Heat Rub

Directions:
1. Set up your Pit Boss. Once it's fired up, set the temperature to 350°F. If you're using charcoal or gas, set it up for medium high heat.
2. Bake the fries according to manufacturer's instructions. Once the fries are done, place them in a large bowl and add the olive oil and Sweet Heat Rub. Toss the fries to coat. Once everything is well coated with the oil and seasoning, spread the fries on a baking sheet.
3. Top the fries with the chili and the shredded cheddar cheese. Place the baking sheet on the grill and grill for 7-10 minutes, or until the cheese is melted and bubbly, and the chili is warm all the way through.
4. Remove the baking sheet from the grill and serve the fries immediately.

Smoked Apple Crepes

Servings: 6
Cooking Time: 60 Minutes
Ingredients:
- 1/2 Cup Apple Juice
- 2 Lbs Apples
- 2 Tbsp Brown Sugar
- 5 Tbsp Butter
- 3 Tbsp Butter, Melted
- Tt Caramel
- 3/4 Tsp Cinnamon, Ground

- Tt Cinnamon-Sugar
- 3/4 Tsp Cornstarch
- 2 Eggs
- 1 Cup Flour
- 2 Tsp Lemon Juice
- Pit Boss Tennessee Apple Butter Seasoning
- 1/2 Cup Water
- 3/4 Cup Milk

Directions:

1. Fire up your Platinum Series KC Combo and preheat to 225°F. If using a gas or charcoal grill, set it up for low, indirect heat.
2. Peel, halve, and core apples.
3. Season apples with Tennessee Apple Butter then place directly on the grill grate, and smoke for 1 hour.
4. Meanwhile, prepare crêpe batter: combine eggs, milk, water, flour, and 3 tbsp of melted butter in a blender, and blend until smooth.
5. Refrigerate for 30 minutes.
6. Remove apples from grill, cool slightly, then slice thin.
7. Place a cast iron skillet on the grill and melt 3 tbsp butter with brown sugar, cinnamon, cornstarch, apple and lemon juices. Cook for 5 minutes until thick.
8. Add apples and cook for another 3 to 5 minutes, stirring to coat apples in sauce.
9. Remove from grill and set aside.
10. Preheat griddle to medium-low. If using a standard grill, preheat a cast iron skillet on medium-low heat.
11. Melt 1 teaspoon of butter on the griddle.
12. Then add ½ cup of batter, and spread with the bottom of a metal spatula, working quickly, as the batter cooks fast.
13. Cook one minute per side, until edges begin to brown. Remove from griddle, set aside, and repeat with remaining batter.
14. Spoon ¼ cup of apple filling into the center of each crêpe, then quarter-fold into a triangle.
15. Serve warm with additional apple filling, drizzle of warm caramel, and a dusting of cinnamon-sugar.

Chocolate Bacon Cupcakes

Servings: 12
Cooking Time: 120 Minutes
Ingredients:

- 1 Lb Bacon
- 1 1/2 Tsp Baking Powder
- 1 1/2 Tsp Baking Soda
- 1 Cup Cocoa, Powder
- 2 Egg
- 1 3/4 Cups Flour
- 1 Cup Milk, Whole
- 1/2 Cup Oil
- 1 Tsp Salt
- 2 Cups Sugar
- 2 Tsp Vanilla

Directions:

1. Start your Pit Boss on SMOKE with the lid open until a fire is established in the burn pot (3-7 minutes). Preheat to 250°F.
2. Once your grill is preheated, place bacon strips on the grates. Smoke for 1hr-1 ½ hours or until desired crispiness is achieved.
3. Remove the bacon from the grill and set aside.
4. Increase set the temperature to 350°F and preheat.

5. Mix the rest of the ingredients in a bowl with an electric mixer until it is nice and smooth.
6. Pour the mixture into a cupcake tin.
7. Transfer the tin to your grill and bake for about 20 - 25 minutes.
8. Allow the cupcakes to cool on a wire rack. Once cooled, top with your favorite premade icing and a half of strip of the bacon. Serve and enjoy!

Lemon Chicken, Broccoli & String Beans Foil Packs

Servings: 4
Cooking Time: 20 Minutes
Ingredients:

- 2 Cups Broccoli
- 3 Tbsp Butter, Melted
- 4 Chicken, Boneless/Skinless
- 1 Garlic, Minced
- 1 1/2 Tsp Italian Seasoning, Dried
- 1 Lemon, Sliced
- Pepper
- Salt
- 1 Cup String Beans

Directions:

1. Start your grill on smoke with the lid open until a fire is established in the burn pot (3-7 minutes). Preheat to 450F.
2. Lay four 12 x 12 inch pieces of foil out on a flat surface, then place one chicken breast in the middle of each foil.
3. Divide the broccoli and string beans between the four foil packs. Thinly slice the lemon, split them between each foil pack, and place the slices on, in and around the chicken and vegetables.
4. Mix the butter, garlic, juice of the remaining lemon, and Italian seasoning together, and then brush over the chicken and vegetables. Sprinkle with salt and pepper to taste.
5. Fold the foil over the chicken and vegetables to close the pack, and pinch the ends together so the pack will remain closed.
6. Grill for 7-9 minutes on each side. Turn off grill, remove the foil packets, and serve immediately.

Bananas Foster

Servings: 4
Cooking Time: 10 Minutes
Ingredients:

- 1/3 Cup Banana Nectar
- 4 Bananas, Quartered
- 3/4 Cup Brown Sugar
- 1/4 Cup Butter
- 1/2 Tsp Cinnamon, Ground
- 1/3 Cup Dark Rum
- Vanilla Ice Cream

Directions:

1. Fire up your Pit Boss Griddle and preheat to medium he. If using a gas or charcoal grill, preheat a cast iron skillet.
2. Place a large skillet on the griddle, then melt butter in t skillet. Whisk in brown sugar and cinnamon, stirring until sugar dissolves.
3. Add the banana nectar and bananas. Stir to coat

Once the bananas begin to soften and turn brown, add the
n. Stir, then ignite the sauce with a stick lighter. After the
nes subside, simmer the sauce for 2 minutes.

Divide the bananas among 4 scoops/bowls of vanilla ice
am, then spoon the warm sauce over the top of the ice
am. Serve immediately.

Double Stuffed Sweet Potatoes

vings: 6
king Time: 45 Minutes
redients:

2 Bacon, Strip
1/4 Cup Green Onion
2 Potato, Sweet
1 Cup Shredded Cheddar Cheese

ections:

Prepare to stuff yourself with Double Stuffed Sweet
atoes.

Fill the hopper with your desired blend of hardwood
lets and preheat your grill to 400°F with the flame broiler
y closed. Bake the sweet potatoes for 30 minutes or until

Remove potatoes from the grill and cut them in half
gthwise). Next, scoop out the potato into a mixing bowl.
ng a fork or electric mixer, diligently mash the potato and
urn it home to the skins. Load the tops with green onion,
on and cheese.

Return the newly loaded skins to the grill for 10 minutes
until the cheese has melted. Garnish with salt, pepper and
r cream for an appetizer that will surely morph into a full
al.

Five Cheese Mac And Cheese By Chef Shaun O'neale

vings: 6 - 10
king Time: 60 Minutes
redients:

5 Tbsp All-Purpose Flour
4 Strips Bacon
Black Pepper
2 Cups Breadcrumbs
4 Oz Brie
4 Oz Brie Cheese
½ Cup Butter, Melted
12 Oz Cheddar Cheese, Grated
3 Cloves Garlic, Minced
2 Tbsp Extra Virgin Olive Oil
1 Tsp Fresh Grated Nutmeg
1 Tsp Ground Cayenne
8 Oz, Grated Gruyere Cheese
1 Cup Heavy Cream
1, Minced Jalapeno Pepper
4 Oz Mozzarella Cheese, Grated
2 Tbsp Parsley, Minced Fresh
12 Oz Raclette
To Taste Salt
5 Tbsp Unsalted Butter
4 Oz Whole Milk, Warm
1 Yellow Onion, Diced

ections:

1. Heat your Pit Boss Pellet Grill to 350 degrees with the
heat shield closed. Bring a large saucepan of water to a boil.
Add the pasta and cook according to the package instructions
for al dente. Drain.
2. Heat the oil in a large saucepan over medium-high heat.
3. Add the onion and cook for about 5 minutes, stirring often,
until lightly colored, then add the garlic and the jalapeño and
cook for 2 more minutes.
4. Reduce the heat to medium, add the butter, and stir until
melted. Add the flour and cook, stirring often, for 5 minutes to
form a light roux.
5. Add the cheeses, the milk, and cream, reduce the heat to
medium-low, and cook, stirring often, until the cheese is
melted, and a smooth sauce comes together, about 7 minutes.
6. Stir in the cayenne and truffle oil, then add the pasta and
stir to fully coat it in the sauce. Season with salt and pepper.
Transfer the mixture to a 12-inch cast-iron skillet and cover
with aluminum foil.
7. Place on the grill and bake for 20 minutes. Remove the foil
and cover the mac and cheese with the breadcrumbs.
8. Return to the grill and bake for another 15 to 20 minutes,
until the cheese is bubbling and the breadcrumbs are golden
brown. Serve family style right out of the skillet.

Cherry Cobbler

Servings: 8
Cooking Time: 45 Minutes
Ingredients:
- 1 Tsp Baking Powder
- 3 Tbsp Butter, Melted
- 1 Cup Flour
- Ice Cream, Prepared
- 1/4 Tsp Salt
- 3/4 Cup Sugar
- 1/2 Cup Milk

Directions:
1. Preheat your Grill to 350 degrees F.
2. In a bowl, combine flour, sugar, baking powder, salt and
mix to incorporate. Stir in butter and milk and mix until
combined. In a cast iron pan, dump in cherry pie filling and
pile on the prepared topping to cover.
3. Place in your Grill and bake for about 45 minutes, or until
the topping is golden brown.
4. Let cool for a couple minutes and serve with ice cream.

Pit Boss Chicken Pot Pie

Servings: 6
Cooking Time: 60 Minutes
Ingredients:
- 2 Chicken, Boneless/Skinless
- 1 Cream Of Chicken Soup, Can
- 1 Tsp Curry Powder
- 1/2 Cup Mayo
- 1 1/2 Cups Mixed Frozen Vegetables
- 1 Onion, Sliced
- 2 Frozen Pie Shell, Deep
- 1/2 Cup Sour Cream

Directions:
1. Start your Grill on "smoke" with the lid open until a fire is
established in the burn pot (3-4 minutes). Preheat to 425F.

2. Cut the onion in half and place on the grates of the grill. If you''re using fresh chicken breasts, barbecue the chicken at the same time as the onions. The chicken is fully cooked when the internal temperature reached 170F. While the onion and chicken are cooking, prepare the pie crust by putting one crust in a pie plate. When the chicken and onions are done, shred chicken and chop onion into small pieces and place in the prepared pie plate along with the mixed vegetables.

3. Combine cream of chicken soup, mayo, sour cream, and curry powder in a bowl. Pour into the pie crust with the chicken and mix to combine. Wet the sides of the bottom crust with a small amount of water and top with the second pie crust. Push gently along the sides of the crust to seal the two pie crusts together.

4. Place in the and bake for 40 minutes, or until the crust is golden brown. Serve hot.

Bourbon Bacon Brownies

Servings: 16
Cooking Time: 60 Minutes
Ingredients:
- 2 Cup All-Purpose Flour
- 1/4 Cup Bourbon
- 1 Cup Brown Sugar
- 1 Cup Canola Oil
- Caramel Sauce
- 1.5 Cup Cocoa Powder
- 1 Tablespoon Hickory Honey Sea Salt
- 2 Tablespoon Instant Coffee
- 6 Large Eggs
- 1/2 Teaspoon Pit Boss Smoked Infused Hickory Honey Sea Salt
- 1 Cup Powdered Sugar
- 6 Slices Bacon, Raw
- 4 Tablespoons Water
- 3 Cups White Sugar

Directions:
1. Start up your Pit Boss. Once it's fired up, set the temperature to 400°F.
2. In a large mixing bowl, whisk together the cocoa, powdered sugar, white sugar, instant coffee and flour.
3. To the flour mixture, add the eggs, oil and water until just combined.
4. Spray the 9 x 13 pan well with cooking spray.
5. Pour half the batter in the pan, drizzle with caramel.
6. Pour other half of batter on top and drizzle with caramel again and add candied bacon to the top.
7. Bake the brownies in the smoker for 1 hour, or until a toothpick inserted in the center of the pan comes out clean.
8. Remove from the smoker and allow to cool before slicing.

Cheesecake Skillet Brownie

Servings: 2
Cooking Time: 30 Minutes
Ingredients:
- 1 Box Brownie Mix
- 1 Package Cream Cheese
- 2 Egg
- 1/2 Cup Oil
- 1 Can Pie Filling, Blueberry
- 1/2 Cup Sugar
- 1 Tsp Vanilla
- 1/4 Cup Water, Warm

Directions:
1. Combine all brownie ingredients and mix. In a separate bowl, combine cream cheese, sugar, egg and vanilla and mix until smooth. Grease skillets and pour in brownie batter. To with cheesecake and cherry pie filling, using a knife to blend give it that marbled look.
2. Place in your Grill at 350F and bake for about 30 minut
3. Let cool for about 10 minutes and enjoy!

Smoky Skillet Pimento Cheese Cornbread

Servings: 4
Cooking Time: 30 Minutes
Ingredients:
- 2 Tsp Baking Powder
- 2 Cups Buttermilk, Low Fat
- 1/2 Cup Cornmeal, Yellow
- 2 Egg
- 1 1/2 Cups Flour, All-Purpose
- 16 Oz Pimento Cheese Spread
- 2 Tbsp Pit Boss Bacon Cheddar Seasoning
- 1/4 Cup Sugar

Directions:
1. Preheat the grill to 350°F. Place a cast iron skillet in the grill to preheat.
2. In a bowl, mix together the eggs, buttermilk, Bacon Cheddar Seasoning, and pimento cheese spread. Add in the sugar, baking powder, cornmeal and flour. Mix until well combined.
3. With cooking gloves, carefully remove the cast iron ski from the grill, grease it, and add the cornbread batter.
4. Grill for 25-30 minutes, or until the cornbread is golder and pulling away from the edges of the skillet.

Cheesy Garlic Pull Apart Bread

Servings: 2
Cooking Time: 20 Minutes
Ingredients:
- 1 Loaf Bread, Sourdough Round
- 2 1/2 Tbsp Butter, Salted
- 8 Oz Fontina Cheese
- 1 Grated Garlic, Roasted
- 1/4 Cup Parsley, Minced Fresh
- 1 Tsp Red Flakes Pepper
- 1 Pinch Salt

Directions:
1. Start your Grill on ''smoke'' with the lid open until a fir established in the burn pot (3-7 minutes). Preheat to 300F.
2. In a small bowl, add the soft butter, grated garlic, red pepper flakes, sea salt, and ¼ cup of the chopped parsley, a whisk together. With a bread serrated knife, cut 1-inch slice into the bread, not cutting all the way through the bottom o the load. With a butter knife, spread a thin layer of the butte mixture on each slice of the bread. Take the serrated knife again, and cut across the loaf to form 1 inch squares. Next, s the cheese into small thin slices, then stuff one slice into eac bread opening. Place the bread on a baking sheet, and cover tightly with aluminum foil. Place on the grill for about 10 minutes, remove the foil, and grill for a few more minutes u

top is nicely golden and the cheese is oozing. Remove from grill, sprinkle with fresh parsley leaves, then serve.

Cheesy Potato Casserole

Servings: 15
Cooking Time: 105 Minutes
Ingredients:

1 Cream Of Celery Soup, Can
1 Family Size Cream Of Mushroom Soup, Can
Pan Spray
1 - 10 Oz Pic Sweet Frozen Seasoning Blend
Pit Boss Steak Seasoning
1 - 32 Oz Bag Potato, Frozen Cubes
8 Oz Sour Cream
1 Lb Cubbed Valveeta Cheese Sauce

Directions:

Start Grill at 350 degrees
Spray foil pan with pan spray
Place all ingredients into mixing bowl except potatoes and x well
Place potatoes into mixing bowl with mixture and mix l.
Empty potatoes into foil pan.
Cover with aluminum foil and bake at 350 for 1 hour.
Remove foil and stir thoroughly, bake for 30 minutes re or until bubbly

8. Let rest at least 15 minutes before serving.

Eggs Benedict

Servings: 6
Cooking Time: 15 Minutes
Ingredients:
- 1 Biscuit Dough, Tube
- 6 Egg
- 16 Ham, Sliced
- 1 Packet Hollandaise Sauce, Package

Directions:
1. Start by preheating your Grill to 350°F with the flame broiler completely closed to allow for true convection cooking.
2. Grease a muffin tin and crack an egg in each cup. Place on the grate of the for about 10 minutes or until the whites are fully cooked.
3. At the same time, place your biscuit dough on a greased pan. Follow the directions on the packaging but bake on the . Place 2 slices of ham per biscuit on the pan as well.
4. While the ham, eggs, and biscuits are cooking, prepare the Hollandaise Sauce according to the directions on the packet.
5. When everything is fully cooked, cut a biscuit in half, and stack one or two slices of ham, 1 egg and a dollop of Hollandaise sauce. Repeat for each half biscuit. Serve with fresh fruit.

BEEF RECIPES

Pepper Jack Bacon Burger

Servings: 7
Cooking Time: 16 Minutes
Ingredients:
- 14 Bacon, Strip
- 3 Lbs Chuck Beef, Ground
- 7 Burger Buns
- 4 Cloves Garlic, Minced
- 1 Onion, Chopped
- 1 Tsp Pepper
- 8 Oz Pepper Jack Cheese, Sliced
- 2 Tomato, Sliced

Directions:
1. Start your Pit Boss Grill on "smoke" with the lid open until a fire is established in the burn pot (3-7 minutes). Preheat to 400°F.
2. In a bowl, mix together the ground chuck, garlic, onion, and pepper. Separate the beef mixtures into about 7 equal bundles and form hamburger patties.
3. Brush the grate with oil, then add the patties and grill them on about 5-8 minutes on each side, or until desired doneness.
4. Remove the burgers from the grill. On the bottom half of the burger bun, add two tomato slices, top with a slice of pepper jack cheese, add the patty,
5. Place another slice of cheese on top, add two slices of bacon and top it off with the other half of the burger bun and serve.

Smoked Brisket With Sweet Heat Rub

Servings: 10
Cooking Time: 600 Minutes
Ingredients:
- 4 Tbsp Apple Cider Vinegar
- 10Lb Trimmed Brisket
- 2 Cups Broth, Beef
- Pit Boss Sweet Heat Rub
- 2 Tbsp Worcestershire Sauce

Directions:
1. Trim the fat cap from your brisket, leaving enough fat to baste the meat during the smoke process.
2. Generously coat the brisket with Pit Boss Sweet Heat rub, and massage into the brisket.
3. In a bowl, whisk together the apple cider vinegar, Worcestershire sauce and beef broth, then pour into a clean spray bottle.
4. Preheat your Pit Boss Smoker to 225°F. Once the smoker is up to temperature, place the brisket inside and insert the temperature probe. Smoke for 10 to 12 hours, or until the internal temperature of the brisket reaches 200°F at the thickest part. Once an hour, spray the brisket with the mop sauce to baste it.
5. Once the brisket is done, remove from the smoker, allow to rest for 30 minutes under tin foil, then slice and enjoy!

Texas Twinkies

Servings:7-14
Cooking Time:40mins

Ingredients:
- 14, slices bacon
- ½ cup bbq sauce
- 1 lb. brisket
- 8 oz. cream cheese
- 1 tsp cumin
- 14 large jalapeños
- ½ tsp pepper
- 1 cup pepper jack cheese, grated
- 2 tsp pit boss hickory bacon rub
- ½ tsp salt

Directions:
1. Fire up your Pit Boss and preheat to 400° F. If using a ga or charcoal grill, set it for medium-high heat.
2. In a food processor, combine the brisket, Hickory Bacon cumin, salt, pepper, pepper jack and cream cheese. Pulse several times until well combined. Transfer to a bowl and place into refrigerator to chill while preparing jalapeños.
3. Place jalapeños on a sheet tray. Cut each in half lengthwise and remove the seeds and rib with a spoon or by hand, then discard. Note: we recommend using gloves when handling jalapenos, as the seeds can be very hot.
4. Fill each jalapeño half with cream cheese mixture until full, then place other jalapeño half on top. Wrap each jalapeñ with a slice of bacon, then skewer crosswise with toothpicks
5. Place a mesh, metal pan on grill grate and transfer jalapeños to pan. Cover grill and cook for 35 minutes.
6. Open grill and baste jalapeños generously with BBQ sa close grill and continue to cook another 5 minutes.
7. Remove from grill and serve hot.

Breakfast Cheeseburger

Servings: 2
Cooking Time: 10 Minutes
Ingredients:
- 4 Bacon, Strip
- 6 Ounce Lean Beef, Ground
- 2 Burger Buns
- 2 Cheese, Sliced
- 2 Egg
- Pepper
- Salt

Directions:
1. Start your Grill on "smoke" with the lid open until a fire established in the burn pot (3-7 minutes). Preheat to 400°F.
2. Take the ground beef and divide it into two thin patties Brush the grate with oil, then add the patties and grill them about 2-5 minutes on each side, or until the desired donenes pressing down to get a good sear.
3. Remove the burgers from the grill, then build your burg Starting with the bottom bun or bread slice, add the patty, t a slice of American cheese, top with bacon, hash browns, an egg over easy, and finish with the top bun or bread slice. No it's ready to serve!

Skillet Shepherd's Pie

Servings: 4 - 6
Cooking Time: 40 Minutes
Ingredients:

2 Tbsp All-Purpose Flour
1 Cup Beef Broth
½ Tsp Black Pepper
2 Tbsp Butter
1 Cup Cheddar Cheese, Grated
4 Oz. Cream Cheese
3 Garlic Cloves, Minced
1 Lb. Ground Beef
1 Tbsp Italian Parsley
1 Tbsp Kosher Salt
1 Tbsp Olive Oil
½ Cup Minced Onion
1 ½ Cup Peas, Frozen
2 Tsp Pit Boss Pulled Pork Rub
1 Tsp Rosemary, Finely Chopped
1 ½ Lbs. Russet Potatoes, Peeled And Quartered

ections:

Fire up your Pit Boss and preheat to 400°F. If using a gas charcoal grill, set the temp to medium-high heat.

In a cast iron Dutch oven, bring potatoes and just enough ter to cover to a boil. Add salt and cook until tender, 12 to minutes. Drain potatoes, and return to pot. Add cream ese, butter, ½ teaspoon salt, ½ teaspoon black pepper, and sh until smooth. Set aside.

Place cast iron skillet on grill and heat oil. Add onion and té 2 minutes, then add garlic and sauté until fragrant. Add und beef, Pulled Pork Rub, and rosemary, and cook, stirring asionally, breaking up the meat until browned.

Sprinkle flour over beef and stir until combined. Add the th and cook, stirring until thickened, about 3 minutes.

Add a layer of peas over beef and sprinkle with parsley. lop mashed potatoes on top of peas and spread evenly.

Increase temperature to 450° F. Cover and cook for 5 utes, then top with grated cheese. Cover and cook and itional 5 to 7 minutes, until cheese is melted, and edges of atoes begin to brown. Serve hot.

Tomahawk Prime Rib

vings: 10 - 12
king Time: 240 Minutes
redients:
1 Stick Of Butter
3/4 Cup Extra-Virgin Olive Oil
5 Garlic, Cloves
Pit Boss Sweet Heat Rub
2 Tablespoon Rosemary, Fresh
Tomahawk Prime Rib
2 Cups White Wine
1 Cup Worcestershire Sauce

ections:

Cook the baste. Melt 1 stick of butter in saucepan with 2 ves garlic. Add 2 cups white wine of your choice with ugh Worcestershire Sauce to make a brown iced tea color.

Start your Pit Boss on SMOKE Mode with the lid open. Let pellets catch fire in the burn pot, close the lid, and heat r grill to 250°F.

Apply the baste all over the prime rib and smoke at 250°F il it reaches an internal temp of 120°F.

Apply the dry rub – Blend: 2-3 cloves of garlic, 2 tbsp h rosemary, ½ cup Extra Virgin Olive Oil, ¼ cup of Pit Boss et Heat Rub. Pour over prime rib and rub all over.

5. Raise grill temp to 425°F, open the Flame Broiler Plate and sear until the meat reaches an internal temperature of 125°F-135°F.

Bbq Brisket Burnt Ends

Servings: 6-8
Cooking Time: 420 Minutes
Ingredients:
- 1 Brisket Point
- Georgia Style Bbq Sauce (Mustard Base)
- As Needed Pit Boss Chop House Steak Rub

Directions:
1. Turn your grill to "smoke" mode, let the fire catch and then set to 250°F.
2. Place your brisket on the grates, cook for 6 to 7 hours or until the internal temperature reaches 190°F
3. Remove from the grill and cut into 1-inch cubes. Toss brisket cubes with seasoning and your favorite BBQ sauce into a pan.
4. Place the pan in the grill for 2 hours, stirring half-way through.

Smoked Tri Tip With Java Chophouse

Servings: 4
Cooking Time: 90 Minutes
Ingredients:
- 3 Tbsp Olive Oil
- 2 Tbsp Pit Boss Java Chophouse Seasoning
- 1 - 3 Pound Fat Cap And Silver Skin Removed Tri-Tip Roast

Directions:
1. Start up your Pit Boss Pellet Grill or Smoker. Once it's fired up, set the temperature to 225°F.
2. Rub the tri-tip with olive oil and generously season on all sides with Java Chop House.
3. Place the tri-tip on the smoker rack and smoke until the internal temperature reads 140°F, or about 1 ½ hours.
4. Remove the tri-tip from the smoker and allow to rest for 10 minutes. Slice the tri-tip against the grain and serve.

Tomahawk Steak With Apple Butter

Servings: 2 – 4
Cooking Time: 215 Minutes
Ingredients:
- Apple Corer Or Metal Spoon
- 3 Lbs Gala Apples
- 1 Lemon
- Pit Boss Chop House Steak Rub
- 1 Tbsp Pit Boss Tennessee Apple Butter Rub
- Sugar
- 4 Cups Water

Directions:
1. Fire up your Pit Boss and preheat to 400°F. If using a gas or charcoal grill, set heat to medium-high heat.
2. Core and halve the apples. Place apples skin-side down on a sheet tray and season with Tennessee Apple Butter and set aside.
3. In a cast iron pot, combine the apple cores with the juice and zest from one lemon. Cover the mixture with water, transfer to the grill and bring to a boil. Reduce heat to 225° F.

Place the apples directly on the grill grate (skin-side down) and cook for 1 hour.

4. After 1 hour, remove cast iron pot from the grill. Strain liquid, discard cores, return liquid to pot, and whisk in sugar. Cover with lid and return to grill. Allow to simmer for another hour.

5. Add smoked apples to the pot and continue to simmer for 20 minutes. Remove pot from grill and purée apple mixture in a blender. Pour apple purée back into pot and return to grill. Increase heat to 375° F and simmer for 20 minutes. Remove from grill and allow to cool slightly.

6. Reduce heat on grill to 225° F. Season the tomahawk steak with Pit Boss Chop House Steak Rub on both sides. Place the steak on the grill grates, insert a temperature probe, and grill, undisturbed, for 45 minutes, or until the steak reaches an internal temperature of 120°F

7. Remove steak from grill and set aside. Open the Sear Slide on your Pit Boss and increase temperature to 400°F. Return tomahawk to grill and sear over open flames, about 2-3 minutes per side.

8. Pull the steak off the grill and allow it to rest for 10 minutes. Ladle reserved apple butter over steak and serve.

Easy Beef Brisket With Chophouse Steak Rub

Servings: 12
Cooking Time: 480 Minutes
Ingredients:
- As Needed, Pit Boss Chop House Steak Rub
- 1, 10 To 12 Lb Whole Beef Brisket

Directions:
1. Turn your grill to "smoke" mode, let the fire catch and then set to 250°F.
2. While the grill is heating up, trim your brisket of excess fat, score the meat against the grain and season with Chop House Steak Rub or your favorite seasoning.
3. Place your brisket on the grates, fat side up and cook for 7-8 hours or until the internal temperature reaches 190°F. If the meat is not probe tender, keep cooking until your temperature probe can easily slide into the meat with little to no resistance.
4. Remove from the grill and allow to rest for 20-30 minutes.
5. Slice against the grain and enjoy!

Standing Rib Roast

Servings: 4
Cooking Time:240 Mins
Ingredients:
- 1 tbsp cracked black pepper
- 1/2 tbsp granulated garlic
- 1/2 tbsp granulated onion
- 2 tbsp kosher salt
- 1 tbsp olive oil
- 2 tsp oregano, dried
- 1/2 tbsp parsley, dried
- 5 1/2 lbs prime rib roast, bone-in
- 2 tsp smoked paprika

Directions:
1. Place the roast in a glass baking dish. In a small mixing bowl, combine the salt, pepper, granulated garlic, granulated onion, parsley, oregano and smoked paprika. Season the entire

roast with the spice blend, then cover and refrigerate overnight.

2. One hour prior to cooking, remove roast from the refrigerator, uncover, and let it sit out at room temperature
3. Fire up your Pit Boss pellet grill on SMOKE mode and le run with lid open for 10 minutes then preheat to 225° F. If using a gas or charcoal grill, set it up for low, indirect heat.
4. Place seasoned roast on a cast iron skillet, drizzle with olive oil, and transfer to the grill. Smoke the roast for 1 hou 45 minutes, or until internal temperature reaches 120° F. Remove from the grill and allow roast to rest for 15 minute:
5. Increase the grill temperature to 450 F, then return roa to grill for an additional 10 to 15 minutes. Allow roast to re: for 15 minutes, slice and serve warm.

Chili Pepper Rubbed Brisket

Servings: 12
Cooking Time: 720 Mins
Ingredients:
- 2 ancho peppers, dried
- 1/2 cup apple cider vinegar
- 9 arbol chilies, dried
- 12 lbs beef brisket, packer cut
- 2 tsp coriander
- 1 tbsp cumin seed, whole
- 2 tsp garlic, granulated
- 1/4 cup kosher salt
- 2 tsp oregano, dried
- 2 tsp smoked paprika
- 3 cups water

Directions:
1. Fire up your Pit Boss on SMOKE mode and let it run wi the lid open for 10 minutes.
2. Close the lid and turn up the temperature to 350°F. Let come to temperature. If using a gas or charcoal grill, set it u for medium heat.
3. Place the dried peppers in a large cast iron skillet, then transfer to the grill and cook for 5 minutes, or until fragrant and hot to the touch. Remove from the skillet, and set aside cool.
4. Add cumin and coriander to the hot skillet, and toast fc minute. Remove seeds from the skillet and cool.
5. Remove stems from ancho peppers, then transfer all chilies to a food processor. Pulse a few times to get going, th process on high for 2 minutes, until coarse-ground.
6. Add in garlic, oregano, smoked paprika, and salt. Pulse times to incorporate, then transfer mixture to a bowl.
7. Remove brisket from packaging, set on a cutting board and blot dry with paper towels.
8. Use a sharp knife to trim the brisket. Start trimming wi the fat side down. Trim the silver skin from the flat side, the remove the sides and corners. Remove the fat from around point. Turn the brisket over and trim any excess fat, leaving around ¼-inch fat thickness.
9. Season the whole brisket with chili pepper rub, then se aside.
10. Fire up your Pit Boss and preheat to Smoke setting. If using a gas or charcoal grill, set it up for low, indirect heat.
11. Place the brisket on the grill, then increase the temperature to 250 F, and smoke until the internal temperature reaches 165°F. After 2 hours, start spraying th brisket every 30 minutes to help retain moisture.

Wrap the brisket tightly in Pit Boss butcher paper, then return to the grill and continue to smoke until the internal temperature reaches 200°F.

Remove the brisket from the gill and rest for 1 to 2 hours in an insulated cooler before slicing.

Leftover Brisket Tostadas With Beans & Cheese

Servings: 4
Cooking Time: 30 Minutes
Ingredients:
- 2 Cups Leftover Chopped Brisket
- Lime, Wedges
- Pickled Jalapeno
- 1 Cup Refried Beans
- ½ Cup Salsa
- 8 Tostada Shells
- ½ Cup Shredded Cheddar Cheese

Directions:
Start up your Pit Boss. Once it's fired up, set the temperature to 300°F.

Assemble the tostadas: smear a tostada shell with refried beans and top with cheese and brisket. Repeat with a second shell and place on top of the first.

Grill the tostadas for 5-10 minutes, or until everything is warmed through and the cheese is melty. Remove from the grill.

Top the tostadas with tomatoes, cilantro, pickled jalapenos, etc and serve immediately!

Pan Seared Ribeye Steak

Servings: 2
Cooking Time: 20 Mins
Ingredients:
- , 4 tbsp butter, room temp
- 1 tsp olive oil
- 1 tsp parsley, chopped
- tt pit boss chop house steak rub
- 1 ribeye steak, 1 to 1.5 inch thick
- 1 tsp scallion, sliced thin

Directions:
Season steak with Pit Boss Chop House Rub, then refrigerate for 1 hour.

In a small bowl, use a fork to mash up butter and 1 teaspoon of Pit Boss Chop House Rub. Transfer compound butter to a sheet of parchment paper, roll, and refrigerate for 1 hour.

Remove steak from the refrigerator, then place a covered cast iron skillet on the grill.

Start up your Pit Boss Grill on SMOKE mode, with the lid open, and let it run for 10 minutes.

Turn your grill up to 400°F and let it come to temperature. Using a gas or charcoal grill, set it up for medium-high heat.

Remove the lid from the skillet. Open the sear slide. Add then sear steak 1 to 2 minutes per side.

Add 3 tablespoons of butter ½ to 1 tablespoon at a time, tilting the pan, and using a spoon to baste the steak.

Continue searing, adding and basting with butter for an additional 3 to 5 minutes.

Remove steak from the skillet, rest for 5 minutes, then serve warm with additional compound butter and fresh herbs.

Smoked Meatloaf

Servings: 8
Cooking Time: 180 Minutes
Ingredients:
- 2 Tsp Apple Cider Vinegar
- 2 Lbs Beef, Ground
- 1/2 Tsp Chipotle Pepper Flakes
- 3 Cups Crushed Chips Corn Tortillas
- 2 Grated Garlic, Cloves
- 2/3 Cup Ketchup
- 1 Small Grated Onion, Chopped
- 4 Oz Into Sticks Pepper Jack Cheese, Sliced
- 2 Tbsp Pit Boss Competition Smoked Rub
- 1 Lbs Pork, Ground
- 1/4 Cup Tomato Paste
- 1 Tsp Worcestershire Sauce

Directions:
1. Preheat your Pit Boss Grill to 250°F.
2. First make the glaze: in a bowl, combine the ketchup, tomato paste, vinegar, Worcestershire, chipotle flakes and Pit Boss Competition Smoked Seasoning. Whisk well to combine and set aside.
3. In a large bowl, mix together the crushed corn chips, eggs, onion and garlic. Add 2/3rds of the glaze to this mixture, reserving the rest for glazing the meatloaf. Mix well to combine and allow to sit until the corn chips have hydrated.
4. Add the ground beef and pork to the corn chip mixture and mix until everything is well distributed.
5. Form the meatloaf into a log and push the sticks of pepper jack cheese into the center of the meatloaf and cover with the meat mixture. Loosely wrap in tin foil and poke holes in the foil with a knife to allow smoke to penetrate.
6. Grill for 1 ½ hours covered, then remove the top half of the tin foil, glaze with reserved glaze, and grill for another 1 ½ hours or until the internal temperature is 165F.

Barbecue Stuffed Beer Can Burgers

Servings: 4
Cooking Time: 60mins
Ingredients:
- 8 bacon slices
- beer, can
- 1/2 lb cheddar jack, cubed
- 2 1/2 lbs ground beef
- 1 jalapeno pepper, minced
- tt pit boss kansas city barbecue rub
- 1 white onion, caramelized

Directions:
1. Fire up your Pit Boss Platinum Series KC Combo and preheat to 300°F. If using a gas or charcoal grill, set it up for medium-low heat.
2. Place ground beef in a mixing bowl, season with Kansas City Barbecue Rub, then mix by hand. Form 4, 10 ounce balls, then use a can (any 12 ounce aluminum can will work), and press the can down the center of each ball, creating a small beef bowl. Press along the sides and roll to create a beef bowl, approximately 3 ½ inches tall.
3. Wrap beef with 2 pieces of bacon, then fill with cheese, caramelized onion, and minced jalapeño. Set filled burgers in a large cast iron skillet, then transfer to the grill. Cook for 25

minutes in the skillet, then transfer burgers to the top rack. Increase the temperature to 325°F, and cook an additional 25 to 30 minutes, rotating halfway. Remove from the grill, top with extra jalapeño, rest for 5 minutes, then serve warm.

Bbq Brisket Queso

Servings: 6
Cooking Time: 15 Minutes
Ingredients:
- ½ Cup Barbecue Sauce
- 1 Cup Brisket, Pulled
- 2 Tablespoons Butter
- 1 Pound American Or Velveeta Cheese, Cubed
- 1 Cup Green Chili, Chopped
- 1 Cup Heavy Cream
- Serving Pickled Jalapeno
- Serving Salsa
- 1 Cup Tomato, Diced
- Serving Tortilla Chip
- ½ Of One Finely Diced White Onions

Directions:
1. Fire up your Pit Boss and set the temperature to 300°F. If you're using gas or charcoal, set your grill for medium low, indirect heat.
2. Let the grilling skillet heat up on the grill. Then, add the 2 tablespoons of butter and finely diced onion and sauté the onions until they are soft and translucent.
3. Next, pour in the heavy cream and bring it to a simmer. Once the cream is simmering, add the cubed cheese, diced tomatoes, and chopped green chilis. Make sure to stir the mixture consistently until the cheese is completely melted.
4. In a separate bowl, combine the brisket with the barbecue sauce and toss until the brisket is fully covered.
5. When your queso is ready, pour it into a serving bowl and top with the brisket, salsa, and jalapenos. You can even add fresh cilantro as a garnish.
6. Serve the queso with tortilla chips while it's hot and fresh and enjoy.

Rib-eye Steaks With Herb Butter

Servings: 2
Cooking Time:55 Mins
Ingredients:
- 1/4 Cup Butter, Room Temp
- 2 Cloves Garlic, Minced
- 1 Teaspoon Horseradish, Prepared
- 1 Tablespoon Mustard, Dijon
- 1/4 Cup Olive Oil
- 1 Tablespoon Parsley, Minced Fresh
- 2 Teaspoon Pepper
- 1/4 Cup Red Wine, Dry
- 1 Tablespoon Rosemary, Springs
- 4 - 3/4 Lbs Steak, Bone-In Ribeye
- 1 Tablespoon Vinegar, Red Wine
- 1 Teaspoon Worcestershire Sauce

Directions:
1. Combine olive oil, red wine, rosemary, vinegar, mustard, pepper, Worcestershire sauce, and garlic in a large plastic bag, add steaks and seal. Marinate overnight in the fridge.

2. Start your Grill on "smoke" with the lid open until a fire established in the burn pot (3-4 minutes). Leave on "smoke" mode.
3. Remove steaks from the bag and discard marinade.
4. Place on the grates of your Grill and smoke for 40 minu
5. While the steaks are smoking, combine butter, parsley, and horseradish in a bowl. Set aside.
6. After 40 minutes of smoking, remove the steaks from the grill. Open the Flame Broiler Plate and crank up the temperature to "HIGH". Let the grill preheat for about 15 minutes. Return the steaks to the grates and sear both sides until the internal temperature reaches:
7. 125°F for rare,
8. 130°F for medium-rare
9. 140°F for medium,
10. 160°F for well done.
11. For medium rare steaks, this should take about 15 minutes.
12. Top with the herb butter and enjoy.

Mustard Crusted Prime Rib

Servings: 8
Cooking Time: 195 Minutes
Ingredients:
- 1 (3 Rib) Beef, Prime Rib Roast
- 1 Tbsp Black Pepper
- 2 Tbsp Garlic, Crushed
- 1 Cup Mustard, Whole Grain
- 2 Tbsp Salt, Kosher

Directions:
1. Preheat your Grill to 450°F.
2. Combine salt, black pepper, mustard and garlic in a bowl. Evenly rub the seasoning all over coating the entire surface the roast.
3. Once your grill is preheated, place the roast on the grate ensuring the ribs are facing the back end of the grill. Once the roast is placed on the grill, shut the lid to the grill.
4. After 45 minutes, lower the temperature of the grill to 325°F. Cook for an additional 2.5 hours or until the internal temperature reaches 125°F. Remove the roast, letting it rest for about 15 minutes. Slice and enjoy!

Texas Chuck Roast Chili

Servings: 4
Cooking Time:150mins
Ingredients:
- 1 cup beef stock
- 1/2 tsp black pepper
- 1/3 cup chili powder
- 1/2 tsp chipotle powder
- 2 1/2 lbs chuck roast, cut in 2-inch cubes
- to taste, cilantro
- 15 oz crushed tomatoes
- 1 tbsp cumin, ground
- 2 tbsp diced green chili peppers
- 3 garlic cloves, minced
- to taste, jalapeño
- 1 jalapeño, minced
- 1 1/2 tsp kosher salt
- 1 lime, zest & juice
- 1 tbsp olive oil

1 1/2 tsp oregano, dried

to taste, red onion

1 red onion, diced

to taste, sour cream

ections:

Fire up your Pit Boss pellet grill on SMOKE mode and let it
with lid open for 10 minutes then preheat to 400° F. If
ng a gas or charcoal grill, set it up for medium-high heat. Set
ep cast iron skillet or Dutch oven on the grill and allow to
heat.

Place cubed chuck roast in a shallow pan then season with
and pepper.

Add the oil to the Dutch oven then sear the beef on all
es. Remove seared beef and set aside.

Add the onions, garlic, and jalapeño to the pot. Stir then
son with salt and pepper. Sauté for 3 minutes, then push all
ons to the sides of the pot, creating a hole in the center. Add
chili powder, cumin, oregano, and green chilis. Cook for 1
ute, until the spices are fragrant, then reincorporate the
ons. Stir in the beef stock, then bring to a hard simmer.

Return the seared beef to the Dutch oven, and stir to coat.
r the crushed tomatoes in a single layer over the top of the
f. Cover the pot and reduce the grill temperature to 300 F.
ise the beef chili for 2 to 2 ½ hours, until beef is fork-
der.

Remove from the grill, then stir in lime zest and juice.
w chili to sit for 10 minutes, then serve warm with your
orite chili toppings.

Grilled Tri Tip With Cajun Butter

vings: 2

king Time: 20 Minutes

redients:

4 Tablespoons Beef & Brisket Rub

1/3 Cup Brown Sugar

1 Stick Unsalted Softened Butter

1/2 Tsp Cayenne Pepper

1 Garlic Clove, Minced

2 Tablespoons Olive Oil

Juice From 1 Orange

1 Tbsp Paprika, Powder

1/3 Cup Soy Sauce

3 - 4 Pounds Trimmed Tri Tip Roast

2 Tablespoons Worcestershire Sauce

ections:

Add the brown sugar, orange juice, Worcestershire sauce,
aced garlic and soy sauce to a resealable plastic bag. Add the
ip to the bag, seal it, and massage the meat to help coat it
nly with the marinade. Place the bag in the refrigerator and
w the tri tip to marinate for 2 hours.

Remove the bag from the refrigerator and drain the
rinade. Remove the steak from the bag and pat dry with
er towels.

In a small mixing bowl, combine the softened butter with
blespoons of Beef & Brisket Seasoning, paprika, and
enne. Mix the butter until well combined. Set aside.

Rub the tri tip down with the olive oil and season
erously with the remaining Beef & Brisket Seasoning.

Fire up your Pit Boss Grill and set the temperature to
°F. If you're using a gas or charcoal grill, set it up for high
t. Insert a temperature probe into the thickest part of the
ak and place it on the grill. Sear the tri tip on the grill for 3-5
utes, then flip it and sear for another 3-5 minutes.

6. Turn the temperature down to 250°F, then grill the tri tip
for 15 more minutes until the internal temperature reaches
135°F.

French Dip Sliders With Smoked Provolone Cheese

Servings:8 - 12
Cooking Time:60mins
Ingredients:
- 1 ¾ cup beef stock
- 3 lbs. beef top round roast, boneless
- 1 tbsp olive oil
- 2 tbsp pit boss chop house steak rub
- 1 8 oz. block of provolone cheese
- 1 red onion, sliced thinly
- ¼ cup sherry
- 1 dozen slider rolls, sliced

Directions:
1. Fire up your Pit Boss Lockhart grill and preheat to 400°F.
If using a gas or charcoal grill, set it up for medium-high heat.
2. Rub roast with olive oil, then season with Pit Boss Chop
House Steak Rub.
3. Place red onion in the bottom of a cast iron skillet and set
roast on top. Transfer to grill and roast for 15 minutes. Reduce
grill temperature to 325°F then add beef stock and sherry, and
continue to cook another 30 minutes, or until 125 to 130°F
internal temperature is reached.
4. Remove from grill and allow the roast to rest for 10
minutes, then slice thinly.
5. Assemble sliders on sheet tray by placing sliced beef on
the bottom half of each roll. Top with onion and provolone
cheese, then place top half of roll on top of cheese. Transfer jus
into a metal gravy boat or porcelain ramekin and reserve for
serving.
6. Transfer rolls back into cast iron skillet and return to grill
for 5 minutes, until cheese melts. Serve hot with jus for
dipping

Jalapeno Burgers With Bacon And Pepper Jack Cheese

Servings: 4
Cooking Time: 30 Minutes
Ingredients:
- 4 Slices, Raw Bacon
- 1/2 Cup Prepared Barbecue Sauce
- 1 Pound Ground Beef
- Hickory Bacon Seasoning, Plus More For Sprinkling
- 2 Thinly Sliced Jalapeno Peppers
- 1/2 Cup Olive Oil
- 4 Onion Burger Buns
- Onion, Crispy
- 4 Pepper Jack Cheese, Sliced

Directions:
1. Fire up your Pit Boss and set the temperature to 350°F. If
using a gas or charcoal grill, set it up for medium high heat.
2. Make the burgers: in a large bowl, mix together the
ground beef and Hickory Bacon seasoning until the seasoning
is well incorporated. Use the Burger Press to make burger
patties. Repeat until all the ground beef is gone.
3. In a small bowl, toss the sliced raw jalapenos with the
olive oil and place them in the vegetable grill basket. Grill the

jalapenos, stirring occasionally, until soft and charred in some spots. Remove from the grill and set aside.

4. Place the bacon on the vegetable grill basket and grill for 5-7 minutes, or until the bacon is crispy and brown. Remove from the grill and set aside.

5. Grill the burgers: place the burger patties on the grill and, if desired, sprinkle more Hickory Bacon seasoning on the patties. Grill the burgers for 5 minutes on one side, then flip and top with a slice of pepper jack cheese and grill for another 5-7 minutes, or until the internal temperature of the burgers is 135-140°F.

6. Remove the burgers from the grill and place on an onion bun. Top with the bacon, grilled jalapenos, crisped onions, and a spoonful of barbecue sauce.

Smoked Brisket Chili

Servings: 6-8
Cooking Time: 120 Minutes
Ingredients:
- 4 Tablespoon Chipotles In Adobo, Diced
- 1 Cup Cooked Bacon, Chopped
- 1 (12 Oz) Beer, Any Brand
- 1 (Drained And Rinsed) Black Beans, Can
- 3 Cups Diced Cooked, Fat Trimmed Brisket
- 2 Tablespoon Chili Powder
- 1/2 Can Corn Kernels, Drained
- 1/2 (Drained) Corn, Can
- 1 Tablespoon Cumin
- 1 Green Hatch Chilies, Can
- 1 Can Kidney Beans, Drained And Rinsed
- 1 Red Onion, Diced
- 1 Tablespoon Pit Boss Beef And Brisket Seasoning
- 1 (15 Oz) Tomato Sauce

Directions:
1. In a sauce pan, sauté the red onion, bacon, and 2 tablespoons of the beer in oil or butter on medium heat until the onions are caramelized, and the bacon is cooked.
2. Preheat your Pit Boss grill to 250°F. Grill for 2 hours, or until the chili is bubbling and brisket is tender.
3. Remove from the grill and serve.

Grilled Steak Recipe

Servings: 2-4
Cooking Time: 25 Minutes
Ingredients:
- Pit Boss Steak Seasoning
- 2 (1 1/4 Thick) Steak, Bone-In Ribeye

Directions:
1. Make some perfectly grilled steaks and add some Chop House Steak Rub seasoning too!
2. No more than an hour before grilling, let steaks come to room temperature.
3. Generously sprinkle Chop House Steak Rub to both sides of each steak, allowing time for the rub to melt into the meat.
4. Fire up your Pit Boss Grill and set temperature to 400°F.
5. Once the grill reaches temperature, Place steaks directly on the grill. For a medium done steak, sear each side for 5-7 minutes, flipping the steaks only one. Adjust time to your desired doneness.
6. Remove steaks from the grill, cover with tin foil, and let it sit 10 minutes before slicing and serving. Note: Use tongs to

flip steaks. Do not flip steaks with a fork or cut into the mea until ready to serve. Any cuts or punctures in the meat will cause juices to escape and dry out your steak.

Chili Bratwurst

Servings: 4
Cooking Time: 45 Minutes
Ingredients:
- 1 Chopped Chipotle In Adobo
- 3 - 4 Cans Of Beer, Any Brand
- 4 Bratwursts, Raw
- 4 Bratwurst Buns
- ½ Cup Prepared Nacho Cheese Sauce
- 1 Cup Chili, Prepared
- Caramelized Onions
- Sweet Rib Rub

Directions:
1. Set up your Pit Boss. Once it's fired up, set the temperature to 350°F. If you're using charcoal or gas, set th temperature to medium high.
2. Place a pot filled with beer, Sweet Rib Rub, caramelized onions and raw brats. Place on grill and par-boil for 20 minutes.
3. Grill the brats for 7-10 minutes, or until internal temperature of the brats is 160°F. Remove the brats from th grill and allow them to rest for 5 minutes.
4. While the brats rest, place the chili in a sauce pan, and place the sauce pan on the grill. Heat the chili all the way through.
5. In a separate sauce pan, add the nacho cheese to the pa add adobo chili peppers and a shake of Sweet Rib Rub. Plac the saucepan on the grill and heat until warm all the way through.
6. Assemble the brats: place a brat in a bun, then top with spoonful of chili and a spoonful of nacho cheese. Serve immediately.

Easy Shepherd's Pie With Tri Tip

Servings: 4
Cooking Time: 30 Minutes
Ingredients:
- 1 Cup Beef Broth
- 2 Tablespoons Unsalted Butter
- 2 Tablespoons Chophouse Steak Seasoning
- 2 Tablespoons Flour
- 1 Cup Mashed Potatoes, Prepared
- 2 Cups Tri-Tip, Diced
- 2 Cups Mixed Frozen Vegetables, Thawed

Directions:
1. Start up your Pit Boss. Once it's fired up, set the temperature to 350°F.
2. In the sauce pan, add the butter and flour over medium low heat. Cook the flour and butter for about 1 minute, or u the flour smells toasty. Slowly add in the beef broth, whiski constantly. Cook for 5 minutes, or until the gravy is thick, a then add the Chophouse Steak. Set aside.
3. Toss the vegetables and tri-tip with the gravy and divic equally into the ramekins. Top the ramekins with mashed potatoes and grill the shepherd's pies for 10-15 minutes, or until warm all the way through and the filling is bubbling. Remove from the grill and serve immediately.

Barbecue Brisket Tacos

Servings: 4
Cooking Time: 15 Minutes
Ingredients:

- ½ Tablespoon Applewood Bacon Seasoning
- 1 Cup Barbecue Sauce
- 2 Cups Cooked Brisket, Cooked And Chunked
- Cilantro, Chopped
- 1 Bag Coleslaw, Prepared
- 8 Corn Tortillas
- Green Onions, Sliced
- 1 Lime, Juiced
- 1/4 Cup Fried Onion, Crispy
- 1 Chipotle Pepper, Diced Finely
- 1/2 Cup Sour Cream

Directions:

Start up your Pit Boss. Once it's fired up, set the temperature to 350°F

In a large aluminum pan, toss together the brisket, barbecue sauce and Pit Boss Smoke Infused Applewood Bacon Rub. Cover the aluminum pan with foil and grill for 15-20 minutes until hot and bubbly.

In a salad bowl, mix together the sour cream, lime juice, diced chipotle, green onion, cilantro and coleslaw mix.

Remove the brisket from the grill and top the corn tortillas with the brisket and chipotle slaw. Garnish with more cilantro and a few fried onion strips.

Leftover Tri Tip Breakfast Sandwich

Servings: 4
Cooking Time: 10 Minutes
Ingredients:

- 4 Slices Cooked And Sliced In Half Bacon
- 4 Cheddar Cheese, Slices
- 4 Eggs
- 4 Split And Toasted English Muffins
- 1 Cup Cook Thinly Sliced Tri-Tip Roast

Directions:

Start up your Pit Boss. Once it's fired up, set the temperature to 350°F.

In a heavy saucepan, bring water to a bare simmer. Using a spoon, stir the water to form a whirlpool and crack an egg into the water. Poach the egg for 5-7 minutes, or until the white is set but the yolk is still runny. Repeat with the remaining eggs.

Assemble the sandwiches: top each sandwich with a slice cheddar cheese, two halves of a bacon slice, tri-tip, and a poached egg.

Grill for 5 minutes, or until everything is warmed through and the cheese is melted. Serve immediately.

Smoked Beef Back Ribs

Servings:2 – 4
Cooking Time:260mins
Ingredients:

- 2 racks beef back ribs
- ½ tbsp black pepper
- ⅓ cup pit boss chop house steak seasoning

Directions:

1. Fire up your Pit Boss and preheat pellet grill to 250°F. If using a gas or charcoal grill, set it up for low heat.
2. Place the ribs on a sheet tray, then remove the membrane from the back of the ribs: Take a butter knife and wedge it just underneath the membrane to loosen it. Using your hands, or a paper towel to grip, pull the membrane up and off the bone. Rub each rack generously with Pit Boss Chop House Steak seasoning and black pepper.
3. Place the ribs on the grill and smoke for 2 hours. Increase the temperature to 300°F and cook an additional 45 to 60 minutes, or until the ribs reach an internal temperature of 205°F. Be sure and flip the ribs halfway to achieve good bark.
4. Remove ribs from the grill and wrap in butcher paper. Allow ribs to rest for 20 minutes, then slice and serve hot.

Reverse Sear Tomahawk Chop With Peppercorn And Thyme

Servings: 4
Cooking Time: 60 Minutes
Ingredients:

- 2 Tbsp Coarsely Ground Black Peppercorns
- 1 Melted Stick Butter, Salted
- 2 Tablespoons Chophouse Steak Seasoning
- 2 Tbsp Sea Salt
- 2 Tsp Sprigs Fresh Thyme, Minced
- 2 Steaks, Tomahawk

Directions:

1. In a small mixing bowl, add the black peppercorns, sea salt, Chophouse Seasoning, and fresh thyme. Mix together and reserve half the seasoning.
2. Place your Tomahawk Steaks onto a sheet pan covered with butcher paper, foil, or parchment paper. Generously season the steaks with the seasoning mixture and rub it into the steaks. Let steaks sit for 1-2 hours if you would like the seasoning to penetrate the meat.
3. Fire up your Pit Boss and set the temperature to 225°F. If you're using a gas or charcoal grill, set it up for low, indirect heat. Insert a temperature probe into the thickest part of one of the tomahawk chops and place them in the center of the grill. If you have 2 temperature probes insert another into the other steak. Grill until the internal temperature of the steaks reaches 110°F, about 30-40 minutes.
4. Once the steaks reach their internal temperature, remove them from the grill and set aside. Increase the grill temperature to 450-500°F. While the grill is heating up melt one stick of butter and add the reserved seasoning to the melted butter. Mix together and brush the steaks with the butter making sure to evenly coat both sides of the steaks.
5. Place the steaks back on the grill over an open flame and sear for 3-5 min per side to reach 130°F-140°F. Remove the steaks from the grill, let them rest for 5 minutes and slice and serve immediately.

Poor Man's Burnt Ends

Servings: 6
Cooking Time: 480 Minutes
Ingredients:

- 1/2 Cup Bbq Sauce
- 1/4 Cup Brown Sugar
- 3 Pound Chuck Roast

- 4 Tablespoons Pit Boss Sweet Heat Rub

Directions:

1. Fire up your Pit Boss Smoker and set the temperature to 275°F.
2. Season your chuck roast liberally on all sides with Sweet Rib Rub. Insert a temperature probe into the thickest part of the chuck roast and place the roast on the smoker.
3. Smoke the roast until the internal temperature reaches 165°F. Wrap the chuck roast in aluminum foil and return to the smoker until the internal temperature is 195°F, about 1 hour.
4. Remove the wrapped roast from the smoker and allow to rest for 15-20 minutes. Cut into 3/4 inch cubes and transfer to a disposable aluminum pan. Sprinkle with 1/4 cup brown sugar and drizzle with most of the BBQ sauce, reserving a couple of tablespoons for later. Toss to coat all the burnt ends with the sauce.
5. Place the pan on the grill, close the lid and cook for an additional 1 1/2 to 2 hours, or until the sauce is thickened and the burnt ends are tender. Remove from the smoker and serve.

Cowgirl Steak & Eggs On The Griddle

Servings: 2
Cooking Time:15 Mins
Ingredients:

- , 1 lbs cowgirl ribeye steak
- 4 eggs
- 1/2 jalapeno pepper, minced
- 1 tbsp olive oil
- tt pit boss chop house steak rub
- 1 scallion, sliced thin
- 1 lb yukon gold potatoes

Directions:

1. Fire up your Pit Boss griddle and preheat to medium-high flame.
2. Season steaks generously with Pit Boss Chop House Rub. Drizzle olive oil on the hot skillet, then sear steaks for 5 to 7 minutes per side, depending on thickness, for medium-rare.
3. After the final sear, quickly sear edges, then add a tablespoon or two of butter, and quickly baste the steaks, turning with tongs. Transfer steaks to a cutting board, to rest for 5 minutes.
4. Meanwhile, halve the par-boiled potatoes. Season with more Chop House Rub.
5. While steaks are resting, sear potatoes in 1 tablespoon of butter, 2 minutes per side. Add jalapeño and scallions at the end, then remove from the griddle.
6. After the first turn of the potatoes, add remaining butter and a drizzle of olive oil in the middle of the griddle. Crack 4 eggs on top. Cook for 2 minutes, or until the white is opaque, but yolk remains runny.
7. Plate sliced steak with 2 sunny-side-up eggs and potatoes.

Spicy Chopped Brisket Sandwich With Sauce And Jalapeno

Servings: 4
Cooking Time: 10 Minutes
Ingredients:

- 3 Cups Cooked And Chopped Brisket
- Dill Pickle, Slice
- Pickled Jalapeno, Sliced

- 4 Sandwich Buns
- 1 Cup Spicy Barbecue Sauce
- White Onion, Sliced

Directions:

1. Fire up your Pit Boss and set the temperature to 350°F. you're using gas or charcoal, prep your grill to cook with medium indirect heat.
2. Add the chopped brisket and spicy barbecue sauce to th aluminum pan and mix well. The brisket should be fully coat with sauce. If 1 cup is not enough, feel free to more sauce ¼ cup at a time.
3. Cover the aluminum pan tightly with foil and place it in the center of the grill. Close the lid and cook the brisket for about 10 minutes or until it's heated all the way through.
4. Remove the brisket from the grill and pile the meat on t of the sandwich buns. Top the brisket sandwich with pickle slices, jalapeno slices, and sliced onions. Serve immediately.

Cheesesteak Sloppy Joes

Servings: 6
Cooking Time:10 Mins
Ingredients:

- 1 tsp beef & brisket rub
- 3/4 cup beef stock
- 2 tbsp butter
- 1 tbsp cornstarch
- 1 green bell pepper, chopped
- 1 lb ground beef
- 6 hamburger buns
- 2 tbsp ketchup
- 8 oz mushrooms, sliced
- 8 oz provolone, grated
- 1 1/2 tbsp worcestershire sauce
- 1 yellow onion, chopped

Directions:

1. Fire up your Pit Boss Griddle and set the right half to medium heat.
2. Add the ground beef and cook for 5 minutes, until browned. Slide to the left side of the griddle to keep warm.
3. Add the butter, onions, bell pepper, and mushrooms, ar sauté for 3 minutes, then mix in the ground beef. Season wit Beef & Brisket, then stir in ketchup and Worcestershire sauc
4. In a small bowl, mix beef stock and cornstarch together then pour over the vegetable and beef mixture. Continue stirring for 1 minute, until thickened.
5. Turn off griddle, then fold in the provolone cheese unti melted. Serve warm on hamburger buns.

Smoked Beef Short Ribs

Servings: 4
Cooking Time: 360 Minutes
Ingredients:

- 1 Cup Apple Cider Vinegar
- 1 Cup Apple Juice
- 4 Tablespoon Olive Oil
- 4 Tbsp Pit Boss Beef And Brisket Rub
- 2 1/2 Pounds (Or 6 Large) Beef Short Rib(S)

Directions:

1. Start up your Pit Boss. Then, set the temperature to 22
2. In a food-safe spray bottle, combine the apple cider vinegar and apple juice. Set aside.

Flip the beef short ribs over, bone side up, and pull off the
k membrane. Discard. Flip the short ribs right side up and
1 any excess fat from the top. Generously rub down the
rt ribs with olive oil and Beef and Brisket Rub.

Place the beef ribs on the center rack. Smoke for about 2
rs, until the short ribs have developed a crust and are a
1 lacquered brown.

After 2 hours, remove the beef short ribs from the smoker,
ce in the heat-proof baking dish, and pour the apple cider
egar and apple juice into the dish. Cover tightly with foil
1 smoke for another 1 ½-2 hours or until the ribs are fall-
rt tender and register 200°F. Remove from the smoker and
ve immediately.

How To Make Homemade Hot Dogs

vings:36
king Time:120mins
redients:

1/3 lbs binder flour
1 tbsp black pepper
2 tsp coriander
1 3/4 cup distilled ice water, divided
1 tbsp garlic powder
7 1/2 lbs ground beef
5 lbs ground pork
2 tsp mace
3 1/2 oz maple cure
1/4 cup mustard powder
3 tbsp paprika
1/4 cup salt
24 - 26 mm sheep casings, pre-flushed

ections:

In a glass bowl or measuring cup, cover sheep casings in
m water and let soak for 1 hour.

In a small bowl, whisk together paprika, mustard powder,
ck pepper, garlic powder, coriander, mace, and salt. Set
le.

In a large tub, combine ground beef and ground pork. Mix
ether by hand, then add maple cure and ¾ cup plus 2
lespoons of distilled ice water. In a medium bowl, whisk
ether seasoning with binder flour and then add ¾ cup plus
blespoons of water. Add to the meat mixture.

Mix meat mixture by hand for 5 minutes, until the meat is
xy. Divide mixture into 2 large bowls. Refrigerate one bowl,
ile the mixture in the other bowl is stuffed.

Prepare the sausage stuffer and fit sheep casing over a ½
1 horn. Place a sheet tray, with a bit of water on it,
lerneath the nozzle of the stuffer and start filling the
ings.

Once the casings are filled, twist off into desired lengths.
rigerate overnight.

Fire up your Pit Boss Platinum Series Lockhart and
heat to 250°F. If using a gas or charcoal grill, set it up for
, indirect heat. Pull open both side handles to increase the
el of smoke and temperature in the smoking cabinet.

Remove hot dogs from the smoking cabinet and either
by hot with your favorite toppings, or place in an ice water
h for 15 minutes, dry at room temperature and refrigerate
reeze for future use.

Bacon Smoked Brisket Flat

Servings: 4
Cooking Time:480 Mins
Ingredients:
- 1/2 lbs bacon
- 4 lbs brisket flat, trimmed
- tt pit boss lonestar brisket rub

Directions:
1. Start up your Pit Boss on SMOKE mode and let it run with the lid open for 10 minutes.
2. Increase your grills temperature to 250°F. If using a gas or charcoal grill, set it up for low, indirect heat.
3. Place the brisket in a foil-lined aluminum pan. Season the fat side of the brisket with Pit Boss Lonestar Brisket Rub, then flip and season the meat side with additional rub.
4. Transfer the brisket to the grill and smoke for 1 hour.
5. Use tongs to flip the brisket over, so the fat side is up, then drape half the bacon slices over the brisket. Smoke for 2 hours, then remove the browned bacon, and set aside.
6. Lay the remaining raw bacon strips over the brisket, and continue cooking until these new bacon strips are browned and the internal temperature of the brisket reads 202°F, which will likely take an additional 3 to 4 hours cook time.
7. Remove the brisket from the grill, and rest for 1 hour, then slice thin. Serve warm.

Philly Cheese Steaks

Servings: 6
Cooking Time: 45 Minutes
Ingredients:
- 2 Green Bell Pepper, Sliced
- 6 Hot Dog Bun(S)
- 2 Cups Mozzarella Cheese, Shredded
- 1 Quart Mushroom
- 1 Onion, Sliced
- Pepper
- Salt
- 2 Thick Steak, Flank

Directions:
1. Start your Grill on SMOKE with the lid open until a fire is established in the burn pot (10 minutes).
2. Preheat to 250°F.
3. Season both sides of your steaks with salt and pepper to your liking. We're going to reverse sear these steaks, so place on the grates of your preheated Grill. You'll want to cook the steaks until the internal temperature reaches 130°F (for medium-rare). Follow these internal temperatures if you'd like to cook your steak more/less done:
4. Rare: 125°F
5. Medium Rare: 130°F
6. Medium: 140°F
7. Well Done: 160°F
8. If you're cooking your steaks medium rare, it will take around 45 minutes depending on how thick the steaks are.
9. While the steaks are cooking, slice up the onion, mushrooms, and peppers thinly and sauté until soft.
10. When the steaks have reached your desired internal temperature, remove steaks from the grill and let them rest for 15 minutes. In the meantime, open up your flame broiler and crank up the grill to HIGH. Sear each side of the steak for about 1 minutes each.
11. Rest steaks again for 10 minutes.

12. Slice steak thinly, combine with the sautéed vegetables and fill a hot dog bun generously with the mixture.

Java Chophouse Steak Tips With Mashed Potatoes

Servings: 4-6
Cooking Time: 60 Minutes
Ingredients:
- 1 Cup Beef Broth
- 1 Stick (Room Temperature) Butter, Unsalted
- 2 Tablespoon Flour, All-Purpose
- 1 Tablespoon Pit Boss Java Chophouse Seasoning
- 4 Tablespoon Pit Boss Java Chophouse Seasoning, Divided
- 2 Pounds Medium Russet Potatoes, Peeled And Cut (Large Chunks)
- 2 Pounds Strip Sirloin
- 1/2 To 1 Cup Whole Milk, Warm

Directions:
1. For the mashed potatoes: add the potatoes to a large pot and add enough cold water to cover the potatoes. Bring to a simmer over medium heat until the potatoes are tender enough to be pierced with a fork, about 40 minutes. Drain the potatoes.
2. Add the potatoes to a large mixing bowl. Add the butter, 1 tablespoon of Java Chop House and ½ cup of warm milk. Mash until smooth and lump free. If potatoes are too thick, add more milk, a tablespoon at a time, until you reach your desired consistency.
3. For the steak tips: preheat your Pit Boss grill to 350°F. Season the steaks generously on both sides with 2 tablespoons of Java Chop House seasoning and grill for 8-10 minutes per side. When steaks are done, remove from grill, allow to rest for 15 minutes, then cut into chunks.
4. While the steak is resting, add the butter to a small saucepan over low heat. Once the butter is melted, whisk in the flour and cook for 2 minutes until the flour smells toasted. Slowly whisk in the beef broth and remaining 2 tablespoons of Java Chop H ouse seasoning and cook the gravy over low heat until thickened. Remove from heat and toss the steak tips in the gravy.
5. Serve steak tips over mashed potatoes. Enjoy!

Reverse Seared T-bone Steak

Servings: 1 - 2
Cooking Time: 64 Minutes
Ingredients:
- Pit Boss Java Chop House Rub
- 1 Steak, T-Bone

Directions:
1. Preheat your Pit Boss Grill to 250°F then close the lid 10-15 minutes.
2. As the is preheating to the perfect temperature, spice the T-bone with your favorite steak rub.
3. Lay the steak on the grill for roughly 60 minutes or until the steaks reach an internal temperature of 105 to 110°F. Remove the steaks and set aside.
4. Crank up the heat to 450°F and open the flame broiler.
5. Place the steak over the flame broiler and sear for about 2 minutes a side, 4 minutes in total. You know when your steak is done once the internal temperature reaches 130 to 135°F (for medium-rare). Follow the below internal temperature for your cooking preference:

6. Rare: 125°F
7. Medium Rare: 130°F
8. Medium: 140°F
9. Well Done: 160°F
10. Once reached for personal preference, take the steaks the grill and eat! Enjoy!

Texas Style Smoked Brisket

Servings:10-12
Cooking Time:480 Mins
Ingredients:
- 1 cup apple cider vinegar
- 1/2 (any brand) beer, can
- pit boss beef and brisket rub
- 10-12 pound whole beef brisket
- 2 tablespoons worcestershire sauce

Directions:
1. Remove the brisket from the refrigerator. Trimming a cold brisket is easier than trimming a room temperature brisket.
2. Flip the brisket over so that the pointed end of the meat facing under. Cut away any silver skin or excess fat from the flat muscle and discard.
3. Next, there will be a large, crescent shaped fat section of the flat of the meat. Trim that fat until it is smooth against the meat so that it looks like a seamless transition between the point and flat.
4. Flip the brisket over and trim the fat cap to ¼ inch thick
5. Generously season the trimmed brisket on all sides with the Pit Boss Beef and Brisket Seasoning.
6. In a bowl, mix together the beer, apple cider vinegar and Worcestershire sauce to make mop sauce.
7. Preheat your Pit Boss Smoker to 225°F.
8. Place the brisket in the smoker, insert a temperature probe, and smoke until the internal temperature reads 165 about 8 hours.
9. Baste the brisket with the mop sauce every 2 hours to keep it moist.
10. Once the brisket reaches 165F, remove from the smoker wrap in butcher paper, folding the edges over to form a leakproof seal, and return to the smoker seam-side down for another 5-8 hours, or until the brisket is tender enough to slide in a probe with little to no effort (around 203°F).
11. Remove the brisket from the smoker and allow to rest 1 hour before slicing.

Grilled Skirt Steak

Servings: 1-2
Cooking Time: 5 Minutes
Ingredients:
- 2 Cloves Garlic, Chopped
- 1 Lemon, Juice
- 2 Tablespoons Mustard, Grainy
- 1/4 Cup Olive Oil
- 2 Tablespoons Pit Boss Java Chophouse Seasoning
- 2 Pounds Skirt Steak, Trimmed
- 1 Tablespoon Worcestershire Sauce

Directions:
1. In a small bowl, mix together the Pit Boss Java Chophou Seasoning, oil, garlic, lemon juice, and Worcestershire.

nerously rub the mixture all over the skirt steak and allow
marinate for 45 minutes.

Start up your Pit Boss on smoke. Once it's fired up, set the
mperature to 400°F.

Grill the skirt steaks for 3-5 minutes on each side or until
e steak is done to the desired degree of doneness.

Remove the steaks from the grill and allow to rest for 5
nutes before slicing and serving.

Georgia Bbq Smoked Brisket Sandwich

rvings: 4
oking Time: 450 Minutes
gredients:

½ Cup Barbecue Sauce
¼ Cup Beef Broth
2 Tablespoons Bourbon
1, 3 Pound Brisket Flat, Trimmed
4 Kaiser Rolls
½ Cup Peach Preserves
Sliced Pickles
4 Tablespoons Pulled Pork Rub
Sliced White Onions

rections:

Start up your Pit Boss smoker. Once it's fired up, set the
mperature to 225°F.

Generously rub the brisket with the Pulled Pork Rub. Set
de.

In a bowl, mix together the barbecue sauce, peach
eserves and bourbon. Set aside.

Place the brisket in the smoker and smoke for 5 hours, or
til the internal temperature reaches 170°F. Once the brisket
aches temperature, remove from the smoker, place the
sket in foil and pour the beef broth over the top. Wrap the
sket tightly in aluminum foil and return to the smoker for
other 2 hours, or until the internal temperature reaches
0°F.

Remove the brisket from the grill, unwrap the brisket,
card the foil, and brush the brisket generously with the
ach glaze mixture. Place the brisket back on the smoker and
oke for 30 minutes, or until the brisket is shiny and glazed.
move the brisket from the grill and rest for 10 minutes,
ered in foil.

Once the brisket has rested, slice thickly against the grain
l top the Kaiser rolls with the brisket slices, onion slices and
kle slices. Serve immediately.

Bacon Mac And Cheese Stuffed Sliders

rvings: 5
oking Time: 20 Minutes
gredients:

16 Oz Lean Beef, Ground
Hawaiian Rolls
1 Box Mac And Cheese, Prepared
Mustard, Ground
Pit Boss Smoke Infused Applewood Bacon Rub

rections:

Cook your favorite prepared mac and cheese. Follow the
tructions on the box.

Turn your grill onto smoke until the flame catches, then
n it to 400°F.

3.   Put the ground beef into a bowl and generously add the
Applewood Bacon Rub. Mix with your hands until the meat
looks evenly coated.
4.   Separate the meat out into 3oz balls, disperse or toss the
remnants.
5.   Split the balls in half, and add half of the meat to the
bottom of the Pit Boss 3-in-1 Burger Press, then add a
tablespoon of mac and cheese (it works better if you kind of
make a bowl in the center of the meat). Then add the
remaining half of the 3oz ball on top of the mac and cheese.
6.   Use the Pit Boss 3-in-1 Burger press to create the perfect
patty!
7.   Add the sliders to the grill, flip every 5 minutes for about
15-20 minutes depending on how cooked you like your
burgers.
8.   You can also toast your buns at this time if you'd like.
9.   Pull the sliders (and the buns) from the grill, add the
stone ground mustard and whatever else your tummy may
desire – and dig in!

Prime Rib Roast

Servings:8
Cooking Time:30 Mins
Ingredients:
- 2 tsps black pepper
- 10 cloves garlic, minced
- pit boss steak seasoning
- 2 lbs prime rib roast
- 2 tsps salt

Directions:
1.   Preheat the grill then increase the temperature to 400°F.
2.   Rub roast garlic, salt, pepper and some Chop House Steak
Rub.
3.   Insert meat thermometer sideways into the center of the
roast so that the shaft is not visible, avoiding fat and bone.
4.   Cook in a closed grill, maintaining constant heat, until the
thermometer reads 145°F(63°C) for medium-rare for about 50
minutes, or cook until desired doneness.
5.   Remove roast to cutting board; tent with foil for 5 to 10
minutes. Serve with mashed potatoes and asparagus on the
side.

Smoked Beef Caldereta Stew

Servings: 12
Cooking Time:240 Mins
Ingredients:
- 1/2 cup cheddar cheese, grated
- 2 lbs, cut into 1 1/2" cubes chuck roast
- 4 garlic cloves, chopped
- 1 tsp kosher salt
- 2 tbsp olive oil
- 2 large yukon gold potatoes
- 5 chopped serrano peppers
- 2 tbsp tomato paste
- 2 cups tomato sauce
- 2 cups water

Directions:
1.   Place beef in a cast iron skillet, then transfer to smoking
cabinet. Make sure that the sear slide and side dampers are
open, then increase temperature to 375°F, to ensure the
cabinet maintains temperature between 225°F and 250°F (If

you're cooking on a different Pit Boss Pellet Grill, set the temperature to 225°F).

2. Smoke beef for 1½ hours, then turn cubed beef, and smoke an additional 1½ hours.

3. Place cast iron Dutch oven on the grill, over flame. Add olive oil, potatoes, and carrots. Cook for 3 to 5 minutes, stirring occasionally. Then add leeks and garlic and cook for 2 minutes, until fragrant.

4. Remove skillet from smoking cabinet and add beef pieces to potato mixture.

5. Add tomato sauce, tomato paste, water, and serrano peppers. Bring to a boil, then cover with lid. Set temperature to 275°F, and allow stew to simmer for 1 hour, until beef and potatoes are tender.

6. Add liver and cheese, and gently stir to combine, until the sauce thickens and cheese has melted.

7. Add bell peppers and olives. Stir, cover and cook an additional 2 minutes. Season with salt, and serve hot.

The Boss Burger

Servings: 10
Cooking Time: 85 Minutes
Ingredients:
- 4 Lbs Beef, Ground
- 1 Loaf Bread, Sourdough Round
- 1/2 Cup Butter
- Condiments (Ketchup, Mustard, Relish, Etc.)
- Lettuce
- 3 Cups Mushroom
- 3 Onion, Chopped
- Pit Boss Kansas City Bbq Sauce
- Pit Boss Mandarin Habanero Spice
- 1 Lbs Pork, Ground
- Red Onion, Chopped
- 1 Bag Shredded Cheddar Cheese
- Tomato, Sliced

Directions:
1. Start your Grill on "smoke" with the lid open until a fire is established in the burn pot (3-4 minutes). Preheat to 300°F.

2. In a large bowl, mix together the ground beef, ground pork, eggs, barbecue sauce, and seasoning until combined. Do not over mix as this will cause the meat to be tough after cooking. Split the mixture into two equal parts.

3. Melt the butter in a pan over medium heat and sauté the onion mushrooms until golden.

4. In a cast iron pan, flatten one half of the meat mixture into the bottom, taking care to work meat slightly up the sides of the pan. Sprinkle in half of the bag of cheese. Pour in onion mixture and top with the rest of the cheese.

5. On a clean work surface, mold the second half of the meat mixture into a circle and cover the filling to complete the burger. Make sure that the top and bottom meat patties are secured together so that the filling cannot be seen.

6. Place the cast iron pan in the Grill for 1 hour - 1 hour 15 minutes, or until the internal temperature reaches 160°F. Crank up the to "HIGH" and open the flame broiler. Flip the burger out of the cast iron pan onto the grates and sear each side for 5 minutes, to get those beautiful grill marks.

7. To serve: You can make an enormous burger like we did, or you can cut it like a pie into slices to be served on regular hamburger buns with your desired condiments.

8. Either way, ENJOY!

Bacon Wrapped Steaks

Servings: 4
Cooking Time: 15 Minutes
Ingredients:
- 1/2 Teaspoon Black Pepper
- 3 Tablespoons/ Small Chunks Butter, Unsalted Melted
- 3 1/2 Teaspoons Chives, Chopped
- 12 Large Peeled Garlic, Cloves
- 1/4 Cup Olive Oil
- Salt, Kosher
- 4 (6 - To 7 - Ounce) 1 Inch Thick Steak, Beef
- 1/2 Teaspoon Dried Thyme, Fresh Sprigs

Directions:
1. Fire up your Pit Boss Grill and turn heat to the HIGH setting. Make sure the Flame Broiler Plate is open.

2. While your grill is heating up, mix the melted butter, olive oil, kosher salt, pepper, garlic, chives, and thyme into a bowl.

3. Wrap the bacon around the sides of the steaks and hold place with a toothpick.

4. Baste the top and bottom of the steaks with the mix using a basting brush.

5. Place the steaks on the grill and brown for 5 minutes on each side.

6. Remove steaks once internal temperature has reached level of desired doneness.

7. Rare = 120°F

8. Medium Rare: 130°F

9. Medium: 140°F

10. Well Done: 160°F

11. After removing the steaks, let them rest for at least 5 minutes.

Grilled Flank Steak Fajitas

Servings: 1
Cooking Time: 30 Minutes
Ingredients:
- 1 Green Bell Pepper, Sliced
- 3 Tbsp Olive Oil
- 1 Onion, Diced
- Pit Boss Sweet Heat Rub
- 1 Red Bell Peppers, Sliced
- 1 -16Oz Steak, Flank
- 8 Tortilla, Corn
- 1 Yellow Bell Pepper, Sliced

Directions:
1. Rub flank steak with 1 tbsp olive oil and Sweet Heat Rub Grill seasoning. Cover and marinate in the refrigerator for 1 hour.

2. Lightly brush peppers and onion with olive oil.

3. Light your Pit Boss to 400°F. Place pepper and onion on grill and cook 5 minutes per side. Watch carefully to ensure the peppers and onion do not burn.

4. Remove peppers and onion from grill and toss lightly with remaining olive oil in a medium sized bowl. Transfer peppers and onions to a cutting board and slice into strips. Set aside.

5. Place flank steak directly on grill. Cook until medium rare (an internal temperature of 165°F).

6. Remove flank steak from the grill and transfer to cutting board. Let meat rest for 5 minutes, then slice against the grain into strips.

Place flank steak, peppers, and onions in a platter and ve immediately with warm tortillas, salsa, guacamole, sour am, shredded cheese, thinly sliced iceberg lettuce, or your rite fajita toppings.

Beer Braised Beef Dip Sandwiches

vings: 4
king Time:180 Mins
redients:

12 oz beer, porter or stout
1/2 black pepper
2 1/2 lbs chuck roast
4 hoagie rolls, sliced lengthwise
1/4 cup horseradish sauce
1 tbsp kosher salt
1 tbsp parsley, chopped
1 red onion, cut into thick rings
1/2 tbsp worcestershire sauce
1 yellow onion, cut into thick rings

ections:

Fire up your Pit Boss pellet grill on SMOKE mode and let it with lid open for 10 minutes then preheat to 450° F. If ng a gas or charcoal grill, set it up for high heat.

Set the chuck roast on a sheet tray, then season with salt pepper. Place onions in a cast iron skillet or Dutch oven a lid. Set aside.

Sear the chuck roast on the grill, 3 minutes per side, then sfer to the skillet set on top of the onions. Add the rcestershire sauce and beer to the skillet, along the side of roast. Cover and reduce the temperature to 325°F. Braise roast for 2 ½ to 3 hours, until tender.

Remove the roast from the grill, add parsley, then pull rt and toss in reduced pan jus and onions.

Serve warm on hoagie rolls with horseradish sauce.

Philly Cheesesteak Rolls With Puff Pastry

vings: 4
king Time:25mins
redients:

4 oz american or jack cheese, shredded, divided
2 tbsp butter
to taste, chop house steak rub
to taste, chop house steak rub (for sauce)
3 oz cream cheese
1 egg, beaten
1 tbsp flour
1 tbsp flour (for sauce)
1 puff pastry sheet, thawed
1 lb sandwich steak, shaved/sliced thin
1 tbsp vegetable oil
1 cup yellow onion, sliced thin
2/3 cup milk

ections:

Fire up your Pit Boss pellet grill on SMOKE mode and let it with lid open for 10 minutes then preheat to 400° F. If ng a gas or charcoal grill, set it up for medium-high heat. heat the griddle to medium flame.

Add oil to the griddle, then cook steak for 2 to 3 minutes, ning with a spatula. Add onions, season with Chop House cook another minute to soften. Transfer steak and onions bowl, then set aside to cool.

3. Meanwhile, melt butter in a sauté pan on the griddle. Stir in flour, then cook for 1 minute. Whisk in milk, then add cream cheese, and 2 ounces of shredded cheese. Whisk until smooth, then remove from the griddle to cool slightly. Use half of the sauce in the pastry, and the other half for serving/dipping once baked.

4. Flour your rolling surface, then set the pastry sheet on top of the flour. Roll the pastry sheet into a 10 to 12 inch square, then cut into 4 squares.

5. Spoon cheese sauce on each pastry square, then divide the steak and onion mixture among the pastries. Top each with remaining shredded cheese, brush sides with beaten egg, then fold pastries over, corner to corner. Secure the seams by pressing down with a fork. Brush the top with beaten egg, then place on a sheet tray.

6. Place the sheet tray on the grill and bake for 18 to 20 minutes, until golden. Remove from the grill, cool for 5 minutes, then cut in half and serve warm with cheese sauce.

Beef Kefta

Servings: 4
Cooking Time:10 Mins
Ingredients:

- bamboo skewers, soaked in warm water
- 1 tbsp blackened saskatchewan rub seasoning
- 3 tbsp cilantro, chopped
- for topping, cucumbers
- 1 tsp cumin
- 2 lbs ground beef
- 1 tsp paprika
- 3 tbsp parsley, chopped
- pitas
- 1 red onion, grated
- for topping, tomatoes
- to taste, tzatziki sauce

Directions:

1. In a mixing bowl, combine ground beef, onion, Blackened Saskatchewan, cumin, paprika, cilantro, and parsley. Mix well, then cover and refrigerate for 1 hour to allow the flavors to blend.

2. Fire up your Pit Boss pellet grill on SMOKE mode and let it run with lid open for 10 minutes then preheat to 425° F. If using a gas or charcoal grill, set it up for medium-high heat.

3. Prepare kebabs: take small amounts of ground beef kefta and shape into popsicle-size cylinders. Skewer the meat, squeezing it to mold it to the skewer.

4. Grill kefta 3 to 5 minutes per side, then remove from the grill and serve warm with pitas, tzatziki sauce, and your favorite fresh veggies.

Carne Asada Tacos

Servings: 4
Cooking Time: 10 Minutes
Ingredients:

- 1/2 Tsp Black Pepper
- 1 Tsp Garlic Powder
- 2 Lime, Juiced
- 1 Tsp Salt
- 1 1/2 Lbs Steak, Skirt
- 8 Tortilla

Directions:

1. Start your Grill on "smoke" with the lid open until a fire is established in the burn pot (3-7 minutes).
2. Preheat to 400°F Place the steaks on the grill, and grill them for 4-8 minutes, then flip the steaks and grill for an additional 4-8 minutes.
3. Remove steaks from the grill, loosely cover them with foil, and let them sit for 5-10 minutes. Next chop the steaks into pieces and serve with tortillas and any desired toppings.

Reverse Seared Picanha Steak

Servings: 4
Cooking Time:120 Mins
Ingredients:
- olive oil
- 3 lbs picanha steak, top sirloin cap, fat cap removed
- tt pit boss chop house steak rub

Directions:
1. Fire up your Pit Boss Platinum Series KC Combo and preheat to 225°F. If using a gas or charcoal grill, set it up for low, indirect heat.
2. Generously season both sides of steak with Chop House, insert temperature probe, and place steak directly on the grill grate.
3. Cover grill and cook 1 ½ to 2 hours, or until internal temperature reads 125°F to 130°F.
4. Remove steak from grill, then preheat KC Combo griddle to medium-high flame. Heat olive oil on the griddle, then sear steak 2 minutes per side on all sides.
5. Remove steak from the griddle, and allow to rest on a cutting board for 10 minutes. Slice steak, against the grain, and serve warm.

Cowboy Beans With Leftover Brisket

Servings:6 - 8
Cooking Time:180mins
Ingredients:
- 1 cup bbq sauce
- 2 cups brisket, chopped
- 1 10 oz can diced tomatoes with green chilis
- 6 garlic clove, minced
- 2, chopped jalapeno peppers
- 1 tsp kosher salt
- 1 lb. pinto beans, dried
- 2 tbsp pit boss pulled pork rub
- water
- 1 tbsp worcestershire sauce
- 1 yellow onion, chopped

Directions:
1. Fire up your Pit Boss and preheat to 400°F. If using a gas or charcoal grill, set it up for medium-high heat.
2. Rinse pinto beans thoroughly in a mesh strainer and pour into cast iron Dutch oven.
3. Add water, chopped brisket, diced tomatoes, onion, garlic, jalapenos, Pulled Pork Rub, and Worcestershire sauce to the Dutch oven. Transfer pot to the preheated grill and let come to a boil.
4. Cover the pot and reduce the grill temperature to 300° F. Cook for one hour, stirring occasionally, then add salt.
5. Continue to simmer beans another 1 ½ to 2 hours, or until beans are soft. Serve and enjoy!

Smashed Cheeseburgers

Servings: 4
Cooking Time:10mins
Ingredients:
- 1/2 lb bacon, half slices
- 1 tbsp butter
- 8 cheddar cheese, slices
- 2 lbs ground beef
- 4 hamburger buns
- 1 jalapeño, sliced thin
- pit boss chop house steak rub
- 1 yellow onion, sliced thin

Directions:
1. IIn a mixing bowl, add ground beef and season with Ch House. Divide into 12 meatballs.
2. Fire up your Pit Boss Griddle and heat the griddle over medium heat, then add bacon slices. Render out fat, then caramelize onion in bacon fat, plus butter.
3. Lay out burger buns to toast, then turn off the burner, keeping the buns in place to keep warm.
4. Move bacon and onions to the side to keep warm, then, place 6 meatballs in their place. Using a metal spatula or stainless steel mixing bowl, smash down each meatball to ¼ inch thickness. Sear 1 to 2 minutes per side. Place cheese or of 6 patties, then top with the other. Repeat this step with tl remaining 6 meatballs.
5. Assemble each smashed burger: bottom bun, cheeseburger stack, bacon, caramelized onions, sliced jalap top bun.

Smoked Kielbasa Dogs

Servings:12
Cooking Time:300mins
Ingredients:
- 1 tsp all spice, ground
- 2 tsp black peppercorns, ground
- 3 tbsp brown sugar
- 1 cup distilled ice water, divided
- 1 1/2 tsp garlic powder
- 1 1/2 lbs ground beef
- 5 lbs ground pork
- 32 - 35 hog casings
- 2 tbsp kosher salt
- 2 tsp marjoram, dried
- 1 1/2 tsp paprika
- 1 1/4 tsp speed cure, pink salt curing

Directions:
1. In a glass bowl or measuring cup, cover hog casings in warm water and let soak for 1 hour.
2. In a small bowl, whisk together brown sugar, salt, blac pepper, marjoram, garlic powder, paprika, allspice, and spe cure.
3. In a large tub, combine ground pork and ground beef. N together by hand, then add seasoning and distilled ice wate Mix mixture by hand for 1 minute, until seasoning is incorporated throughout.
4. Prepare the sausage stuffer, and fit one hog casing ovei 1 to 1 ¼ inch horn. Place a sheet tray, with a bit of water on underneath the nozzle of the stuffer and start filling the casings.
5. Once the casings are filled, twist off into desired length and refrigerate overnight.

Hang the links with S-hooks from the top rack of your
:khart Grill or Vertical Smoker. Smoke on SMOKE mode for
ours, then increase grill temperature to 300°F, which will
se the temperature of the smoking cabinet to 170°F. If using
ertical smoker, keep smoking on SMOKE mode. Continue
oking the sausage for another 1 to 2 hours, until the
ernal temperature of the sausage reaches 155° F.

Remove sausage from the smoking cabinet and either
oy hot with your favorite toppings, or place in an ice water
h for 15 minutes, dry at room temperature and refrigerate
reeze for future use.

Peppered Spicy Beef Jerky

vings: 4-6
oking Time: 240 Minutes
redients:
- 1 12 Oz Bottle Dark Beer
- 1/4 Cup Brown Sugar
- 2 Tbsp Coarse Black Pepper
- 4 Tbsp Garlic Salt
- 2 Tbsp Hot Sauce
- 2 Tablespoons, Divided Pit Boss Sweet Heat Rub
- 1 Tablespoon Quick Curing Salt
- 1 Cup Soy Sauce
- 2 Pounds Trimmed Flank Steak
- ¼ Worcestershire Sauce

rections:
When you are ready to smoke your jerky, remove the beef
m the marinade and discard the marinade.

Fire up your Pit Boss Smoker and set the temperature to
0°F. If using a sawdust or charcoal smoker, set it up for
dium low heat.

Arrange the meat in a single layer directly on the smoker
ite. Smoke the beef for 4-5 hours, or until the jerky is dry
t still chewy and still bends somewhat.

4. Remove the jerky from the grill with tongs and transfer to
a resealable plastic bag while still warm. Let the jerky rest for
1 hour at room temperature.
5. Squeeze any air out of the resealable plastic bag and
refrigerate the jerky. It will keep for several weeks. Enjoy!

Reverse Seared Ny Steak

Servings: 4
Cooking Time: 68 Minutes
Ingredients:
- 4 Tbsp Butter
- Pit Boss Steak Seasoning
- 4 - 1 1/2" Steak, New York Strip

Directions:
1. Preheat your Pit Boss Pellet Grill to 250°F then close the
lid 10-15 minutes.
2. As the grill is preheating to the perfect temperature, spice
the steaks with the Chop House steak rub.
3. Lay the steaks on the grill for roughly 60 minutes or until
the steaks reach an internal temperature of 105 to 110
degrees F. Remove the steaks and set aside.
4. Crank up the heat to 500°F, open the Flame Broiler plate
and let the grill preheat.
5. Place the steaks back on the grill and sear for 4 minutes.
Don't forget to add 1 TBSP of butter for flavor to each steak.
You know when your steak is done once the internal
temperature reaches 130 to 135°F (for medium-rare). Follow
the below internal temperature for your cooking preference:
6. Rare: 125°F
7. Medium Rare: 130°F
8. Medium: 140°F
9. Well Done: 160°F
10. Once reached for personal preference, take the steaks off
the grill and let them rest for 5 to 10 minutes before eating.
ENJOY!

CHICKEN RECIPES

Grilled Chicken Fajita Quesadillas

Servings: 4
Cooking Time: 45 Minutes
Ingredients:
- 2 Chicken, Boneless/Skinless
- 1 Tsp Chilli, Powder
- 1 Tsp Garlic Powder
- 1/2 Green Bell Pepper, Sliced
- 1 Cup Mexican Cheese, Shredded
- 1/2 Onion, Sliced
- 1/2 Tsp Oregano
- 1 Tsp Paprika, Powder
- 1/4 Tsp Pepper
- 1/2 Red Bell Peppers
- Salsa
- Sour Cream
- 4 Tortilla
- 1/2 Yellow Bell Pepper, Sliced

Directions:
1. Preheat your Grill to 350F.
2. Combine spices in a bowl and season chicken breasts. Leave a little bit of seasoning for the vegetables.
3. Place chicken on the grates and cook for 30 minutes, flipped halfway through.
4. In a Vegetable Basket, combine all vegetables and season with the remaining spice mixture.
5. Open up the flame broiler and saute over the open flame for about 15 minutes, or until the vegetables are cooked to your liking.
6. On a tortilla, layer cheese, vegetables, sliced chicken and more cheese. Fold the tortilla and place over the open flame on your Grill. Sear until the tortilla is nicely toasted and the cheese is melted. Cut and serve with salsa and sour cream.

Beer Brined Smoked Cornish Hens

Servings: 4
Cooking Time: 150 Minutes
Ingredients:
- 2 Tbsp Ales Pepper
- 12 Cups Beer Brine
- 2 Cornish Game Hens
- 2 Lemons
- 6 Rosemary Sprigs
- Salt & Freshly Ground Black Pepper
- 12 Thyme Sprigs

Directions:
1. Set your Pit Boss Lockhart grill to 300°F (I have found the setting the grill at 300 will keep the top smoker temp between 200°F and 215°F, this could vary depending on the air temp and general weather conditions. You want to keep the upper smoking cabinet between 200°F and 215°F) If you're using a vertical smoker, set temp to 200°F.
2. Stuff your hens with the rosemary, thyme, and lemons. Coat the skin with the ales pepper and freshly ground black pepper.
3. Truss your hens and tie a small loop at the legs so you can hang your birds. Hang them in the Lockhart smoker and insert a probe thermometer, cook to an internal temp of 155°F.
4. Remove the hens to rest. Final temp should be 160°F.

5. Serve these with some great creamed kale or charred asparagus.

Keto Chicken Crust Pizza

Servings: 4
Cooking Time: 35 Minutes
Ingredients:
- ½ Cup Alfredo Sauce
- 1 Tbsp Butter
- ¾ Lb. Shredded Chicken
- 2 Large Eggs
- 2 + 6 Divided Garlic Clove, Minced
- 1 ½ Cups Heavy Cream
- ¾ Cup Kale
- ¼ Cup Mushroom
- 1 Cup Grated Parmesan Cheese
- Pit Boss Champion Chicken Rub
- 2 Tbsp Red Onion, Diced
- ½ Tsp Salt

Directions:
1. Fire up your Pit Boss and preheat to 400° F. If using a gas or charcoal grill, set heat to medium-high heat. Place pizza stone on grill grates and allow to preheat. Line a pizza peel with parchment paper and set aside.
2. In a medium bowl, stir together the shredded chicken, grated Parmesan cheese, minced garlic, and sea salt. Whisk eggs lightly in a small bowl then add to chicken mixture. Mix until well combined.
3. Spread the chicken crust pizza "dough" onto the parchment paper on the pizza peel, as thinly as possible (about ¼" thick).
4. Using the pizza peel, transfer the parchment to the preheated pizza stone. Grill for 15 to 20 minutes, until firm and golden on the edges. Remove from the grill and let rest for 5-10 minutes.
5. Top pizza crust with alfredo sauce, kale, mushrooms, red onion and additional parmesan cheese. Return to the grill for 10 to 15 minutes, until the cheese is melted. Slice and serve!

Grilled Parmesan Garlic Chicken Wings

Servings: 4
Cooking Time: 25 Minutes
Ingredients:
- 4 Tbsp Butter
- 4 Lbs Chicken Wings, Trimmed And Patted Dry
- 4 Garlic Cloves, Chopped
- 2 Tbsp Olive Oil
- 1/2 Cup Parmesan Cheese, Grated
- 2 Tbsp Parsley, Chopped
- Tt Pit Boss Champion Chicken Seasoning

Directions:
1. Lay chicken wings out on a sheet tray, blot with paper towel, then season with Champion Chicken.
2. Fire up your Pit Boss grill and preheat to 400°F. If using gas or charcoal grill, set it up for medium-high heat.
3. Transfer wings to grill and cook for 20 to 25 minutes, turning every 5 minutes, until lightly browned. Remove wings from the grill and set on a sheet tray. Place in the smoking cabinet to keep warm while preparing the garlic butter.

Melt butter and olive oil in a cast iron skillet, then add
[gar]lic and simmer until fragrant. Remove from the grill.

Transfer chicken wings to a large bowl and pour garlic
[bu]tter over the wings. Add cheese and parsley, then toss well
[to c]oat. Serve warm with additional sprinkling of parmesan
[che]ese.

Lemon Garlic Parmesan Chicken Wings

[Ser]vings: 4 -8
[Coo]king Time: 30 Minutes
[Ing]redients:

2 Tablespoons Unsalted Butter, Melted
2 Lbs Chicken Wings, Trimmed And Patted Dry
3 Cloves Garlic, Minced
Juice Of 1 Lemon
2 Tablespoons Mustard, Dijon
¼ Cup Olive Oil
¼ Cup Shredded Parmesan Cheese
2 Tablespoons Parsley, Chopped
2 Tablespoons Champion Chicken Seasoning
[Dir]ections:

Set up your Pit Boss Grill. Once it's fired up, set the
[tem]perature to 350°F. If you are using a charcoal or gas grill,
[set] the temperature to medium high heat.

In a large resealable bag, combine the olive oil, minced
[gar]lic, lemon zest, lemon juice, Dijon mustard, Champion
[Chi]cken Seasoning, and chopped parsley. Seal the resealable
[bag] and give it a good shake to mix the ingredients.

Once the chicken has finished marinating, remove the
[chi]cken from the marinade and drain. Place the chicken wings
[on] the wing rack.

Place the wing rack on the grill and insert a temperature
[pro]be into the thickest part of one of the wings. Grill the wings
[for] 5 minutes, then rotate, and grill for another 5-10 minutes,
[u]ntil the internal temperature of the wings reaches 165°F.

Toss the wings in the large bowl with the melted butter
[and] shredded Parmesan until well coated. Serve immediately.

Grilled Whole Chicken With Sausage & Apple Stuffing

[Ser]vings: 4
[Coo]king Time: 90 Minutes
[Ing]redients:

¼ Tbsp Black Pepper
1 Tbsp Butter, Unsalted
1 Celery, Stalk
¾ Cup Chicken Broth
¼ Tbsp Dried Sage
1 ½ Cup Dry Stuffing, Unseasoned
1 Granny Smith Apple, Chopped
8 Oz. Italian Sausage, Casings Removed
½ Tbsp Olive Oil
3 Tbsp Pit Boss Tennessee Apple Butter Rub
¼ Tbsp Salt
¼ White Onion, Chopped
½ White Onion, Sliced
3-4 Lb. Whole Chicken
[Dir]ections:

1. Fire up your Pit Boss and preheat to 400°F, with the lid
closed. If using a gas or charcoal grill, set it up for medium-
high heat.
2. Meanwhile, rinse chicken thoroughly and dry with paper
towel. Place sliced onion in cast iron pan and set chicken on
top. Place stuffing inside chicken cavity. Sprinkle Tennessee
Apple Butter seasoning all over chicken and rub into skin.
Tuck wings under.
3. Transfer to pellet grill and cook for 45 minutes. Add 1 cup
chicken stock to pan, rotate and cook an additional 30 minutes.
Remove from grill when internal temperature reaches 165° F
and there is even browning. Allow chicken to rest for 15
minutes, then carve and serve.

Marinated Grilled Chicken Wings

Servings: 4-6
Cooking Time: 30 Minutes
Ingredients:

- 1/2 Bottle Beer, Any Brand
- 2 Lbs Chicken Wings, Whole
- 2 Tablespoon Honey
- 1 Tablespoon Pit Boss Sweet Heat Rub
- 2 Tablespoon Rice Wine Vinegar
- 1/2 Tablesoon Sesame Oil
- 1/4 Cup Soy Sauce
- 1 Tablespoon Sriracha Hot Sauce

Directions:

1. In a large glass or plastic bowl, combine the beer, soy
sauce, honey, rice wine vinegar, sriracha, sesame oil and Pit
Boss Sweet Heat Seasoning. Whisk well to combine.
2. Add the chicken wings to the marinade and toss well to
combine. Cover with plastic wrap and refrigerate for 2 hours
and up to 24 hours.
3. Remove chicken wings from refrigerator, drain marinade
and pat dry. Preheat Pit Boss Grill to 350F. Place the wings on
a grill pan and grill for 20-25 minutes, or until the wings'
internal temperature is 165F. Remove from the grill, serve and
enjoy!

Alabama White Sauce On Crispy Chicken Quarters

Servings: 4
Cooking Time: 55 Minutes
Ingredients:

- 2 Cups Alabama White Sauce
- 1 Tbsp Champion Chicken
- 4 Chicken Leg Quarters
- 1 Tbsp Olive Oil

Directions:

1. Place chicken leg quarters on a sheet tray lined with
aluminum foil. Gently pull away the skin from the chicken leg
quarters, then drizzle inside and out with olive oil. Season the
chicken leg quarters all over and under the skin with
Champion Chicken. Let chicken sit out at room temperature
for 1 hour.
2. Fire up your Pit Boss grill and preheat to 450°F with the
Sear Slide open. If using a gas or charcoal grill, set it up for
medium-high heat and direct heat.
3. Sear the leg quarters on all sides over direct flame until
crispy and golden brown. Transfer to indirect heat and close
the sear slide. Reduce temperature to 350° F and grill the

chicken for 45 minutes, turning occasionally, until chicken registers an internal temperature of 165° F.
4.   Remove chicken from grill and allow to rest for 10 minutes. Serve chicken hot with a generous drizzling of Alabama white sauce*.

Southern Fried Chicken Sliders

Servings: 8
Cooking Time: 30 Minutes
Ingredients:
- 8 Slider Buns
- ½ Cup Buttermilk
- 4 Horizontally Cut Chicken Breasts
- 2 Cups Flour, All-Purpose
- 1 Tablespoon Hot Sauce
- ¼ Cup Mayonnaise
- 2 Quarts Cooking Canola Or Soybean Oil
- ½ Cup Spicy Bread And Butter Pickle Slices
- ½ Tablespoon Champion Chicken Seasoning

Directions:
1.   Fire up your Pit Boss to 350°F. If you're using a gas or charcoal grill, set it up for medium heat.
2.   Place a deep cast iron pan on the grill and fill it with about 3 inches of cooking oil. Place a temperature probe into the oil.
3.   While the oil heats, combine the buttermilk, hot sauce and Champion Chicken seasoning in a resealable plastic bag. Seal and shake to mix, then place the chicken in the bag and turn to coat.
4.   Place the flour on a plate and dip the chicken in the flour to coat. Place the chicken on a wire rack set on a baking sheet and allow the coated chicken to set for 10 minutes, then dip again in the flour.
5.   Once the oil in the cast iron pan reaches 350°F, place a temperature probe in a piece of chicken and fry the chicken, 2-3 pieces at a time. The oil temperature in the pan will drop by 25-30 degrees, so make sure not to put more than 3 pieces of chicken in the pan or your chicken will be greasy.
6.   Fry the chicken until golden brown, crispy, and the internal temperature of the chicken is 170°F. Remove the chicken and place on a plate lined with paper towels. Allow the chicken to drain and rest for 5 minutes. Fry the remaining chicken pieces, reinserting the temperature probe.
7.   Once the chicken is all fried, place the chicken on the slider buns, top with spicy bread and butter pickles, and a swoop of mayo, serve immediately.

Beer Can Chicken

Servings: 4
Cooking Time: 75 Minutes
Ingredients:
- 1 Beer, Can
- 1 Chicken, Whole
- Pit Boss Lemon Pepper Garlic Seasoning

Directions:
1.   Preheat your Grill to 400 degrees F.
2.   Season the chicken all over with spices. Open the can of your favorite pop/beer and place the opening of the chicken over the can. Make sure that the chicken can stand upright without falling over. Place on your Grill and barbecue until the internal temperature reaching 165 degrees F (about an hour).
3.   Remove from grill, slice and serve hot.

Hibachi Chicken

Servings: 4
Cooking Time: 10 Minutes
Ingredients:
- To Taste, Blackened Sriracha Rub Seasoning
- To Taste, Blackened Sriracha Rub Seasoning (For Vegetables)
- 2 Cups Broccoli Florets, Blanched
- 1 Tbsp Brown Sugar
- 1 Tbsp Butter, Unsalted
- 1 1/2 Lbs Chicken Breast, Boneless, Skinless, Sliced Thin
- 1 Tbsp Cilantro, Chopped
- 3 Garlic Cloves, Minced
- 2 Garlic Cloves, Minced (For Vegetables)
- 1 Tsp Ginger, Grated
- 1 Tsp Ginger, Grated (For Vegetables
- 1/2 Lime, Juiced
- 1/2 Red Bell Pepper, Sliced Thin
- For Serving, Rice Noodles, Cooked
- 2 Scallions, Chopped
- 1 Tbsp Sesame Oil
- 2 Tbsp Sesame Oil, Divided
- 1 Cup Snap Peas, Blanched
- 1/4 Cup Tamari
- For Serving, Toasted Sesame Seeds
- 1 Tbsp Vegetable Oil
- 1 Tbsp Vegetable Oil (For Vegetables)
- For Serving, Yum-Yum Sauce

Directions:
1.   Fire up your Pit Boss Griddle and set it to medium-high heat. When hot, add 1 tablespoon of sesame oil and vegetable oil. Immediately add the chicken and season with Blackened Sriracha. When the chicken starts to brown, flip it over to brown the other side.
2.   Add the garlic, ginger, soy sauce, brown sugar, butter, and the remaining tablespoon of sesame oil and stir. Turn the heat down to medium-low and let the mixture simmer for 3 minutes, until it thickens and adheres to the chicken. Add lime juice, cilantro, and scallions, then remove the mixture from griddle.
3.   After starting the sauce for the chicken, sauté the vegetables: Add sesame oil and vegetable oil to the other side of the griddle. Quickly sauté broccoli, snap peas, and red bell pepper with garlic and ginger. Season with Blackened Sriracha. Remove from the griddle after 2 minutes.
4.   Serve hibachi chicken warm with sautéed vegetables, toasted sesame seeds, rice noodles, and Yum-Yum sauce if desired.

Sweet And Sour Chicken Drumsticks

Servings: 4
Cooking Time: 150 Minutes
Ingredients:
- 3 Tbsp Brown Sugar
- 8 Chicken Drumsticks
- Garlic, Minced
- Ginger, Minced
- 2 Tbsp Honey
- 1 Cup Ketchup

½ Lemon Lemon, Juice
1/2 Lime, Juiced
2 Tbsp Rice Wine Vinegar
¼ Cup Soy Sauce
1 Tbsp Sweet Heat Rub

rections:

In a mixing bowl, combine the ketchup, soy sauce, rice ne vinegar, brown sugar, honey, ginger, garlic, lemon, lime d Sweet Heat Rub. Reserve half of the mixture for dipping ce and set aside. Use the remaining half and pour into a ge resealable plastic bag. Add the drumsticks and seal bag. frigerate for at least 4-12 hours. Remove chicken from bag, carding marinade.

Fire up your Pit Boss Grill and set the temperature to 5°F. If you're using a gas or charcoal grill, set it up for low-dium heat. Smoke the chicken over indirect heat with grill closed for 2 – 3 hours, turning once or twice, until the cken reaches 180°F. During the last half hour, feel free to sh more glaze on.

Remove from grill, and let stand for 10 minutes. Feel free add more sauce if desired or use it as a dipping sauce for the msticks.

Cajun Chicken Carbonara

vings: 2
oking Time: 20 Minutes
gredients:
2 Slices Thick-Cut Bacon
1 Tbsp Cajun Seasoning
8 Oz. Chicken Breast
4 Egg, Yolk
1 Tbsp Garlic Clove, Minced
1 ¼ Cup Heavy Cream
2 Tbsp + 1 Tbsp Divided Italian Parsley
1 ½ Tbsp Divided Olive Oil
½ Cup Grated Parmesan Cheese
½ Tbsp Pit Boss Hickory Bacon Seasoning
¼ Tbsp Red Chili Flakes
1 Tbsp Scallions
½ Lb. Spaghetti

rections:

Fire up your Pit Boss and preheat to 400°F. If using a gas charcoal grill, set the temp to medium-high heat. In a dium bowl, combine chicken, Pit Boss Hickory Bacon soning, Cajun seasoning, and ½ tablespoon of olive oil. Toss combine. Set aside or place in a bag and marinate in the rigerator for 30 minutes to 1 hour.

Place tenders on preheated grill and cook for 3 minutes side. Remove from grill and place on a cutting board to t for 5 minutes. Slice thinly on the diagonal and set aside.

In a large stock pot, boil pasta per package instructions. ain and set aside.

In a large skillet heat 1 tablespoon of oil over medium t. Sauté bacon, stirring frequently, for 3 minutes or until sp. Add garlic and cook for one minute. Lower heat to low d add in drained pasta. Using tongs, gently toss pasta to coat il and bacon.

In a mixing bowl, whisk together heavy cream, parmesan, yolks, and 2 tablespoons of parsley. Slowly pour over pasta, ntinuously stirring, as to not scramble eggs. After 2 minutes, sauce will thicken. Add in chicken and lemon zest, and tly stir another minute. Transfer to serving dishes and nish with additional parsley and red chili flakes.

Peanut Butter And Jelly Chicken Wings

Servings: 4
Cooking Time: 35 Minutes
Ingredients:
- 1 Tsp Black Peppercorns, Ground
- 2 Tbsp Brown Sugar
- 4 Lbs Chicken Wings, Trimmed And Patted Dry
- 2 Tbsp Honey
- 1/4 Cup Peanut Butter
- 10 Oz Peanuts, Whole
- 2 Tsp Pit Boss Sweet Rib Rub
- 1/2 Red Onion, Minced
- 1/2 Cup Strawberry Preserves
- 1 Tbsp Thai Chili Sauce
- 1/4 Cup Worcestershire Sauce

Directions:
1. Place chicken wings in a 9 x13 glass baking dish. Pour mixture over chicken, cover with plastic wrap, and refrigerate for 2 hours.
2. Fire up your Pit Boss Platinum Series KC Combo and preheat grill to 400° F. Preheat griddle to medium-low flame. If using a gas or charcoal grill, set it to medium-high heat.
3. Place wings directly on grill grate, over indirect heat, and cook for 20 to 25 minutes, rotating wings every 5 minutes.
4. Meanwhile, place shelled peanuts on the griddle, turning occasionally with a metal spatula for 5 to 7 minutes, to lightly roast. Remove from the griddle and set aside to cool.
5. Remove wings from grill and allow to rest for 5 minutes. While wings are resting, shell the peanuts, and transfer to a resealable plastic bag. Use a rolling pin to crush the peanuts, then scatter peanuts on top of the chicken wings. Serve warm.

Whole Smoked Chicken With Honey Glaze

Servings: 4
Cooking Time: 40 Minutes
Ingredients:
- 1 Tablespoon Honey
- 1 ½ Lemon
- 4 Tablespoons Pit Boss Champion Chicken Seasoning
- 4 Tablespoons Unsalted Butter
- 1, 4 Pound Chicken, Giblets Removed And Patted Dry

Directions:
1. Start up your Pit Boss Smoker. Once it's fired up, set the temperature to 225°F.
2. In a small saucepan, melt together the butter and honey over low heat. Squeeze ½ lemon into the honey mixture and remove from the heat.
3. Smoke the chicken, skin side down until the chicken is lightly browned and the skin releases from the grate without ripping, about 6-8 minutes.
4. Turn the chicken over and baste with the honey butter mixture.
5. Continue to smoke the chicken, basting every 45 minutes, until the thickest part of the chicken reaches 160°F.

Chicken Fajita Omelet

Servings: 4
Cooking Time: 12 Minutes

Ingredients:

- 1 Cup Bell Pepper, Sliced Thin
- To Taste, Blackened Sriracha Rub Seasoning
- 2 Tbsp Butter
- 1 Cup Cheddar Jack Cheese, Shredded
- 8 Oz Chicken Breast, Boneless, Skinless, Sliced Thin
- 6 Eggs, Beaten
- 1 Tbsp Heavy Cream
- 1 Jalapeño, Minced
- 1/2 Lime
- 1 Cup Red Onion, Sliced Thinly
- 1/3 Cup Salsa Roja
- 2 Tbsp Sour Cream
- 1 Tbsp Vegetable Oil, Divided

Directions:

1. Fire up your Pit Boss Griddle and preheat to medium heat. If using a gas or charcoal grill, preheat a cast iron skillet.
2. Drizzle sliced chicken breast with 1 teaspoon oil, then season with Blackened Sriracha.
3. Drizzle the remaining oil on the griddle, then add the chicken. Sauté for 2 minutes, then add the bell peppers and onions. Season with additional Blackened Sriracha and continue to sauté another 2 minutes, then deglaze with fresh squeezed lime juice. Remove mixture from the griddle, set aside.
4. Turn the griddle down to low, then whisk the eggs (3 per omelet) and heavy cream.
5. Melt 1 tablespoon of butter on the griddle. Quickly pour the eggs over the melted butter.
6. Flip the eggs, then add ¼ cup of cheese and divide all but ½ cup of the reserved filling into the middle of each egg. Add additional cheese and some minced jalapeño. Fold the egg over to shape the omelet.
7. Transfer the omelet to a plate and top with additional filling, cheese, salsa, sour cream, and jalapeño. Serve warm.

Bossin' Buffalo Chicken Wings

Servings: 4-6
Cooking Time: 25 Minutes
Ingredients:

- Bleu Cheese Dip
- ⅔ Cup Buffalo Sauce
- Celery
- 2 Lbs. Chicken Wings
- ½ Cup Pit Boss Sweet Heat Rub

Directions:

1. Fire up your Pit Boss and preheat to 450° F. If using a gas or charcoal grill, set heat to high heat.
2. Rub wings generously with Pit Boss Sweet Heat Rub and transfer to wing rack.
3. Place rack on grill and cook for 20 minutes, rotating after 10 minutes.
4. Baste with sauce, then cover and grill an additional 5 to 7 minutes. Note: your cooking time will vary depending on the size of the wings. When done, wings should have an internal temperature of 165°F.
5. Remove wings from grill and transfer to a baking sheet and let rest for about 5 minutes.
6. Transfer wings to a large bowl and coat with the Buffalo Sauce. Shake the bowl around gently to combine or use a spatula to ensure every wing is coated.
7. Serve hot with extra sauce, celery, and bleu cheese dip.

Chicken Lollipops With Sticky Asian Sauce

Servings: 3
Cooking Time: 45 Minutes
Ingredients:

- To Taste, Blackened Sriracha Rub Seasoning
- 1/4 Cup Brown Sugar
- 3 Lbs Chicken Drumsticks
- 2 Garlic Cloves, Minced
- 2 Tbsp Honey
- 1" Knob Of Ginger Root, Grated
- 2 Tsp Sesame Oil
- For Garnish, Sliced Scallions
- 3 Tbsp Sweet Chili Sauce
- 1/4 Cup Tamari
- For Garnish, Toasted Sesame Seeds
- 2 Tsp Vegetable Oil

Directions:

1. Prepare lollipops: Use a sharp knife coupled with kitchen shears to cut around the leg, just below the knuckle, then tear/clip off. Cut out loose skin, tendons, and clip the small bone against the leg, then push the meat down. Transfer to a sheet tray while repeating with remaining chicken legs. Season with Blackened Sriracha.
2. Fire up your Pit Boss pellet grill on SMOKE mode and let run with lid open for 10 minutes then preheat to 350° F. If using a gas or charcoal grill, set it up for medium heat.
3. Place the chicken lollipops on the grill, over indirect heat and cook for 25 to 30 minutes, flipping and rotating occasionally, until an internal temperature of 165° F is reached.
4. Remove from the grill and rest for 10 minutes.
5. While lollipops are resting, prepare the sauce: Place a small cast iron skillet on the grill. Add sesame oil, vegetable oil, honey, sweet chili sauce, brown sugar, tamari, ginger, and garlic. Whisk to combine, then bring to a simmer. Simmer for minutes until sauce thickens and sugar is dissolved.
6. Remove skillet from the grill, cool for 5 minutes, then roll each lollipop in the sauce. Transfer to a platter, and garnish with scallions and toasted sesame seeds. Serve warm.

Garlic Sriracha Chicken Wings

Servings: 6-8
Cooking Time: 160 Minutes
Ingredients:

- 1 Cup Buffalo Sauce
- 6 Lbs Chicken Wings
- 2 Tbsp Garlic Powder
- 1 Tsp Pepper
- Divided By 2 Tbsp And ½ Tbsp Pit Boss Sweet Heat Rub
- 1 Tsp Salt
- ⅓ Cup, Divided Sriracha Sauce

Directions:

1. In a non-stick sauce pot, add the remaining Sriracha and buffalo sauce. Stir to combine and set aside.
2. Fire up your Pit Boss and preheat to 250° F. If using a gas or charcoal grill, set it to low heat with indirect heat. Place marinated wings directly on grill grate and cook (covered) for 1 hour 15 minutes.
3. Flip wings and baste each piece with Sriracha sauce. Season with additional Pit Boss Sweet Heat Rub, cover, and continue to grill for an additional 1 hour 15 minutes.

Remove wings from grill and place on sheet tray. Baste h additional sauce, then open Sear Slide and return wings he grill. Grill for 3-5 minutes, rotating often, until wings in to char lightly.

Transfer wings to a serving tray, baste with remaining ce and serve!

Jerk Chicken Wings

vings: 0
king Time: 0 Minutes
redients:

1 Tsp Allspice, Ground
3 Lbs Chicken Wings, Split
1/2 Tsp Cinnamon, Ground
4 Garlic Cloves, Smashed
2 Tsp Ginger, Grated
1 Habanero Pepper, Chopped
2 Tbsp Honey
2 Tbsp Lemon Juice
1/3 Cup Lime Juice
1/2 Tsp Nutmeg, Ground
1/2 Cup Olive Oil
1/4 Cup Poblano Pepper, Chopped
1 Tbsp Tamari
2 Tsp Thyme, Dried
1/2 Cup Yellow Onion, Chopped

ections:
Add chicken to a large resealable plastic bag.
In the bowl of a food processor, add the garlic, onion, ger, peppers, tamari, honey, lime juice, lemon juice, thyme, pice, cinnamon, nutmeg, and oil. Process on low for 1 ute, then transfer marinade to the bag. Seal the bag and ce in the refrigerator for at least 2 hours, up to overnight.
Fire up your Pit Boss pellet grill on SMOKE mode and let it with lid open for 10 minutes then preheat to 425° F. If ng a gas or charcoal grill, set it up for medium-high heat.
Remove wings from the marinade, and discard remaining rinade. Place wings on the grill and cook for 15 to 20 autes, flipping every 5 minutes, until an internal nperature of 165 F is reached.
Remove wings from the grill and serve warm.

Bacon-wrapped Stuffed Chicken Breasts

vings: 4 - 6
king Time: 270 Minutes
redients:

5 Oz Frozen Spinach, Thawed, Strained
8 Bacon Slices
1 Tbsp Butter
4 Chicken Breasts, Boneless, Skinless, Butterflied
2 Garlic Clove, Minced
1 Cup Italian Cheese Blend, Shredded
8 Oz Mushrooms, Sliced Thin
1 Tbsp Olive Oil
1 Tbsp Pit Boss Hickory Bacon Rub
1 Yellow Onion, Chopped

ections:
Fire up your Pit Boss KC Combo and preheat both grill griddle to 375°F. If using a gas or charcoal grill, set heat to dium heat. For all other grills, preheat cast iron skillet on l grates.

2. Heat olive oil and butter on griddle, then add mushrooms and cook for about 3 minutes, stirring frequently. Add chopped onion and garlic and cook for 2 minutes. Add spinach and sauté another minute, then transfer vegetables to a heat-safe bowl to cool slightly.
3. Season the butterflied chicken breasts with Hickory Bacon, coating both sides. Sprinkle half of cheese over each butterflied chicken breast, followed by the sautéed vegetables, and the remaining half of the cheese.
4. On a metal sheet tray, lay out two bacon slices. Gently fold chicken breast halves together and place on top of bacon slices, then wrap tightly with bacon. To secure, tuck ends of bacon underneath, or insert a toothpick to hold it together. Repeat with remaining breasts.
5. Arrange the chicken breasts, bacon seam down, directly on the grill grate and grill, turning once or twice, until the bacon is crisp and golden brown, about 25 to 30 minutes, or until internal temperature reaches 165°F.
6. Remove from grill, allow to rest for 5 minutes, remove any toothpicks, then serve hot.

Cheesy Chicken

Servings: 4
Cooking Time: 45 Minutes
Ingredients:

- 4 Aged Chedder Cheese, Sliced
- 32 Oz Chicken Broth
- 1 Tsp Extra-Virgin Olive Oil
- Pit Boss Sweet Heat Rub And Grill
- 4 Plump Chicken, Boneless/Skinless

Directions:
1. Fill your hopper with your choice of pellets (we chose Competition Blend), preheat your grill to 350°F.
2. Remove the chicken from the brine. Pat the breasts dry and lightly brush olive oil on both sides of the chicken. Take your knife and slice diagonally across the top of each breast. Sprinkle a lit amount of Pit Boss Sweet Heat Rub and Grill on each side.
3. Barbecue your chicken breasts for 30 minutes. Next, place a slice of cheddar cheese on top of each breast.
4. Heat for another 5-10 minutes or until the cheese has fully melted into the incisions you made earlier. Remove and serve for a tender chicken breast with a spicy kick and hot cheesy center. You'll receive too much credit for a recipe this easy.

Champion Lollipop Drumsticks

Servings: 4-6
Cooking Time: 75 Minutes
Ingredients:

- 1 Cup Barbecue Sauce
- 10 Tablespoons Butter, Salted
- 12 Chicken Drumsticks
- 1 Cup Hot Sauce
- Pit Boss Champion Chicken Seasoning
- Blue Cheese Or Ranch Dressing

Directions:
1. Start up your Pit Boss. Then, set the temperature to 300°F.
2. Rinse chicken and pat dry with a paper towel.
3. Chop the very top of the drumstick on the larger, meaty side so the lollipops sit flatly. On the small end of the

drumstick, about an inch above the knuckle, use a sharp knife or kitchen shears to cut the skin and tendons all the way down to the bone and pull the skin and cartilage off the knuckle.

4.   Remove the tiny, sharp bone that sits right against the exposed chicken leg. Then, push all the meat and skin down to form the lollipop ball. Use your knife or shears to remove any excess tendons.

5.   Season each lollipop generously with Champion Chicken seasoning and place in the aluminum pan with the flat side done and bones standing straight up. Then, cut 10 tablespoons of butter into cubes of 1 tablespoon each and place evenly throughout the rows of lollipops.

6.   Cook lollipop drumsticks on your Pit Boss at 300°F for 1 hour; checking back every 20 minutes to baste the meat with the melted butter on the bottom of the pan.

7.   For the Sauce: add your favorite bbq sauce into one aluminum loaf pan. Then, add 1 cup of hot sauce and 10 tablespoons of butter into the other aluminum loaf pan. Place them on the grill 5 minutes before your chicken is done. Stir well once it's warm and the butter has melted.

8.   After 1 hour, use a thermometer to check the internal temperature of the lollipops. They will be ready to glaze when the temperature reaches 165°F.

9.   Once ready, dip 6 lollipops in the bbq sauce and 6 in the buffalo sauce making sure to hold the leg and cover the meat entirely. Then, place the lollipops on the wing rack and put back on the grill for 15 more minutes or until the sauce is set.

Crispy And Easy Bbq Chicken Wings

Servings: 4
Cooking Time: 40 Minutes
Ingredients:
- 1 Pack Chicken Wings
- Extra Virgin Olive Oil
- Champion Chicken Seasoning

Directions:
1.   Set grill to 350°.
2.   Blot the defrosted chicken wings dry with paper towels.
3.   Brush oil onto each side of the wings and sprinkle with seasoning.
4.   Grill at 350° for 40 minutes or until wings are crispy. Flip halfway through. Serve hot.

Zesty Chile Cilantro Lime Chicken Wings

Servings: 4
Cooking Time: 20 Minutes
Ingredients:
- 1 Tsp Ancho Chili Powder
- 2 Tsp Blackened Sriracha Rub Seasoning
- 2 Lbs Chicken Wings, Split
- 2 Tbsp Cilantro, Chopped, Divided
- 1 Tsp Cumin
- 1 Lime, Zest & Juice
- 1 1/2 Tbsp Olive Oil

Directions:
1.   In a medium bowl, combine 1 tablespoon of cilantro, lime juice and zest, olive oil, Blackened Sriracha, ancho chili powder, and cumin.
2.   Place chicken wings in a resealable gallon bag and add cilantro mixture. Transfer to the refrigerator and marinate for 1 hour, turning occasionally.

3.   Fire up your Pit Boss Platinum Series KC Combo and se to 350° F. If using a gas or charcoal grill, set it up for mediur heat.

4.   Remove chicken wings from the marinade and place or the grill over indirect heat. Grill for 15 to 18 minutes, turnin and rotating every 3 to 5 minutes.

5.   Remove chicken wings from the grill, garnish with remaining cilantro, and serve warm.

Buffalo Wing Chicken Drumsticks

Servings: 4
Cooking Time: 30 Minutes
Ingredients:
- Buffalo Style Dry Rub
- Carrot, Stick
- Celery, Stick
- 12 Chicken, Drumsticks

Directions:
1.   Preheat your Grill to 350 degrees F.
2.   Generously sprinkle the Buffalo Wing Rub all over the drumsticks. Hang each drumstick by the bone on the Wing Rack. Place in the for about 30 minutes.
3.   Serve hot with celery and carrot sticks. Enjoy!

Chicken Cordon Bleu

Servings: 8
Cooking Time: 75 Minutes
Ingredients:
- 8 Chicken, Boneless/Skinless
- 1 Cup Mozzarella Cheese, Shredded
- Pit Boss Lemon Pepper Garlic Seasoning
- 8 Prosciutto, Sliced

Directions:
1.   Preheat your Grills to 250 degrees F.
2.   Pound each chicken breast with a mallet or cast iron pa so that it's about ½ inch thick.
3.   On a piece of prosciutto, sprinkle mozzarella cheese an roll up. Place in the middle of a chicken breast and wrap the chicken around the prosciutto roll. Sprinkle with Lemon Pepper seasoning.
4.   Smoke for an hour to 75 minutes, or until internal temperature reaches 165 degrees F.

Grilled Sweet Heat Chicken Wings

Servings: 4
Cooking Time: 40 Minutes
Ingredients:
- 16 Chicken, Wing
- 3 Tbsp Lime, Juiced
- Pit Boss Sweet Heat Rub

Directions:
1.   We are fans of wings. They"re a great way to try out ne seasonings and, lets be honest, they"re a breeze to cook. Th recipe serves 2–4.
2.   Rinse the chicken wings under cold running water and blot dry with paper towels. Arrange the wings lengthwise o baking dish. Drizzle lime juice evenly over wings.
3.   Shake Sweet Heat Rub Grill seasoning over the wings, turning the wings to coat evenly.

Light your ceramic charcoal barbecue to 350°F. Place the
[he]at deflector in the barbecue and place grate over top heat
[def]lector.

Place the wings directly on the grate. Grill over indirect
[hea]t until crispy, about 20–25 minutes per side. Transfer
[win]gs to a platter and serve with your favorite dipping sauce.

Fig Glazed Chicken With Cornbread Stuffing

[Ser]vings: 10
[Coo]king Time: 120 Minutes
[In]gredients:

Black Pepper
6 Tablespoons (For The Chicken) Butter, Unsalted
3 Chicken, Whole
2 1/5 Cups (Replace With Craisins For A Different Flavor)
[Dri]ed Figs, Chopped
1 Egg
2 Tablespoon Extra-Virgin Olive Oil
1/2 Cup Heavy Cream
1/2 Cup Honey
Kosher Salt
4 Tablespoon Lemon, Juice
1/2 Onion, Chopped
Pit Boss Champion Chicken Seasoning
1 1/2 Teaspoon Finely Chopped Rosemary, Fresh
1 Pound Sweet Italian Sausage
3 Cups Water, Warm
[Di]rections:

Mix figs, honey, lemon juice, and warm water. Cover with
[pla]stic wrap and let figs soften for 30 minutes. Strain the figs
[and] reserve the liquid for glaze.

Heat olive oil over medium heat and sauté the onions with
[ros]emary. Add the sausage. Cook until browned. Place into a
[lar]ge bowl, add the cornbread and figs. Season with Pit Boss
[Ch]ampion Chicken Seasoning. Stir. In a separate bowl, Stir
[tog]ether egg, heavy whipping cream, and chicken stock. Pour
[ov]er the cornbread/fig mix and stir together. Set aside.

Rinse chickens and pat dry. Season liberally with Pit Boss
[Ch]ampion Chicken Seasoning, kosher salt and black pepper.
[Do]n't forget the cavity! Stuff cavities with Stuffing. Top each
[chi]cken with 2 tablespoons butter.

Preheat your Pit Boss to 300°F. Place in a roasting tray
[and] cook until internal temp reads 165°F.

While chickens cook, place the fig liquid, balsamic vinegar
[and] butter over. Reduce to thicken and baste chickens with
[abo]ut 160°F or 10 minutes before finished. Rest for 10
[mi]nutes. Carve and serve!

Loaded chicken Nachos

[Ser]vings: 6-8
[Coo]king Time: 10 Minutes
[In]gredients:

1 Can Black Beans, Rinsed And Drained
1 Cup Cheddar Cheese, Shredded
2 Cups Chicken, Diced
(If Desired) Cilantro
1 Can Corn Kernels, Drained
(If Desired) Pickled Jalapeno Peppers
1/2 Tablespoon Pit Boss Champion Chicken Seasoning
1/2 Red Onion, Diced
1/2 Cup Salsa

• 1/4 Cup Sour Cream
Directions:
1. On a large sheet pan, spread out half the tortilla chips,
then cover with half the shredded cheese and one cup of
chicken. Sprinkle with half of Champion Chicken seasoning.
Top with the rest of the tortilla chips, cheese, chicken and
remaining seasoning.
2. Turn your Pit Boss Grill to 350F. Grill for 5-7 minutes, or
until the cheese is melted and bubbly and everything is
warmed all the way through. Remove the pan from the grill.
3. Top the nachos with the black beans, corn, diced red
onion, sour cream, cilantro and pickled jalapenos. Serve and
enjoy!

Grilled Chicken Kabobs

Servings: 6
Cooking Time: 15 Minutes
Ingredients:
• 3 (Cut Into 1 Inch Cubes) Chicken Breast, Raw
• 2 Cloves Garlic, Minced
• 2 Tablespoons Honey
• 1 Pound Of Button (Destemmed And Cut In Half)
Mushroom
• 1/2 Cup Olive Oil
• 1 Red (Cut Into Quarters And Seperated) Onion
• 1 Green (Cut Into Large Chunks) Bell Pepper
• 2 Tablespoons Pit Boss Competition Smoked Seasoning
• 2 Tablespoons Soy Sauce
Directions:
1. To make the marinade: In a large bowl, combine the olive
oil, soy sauce, honey, garlic and Competition Smoked. Add the
chicken and mix well. When the chicken is covered completely,
allow it to marinate for 2-12 hours.
2. In a large, shallow baking dish, soak the kabob skewers
for a minimum of 2 hours and up to 12 hours.
3. Once the chicken has finished marinating and the skewers
are finished soaking, drain the water from the skewers and
remove the chicken from the marinade.
4. Start your Pit Boss on "smoke". Once it's fired up, set the
temperature to 350°F.
5. Thread a piece of chicken, followed by a piece of pepper,
mushroom, and onion. Repeat until the skewers are full.
6. Grill the kabobs for 5 minutes on one side, then flip and
grill for 5 more minutes or until the chicken reaches an
internal temperature of 180°F. Remove from the grill and
serve.

Bbq Chicken Stuffed Bell Peppers

Servings: 4
Cooking Time: 15 Minutes
Ingredients:
• ½ Cup Barbecue Sauce
• 4 Bell Pepper
• ½ Cup Cheddar Cheese, Shredded
• 2 Cups Leftover Chicken, Chopped
• 2 Tablespoons Champion Chicken Seasoning
Directions:
1. Wash and slice the bell peppers in half, long ways. Deseed
them and set aside.
2. Preheat your Pit Boss. Once it's fired up, set the
temperature to 350°F.

3. In a large bowl, mix together the cheese, chicken, Champion Chicken Seasoning, and barbecue sauce, then stuff inside the pepper halves.
4. Grill the peppers for 7-10 minutes or until the peppers are softened and the filling is heated through and melted. Remove from the grill and serve.

Chicken Enchiladas

Servings: 6
Cooking Time: 45 Minutes
Ingredients:
- 2 Cups Chicken, Shredded
- 1 (12 Oz) Package Colby Jack Cheese, Shredded
- 1 Enchilada Sauce, Can
- 1 Can Green Chiles, Drained
- 1 Onion, Diced
- 1 Tablespoon Pit Boss Sweet Rib Rub
- 1 Cup Sour Cream
- 1 Package Flour Tortilla

Directions:
1. Start up your Pit Boss. Then, set the temperature to 300°F.
2. In a bowl, mix - the chicken, green chiles, Sweet Heat seasoning, sour cream, diced onion, and half the bag of shredded cheese.
3. Place a large spoonful of the chicken mixture in the center of a tortilla and roll it up. Repeat with the remaining tortillas, then place in the baking pan, and pour the enchilada sauce over the tortilla pans. Top with the remainder of the shredded cheese.
4. Wrap the top of the pan tightly in aluminum foil and grill for 45 minutes or until the enchilada sauce is bubbly. Remove from the grill and serve.

Pulled Chicken Corn Fritters

Servings: 8
Cooking Time: 45 Minutes
Ingredients:
- 2 Tsp Baking Powder
- 1 Cup Cheddar Jack Cheese, Shredded
- 1 1/2 Lbs Chicken Breast, Bone-In
- 3/4 Cup Corn Kernels, Drained
- 2 Eggs
- 3/4 Cup Flour
- 1 1/2 Tsp Lemon Juice
- 3 Tbsp Mayonnaise
- Olive Oil
- 2 Tbsp Parsley, Chopped
- 2 Tsp Pit Boss Champion Chicken Seasoning, Divided
- 1 Tbsp Scallions, Chopped
- 2 Tbsp Sour Cream
- 1 Yellow Onion, Chopped
- 1/3 Cup Milk

Directions:
1. Fire up your Platinum Series KC Combo and preheat to 425° F. If using a gas or charcoal grill, set it up for medium-high heat.
2. Remove skin from chicken breast. Drizzle chicken with olive oil, then season with 1 teaspoon of Champion Chicken. Place directly on grill grate, over indirect heat and grill for 25 minutes, until internal temperature is 165° F. Remove from the grill and rest for 10 minutes, then pull chicken.

3. In a mixing bowl combine onion, corn, eggs, parsley, mi cheese, and pulled chicken.
4. In a separate mixing bowl, whisk together remaining teaspoon of Champion Chicken, flour and baking powder. Combine with the wet ingredients, then cover with plastic wrap and refrigerate for 2 hours.
5. Prepare dip: whisk together mayonnaise, sour cream, scallions, parsley, and lemon juice. Refrigerate until fritters a ready to serve.
6. Preheat griddle over medium-low flame.
7. Drizzle vegetable oil on the griddle, then add ¼ cup of fritter mixture to the griddle and cook 3 to 4 minutes per si adding additional oil if needed.
8. Transfer fritters to a wire rack lined sheet tray. Allow to cool for 2 minutes, then serve warm with dip.

Jerk Chicken Kebabs

Servings: 4
Cooking Time: 12 Minutes
Ingredients:
- 1 Tablespoon All Spice, Ground
- 2 Lbs Chicken, Boneless/Skinless
- 1 Tablespoon Cinnamon, Ground
- 1/4 Cup Extra-Virgin Olive Oil
- 3 Garlic, Cloves
- 2 Inch Piece Ginger, Fresh
- 3 Green Onion
- 1 Lime, Juiced
- 1 Tablespoon Nutmeg, Ground
- 1 Cup Orange Juice, Fresh
- Pepper
- 1 Red Onion, Chopped
- Salt
- Skewers
- 1/4 Cup Soy Sauce
- 1/4 Cup Thyme, Fresh Sprigs

Directions:
1. Soak the bamboo skewers in water for about 30 minute (the longer the better).
2. In a food processor, combine orange juice, oil, soy sauce thyme, allspice, nutmeg, cinnamon, garlic, onions, ginger, lin juice, salt and pepper. Puree until smooth.
3. In a large resealable bag, pour all but 1/4 cup of the mixture in along with the sliced up chicken breasts. Seal the bag and marinate in the fridge for 2 - 3 hours.
4. Preheat your Grill to 450 degrees F.
5. Skewer the chicken and grill for about 7 minutes. Flip a continue grilling for about 5 minutes, or until the chicken is cooked through and grill marks appear. Serve with the remaining 1/4 cup of marinade.

Pulled Chicken Jalapeno Sliders

Servings: 8-10
Cooking Time: 180 Minutes
Ingredients:
- 3 Pounds Boneless Skinless Chicken Breasts
- 8-10 Slices Cheese Of Choice
- 1/2 Cup Chicken Broth
- Pickled Jalapeños
- 1 Tsp Pit Boss Smoked Infused Sweet Mesquite Jalapen Sea Salt

1/2 Cup Salsa Verde
1 Package Slider Buns
3 Tablespoons Sweet Heat Rub

ections:

Add the chicken breasts, chicken broth, and salsa verde to isposable aluminum foil pan. Season everything generously h Sweet Heat and 1 tsp of Pit Boss Smoked Infused Sweet squite Jalapeno Sea Salt. Cover tightly with aluminum foil.

Fire up your Pit Boss Grill and set the temperature to °F. Place the aluminum foil pan on the grill and cook for 3-ours, or until the chicken is completely cooked (165°F rnal temperature), tender, and falling apart. Remove from grill and let cool slightly.

Shred the chicken with the meat claws and toss with the et Heat rub. Then, build the sliders: top the slider buns h a scoop of the pulled chicken, a slice cheese, and a few es of pickled jalapeños. Serve immediately.

Grilled Honey Chipotle Chicken Wings

vings: 4 - 8
king Time: 30 Minutes
redients:

2 Chipotles Chopped In Adobo
1 Apple Cider Vinegar
2 Tablespoons Balsamic Vinegar
¼ Cup Brown Sugar
2 ½ Lbs Chicken Wings, Trimmed And Patted Dry
¼ Cup Honey
½ Cup Ketchup
¼ Cup Adobo Sauce
2 Tablespoons Sweet Rib Rub
2 Teaspoons Worcestershire Sauce

ections:

Fire up your Pit Boss Grill. Once it's fired up, set the perature to 350°F. If you're using a charcoal or gas grill, set the grill for medium high heat.

In a large bowl, whisk together the apple cider vinegar, chup, brown sugar, honey, chopped chipotle peppers with bo sauce, balsamic vinegar, Worcestershire sauce, and et Rib Rub. Whisk the glaze until it's well combined.

Add the wings to the glaze and place the bowl in the igerator. Marinade the chicken wings for up to 12 hours. e the wings have finished marinating, remove the chicken gs from the marinade and place the chicken wings onto the g rack.

Once all the wings have been placed on the wing rack, ce the wing rack on the grill. Insert a temperature probe the thickest part into one of the wings and grill the wings 5 minutes, and then rotate the rack 180° and grill for ther 5 minutes. Remove the wings once they have an rnal temperature of 165°F and the juice from the chicken s clear.

Remove the wings from the grill and serve immediately.

Grilled Chicken Burrito Bowls

vings: 4
king Time: 20 Minutes
redients:

1 Avocado
1 Can Black Beans, Rinsed And Drained
1 ½ Pounds Boneless Skinless Chicken Strips

- 1 Tablespoon Cilantro, Chopped
- 1 Can Corn Kernels, Drained
- Juice From 1 Lime
- ½ Lime Lime Juice
- 1 ½ Cups Long Grain White Rice
- 2 Tablespoons Olive Oil
- 2 Tablespoons Pit Boss Sweet Heat Rub
- ¼ Cup Salsa
- 1 Teaspoon Salt
- ½ Cup Shredded Mexican Blend Cheese
- ¼ Cup Sour Cream

Directions:

1. Fire up your Pit Boss and set the temperature to 350°F. If using a gas or charcoal grill, set it up for medium heat.
2. Place the rice in a fine mesh sieve and rinse under cold water for 2-5 minutes, or until the water runs clear. Add the rice to a pot with 2 cups of water and 1 teaspoon of salt and bring to a boil on the stove top. Once the rice boils, drop the temperature to a simmer, place the pot lid on top securely, and let the rice cook for 20-25 minutes.
3. Once the time is up, remove the rice from the heat, and allow it to steam with the lid on for a further 10 minutes. Remove the lid from the rice, add the lime juice and cilantro, and fluff the rice with a fork. Set aside.
4. Grill the chicken for 5-7 minutes, or until the chicken reaches an internal temperature of 165°F and is golden and charred in some spots. Remove the chicken from the grill and allow it to rest for 5 minutes before slicing into bite sized pieces.
5. To assemble the burrito bowls: place a large scoop of cilantro lime rice into a bowl. Top with slices of grilled chicken, a scoop of black beans, a scoop of corn, salsa, cheese, sour cream, and avocado. Serve immediately.

Smoked Queso Dip With Pulled Chicken

Servings: 6
Cooking Time: 65 Minutes
Ingredients:

- To Taste, Ale House Beer Can Chicken Seasoning
- 1 Lb Chicken Breasts, Boneless, Skinless
- 1 Tbsp Cilantro, Chopped
- 1 Tsp Cumin, Ground
- 2 Jalapeños, Chopped
- 2 Tsp Olive Oil
- 1 Bag Tortilla Chips
- 1 Lb White American Cheese, Cubed
- 1 Cup Milk

Directions:

1. Fire up your Pit Boss pellet grill on SMOKE mode and let it run with lid open for 10 minutes then preheat to 350° F. If using a gas or charcoal grill, preheat to medium heat.
2. Score the chicken, rub with olive oil, then season with Ale House Beer Can Chicken.
3. Transfer the chicken to the grill and cook for 8 to 10 minutes, turning occasionally.
4. Remove chicken from the grill, and reduce the temperature to 225° F. Allow the chicken to rest for 10 minutes, then pull apart with 2 forks. Set aside.
5. While the chicken is resting, heat a cast iron skillet on the grill. Partially open the sear slide, then to the skillet add the cubed cheese, jalapeño, milk, and cumin. Stir occasionally, for 5 minutes, until the cheese melts. Fold in the pulled chicken,

then close the lid and allow the dip to smoke for 30 to 45 minutes.

6. Remove from grill and let rest for 5-10 minutes to thicken. Serve warm with fresh cilantro and tortilla chips.

Smoked Chicken Drumsticks

Servings: 4
Cooking Time: 30 Minutes
Ingredients:
- 1/2 Cup Apple Cider Vinegar
- 12 Chicken Drumsticks
- 2 Tablespoons Dijon Mustard
- 1/4 Cup Honey
- 1/4 Cup Ketchup
- 1 Tablespoon Pit Boss Sweet Heat Rub
- 1/2 Cup Soy Sauce

Directions:
1. Start your grill on smoke. Once it's fired up, set the temperature to 225°F. Remove the wings from the marinade and place the drumsticks into the Pit Boss Buffalo Wing Rack.
2. Smoke for 60 minutes, or until a thermometer inserted into the thickest part of the drumstick registers at 170°F.
3. Turn the heat up to 350°F and cook for 5 to 10 minutes to make the skin crisp.
4. Remove from the smoker, serve immediately and enjoy!

Spinach Artichoke Chicken Grilled Cheese

Servings: 2
Cooking Time: 20 Minutes
Ingredients:
- 1/2 Jar Marinated Artichoke Hearts, Drained And Chopped
- 4 Bread, Slices
- 2 Tablespoon Butter, Unsalted
- 2 Chicken Breast, Raw
- 4 Oz Cream Cheese, Softened
- 1/4 Cup Parmesan Cheese, Shredded
- 1 Tablespoon Pit Boss Champion Chicken Seasoning, Divided
- 1 Bag Spinach, Fresh

Directions:
1. Preheat your Pit Boss grill to 350F. Using 1 tablespoon of the Pit Boss Champion Chicken seasoning, season both chicken breasts. When grill is up to temperature, grill chicken breasts until fully cooked, about 7 minutes on each side. Remove from the grill, allow to cool, and slice into bite sized strips.
2. In a large bowl, combine the cream cheese, spinach, artichoke hearts, parmesan cheese, and remaining Champion Chicken seasoning. Mix well until everything is thoroughly combined.
3. On a stovetop, heat a large frypan over medium heat and add the butter. Spread the spinach artichoke mixture onto the bread, add the chicken, and cook until the bread is a deep golden brown and the cheese is melty.
4. Remove from the pan and enjoy!

Grilled Fried Chicken Wings

Servings: 6
Cooking Time: 50 Minutes

Ingredients:
- 4 Lbs Chicken Wings, Whole
- 1 Cup Cornmeal
- 2 Eggs
- 1 Cup Flour
- 2 Tbsp Pit Boss Champion Chicken Rub
- 1 Cup Milk

Directions:
1. Fire up your Pit Boss Pellet Grill and preheat to 300°F. using a gas or charcoal grill, set it up for medium-low heat.
2. Place chicken wings on a sheet tray, then cut off the tip each wing with a knife, or scissors. Pat dry with a paper tow
3. In a mixing bowl, whisk together flour, cornmeal, and Champion Chicken. Set aside.
4. In another mixing bowl, whisk together milk and eggs. aside.
5. Form "breading" station: wings, egg wash, seasoned flo sheet tray. Dunk each wing in egg wash, then coat in season flour. Set aside on a sheet tray, while coating the remaining wings.
6. Place wings directly on the grill rack. Flip/rotate wings every 10 minutes for 45-55 minutes, until golden and "fried crisp."
7. Remove from the grill, rest for 10 minutes, then serve warm.

Buffalo Chicken Egg Rolls

Servings: 4
Cooking Time: 75 Minutes
Ingredients:
- 1/4 Cup Bleu Cheese, Crumbled
- 1/4 Cup Buffalo Sauce
- 1 Lb Chicken Breasts - Boneless, Skinless
- 4 Oz Cream Cheese, Softened
- 8 Egg Roll Wrappers
- 1/2 Jalapeno Pepper, Minced
- Pinch Pit Boss Sweet Heat Rub
- 1/4 Red Bell Pepper, Chopped
- 4 Scallion, Sliced Thin
- 1/4 Cup Sour Cream
- 2 Cups Vegetable Oil

Directions:
1. Fire up your Pit Boss grill and preheat to 200°F. If usin gas or charcoal grill, set it up for low, indirect heat.
2. Season chicken breasts with Pit Boss Sweet Heat Rub, then place on the grill. Smoke for 1 hour, then remove from grill, cool, shred, and set aside.
3. Prepare the filling: In a mixing bowl, use a hand mixer t blend cream cheese, bleu cheese, Buffalo sauce and sour cre
4. Fold in scallions, jalapeño, red bell pepper, and shredde chicken.
5. Prepare egg rolls: Lay an egg roll wrapper on a flat sur and add 3 tablespoons of filling to the middle.
6. Fold the bottom of the wrapper over the top of the filli then fold over each side. Brush the top point of the wrapper with warm water, then roll the wrapper tight. Transfer to a tray while filling the remaining wrappers.
7. Increase the temperature of the grill to 425°F, then set cast iron Dutch oven on the grill. Add vegetable oil and heat 5 minutes.
8. Place 3 egg rolls in heated oil and fry until golden, 1 to minutes per side.

Transfer to a wire rack to cool, then fry the remaining egg
ls, in batches.

Cool egg rolls for 2 minutes, then slice in half and serve
rm with celery sticks and extra Buffalo sauce for dipping.

Buffalo Ranch Chicken Wings

rvings: 4
oking Time: 20 Minutes
gredients:

1 1/2 Tbsp Apple Cider Vinegar
1/2 Cup Butter, Unsalted, Cubed
1/4 Tsp Cayenne Pepper
3 Lbs Chicken Wings, Split
2 Tsp Chives, Minced (Garnish)
1/8 Tsp Garlic, Granulated
2/3 Cup Hot Pepper Sauce
1 Tbsp Ranch Seasoning
To Taste, Sweet Heat Rub
1/2 Tsp Sweet Heat Rub (For Sauce)
1/4 Tsp Worcestershire Sauce

rections:

Fire up your Pit Boss pellet grill on SMOKE mode and let it
a with lid open for 10 minutes then preheat to 425° F. If
ng a gas or charcoal grill, set it up for medium-high heat.

Place chicken wings in a large mixing bowl. Season with
eet Heat.

Prepare sauce: Set a small cast iron pan or saucepan on
e grill. Add the hot pepper sauce, apple cider vinegar,
orcestershire sauce, Sweet Heat, cayenne, and granulated
lic to the skillet, and whisk to combine. When the sauce
gins to bubble, remove the skillet from the grill and whisk in
tter. Transfer the sauce to a mason jar.

Combine 1 cup of the buffalo sauce with ranch seasoning.
. aside.

Place wings on the grill and cook for 20 minutes, flipping
d rotating every 3 to 5 minutes.

Remove wings from the grill when an internal
mperature of 165° F is reached. Transfer to a mixing bowl,
en pour sauce over. Toss to evenly coat. Garnish with fresh
ves and serve warm.

Grilled Hand Pulled Chicken & White Bbq Sauce

rvings: 4
oking Time: 90 Minutes
gredients:

2 Tablespoons Apple Cider Vinegar
1 Clove Garlic, Minced
Juice Of Half Of A Lemon
1 Cup Mayo
1 Tablespoon Olive Oil
½ Teaspoon Paprika, Powder
2 Tablespoons Sugar
1, 3-4 Pound Chicken, Giblets Removed And Patted Dry
4 Tablespoons Champion Chicken Seasoning

rections:

Start up your Pit Boss. Once it's fired up, set the
mperature to 350°F.

In a large bowl, mix all the ingredients for the sauce
gether. Divide the sauce between two bowls and set aside.

On a clean, flat surface, lay your chicken breast side down.
ing the kitchen shears, remove the spine and discard. Open

the chicken up and flip the chicken over so that it lays breast
side up. Press the breastbone down with the heel of your hand
to flatten the chicken.

4. Generously rub the chicken with the olive oil and
Champion Chicken. Place on the grill, skin-side up, on the
grates. Grill for 1 ½ hours, basting with half the reserved sauce
every 20 minutes, until the internal temperature reaches
175°F. Remove the chicken from the grill and cover loosely for
10 minutes.

5. Shred the chicken with forks and discard the skin and
bones. Serve the chicken with the remaining white BBQ sauce.

Loaded Chicken Fries With Cheese And Bacon

Servings: 4
Cooking Time: 20 Minutes
Ingredients:

- 8 Slices Bacon, Cooked And Diced
- 1 12 Oz Bag Cheese, Shredded
- 1 Bag Fries, Frozen
- 2 Tablespoons Green Onions, Diced
- ¼ Cup White Barbecue Sauce

Directions:

1. Start up your Pit Boss. Once it's fired up, set the
temperature to 400°F.

2. Bake the fries on the baking sheet in your Pit Boss
according to the manufacturer's instructions. Once the fries
are done, remove them from the grill and reduce the
temperature to 350°F.

3. Top the fries with the cheese, chicken and bacon. Place
the fries back on the grill and cook for another 5-7 minutes, or
until the chicken is warmed through and the cheese is melted.
Remove the fries from the grill.

4. Top the fries with the white barbecue sauce and green
onions and serve immediately.

Smoked Chicken Lo Mein

Servings: 4 – 6
Cooking Time: 120 Minutes
Ingredients:

- 2 Cup Broccoli
- ¼ Cup Chicken Stock
- 6 - 8 Chicken Thighs, Boneless, Skinless
- 1 Tbsp Chili Flakes
- 1 Tsp Cornstarch
- 4, Chopped Garlic Cloves
- 3 Tbsp Hoisin Sauce, Divided
- Knob Of Fresh Ginger, Grated
- 1, Thin Red Bell Peppers, Sliced
- 1 Tbsp Rice Wine Vinegar
- 8 Scallions, Sliced
- 1 ½ Tbsp Sesame Oil, Divided
- 1 Tbsp, Toasted Sesame Seeds
- 3.5 Oz Shitake Mushrooms, Sliced Thin
- 8 Oz Snow Peas
- 3 Tbsp Soy Sauce
- 2 Tbsp Sweet Chili Sauce
- 3 Tbsp Vegetable Oil
- 1 Lb Vermicelli Noodles, Or Linguini, Cooked And Drained

Directions:

1. In a large bowl, whisk together rice wine vinegar, 1 tablespoon of Hoisin sauce, and 1 tablespoon of sesame oil. Toss chicken to coat and allow to marinate for 1 hour.
2. Fire up your Pit Boss Platinum Series KC Combo and preheat to 225° F. If using a gas or charcoal grill, set it for low, indirect heat. Place chicken directly on the grill grate and smoke for 1 ½ to 2 hours, or until the internal temperature reaches 165° F. Remove it from the smoker, cover with foil, and rest for 10 minutes, then slice thin and set aside.
3. In a glass measuring cup whisk together 2 tablespoons of Hoisin sauce, soy sauce, sweet chili sauce, chicken stock, ½ tablespoon of sesame oil, and cornstarch. Set aside.
4. Preheat griddle to medium flame, then add oil. Working quickly, sauté ginger and garlic for 15 seconds, then add bell pepper and mushrooms and continue cooking for another minute, then add in snow peas and slaw. Toss in cooked pasta, chicken, scallions, and pour sauce over. Cook for one minute until sauce thickens and is well incorporated.
5. Transfer to platter and serve hot. Sprinkle with chili flakes and sesame seeds, if desired.

Champion Beer Can Chicken On The Grill

Servings: 4
Cooking Time: 75 Minutes
Ingredients:
- 3 Tbsp Barbecue Sauce
- 1 Can Beer, Any Brand
- 2 Tbsp Olive Oil
- 4-6 Tbsp Pit Boss Champion Chicken Seasoning
- 1 Whole Chicken

Directions:
1. Remove the chicken from the bag and make sure all the giblets and organs are removed from inside the chicken. Rinse the bird, inside and out, then pat dry.
2. Pour out half a can of beer until you have half a can remaining. Into the can of beer, or a chicken throne, add the barbecue sauce. Set aside.
3. Brush the chicken generously with olive oil and season with Pit Boss Champion Chicken Seasoning. Let the chicken sit for at least 15 minutes with the seasoning on top.
4. Carefully slide the chicken onto the beer can or chicken throne so that the cavity fits snugly. Tuck the chicken wings behind the chicken's back.

Buffalo Chicken Stuffed Peppers

Servings: 6
Cooking Time: 90 Minutes
Ingredients:
- 1 1/2 Tbsp Apple Cider Vinegar
- 3 Tbsp Bleu Cheese, Crumbled
- 1/4 Cup Buffalo Sauce
- 1/2 Cup Butter, Unsalted, Cubed
- 1/4 Tsp Cayenne Pepper
- 3 Celery Stalks, Cut Into Sticks
- 1 Cup Cheddar Jack Cheese, Shredded
- 1 Lb Chicken Breast, Boneless, Skinless
- 3 Oz Cream Cheese, Softened
- 1/8 Tsp Garlic, Granulated
- 2/3 Cup Hot Pepper Sauce
- 12 Jalapeno Peppers
- Mason Jar(S)

- 1/4 Red Bell Pepper, Chopped
- 2 Scallions, Sliced Thin
- Shredded Chicken
- 3 Tbsp Sour Cream
- To Taste, Sweet Heat Rub
- 1/2 Tsp Sweet Heat Rub (For Sauce)
- 1/4 Tsp Worcestershire Sauce

Directions:
1. Fire up your Pit Boss pellet grill on SMOKE mode and le run with lid open for 10 minutes then preheat to 200° F. If using a gas or charcoal grill, set it up for low, indirect heat.
2. Season chicken breasts with Sweet Heat, then place on grill. Smoke for 1 hour, then remove from the grill, and set aside to rest.
3. While the chicken is resting, prepare the Buffalo sauce: Set a small cast iron pan or saucepan on the grill. Open the sear slide and increase the grill temperature to 350° F. Add t hot pepper sauce, apple cider vinegar, Worcestershire sauce Sweet Heat, cayenne, and granulated garlic to the skillet, an whisk to combine. When the sauce begins to bubble, remove the skillet from the grill and whisk in butter. Transfer the sauce to a mason jar.
4. Shred the chicken with 2 forks in the sauce skillet. Set aside.
5. Prepare the filling: In a mixing bowl, use a hand mixer t blend cream cheese, bleu cheese, Buffalo sauce and sour cre Fold in scallions, red bell pepper, and shredded chicken.
6. Prepare the peppers: Cut each jalapeño in half, lengthw Use a paring knife or teaspoon to scrape out the seeds and membrane, then place in a cast iron skillet (might need to divide between 2 skillets). Stuff the mixture into the jalapeñ halves, then top with shredded cheese.
7. Transfer peppers to the grill, with the sear slide closed. Close the lid and cook for 15 to 20 minutes, until peppers begin to soften and cheese has melted.
8. Remove the peppers from the grill, transfer to a serving board or platter, and serve warm with extra Buffalo sauce.

Chicken Pepper Sliders

Servings: 5
Cooking Time: 20 Minutes
Ingredients:
- 16 Oz Chicken, Ground
- 1 Pepper, Anaheim
- Pit Boss Jalapeno Brat Burger Seasoning
- 1 Red Bell Peppers
- Spinach

Directions:
1. Turn your grill onto smoke until the flame catches, then turn it to 400°F.
2. Put the ground chicken into a bowl and generously add the Jalapeno Brat Burger seasoning to the mixture.
3. Dice the Anaheim pepper and add it to the bowl as well
4. Mix with your hands until the meat looks evenly coated
5. Separate the meat out into 3oz balls, disperse or toss th remnants.
6. Use the Pit Boss 3-in-1 Burger press to create the perfe patty! If your chicken is too sticky to use the burger press, w put the 3oz balls into a tinfoil covered pan and placed that o the grill. Allow to cook 20-25 minutes, do not flip.
7. Add the buns to the grill if you'd like them toasted!
8. Remove the chicken sliders (and the buns) from the gri add spinach, red peppers and whatever else you enjoy!

Caution: contents may be hot :)

moked Chicken Legs With Spicy Cola Bbq Sauce

vings: 6
)king Time: 110 Minutes
redients:

- 1/4 Cup Brown Sugar
- 1/2 Tsp Or To Taste Cayenne Pepper
- 6 Chicken, Drumsticks
- 1 Cup Of Your Favorite Cola
- 2 Tbs Competition Chicken Seasoning
- 1 Tbs Honey
- 1/2 Tsp To Taste Hot Sauce
- 1 Cup Ketchup
- 2 Tbs Pit Boss Hot Wing Sauce

ections:

For the chicken:Preheat smoker to 300 degrees.
In a small bowl,Pour hot sauce over legs and toss to coat.
Sprinkle legs with Competition Chicken Seasoning and
: Wing Seasoning.
Toss to evenly distribute seasoning.
Place legs in Grills Wing Rack or lay on grill.
Cook for 1 hour 45 minutes, or until legs reach an internal
perature of 170 degrees.
Brush legs with sauce and return to grill for 5- 10 minutes
llow sauce to cook onto meat.
Serve with extra sauce on the side.Place all ingredients
) a small sauce pan and whisk.
Bring to a boil then immediately reduce to a simmer,
isking often
Allow to simmer for 15 minutes or until sauce is
jinning to thicken
Remove from heat and allow to cool
Pork or Beef, chicken does not have as much
amuscular fats that need to render out to result in tender
at
You can cook chicken at a hotter temperature to ensure
 get tender, moist chicken every time
Use a meat thermometer to know exactly when to pull the
cken off the grill
I pull white meat at 165 degrees, and dark meat, such as
se legs, at 175 degrees

Bourbon Breaded Chicken And Waffles

vings: 8
)king Time: 30 Minutes
redients:

- 1 Shot Of Bourbon
- 3 Cups Bread Crumbs
- 4 Horizontally Half Sliced Boneless, Skinless Chicken
ast
- Butter Flavored Cooking Spray
- 3 Eggs
- 1 Tsp Garlic Powder
- 1 Tsp Paprika, Powder
- Red Velvet Cake Mix
- 16 Oz. Reduced Fat Sour Cream
- Sweet Rib Rub
- ¼ Cup Vegetable Oil
- 1 ¼ Cup Water
- 1 Tbsp Worcestershire Sauce

Directions:
1. Fire up your Pit Boss and set the temperature to 350°F. If you're using a gas or charcoal grill, set up the grill for medium heat.
2. In a large bowl, combine the sour cream, bourbon, Worcestershire sauce, paprika, garlic powder, and Sweet Rib Rub seasoning. Add the chicken, turn the chicken breasts to coat, and cover the bowl. Refrigerate for 4-12 hrs.
3. Remove the chicken from the refrigerator and drain the marinade from the chicken. Mix together 3 cups bread crumbs and 2 tbsp Sweet Rib Rub. Mix the coating together and bread the chicken breasts.
4. Moisten a paper towel with cooking oil and using a pair of tongs, lightly grease the grill rack.
5. Grill or smoke until the internal temperature of the chicken reaches 170°F and the chicken is crispy and golden brown.
6. While the chicken is cooking, mix the eggs, vegetable oil, water, and red velvet cake mix in a bowl with the electric mixer.
7. Add the mix into the waffle iron and cook. Make as many waffles as the mix allows.
8. On a plate, place the cooked chicken on top of the waffles and top with maple syrup or honey.

Asian Bbq Wings

Servings: 6
Cooking Time: 60 Minutes
Ingredients:

- 2 Lbs Chicken, Wing
- 1 Tsp Garlic, Minced
- 1 Tsp Ginger, Fresh
- 1 Tsp Chopped Green Onion
- 1/2 Cup Hoisin Sauce
- 1 Tsp Honey
- 2 Tsp Rice Vinegar
- 2 Tsp Sesame Oil
- 1 Tsp Sesame Seeds
- 1 Tsp Soy Sauce
- 1 Cup Water, Boiling

Directions:
1. Add all ingredients except wings and sesame seeds to a mixing bowl and whisk to incorporate. Add wings to a resealable plastic bag and pour marinade over. Allow marinating for at least 2 hours up to overnight. Remove wings from bag, reserving marinade.
2. Preheat grill to 300°F. Place wings in a grilling basket and cook for 1 hour or until they reach an internal temperature of 165°F.
3. While wings are cooking, pour reserved marinade into a small saucepan and add rice wine vinegar. Over high heat, bring to a boil while whisking often, and reduce by 1/3, or about 10 minutes. Set aside.
4. Brush wings with reduced sauce and allow to cook for 5-10 more minutes or until glaze has set. Remove from smoker, sprinkle with sesame seeds, allow to rest for 5 minutes, and serve.

Buffalo Chicken Pinwheels

Servings: 8
Cooking Time: 10 Minutes

Ingredients:
- 2 T Bleu Cheese, Crumbled
- ½ Cup Buffalo Wing Sauce, Divided
- 1-2, Boneless And Skinless Chicken Breast
- ½ Cup Colby Cheese, Shredded
- 4 Oz. Cream Cheese
- 4, 10" Diameter Flour Tortillas
- 2 Scallions, Thinly Sliced [Reserve 1 Tsp Of Green For Garnish]

Directions:
1. Fire up your Pit Boss Grill and preheat to 375°F. If you're using a gas or charcoal grill, set it up for medium heat. Remove chicken from refrigerator place on grill. Grill chicken for 10 min, turning once. Allow to rest 10 minutes, then shred.
2. In a food processor, add remaining buffalo wing sauce, cream cheese, Colby cheese, bleu cheese, and scallions. Process on low for 20 seconds. Add shredded chicken breast to mixture and pulse about 8 times, or until mixture is fully combined.
3. Place tortillas on a flat work surface and divide filling into quarters. Spread mixture evenly over each tortilla with a rubber spatula.
4. Roll up tortillas and place seam side down on cutting board. Refrigerate for 10 minutes, then slice into ½ inch pieces. Transfer to serving platter and garnish with remaining scallions. Serve with extra buffalo sauce or ranch dressing.

Cajun Bbq Chicken

Servings: 4
Cooking Time: 25 Minutes
Ingredients:
- ½ Cup Barbecue Sauce
- ¼ Cup Beer, Any Brand
- 1 Tablespoon Butter
- 1 Pound Boneless, Skinless Chicken Breasts
- 2 Cloves Garlic Clove, Minced
- ¼ Teaspoon Ground Thyme
- 1 Teaspoon Hot Sauce
- Juice Of 1 Lime
- 1 Tablespoon Olive Oil
- ½ Teaspoon Oregano
- 2 Tablespoons Sweet Heat Rub
- 1 Tablespoon Worcestershire Sauce

Directions:
1. In a small mixing bowl, mix together the Sweet Heat Rub, oregano, and ground thyme.
2. Rub the chicken breasts all over with olive oil, making sure to completely coat the meat. Generously season the chicken breasts on all sides with the Sweet Heat mixture.
3. Fire up your Pit Boss and set the temperature to 350°F. If you're using a gas or charcoal grill, set it up for medium heat. Insert a temperature probe into the thickest part of one of the chicken breasts and place the meat on the grill. Grill the meat on one side for 10-12 minutes, then flip and grill for another 5-7 minutes, or until the chicken breasts are golden brown and juicy and reaches an internal temperature of 165°F.
4. Remove the chicken from the grill and allow to rest for 10 minutes.
5. While the chicken rests, make the sauce. Combine the butter, barbecue sauce, beer, Worcestershire sauce, lime juice, and minced garlic in a heat proof saucepan and place on the grill. Bring the sauce to a boil. Once it boils, remove it from heat, whisk it and serve with the chicken.

Smoked Chicken Quesadilla Ring

Servings: 4-8
Cooking Time: 180 Minutes
Ingredients:
- 2-3 Boneless, Skinless Chicken Breasts
- 1 Jalapeno, Chopped
- 1 Onion, Chopped
- Pit Boss Sweet Heat Rub
- 1, Chopped Red Bell Pepper
- 1-2 Cups Salsa
- 3 Cups Shredded Cheddar Cheese
- 3 Cups Shredded Monterey Or Pepper Jack Cheese
- Taco Sauce
- 20 Taco-Size Tortilla

Directions:
1. Fire up your Pit Boss Grill to Smoke with the lid open u a fire is established (about 5 minutes). Preheat to 350°F. If you're using a gas or charcoal grill, set it up for medium hea Preheat with lid closed for 10-15 minutes.
2. Sprinkle chicken breasts generously in Sweet Heat Rub and rub to coat evenly. Place chicken breasts directly on preheated grill grates and cook for 45 minutes, or until the chicken is completely cooked (165°F internal temperature) tender, and falling apart. Remove from the grill and let cool slightly. Shred with meat claws and set aside. Turn grill up t 375°F.
3. In a large bowl, add the shredded chicken, onion, red b pepper, jalapeno, and taco sauce. Mix to combine then set aside.
4. Cut each tortilla in half. Add about 2 tablespoons each the cheddar cheese, Monterey Jack cheese, and chicken mixture to each tortilla half. Roll the tortillas into cones, starting from the cut edge, making sure not to push the ingredients out of the tortilla.
5. Place the small bowl in the center of the pizza plan and begin to stack quesadilla cones in a ring around the bowl. T points of each cone should be in the center just touching th bowl. Sprinkle cheese over the layer and repeat another lay with the remaining cones, finishing with a final sprinkle of cheese.
6. Remove bowl from the center of the ring and place the pizza pan directly on the grill grates. Cook with the lid close for 15-20 minutes, or until the cheese is melted and the edg are browned and crispy.
7. Fill small bowl with salsa and return to the center of th ring. Serve immediately and enjoy!

Smoked Boneless Chicken Thighs With Teriya Glaze

Servings: 8 - 10
Cooking Time: 55 Minutes
Ingredients:
- 2 Tbsp Ginger Root, Grated
- 5 Lbs. Boneless Skinless Chicken Thighs
- ⅔ Cup Brown Sugar
- 2 Cups Chicken Broth
- 1 Tsp Chinese Five-Spice Powder
- 5 Garlic Cloves, Minced

¼ Cup Honey
1 Tbsp Pit Boss Sweet Heat Rub
½ Cup Soy Sauce
1 Yellow Onion, Minced

rections:

When ready to cook, fire up your Pit Boss and preheat to
5°F. If using a gas or charcoal grill, set it up for low heat.

Remove chicken from marinade and place on a metal
eet tray. Using a mesh strainer, strain the marinade directly
o a cast iron skillet.

3. Place skillet with marinade and chicken on the grill. Allow chicken to smoke for 10 minutes, then increase grill temperature to 400°F.

4. Grill an additional 15 minutes. Make sure to stir marinade periodically. The sauce will begin to reduce and thicken as it cooks.

5. After 15 minutes, baste chicken thighs with marinade, then flip and baste the other sides. Grill an additional 15 minutes, then baste again.

6. Cook until glaze has caramelized and thickened, then remove from grill and serve hot.

PORK RECIPES

Texas Smoked Ribs

Servings: 4
Cooking Time: 240 Minutes
Ingredients:
- 1 Cup Apple Cider Vinegar
- 1 Rack Baby Back Rib
- 2 Tablespoons Whole Grain Mustard
- 2 Tablespoons Olive Oil
- 1 Bottle Pit Boss Sweet Heat Rub
- 1 Tablespoons Worcestershire Sauce

Directions:
1. Remove the ribs from their packaging and pat dry.
2. Flip to back of ribs and score the membrane with a knife, then peel off the membrane.
3. Rub the ribs with the olive oil, followed by a generous amount of Pit Boss Sweet Heat Rub & Grill, on both sides.
4. In a small bowl, mix together the mustard, apple cider vinegar, and Worcestershire. Set aside.
5. Start up your grill. Once it's fired up, set the temperature to 225°F. Add the ribs and smoke for 3 hours.
6. Transfer the ribs onto a foil lined sheet pan and brush both sides with the apple cider vinegar mixture. Wrap the ribs tightly in foil and place back on the smoker for 2 more hours.
7. Carefully remove the ribs from the foil and brush with more of the apple cider vinegar mixture. Place the ribs back on the smoker grates and smoke for 1 additional hour.
8. Remove from the smoker and let rest for 5 minutes before serving.

Next Level Smoked Porchetta

Servings: 6
Cooking Time: 360 Minutes
Ingredients:
- 1 Tbs Ancho Chili Powder
- 1/2 Cup Brown Sugar
- 3 Tbs Grilling Seasoning
- 1 Tbs Chopped Italian Parsley
- 1/2 Cup Maple Syrup
- 1 Tsp Dry Oregano
- 1 Tbs Chopped Oregano, Leaves
- 1/2 Pork, Belly (Skinless)
- 1 Whole Pork, Tenderloins
- 6 Slices Prosciutto, Sliced
- 1 Tbs Chopped Rosemary, Fresh
- 1 Tbs Chopped Sage, Leaves
- 1/2 Cup Sugar, Cure

Directions:
1. Sprinkle Sugar Cure on each side and rub in. (You can cure pork belly without using Sodium Nitrite (in the cure mix) but it is much safer if you use it, so I definitely recommend it).
2. In a small bowl, mix brown sugar, maple syrup, ancho chili powder and oregano, and whisk. Slather on both sides of each pork belly piece.
3. Place pork bag (if you can find a 2 gallon or larger one) or container and refrigerate Rotate and flip each 24 hours.
4. After 3 days remove pork belly and rinse each piece thoroughly.
5. If you do not rinse well the porchetta (or bacon) will be too salty due to the sugar cure.

6. Lay pork belly skin side down on a large cutting board.
7. Lightly score the meat side with diamond cuts to allow the seasoning to penetrate.
8. Lightly sprinkle with grilling seasoning, then coat well with the herb mix.
9. Lay out the prosciutto, then lay the pork tenderloin on t pork belly.
10. Lightly sprinkle tenderloin with seasoning, and wrap th pork belly tightly around it.
11. Use cooking twine to tie up tightly.
12. Season the exterior of the pork belly lightly but evenly with grilling seasoning.
13. Place in smoker with apple wood pellets (recommended at 250°F.
14. Smoke for 6 hours, or until internal temperature reache around 175°F.
15. Remove and allow to rest for 20 minutes. Once it cools, then slice thinly and sear in a hot skillet.
16. Let it cool again for about 10 minutes before serving.

Pork Butt With Sweet Chili Injection

Servings: 6
Cooking Time: 300 Minutes
Ingredients:
- To Taste, Blackened Sriracha Rub Seasoning
- 1/2 Tbsp Blackened Sriracha Rub Seasoning (For Injection)
- 1/4 Cup Butter, Melted
- 2 Cups Chicken Stock
- 1/2 Cup Chicken Stock (For Injection)
- 1 Tbsp Ginger Root, Sliced Thin
- 1/2 Lime, Juiced
- 1 Tbsp Olive Oil
- 5 Lbs Pork Butt, Bone-In
- 1 Red Onion, Sliced
- 1/4 Cup Rice Vinegar
- 1/2 Tbsp Sugar, Granulated
- 2 Tbsp Sweet Chili Sauce

Directions:
1. Place the pork butt on a sheet tray and pat dry with a paper towel.
2. Prepare the injection solution: Whisk together all ingredients in a glass measuring cup (1/2 cup Chicken Stock 1/4 cup melted Butter, 1/4 cup Rice Wine Vinegar, 1/2 tbsp Blackened Sriracha Rub Seasoning, 1/2 Lime juice, 1/2 tbsp granulated Sugar).
3. Use a meat syringe to inject the solution into the pork b spacing every ½ inch.
4. Score the fat cap in a cross-hatch pattern, then rub swe chili sauce on the outside of the pork butt, and season with Blackened Sriracha. Allow to sit at room temperature for 30 minutes.
5. Fire up your Pit Boss and with the lid open, set your temperature to SMOKE mode.
6. Once the fire is lit, preheat to 250° F. If using a gas or charcoal grill, set it up for low, indirect heat.
7. Place the pork shoulder on the grill grate and smoke fo hours.
8. Place a Dutch oven or deep cast iron skillet on the grill. Heat olive oil, then add sliced onion and ginger, and set pork

t on top. Pour in chicken stock, then cover with a tight lid or

Increase temperature to 325° F, and braise for 3 hours,
il pork is tender. Remove the pork from the Dutch oven,
set aside to rest on a sheet tray, or cutting board.
Pull pork, then serve warm with braising jus.

Bbq Smoked Pork Loin

vings: 4
king Time: 120 Minutes
redients:
1 Tbsp Olive Oil
Pit Boss Pulled Pork Rub
3 Lbs Pork Loin, Center-Cut
ections:
Fire up your Pit Boss pellet grill and preheat to 250°F. If
ng a gas or charcoal grill, set it up for low, indirect heat.
Score the fat cap of the loin in a cross-hatch pattern, then
zzle with olive oil, and season with Pit Boss Pulled Pork Rub.
Transfer the pork directly on the grates. Smoke for 1 ½ to
ours, until the internal temperature reaches 145°F.
Remove the pork loin from the gill and rest for 15 minutes,
ore slicing and serving warm.

Grilled Pork Loin With Blackberry Sauce

vings: 4
king Time: 30 Minutes
redients:
2 Tablespoons Balsamic Vinegar
2 Cups Fresh Washed And Dried Blackberries
¼ Cup Seedless Blackberry Preserve
½ Teaspoon Dijon Mustard
Pinch Of Kosher Salt
1 Tablespoon Olive Oil
1 Pound Silver Skin And Extra Fat Removed Pork Loin
2 Tablespoons Sweet Rib Rub
1 Tablespoon Worcestershire Sauce
ections:
Place your pork loin on a flat work surface. Trim the pork
if necessary. Rub the tenderloin all over with olive oil until
fully coated. Once the pork loin is completely coated,
erously season all over with Sweet Rib Rub until every part
he pork loin is coated. Allow the pork tenderloin to rest at
m temperature for 30 minutes.
While the pork loin rests, make the blackberry sauce. In a
ll bowl, place a metal strainer on top combine the fresh
ckberries, seedless blackberry preserves, balsamic vinegar,
rcestershire sauce, Dijon mustard, and Sweet Rib Rub. Mix
l and set aside.
Fire up your Pit Boss Grill and set the temperature to
°F. If you're using a gas or charcoal grill, set it up for
dium heat. Insert a temperature probe into the thickest
t of the pork loin and smoke at 225°F for 4-5 hours, flipping
e, until the pork loin is golden brown and charred in some
ts, and reaches an internal temperature of 145°-165°F.
nove the pork loin from the grill and allow it to rest for 5
utes.
Slice the pork loin thinly and serve with the blackberry
ce.

Pulled Pork Nachos

Servings: 4 - 6
Cooking Time: 270 Minutes
Ingredients:
- ½ Cup Apple Cider
- ½ Avocado, Diced
- 2 Tbsp Cilantro, Chopped
- ¼ Cup Crema
- 2 Tbsp Jalapeno, Chopped
- 1 Cup Marble Jack, Grated
- 2 Tbsp Pit Boss Sweet Heat Rub
- 2 Lbs Pork Shoulder
- 1 Cup Queso Fresco, Crumbled
- ¼ Cup Red Bell Pepper, Chopped
- 1 Tsp Red Chili Flakes
- 2 Tbsp Red Onion, Chopped
- 2 Tbsp Scallions, Chopped
- 10 Oz. Tortilla Chips
- 1 Cup Water

Directions:
1. Fire up your Pit Boss and preheat pellet grill to 225° F. If using a gas or charcoal grill, set it up for low, indirect heat.
2. Combine Sweet Heat and chili flakes, then sprinkle over pork shoulder, rubbing to coat all sides.
3. Place seasoned pork shoulder directly on the grill grate, fat side up, then close the lid and smoke the pork until it reaches an internal temperature of 175° F, about 2 ½ hours.
4. Transfer pork to a disposable aluminum pan, with cider and water. Cover with aluminum foil and cook another 2 hours, or until the pork reaches an internal temperature of 202° F.
5. Remove the pork shoulder from the grill and allow it to rest for 30 minutes before shredding with meat claws.
6. In a cast-iron skillet, build 2 layers of toppings beginning with chips, followed by cheese, red onion, scallions, bell pepper, jalapeno, and cilantro. Transfer to grill for 10 minutes, until cheese is melted.
7. Top nachos with avocado and crema. Serve hot.

Stuffed Pork Shoulder

Servings: 8 - 10
Cooking Time: 240 Minutes
Ingredients:
- Aluminum Foil Aluminum Foil
- 1 Diced Apple
- 1 Cup Broth, Chicken
- 2 Tbsp Butter, Salted
- 1 Diced Onion
- 1 Pork Shoulder Or Pork Butt Roast
- 1 Box Or Bag Of Stovetop Stuffing Mix
- Champion Chicken Seasoning

Directions:
1. Prepare the pork shoulder. Place the pork shoulder on the cutting board, and with a sharp knife, trim any very fatty sections of the pork shoulder and remove. Then, butterfly the shoulder. Beginning on one side, carefully cut a slit horizontally into one side of the pork shoulder and carefully continue to slice almost all the way to the right side, rolling the shoulder as you cut, unfolding the meat like a book, until the pork shoulder is one long strip.
2. Began to make the stuffing by using a medium sized pan and adding 2 tbsp of salted butter to the pan. Add in the onion and apple and let cook for about 5 minutes making sure to stir

in between. Add 2 tbsp of Champion Chicken Seasoning. Add the 1 cup of chicken broth followed by a bag of stuffing mix. Let reduce and mix together very well and remove from heat. Transfer to a bowl and set aside.

3. Once the pork shoulder is butterflied, place some stuff on the roast making sure to leave enough space to roll and tie the roast as well.

4. Starting on one end of the pork shoulder, roll the pork shoulder up into a tight spiral, and set onto the cutting board, seam side down. Cut four even lengths of butcher's twine, and wiggle under the pork shoulder, two inches apart from each other. Tie tightly to hold the roast together and place on a sheet pan.

5. Start your Pit Boss Wood Pellet Grill and set the temperature to 250°F. If you're using a gas or charcoal grill, set it up for medium low heat. Place the aluminum pan in the center of the grill and cook for 3-4 hours, or until the temperature of the pork shoulder reaches an internal temperature of 180°F and is very tender.

6. Remove the pork shoulder from the grill and allow to rest for 15 minutes, then slice and serve.

Pulled Pork

Servings: 6 - 8
Cooking Time: 300 Minutes
Ingredients:
- 1/3 Cup Apple Cider Vinegar
- 4 Cups Chicken Broth
- 1/3 Cup Ketchup
- 2 Tbsp Pit Boss Pulled Pork Seasoning
- 4 Lbs. Pork Shoulder, Bone In

Directions:
1. Preheat your Pit Boss grill to 350°F. In a bowl, combine the chicken broth, ketchup, apple cider vinegar, and 1 tablespoon of Pulled Pork Seasoning. Whisk well to combine and set aside.

2. Generously season the pork shoulder with the remaining 3 tablespoons of Pulled Pork Seasoning on all sides of the pork shoulder, then place on the grill and sear on all sides until golden brown, about 10 minutes.

3. Remove the pork shoulder from the grill and place in the disposable aluminum pan. Pour the chicken broth mixture over the pork shoulder. It should come about 1/3 to ½ way up the side of the pork shoulder. Cover the top of the pan tightly with aluminum foil.

4. Reduce the temperature of your Pit Boss grill to 250°F. Place the foil pan on the grill and grill for four to five hours, or until the pork is tender and falling off the bone.

5. Remove the pork from the grill and allow to cool slightly. Drain the liquid from the pan, reserving about a cup, then shred the pork and cover with the reserved liquid. Serve and enjoy!

Grilled Pork Tenderloin

Servings: 4
Cooking Time: 20 Minutes
Ingredients:
- 2 Tablespoons Brown Sugar
- 2 Tablespoons Olive Oil
- 2 Tablespoons Pit Boss Tennessee Apple Butter Seasoning
- 1 Pork Tenderloin, Trimmed With Silver Skins Removed

Directions:
1. In a small bowl, combine the olive oil, brown sugar, and Tennessee Apple Butter seasoning until well combined. Generously rub the pork tenderloin with the mixture. Allow the pork tenderloin to marinade for 1 hour.

2. Start your Pit Boss on smoke. Once it's fired up, set the temperature to 350°F.

3. Grill the tenderloin for 5-7 minutes on each side, flipping the tenderloin only once and cooking until the internal temperature reaches 140-145°F.

4. Remove the tenderloin from the grill and allow to rest minutes before slicing and serving.

Easy Ribs

Servings: 5
Cooking Time: 240 Minutes
Ingredients:
- 1 Rack Baby Back Rib
- 1 Bottle Pit Boss Sweet Rib Rub

Directions:
1. Remove the ribs from their packaging and pat dry. Flip back of ribs and score the membrane with a knife, then peel the membrane.

2. Generously sprinkle the ribs with Pit Boss Sweet Rib R on both sides of the ribs and rub.

3. Set your Pit Boss Smoker to 250F. Once the smoker is ready, add the ribs and smoke for 4 hours, or until the ribs a tender and the meat is pulling away from the bone.

4. Serve and enjoy!

Smoked St. Louis Style Ribs With Tequila Bbq

Servings: 8
Cooking Time: 240 Minutes
Ingredients:
- 1/2 Cup Brown Sugar
- 2 Garlic, Cloves
- 3 Tbsp Honey
- 1 Cup Ketchup
- 1/2 Squeezed Lime
- 3 Tbsp Molasses
- 1 Jar Mustard
- 2 Slabs Slabs St. Louis-Style Rib Racks
- 1 Bottle Sweet Heat Rub
- 1/4 Cup Tequila Blanco

Directions:
1. First, make the barbecue sauce. In a mixing bowl, add t ketchup, brown sugar, garlic cloves, molasses, honey, tequil lime, and 1 tbsp Sweet Heat Rub. Mix together well until gla is blended together. Set aside.

2. Prepare the ribs. Pat the ribs dry with paper towels, the pull the thin membrane off the back of the ribs and discard. Using a basting brush, coat the meat on both sides with a th layer of mustard and season heavily with Sweet Heat Rub u the ribs are completely coated. Repeat with the second rack ribs. Place the ribs on a baking sheet and refrigerate overni; or for 12 hours if you choose to.

3. Once the ribs have finished marinating, remove them from the refrigerator and set out two sheets of large, heavy duty aluminum foil. Place one rack of ribs on each sheet of f meat-side down, and fold the edges over to form a sealed pouch.

Fire up your Pit Boss Grill and set the temperature to 5°F. If you're using a gas or charcoal grill, set it up for low, direct heat. Place the rib packets on the grill, meat-side up, d smoke for 2-3 hours, or until the ribs are nearly tender.

Remove the ribs from the grill and take the aluminum foil the ribs and place them back onto the grill for another hour. ush generously with the tequila barbecue sauce on both es, then grill for 5 minutes, meat- side up. Baste the ribs one re time with the barbecue sauce, then flip them meat-side wn and grill for a final 5 minutes. The ribs should be sticky d caramelized. Remove the ribs from the grill and serve mediately with the remaining barbecue sauce.

Applewood Bacon Jalapeno Poppers

vings: 6-8
oking Time: 30 Minutes
gredients:
- 2 Teaspoon Pit Boss Applewood Bacon Seasoning
- 1 Pack Cheddar Cheese, Shredded
- 1 Pack Cream Cheese, Softened
- Cut In Half Lengthwise, Destemmed, Deveined And seeded Jalapeno Peppers
- 8 Strips Smoked Applewood Bacon, Cut In Half

rections:

In a large bowl, combine cream cheese, Applewood Bacon soning and cheddar cheese. Mix until completely combined.

Using a spoon, fill the peppers with the cream cheese xture. Wrap each pepper with a half slice of bacon and cure with a toothpick. Repeat until all jalapeno poppers are ished.

Preheat your Pit Boss Grill to 400°F. Place your jalapeno ppers on the grill basket and grill for 15-20 minutes, or until bacon is cooked and crispy.

Serve and enjoy!

Orange Chipotle Ribs

vings: 4
oking Time: 180 Minutes
gredients:
- 1 Tablespoon Adobo Sauce
- 2 (2 1/2-Pound) Racks Baby Back Rib
- 1/3 Cup Firmly Packed Light Brown Sugar
- 1 Tablespoon Chili Powder
- 5 In Adobo Sauce Chipotle Peppers
- 1/3 Cup Leaves Cilantro, Fresh
- 1 Teaspoon Ground Cumin
- 1/4 Cup Honey
- 1/4 Cup Ketchup
- 2 Tablespoons Lime Juice
- 1 Cup Orange Juice, Fresh
- 5 Tablespoons Sweet Heat Rub

rections:

First, make the barbecue sauce. Into the bowl of a blender, 1 ¾ cup of orange juice, cilantro, honey, ketchup, lime juice, hipotles in adobo, adobo sauce, and 1 tablespoon of the eet Heat Rub. Place the lid on the blender and blend until mpletely smooth. Pour into a bowl, reserve ½ cup and set de.

Prepare the ribs. Using the paper towels, pull the mbrane off of the back of the ribs and discard. In the bowl a blender, add the orange juice, brown sugar, chipotle

peppers, chili powder, ground cumin, and Sweet Heat. Place the lid on the blender and blend until smooth. Pour this mixture over the ribs and massage into the meat. Place the ribs in the refrigerator and marinade for 8 hours.

3. Fire up your Pit Boss Grill and set the temperature to 275°F. Place the ribs, meat side up, and grill for 1 ½ hours. Baste the ribs with the reserved barbecue sauce, then BBQ for another 1 ½ hours, or until the ribs are extremely tender. Remove the ribs from the grill and serve with barbecue sauce.

Smoked & Braised Crispy Pork Belly

Servings: 6
Cooking Time: 255 Minutes
Ingredients:
- 1 1/2 Cup Chicken Stock
- Pit Boss Hickory Bacon Rub
- 3 Lbs Pork Belly
- 1 Yellow Onion, Sliced Thin

Directions:

1. Score pork belly fat in a cross-hatch pattern. Season with Pit Boss Hickory Bacon, cover, and refrigerate overnight.
2. Fire up your Pit Boss pellet grill and preheat to 225° F. If using a gas or charcoal grill, set it up for low, indirect heat.
3. Set a cast iron pot on the grill, then place a wire rack over it. Place pork belly, fat side up, on the wire rack, and smoke for 2 hours.
4. Increase temperature to 325°F. Remove the wire rack and transfer pork belly inside the cast iron pot, add onion and stock, then cover and braise for 2 hours, until an internal temperature reaches 185°F.
5. Preheat your Pit Boss griddle over medium flame. If you don't have a griddle, you can use a large cast iron skillet. Place the pork fat side down, on the griddle. Sear, fat side down, for 1 minute, to crisp.
6. Allow pork belly to rest for 15 minutes, then slice thick and serve warm.

Beer Braised Pork Belly

Servings: 4
Cooking Time: 90 Minutes
Ingredients:
- 1, Dark Beer, Any Brand
- 3 Cups Broth, Beef
- 1 Tablespoon Chinese Cooking Wine (Such As Shaoxing) Or Dry Sherry Wine
- 1 Teaspoon Chinese Five Spice Powder
- 2, Smashed Garlic, Cloves
- 1 Inch Knob Ginger, Peeled And Thinly Sliced
- 1 Onion, Sliced
- 2 Pounds Pork Belly, Cut Into 1 Inch Chunks
- 2 Tablespoons Rice Wine Vinegar
- 2 Tablespoons, Dark Soy Sauce, Low Sodium
- 3 Tablespoons Sugar

Directions:

1. Place a heavy dutch oven on a stovetop over medium high heat. Add the pork belly and brown on all sides, about 5 minutes. Once the pork belly has browned, add in the onion, ginger, and garlic, and stir well.
2. Pour the beer, beef broth, soy sauce, dark soy sauce, sugar, Chinese cooking wine, rice wine vinegar, and Chinese five

spice powder into the pan. Place a lid on the pan and bring it to a boil. Once it boils, remove it from the heat.

3.   Fire up your Pit Boss Grill and set the temperature to 325°F. Place the pan of pork belly on the grill and braise for 1 ½ hours, or until the pork belly is falling apart tender and glazed.

4.   Remove the pork belly from the grill and serve immediately.

Perfect Pulled Pork

Servings: 5
Cooking Time: 420 Minutes
Ingredients:
- 1 Bouillon Cube, Chicken
- 2 Tbsp Brown Sugar
- 1/4 Cup Honey
- 3/4 Cup Peach Nectar
- 1 Tbsp Pit Boss Hickory Bacon Rub
- 8Lb Pork Butt Roast, Bone-In
- 1/2 Tbsp Soy Sauce
- 3/4 Cup White Grape Juice
- 2 Tbsp Worcestershire Sauce

Directions:
1.   Fire up your Pit Boss Grill and set at 250°F.
2.   Place pork butt fat side down in a pan.
3.   Using a meat injection needle, inject across the meat in a checkerboard pattern, injecting approximately 1 tablespoon per site.
4.   Try to spend extra time around the bone, as this will help radiate the flavor through the meat while it's cooking.
5.   Sprinkle meat side thoroughly with Pit Boss Hickory Bacon Rub, then rub in while wearing gloves.
6.   Allow to rest 30 minutes before placing on grill. Place in smoker at 250 degrees.
7.   After 3.5 hours, or when internal temperature hits 145 degrees, remove butt, place in pan fat side down, and add seasoning and drizzle with honey.
8.   Cover in foil and return to smoker at 275 degrees.
9.   Check for tenderness when pork butt approaches 190 degrees.
10.   The bone should be showing 1" or more when it is at 194 degrees.
11.   When it's tender, remove from smoker and let rest for 30 minutes to 1 hour.
12.   Wearing "hot" gloves (I like cotton gloves with a nitrile glove pulled over them) remove the bone and hand pull the pork, placing aside any large pieces of fat.

Breaded Pork Chops

Servings: 6
Cooking Time: 10 Minutes
Ingredients:
- 2 Tbsp Apple Cider Vinegar
- 1 Tbsp Brown Sugar
- 2 Tbsp Butter
- 1/8 Tsp Cayenne Pepper
- 2 Eggs, Beaten
- 1/2 Cup Flour
- 1/2 Tbsp Horseradish
- 1/2 Lemon, Juiced
- 1/2 Cup Mayonnaise

- 1 1/2 Cup Panko Breadcrumbs
- 6 Pork Chops, Bone-In
- 1 Tbsp Smoked Hickory Sea Salt
- 1/4 Cup Sour Cream
- 1/2 Tbsp Stone Ground Mustard
- 1/2 Cup Vegetable Oil

Directions:
1.   Place pork chops on a sheet tray, blot dry with a paper towel, then season with Smoked Hickory & Honey Sea Salt.
2.   Place flour, beaten egg and bread crumbs in 3 separate bowls. Dip each pork chop in flour, then beaten egg, then breadcrumbs, then set aside.
3.   Prepare the Alabama White Sauce: In a small bowl, whisk together the mayonnaise, sour cream, apple cider vinegar, brown sugar, spicy brown mustard, horseradish, lemon juice and cayenne. Whisk until fully combined, then set aside.
4.   Fire up your Pit Boss Griddle and set it to medium heat. then add the oil. When oil begins to smoke, add the butter to melt, then lay out the pork chops. Cook pork chops 2 to 3 minutes per side until golden brown and crisp. For thicker chops, add 1 minute per side.
5.   Serve breaded pork chops warm with Alabama White Sauce.

Bacon Wrapped Stuffed Pickles

Servings: 6
Cooking Time: 60 Minutes
Ingredients:
- 13 Strips Bacon
- 3 Bratwursts, Raw
- 1/2 Cup Colby Jack Cheese, Shredded
- 4 Oz Cream Cheese
- 13 Large Dill Pickles, Spears
- Pit Boss Hickory Bacon Rub
- 2 Scallion, Sliced Thin
- 1/4 Cup Sour Cream

Directions:
1.   Fire up your Pit Boss Platinum Series KC Combo and preheat grill to 375°F.
2.   Preheat griddle to medium- low flame.
3.   In a mixing bowl combine cream cheese, sour cream, and scallions.
4.   Use a hand mixer to blend well, then fold in grated cheddar-jack. Set aside.
5.   Cook bratwurst on the griddle. Use a metal spatula to chop up sausage into smaller bits and cook until browned.
6.   Remove from the griddle and set aside on a sheet tray to cool.
7.   Place pickles on a sheet tray. Cut in half, then remove seeds with a small measuring spoon.
8.   Stuff one half of each pickle with cream cheese mixture and top with crumbled bratwurst.
9.   Top with the other pickle half, then wrap in bacon.
10.   Season bacon-wrapped pickles with Hickory Bacon Rub, place in cast iron skillet, then transfer to grill.
11.   Grill pickles for 45 to 55 minutes, until bacon starts to crisp on top. Remove from grill. Serve warm.

Bacon Wrapped Tenderloin

Servings: 5
Cooking Time: 30 Minutes

Ingredients:
- 1 Package Bacon, Thick Cut
- 1/4 Cup Maple Syrup
- 2 Tbsp Olive Oil
- 3 Tbsp Pit Boss Competition Smoked Rub
- 1 Trimmed With Silver Skin Removed Pork, Tenderloin

Directions:

Lay the strips of bacon out flat, with each strip slightly overlapping the other.

Sprinkle the pork tenderloin with 1 tablespoon of the Pit Boss Competition Smoked Rub and lay in the center.

Wrap with bacon over the tenderloin and tuck in the ends.

In a small bowl, mix the olive oil, maple syrup and remaining seasoning together and brush onto the wrapped tenderloin.

Preheat your Pit Boss Grill to 350°F.

When the grill is ready, place your tenderloin on the grill and cook, turning, for 15 minutes.

Increase the grill temperature to 400°F and grill for another 15 minutes or until the internal temperature is 145°F. Serve and enjoy!

Hot And Spicy Ribs

Servings: 4

Cooking Time: 300 Minutes

Ingredients:
- 2 Finely Minced Chipotle In Adobo
- 1 Cup (Any Kind) Barbecue Sauce
- 1/2 Cup Brown Sugar
- 1/4 Cup Honey
- 1/4 Cup Olive Oil
- 1 Rack St. Louis-Style Rib(S)
- 3 Tablespoons Sweet Heat Rub

Directions:

Remove the ribs from their packaging, drain, and pat dry. Using a paper towel, grip the membrane on the back of the ribs and pull off. Discard the membrane and paper towel.

In a small mixing bowl, combine the brown sugar, olive oil, honey, BBQ sauce, and chiles in adobo. Using a basting brush, brush the front and back of the ribs generously with the BBQ mixture. Save the basting brush for later along with half of the sauce.

Generously season the ribs with Sweet Heat rub, making sure to focus especially on the front of the ribs.

Fire up your Pit Boss and set the temperature to 225°F. If you're using a gas or charcoal grill, set it up for low heat. Place the ribs on the grill and smoke at 225°F for 4-6 hours making sure to baste in the sauce every 2 hours.

Remove from the grill and serve with additional barbecue sauce.

Bacon Roses

Servings: 2

Cooking Time: 60 Minutes

Ingredients:
- 1 Pack Bacon, Thick Cut
- 1 Dozen Roses, Fake

Directions:

Start your Grill on "smoke" with the lid open until a fire is established in the burn pot (3-7 minutes). Preheat to 225°F.

2. Roll each piece of bacon tightly, starting on the thicker side of the strip. Take a toothpick and skewer the middle of the bottom of the bacon roll to keep the bacon from unraveling. With a second toothpick, skewer the bacon roll so that the two toothpicks form an "X" at the bottom of the roll of bacon. Do this to every piece of bacon.

3. Place the bacon rolls directly on the grates of your preheated Grill and smoke for an hour, checking on them every 20 minutes.

4. While the bacon is smoking, rip the petals of the fake roses off of the steams.

5. Once the bacon is fully cooked, remove the toothpicks and pierce the bacon in the head of the steam (where the fake flowers once were). If the bacon isn't staying, you can break a toothpick in half and stick it in the tip of the steam, press firmly and try piercing the bacon again.

6. Place in a nice vase with some babies breath and gift to your Valentine.

Hasselback Potatoes With Candied Bacon

Servings: 4

Cooking Time: 30 Minutes

Ingredients:
- 4 Raw Strips Bacon
- 2 Tablespoons Brown Sugar
- Candied Bacon
- 2 Tablespoons Olive Oil
- 2 Tablespoons Pit Boss Hickory Bacon Seasoning
- 4 Potato, Medium
- 1/2 Cup Shredded Cheddar Cheese

Directions:

1. Forgo bland, traditional baked potatoes for this delicious and creative grilled Hasselback potatoes recipe topped with smoked, candied bacon and melted shredded, cheddar cheese. Goes great with your favorite cut of steak or chicken.

Smoked Pork Belly

Servings: 15

Cooking Time: 370 Minutes

Ingredients:
- Peanut Oil
- Pit Boss Mandarin Habanero Spice
- 13 Lbs Pork, Belly (Skin And Fat)
- Salt
- Sweet Barbecue Sauce

Directions:

1. Start your Grill on "smoke" with the lid open until a fire is established in the burn pot (3-4 minutes). Preheat to 250°F.

2. Place the pork belly on the grates of your preheated , meat side down. Smoke until the internal temperature reaches 195°F (this normally takes about 6 hours).

3. Open the flame broiler and flip the pork belly so that the meat side is up. Brush on the BBQ Sauce (on meat side). Sear the fat side for about 5 minutes, or until crispy.

4. Using your grill gloves, remove the pork belly from the grill and wrap in aluminum foil for 15 minutes or until it's cool enough to pull apart with your Meat Claws. Or dice into cubes with a knife. Serve hot.

Pork Belly Burnt Ends

Servings: 4
Cooking Time: 270 Minutes
Ingredients:
- 2/3 Cup Bbq Sauce
- 2 Tbsp Butter, Melted
- 2 Tbsp Honey
- 2 Tbsp Olive Oil
- Tt Pit Boss Blackened Sriracha Rub
- 3 Lbs Pork Belly, Skin Removed

Directions:
1. Fire up your Pit Boss Platinum Series Lockhart and preheat to 225°F. If using a gas or charcoal grill, set it up for low, indirect heat.
2. Cut pork belly into 2-inch cubes and place into a large mixing bowl.
3. Drizzle olive oil over pork belly, then generously season with Blackened Sriracha.
4. Transfer seasoned pork belly to a wire rack and place on the grill grate. Cook for 3 hours.
5. Remove the pork belly from the wire rack and transfer into a foil-lined aluminum pan or disposable foil pan.
6. Whisk together BBQ sauce, melted butter, and honey, then pour mixture over pork.
7. Toss to coat, then cover the pan with aluminum foil and return to the grill rack.
8. Cook for another 1 to 1 ½ hours, until the internal temperature reaches 200° F.
9. Remove the foil, transfer pork belly to a cast iron skillet and place in the center of the grill.
10. Open the sear slide and continue cooking for another 5 to 7 minutes, turning halfway, to crisp up the pork.
11. Remove pork belly from the grill, and serve warm.

Apple Bacon Smoked Ham With Glazed Carrots

Servings: 8-12
Cooking Time: 120 Minutes
Ingredients:
- 1 1/2 Cup Apple Cider
- 3 Tablespoon Apple Cider Vinegar
- 2 Apples
- 1 Lb. Bacon
- 2 Tablespoon Butter, Unsalted
- 2 Tablespoon Cornstarch
- 3 Tablespoon Dijon Mustard
- Pit Boss Smoke Infused Applewood Bacon Rub
- 1/2 Cup Pure Maple Syrup
- 1 Large Bone In Spiral Cut Smoked Ham
- 2 Tablespoon Yellow Mustard

Directions:
1. Turn your grill to smoke mode, let the fire catch and then set to 250 degrees F (121 degrees C).
2. Smoke the bacon directly on the grates for 25 minutes, flipping at the 15-minute mark. Thinly slice the apples while the bacon cooks. Once the bacon is done, set your temperature down to 225 degrees F (107 degrees C).
3. Put the spiral-sliced ham into an aluminum foil roasting pan. Start by adding apple into the first slice and every other slice after that. Fill in all other slices with the bacon strips. Season with Pit Boss Smoke Infused Applewood Bacon Rub. Add any extra apple cider to the bottom of the pan for added flavor.

4. Place ham in the grill for 60 minutes.
5. Meanwhile, in a saucepan, whisk together apple cider, maple syrup, apple cider vinegar, Dijon mustard, yellow mustard, cornstarch and Pit Boss Smoke Infused Applewood Bacon Rub. Bring to a boil. Reduce to a simmer, stirring often until the sauce has thickened and reduced (approximately 1 20 minutes). Stir in the butter until it has completely melted Glaze should thicken more as it stands.
6. After 60 minutes, add carrots into the roasting pan and glaze the entire ham. Glaze again every 30 minutes until do
7. Remove ham from grill and allow to rest covered with for 20 minutes before serving.
8. Serve with remaining warmed up sauce if desired.

Curry Ketchup Pork Ribs

Servings: 4
Cooking Time: 205 Minutes
Ingredients:
- 1 Tsp Chili Powder
- 1 Tbsp Curry Powder
- 1/2 Tsp Ground Mustard
- 2 Tsp Honey
- To Taste, Kansas City Barbecue Rub Seasoning
- 1 Cup Ketchup
- 2 Pork Back Rib Racks, Membrane Removed
- 2 Tsp Smoked Paprika
- 2 Tsp Worcestershire Sauce

Directions:
1. Fire up your Pit Boss Platinum Series Lockhart grill on SMOKE mode and let it run with lid open for 10 minutes the preheat to 225° F. If using a gas or charcoal grill, set it up fo low, indirect heat.
2. Place rib racks on a sheet tray, then season both sides with Kansas City Barbeque Rub. Transfer ribs to the grill an smoke for 1 hour.
3. Meanwhile, prepare the curry ketchup: In a mixing bow add ketchup, curry powder, smoked paprika, chili powder, ground mustard, Worcestershire, and honey and whisk to incorporate. Set aside.
4. Rotate the rib racks and increase temperature to 250 F Cook for another hour, then remove the ribs from the grill a place on butcher paper. Brush ribs with sauce then wrap w paper.
5. Return ribs to the grill. Cook for one more hour, until tender.
6. Remove ribs from the grill, cut open the butcher paper, and baste with remaining curry ketchup. Place racks back o the grill, increase the temperature to 275 F, then cook for a additional 15 minutes. Remove ribs from the grill, cut open butcher paper, and baste with remaining curry ketchup. Pla racks back on the grill, increase the temperature to 275 F, t cook for an additional 15 minutes.
7. Remove ribs from the grill, rest for 10 minutes, then sl and serve warm.

Dry Rub Smoked Ribs

Servings: 4
Cooking Time: 300 Minutes
Ingredients:
- 1 Rack Baby Back Rib
- 1 Tablespoon Olive Oil

Pit Boss Sweet Heat Rub

rections:

Start your Pit Boss on "smoke". Once it's fired up, set the mperature to 225°F.

Remove the membrane from the back of the ribs. Rub the s down with olive oil, then generously coat both sides with eet Heat Rub. For deeper flavor penetration, gently pat the ces into the meat and let sit in the refrigerator for at least hour.

Smoke the ribs for about 5 hours or until the temperature etween 180°F and 195°F, and the meat is dark, glossy and ily tears apart.

When the ribs are finished, remove from the grill and let m rest for 5 minutes before serving.

Egg & Bacon French Toast Panini

vings: 2
oking Time: 10 Minutes
gredients:

6 Bacon Slices
1 Tbsp Black Pepper
4 Brioche Sandwich Slices, Day Old
2 Tbsp Butter
1 Tbsp Cinnamon-Sugar
6 Eggs
1 Tbsp Heavy Cream
1 Tbsp Maple Syrup
1 Tbsp Salt

rections:

Fire up your Pit Boss KC Combo Grill and preheat griddle 375°F. If using a gas or charcoal grill, set heat to medium at. For all other grills, preheat cast iron skillet on grill grates.

Place butter on griddle and spread to coat surface.

In a pie plate, whisk together 2 eggs, heavy cream, and ple syrup.

Soak both sides of bread slices in egg mixture and transfer griddle. Cook for 2 minutes, flipping halfway until egg xture is cooked and golden. Set aside.

Lay bacon on the griddle, and cook 3 minutes per side, til golden.

Transfer to lower right-hand corner of griddle to keep rm.

Crack 4 eggs on top of rendered bacon fat. Season with t and pepper. Cook 1 minute per side, or to desired neness.

Lay eggs on top of French toast, add bacon, then place the er slice of French Toast on top.

Transfer back to griddle for another minute to warm, inkle with extra cinnamon-sugar, then slice in half and ve hot.

Smoked Homemade Breakfast Sausage Links

vings: 3-6
oking Time: 90 Minutes
gredients:

½ Tsp Black Pepper
1 Tbsp Brown Sugar
Ice Water Dried Marjoram
⅛ Tsp Ground Cloves
⅓ Cup Ice Water
20/22 Mm Natural Sheep Casings

- Pit Boss Tennessee Apple Butter Rub
- 2Lbs. Pork Sausage, Ground

Directions:

1. One hour before stuffing, rinse sheep casings thoroughly and let soak in warm water for 60 minutes.
2. In a chilled stand mixing bowl, add the pork sausage, Tennessee Apple Butter, marjoram, cloves, brown sugar, and ice water. Use the paddle attachment and mix on low speed for 5 minutes, until threads appear in the meat. Place mixture in the refrigerator while preparing the sausage stuffer.
3. Thread the sausage stuffer with the prepared sheep casings, then fill the well with the meat mixture. Use one hand to hold the wand to press the meat through the auger, and the other hand guide and fill the casings being careful to avoid air gaps while also not overstuffing the casings.
4. Twist the sausages into 4 to 5-inch links, twisting every other link. Use a sausage pricker to prick any air bubbles out of the links.
5. Place sausage links on a sheet tray and refrigerate overnight.
6. Fire up your Pit Boss Lockhart Grill and set it to Smoke mode. If using a gas or charcoal grill, set it up for low indirect heat.
7. Hang sausage links on S-hooks and place in the smoking cabinet. Increase temperature to 350°F. Smoke links for 1 hour, then increase the temperature to 425°F and cook for another 30 minutes.
8. Remove links from the cabinet and serve hot. For additional browning, sear in cast iron, 1 minute per side.

Pulled Pork Poutine

Servings: 4
Cooking Time: 240 Minutes
Ingredients:

- 2 Tbsp Apple Cider Vinegar
- 1/2 Cup Bbq Sauce
- 1 1/2 Cups Beef Stock
- 2 Tbsp Butter
- For Assembly, Cheese Curds
- 2 Cups Chicken Stock
- 2 Tbsp Flour
- For Assembly, French Fries
- 3 Garlic Cloves, Minced
- 1 Tbsp Olive Oil
- 2 1/2 Lbs Pork Shoulder Roast, Bone-In
- To Taste, Pulled Pork Rub
- For Assembly, Sliced Scallions
- 1/2 Yellow Onion, Minced
- 1/2 Yellow Onion, Sliced

Directions:

1. Fire up your Pit Boss pellet grill on SMOKE mode and let it run with lid open for 10 minutes then preheat to 225° F. If using a gas or charcoal grill, set it up for low, indirect heat.
2. Season the pork shoulder with a pork rub, then transfer to the grill grate, fat side up. Smoke the pork shoulder for 2 ½ hours.
3. Add chicken stock, vinegar, and sliced onion to a Dutch oven. Transfer the smoked pork shoulder to the Dutch oven, then cover and increase the grill temperature to 325° F. Braise the pork shoulder for 1 ½ hours, until tender.
4. When tender, remove the pork from the grill and rest for 20 minutes, then shred.

5. While the pork is resting, prepare the gravy: set a cast iron skillet on the grill. Heat the butter and olive oil in the skillet, then sauté the onion and garlic for 2 minutes, stirring often. Stir in the flour and cook for 1 minute. Slowly add the beef stock, and stir until thickened. Add bbq sauce and simmer for 3 minutes. Remove from the grill and set aside for assembly.

6. Assemble the poutine: spread out a layer of French fries, then layer gravy, pulled pork, cheese curds, additional gravy, and scallions. Serve warm.

Pulled Pork Stuffed Sweet Potatoes

Servings: 4
Cooking Time: 120 Minutes
Ingredients:
- 1/2 Cup Barbecue Sauce
- 1 Finely Diced Red Bell Pepper
- Drained And Rinsed Black Beans, Can
- 1/2 Cup Cheddar Cheese, Shredded
- 2 Tablespoon Olive Oil
- 1 Tablespoon Pit Boss Pulled Pork Seasoning
- 1 Cup Pulled Pork
- 4 Sweet Potatoes, Scrubbed

Directions:
1. Preheat your Pit Boss Grill to 400F. To prepare the sweet potatoes, place on a sheet of aluminum foil. Rub with ½ tablespoon of olive oil and ½ tablespoon Pulled Pork Seasoning, then wrap tightly in foil. Repeat with the remaining sweet potatoes. Grill for 20-30min, or until the sweet potatoes are easily pierced with a knife. Remove from the grill. Allow to cool.

2. Once the sweet potatoes have cooled, cut them in half and scoop out the centers. In a separate bowl, combine the pulled pork and barbecue sauce. Fill the hollowed out sweet potatoes with the pulled pork, black beans, red pepper, and cheese, then place on a sheet pan.

3. Preheat your Pit Boss Grill to 350F. Grill the stuffed sweet potatoes for 10-15 minutes, or until the cheese is melted. Serve immediately and enjoy!

Grilled Tacos Al Pastor

Servings: 8
Cooking Time: 15 Minutes
Ingredients:
- 2 Tsp Annatto Powder
- Cilantro, Chopped
- Corn Tortillas
- 2 Tsp Cumin
- 1 Tsp Granulated Garlic
- 2 Tbsp Guajillo Chili Powder
- Jalapeno Pepper, Minced
- Lime, Wedges
- 1 Tsp Oregano, Dried
- 1/2 Tsp Pepper
- 1/2 Cup Pineapple, Juice
- 1/2 Pineapple, Skinned & Cored
- 2 Lbs Pork Shoulder, Boneless, Sliced Thin
- 1 1/2 Tsp Salt
- 2 Tbsp Tomato Paste
- 2 Tbsp Vegetable Oil
- 1/4 Cup White Vinegar

- Yellow Onion, Chopped

Directions:
1. Prepare marinade: In a mixing bowl, whisk together pineapple juice, vinegar, oil, tomato paste, chili powder, annatto, cumin, granulated garlic, oregano, salt, and pepper. Set aside.

2. Slice pork shoulder into thin slices (around ¼" thick), then place in a resealable plastic bag. Pour marinade over po seal bag, and turn to coat. Refrigerate overnight.

3. Fire up your Pit Boss grill and preheat to 450° F. If usin gas or charcoal grill, set it up for high heat.

4. Remove the pork from the marinade and set on the grill Grill over high heat for 3 to 5 minutes, turning frequently. Transfer to a cutting board to rest for 10 minutes, then slice thin.

5. Grill pineapple for 3 minutes, turning once. Set aside on cutting board, and chop once cooled.

6. Assemble tacos: tortillas, pork, pineapple, jalapeño, oni and cilantro. Serve warm with fresh lime wedges.

Apple Cider & Maple Glazed Ham

Servings: 10 - 14
Cooking Time: 190 Minutes
Ingredients:
- 1 1/2 Cups Apple Cider
- 3 Tbsp Apple Cider Vinegar
- 1/2 Cup Packed Light Brown Sugar
- 2 Tbsp Unsalted Butter
- ¼ Tsp Chili Powder
- 2 Tsp Cornstarch
- 3 Tbsp Dijon Mustard
- ½ Tsp Ground Cinnamon
- ¼ Tsp Ground Cloves
- Large Cast Iron Skillet
- 1/2 Cup Pure Maple Syrup
- 2 Tsp Pit Boss Tennessee Apple Butter Rub
- 1 Spiral-Sliced Ham, Bone-In
- ¼ Tsp Thyme, Dried
- 3 Tbsp Yellow Mustard

Directions:
1. Remove ham from refrigerator and let rest at room temperature for 2-3 hours.

2. Fire up your Pit Boss grill and preheat to 300° F. If usin gas or charcoal grill, set heat to medium-high heat.

3. Create a bed of foil in the bottom of a large cast iron pan making sure to have enough to seal entire ham. Set ham insi foil and add one cup of water to the bottom of pan. Pour som glaze (about ⅓ of mixture) over ham, making sure to coat in between slices. Wrap ham tightly in foil and grill for 2 hours

4. Remove ham from grill and increase temperature to 40 F. Carefully unfold foil to expose ham and pour an additiona ⅓ of glaze over ham. Leave ham exposed and grill for 30 minutes or until edges are golden brown and caramelized.

5. Remove ham from grill and carefully remove foil from underneath ham, so that ham is directly sitting on cast iron. Return to grill, brush with more glaze, and grill another 15 minutes. Remove ham from grill, let rest for 15 minutes, the carve and serve with remaining glaze.

Bbq Pulled Pork Sandwiches

Servings: 12

Cooking Time: 480 Minutes

Ingredients:
- 1 Bottle Bbq Sauce
- Coleslaw, Prepared
- 12 Kaiser Rolls
- 8-10Lbs Pork Butt Roast, Bone-In
- 5 Oz Sugar
- 1 Cup Yellow Mustard

Directions:

Set your Pit Boss Grill to 225°F. While your grill is heating, remove the pork roast from its packaging and place on a cookie sheet. Rub the pork roast down with yellow mustard.

Mix BBQ sauce and sugar in a bowl. Rub the roast down with entire mixture, allowing time for the rub to melt into the meat.

Place the roast in the smoker and cook for 6 hours.

After 6 hours, remove the roast and double wrap in tin foil. Turn the grill up to 250°F and cook the roast for another 2 hours or until the roast is probe tender (around an internal temperature of 204°F). Let the pork butt rest in the foil for up to an hour before pulling.

Cut each Kaiser roll in half, mix pulled pork with some more barbecue sauce and pile on each half of roll. Top with coleslaw and green onions. Don't mix all the pulled pork with barbecue sauce so that you can use the extra pulled pork for different recipes. Serve hot and enjoy!

Competition Smoked Baby Back Ribs

Servings: 4
Cooking Time: 255 Minutes

Ingredients:
- 2 Cups Apple, Juice
- 2 Racks Baby Back Rib
- Pit Boss Competition Smoked Rub
- Southern Style Bbq Sauce

Directions:

Preheat your to smoke mode or 200°F.

Remove the membrane on the back side of the ribs with a knife and a paper towel. Rub with your preferred seasoning or use the Smoke Infused Competition Smoked Rub.

Rub with your preferred seasoning or use the Smoke Infused Competition Smoked Rub.

Place the seasoned baby back ribs on the grates of your grill, meat side up, and smoke for 2 hours.

After 2 hours, remove from the grill and turn the temperature up to 250°F.

Create an aluminum boat for each set of ribs and place the ribs inside. Pour a cup of apple juice over the ribs into the boat and seal the aluminum foil.

Return the ribs to the grill for another 2 hours.

Remove the ribs from the apple juice bath and coat with barbecue sauce.

Turn the temperature of the grill up to 350°F. Return to ribs to the grill after the grill has preheated.

You're just trying to get the barbecue sauce to firm up a bit so only leave your ribs on the grill for about 15 minutes. Don't leave the grill during this step - the sugar from the apple juice and barbecue sauce can burn very easily, so stay close by to supervise.

Let the ribs rest for about 15 minutes off the grill, serve and enjoy!

Raspberry Spiral Ham

Servings: 12
Cooking Time: 120 Minutes
Ingredients:
- 1 Ham, Spiral (Precooked)
- Pit Boss Raspberry Chipotle Spice Rub
- 1/2 Jar Raspberry Jam
- 1 Quart Raspberry, Fresh
- 1/4 Cup Sugar
- 1/3 Cup Water, Warm

Directions:
1. Preheat your Grill to 225F.
2. Season the ham with Raspberry Chipotle Spice, taking care to season in between each slice. Place in your Grill and smoke for about 2 hours.
3. Just before you pull the ham, combine glaze ingredients in a saucepan over medium heat until raspberries are no longer whole and the glaze is runny. If you want a smoother glaze, remove the raspberry seeds by draining the glaze through cheesecloth.
4. Pour glaze over the ham just before serving. Slice and serve hot. Enjoy!

Carolina Mustard Ribs

Servings: 4
Cooking Time: 300 Minutes
Ingredients:
- 1 Rack St. Louis Style Ribs
- 2 Cups Apple Juice
- 1/4 Cup Cider Vinegar
- 1/4 Cup Dark Brown Sugar
- 1/4 Cup Honey
- 1 Tablespoon Hot Sauce
- 2 Tablespoons Ketchup
- 7 Tablespoon Sweet Rib Rub
- 1 Tablespoon Worcestershire Sauce
- 2 Cups, Prepared Yellow Mustard

Directions:
1. Make the sauce for the ribs. In a large mixing bowl, combine 1 cup of the yellow mustard, cider vinegar, dark brown sugar, honey, ketchup, Worcestershire sauce, hot sauce, and 1 tablespoon of the Sweet Rib Rub. Mix well to combine and set in the refrigerator until ready to use.
2. Make the ribs. Using a paper towel, peel the membrane off of the backs of the rib racks and discard. Generously coat the ribs in a thin coat of mustard, and sprinkle all over with Sweet Rib Rub.
3. Fire up your Pit Boss grill and set the temperature to 275F. If you're using a gas or charcoal grill set it up for low, indirect heat. Place the ribs meaty-side up and grill for 2-3 hours. Once the ribs have grilled for 2-3 hours, fill a spray bottle with 2 cups of apple juice and spray the ribs to keep them moist. Continue to grill the ribs, spraying every 45 minutes, until the meat bends slightly at the ends when lifted and is a deep mahogany color, about another 2-3 hours.
4. Remove the ribs from the grill and brush with mustard sauce, then slice and serve immediately.

Scalloped Potatoes With Ham, Corn & Bacon

Servings: 4-6
Cooking Time: 60 Minutes

Ingredients:
- 1 1/2 Cups Cooked Bacon, Chopped
- 1 Tablespoon Butter
- 1 1/2 Cup Cooked Ham, Cubed
- 5-6 Large Potatoes, Red
- Salt And Pepper
- 1 Cup Whole Kernel Corn
- Milk

Directions:
1. Turn your Pit Boss grill to smoke mode, let the fire catch and then set to 350 degrees F (177 degrees C) to preheat.
2. Smear softened butter all over the bottom of a baking dish. Slice potatoes as uniformly as possible.
3. Place enough potatoes in the pan to cover the bottom. Add some of the bacon, ham and corn on top of the potatoes. Repeat this until you've created a few layers and have used all the potatoes, ham, corn and bacon.
4. Add 1 tbsp of butter and cover with milk, till it's almost covering the mixture. Add salt and pepper to taste.
5. Place on the grill for 1 hour and enjoy!

Smoked Rack Of Pork With Sweet Potato, Fennel & Mustard Gravy

Servings: 6
Cooking Time: 360 Minutes
Ingredients:
- 4 Bay Leaves
- 2 Jalapeno Peppers
- 1 Six Bone Rack Of Pork
- 1 Cup Salt
- Salt & Freshly Ground Black Pepper
- 2 Tbsp Smokey Apple Chipotle Rub
- 10 Thyme, Fresh Sprigs
- 1 Gallon Water

Directions:
1. To make the rack of pork: Combine the salt, water, bay, thyme and jalapeño in a large stock pot and bring to a boil, let boil for 10 minutes until salt is dissolved.
2. Remove from heat and let cool completely, add pork to the brine and brine overnight. Remove from the brine and rinse. Pat dry and season with Apple Chipotle seasoning and salt and pepper.
3. Set your Pit Boss Pellet Grill to SMOKE. Place the rack of pork on the smoker with a probe inserted and cook for about 5 to 6 hours or until you reach an internal temp of 140°F.
4. Turn the heat up to 450°F and open the heat shield.
5. Sear the pork on all sides, once seared move to a cutting board and tent with foil, rest for 20 minutes then slice in between each bone and serve.
6. To make the pickled fennel: Place the fennel in a bowl. In a small saucepan over medium low heat, add the pickling spice and toast for about 2 minutes or until fragrant.
7. Add the cider vinegar and bring to a boil over high heat. Add the sugar, salt and water and bring to a boil.
8. Cook for 10 minutes over medium high heat to meld the flavors. Strain over the fennel and set aside to cool. Once cool cover and place in the fridge until ready to use.
9. To make the caramelized sweet potato puree: In a large pan add the olive oil over high heat until the oil is shimmering, add the sweet potatoes and cook browning on all sides.
10. Once the sweet potatoes are caramelized add 1 cup of the water and cook until it has evaporated and repeat the process with the remaining water.
11. In a saucepan add the milk and the cream and warm ov low heat. Once the sweet potatoes are tender add them to a blender with the milk mixture and blend until smooth but b careful not to over process and turn the potatoes into glue.
12. To make the mustard gravy: Add the olive oil to a large pan over medium high heat, once shimmering, add the shall and cook until translucent but not browned.
13. Add the bourbon and cooked until almost entirely reduced. Add the heavy cream and the mustard and cook fo about 8 to 10 minutes stirring often until the sauce thickens and coats the back of a spoon.
14. Stir in the parsley and season with salt and pepper.
15. To make the fried shallots: Place the shallots in a small bowl and cover them with the milk, let soak in the milk for a least 1 hour.
16. Drain the shallots and transfer them to a large Ziplock add the flour, salt and pepper. Seal the bag and shake well to coat all the shallots in the flour. Remove from the bag shakin off the excess flour.
17. Heat the oil to 350°F in a deep pot. Fry the shallots unti golden brown then remove them to a plate lined with paper towels. Season with salt.
18. To put it all together and plate: Spread the puree in a circle in the middle of the plate, place a small handful of the pickled fennel on one side of the puree, Place the pork leani on the fennel, Spoon over the sauce and top with the fried shallots and the micro arugula.

Classic Easter Quiche

Servings: 6
Cooking Time: 40 Minutes
Ingredients:
- 4 Chopped Bacon, Strip
- 4 Egg
- 1/4 Cup Green Bell Pepper, Diced
- Green Onion
- 1 Cup Half - And - Half
- 1 Cup Mozzarella Cheese, Shredded
- 1/4 Tsp Nutmeg, Ground
- 1 At Room Temp Pie Shell, Deep
- 1/4 Cup Red Bell Peppers, Diced
- 1/8 Cup Red Onion, Chopped

Directions:
1. Start up your Pit Boss on SMOKE mode and let it run fo 10 minutes with the lid open.
2. Preheat your grill to 400°F.
3. Place the frozen pie crust in a pie dish. Bake according the directions on the box (bake at 400°F for about 15 minu Don't forget to prick the bottom with a fork!
4. In a medium mixing bowl, whisk the eggs and half and half together until smooth.
5. Pour in the bacon, bell peppers, onion, green onion, nutmeg, and cheese. Lightly whisk together with the egg an half and half.
6. Pour mixture into the pie crust and bake in your Pit Bo for about 25 minutes. You'll know its done when you can sli a tooth pick in and remove it without anything sticking to it
7. Slice and serve hot. Enjoy!

Pulled Pork Taquitos

Servings: 4

oking Time: 300 Minutes
gredients:

- ⅓ Cup Apple Cider Vinegar
- ½ Cup, Plus Extra For Dipping Bbq Sauce
- 4 Cups Chicken Broth
- 1 Teaspoon Chili Powder
- ⅓ Cup Mustard
- 2 Tbsp Olive Oil
- 6 Tbsp Pit Boss Pulled Pork Rub
- 4 Lb. Pork Shoulder, Bone In
- 1 ½ Cup Sharp Cheddar Cheese, Shredded
- ¼ Cup Sour Cream
- 10 Flour Tortillas

rections:

Fire up your Pit Boss grill to 400°F. If using a gas or arcoal grill, set the temp to medium heat. In a bowl, combine chicken broth, mustard, apple cider vinegar, and 1 blespoon of Pulled Pork Seasoning. Whisk well to combine d set aside.

Generously season the pork shoulder with the remaining ablespoons of Pulled Pork Seasoning on all sides of the pork oulder, then place on the grill and sear on all sides until den brown, about 10 minutes.

Remove the pork shoulder from the grill and place in the posable aluminum pan. Pour the chicken broth mixture er the pork shoulder. It should come about 1/3 to ½ way up side of the pork shoulder. Cover the top of the pan tightly th aluminum foil.

Reduce the temperature of your Pit Boss grill to 250°F. ce the foil pan on the grill and grill for four to five hours, or til the pork is tender and falling off the bone.

Remove the pork from the grill and allow to cool slightly. ce on a cutting board and shred with meat claws, reserving out 2.5 cups. Fire up Pit Boss grill to 425°F.

In a mixing bowl, combine sour cream, BBQ sauce, and li powder. Stir in cheddar cheese and pork until well nbined.

Lay each tortilla flat on your work surface and scoop out ¼ cup of pork mixture in the center, lengthwise. Roll up ntly and place seam side down on baking sheet. Repeat with tortillas, then brush tops lightly with olive oil.

Transfer baking sheet to grill and cook for 15-20 minutes 400°F , or until cheese has melted and tortilla edges have ned a golden brown. Serve with extra BBQ sauce for ping and enjoy!

3-2-1 St. Louis Ribs

vings: 4
oking Time: 360 Minutes
gredients:

- 1/2 Cup Brown Sugar
- 6 Tbsp Butter
- 1 Cup Memphis Style Bbq Sauce
- To Taste, Pulled Pork Rub
- 2 St. Louis Style Rib Racks

rections:

Fire up your Pit Boss and with the lid open, set your nperature to SMOKE mode.

Once the fire is lit, preheat to 200° F. If using a gas or rcoal grill, set it up for low, indirect heat.

Remove the membrane on the back of the ribs, trim off ess fat, meat flap, and silverskin, then season both sides of

the ribs with Pulled Pork Rub. Transfer to the grill and smoke for 3 hours.

4. Remove ribs from the grill, and set on 2 sheets of Pit Boss Butcher paper. Sprinkle with the brown sugar, top with the butter cut into small pads, and then wrap the ribs.

5. Return the ribs to the grill and increase temperature to 225° F. Cook for 2 hours.

6. Remove the ribs from the grill and carefully cut open the paper with scissors, being cautious of hot steam.

7. Fold over the paper, baste with Memphis-style sauce, then return ribs to the grill (meat side up). Close the lid and cook ribs another hour, until tender.

8. Remove ribs from the grill, allow to rest for 15 minutes, then slice and serve hot.

Kansas City Style Championship Ribs

Servings: 4
Cooking Time: 210 Minutes
Ingredients:

- Apple Juice
- 2 Racks Baby Back Rib
- 2 Cups Brown Sugar
- 24 Oz Dijon Mustard
- 4 Tbsp Pit Boss Sweet Rib Rub
- Spray Bottle

Directions:

1. Pour Dijon Mustard into a mixing bowl. Mix in brown sugar until mustard taste diminishes and a sweet taste takes over.

2. Generally, you will use a half bag of brown sugar for 2 bottles and the whole bag for 4 bottles. The key is for the tangy mustard taste to turn sweet.

3. When this mix is brushed on the ribs the mix of pork flavor and this glaze will produce a sweet and sassy result. The easiest way to mix is with an electric mixer but a whisk will do nicely. This will become very thick and sticky.

4. Pre-heat Grill for 10 minutes and then set cooking temperature to 275˚.

5. Place ribs, back side down, on the cooking grid. Note: If you are doing multiple slabs, I suggest you use a rib rack. Most Rib Racks will hold 6 slabs. This will allow ribs to cook evenly. The rib rack allows for more slabs since ribs will sit in rack on their edge. Try to put meatier side up.

6. Spray ribs thoroughly with apple juice every 30-40 minutes. Apple Juice not only helps to keep meat moist and juicy while cooking, the acidity also helps to break down the muscles, thus tenderizing as well. I have had people tell me they prefer Pineapple juice or a mixture of apple and pineapple. Personally, I can't tell the difference, but you can experiment for yourself if you want to. The result will be same.

7. Note: How to tell when ribs are done? It is hard to measure temp of a rib with a meat thermometer due to the meat between the bones being so tight. You can get a false reading if the thermometer is touching a bone. Take your tongs and pick up slab in the middle. If the rib folds over and is limp and the meat just begins to pull away from the bone, they are done.

8. Remove ribs from grill and place in a pan (long enough for ribs to fit)

9. Glaze both sides of ribs with a light coat of the sassy glaze. This is a flavor enhancer, not a cover up. Just a light coat is plenty. If you really like the glaze there will generally always

be some left over, and you can add to your desire while on the plate.

10.   Wrap ribs in foil and let stand for 15 minutes
11.   Serve (you can serve in slab form and let each guest cut his own or I like to cut ribs and serve as single bones.
12.   Enjoy!

Bacon Cheese Fries

Servings: 2
Cooking Time: 25 Minutes
Ingredients:
*   2 Bacon, Strip
*   1/2 Cup Colby Jack Cheese, Shredded
*   1/2 Package Fries, Frozen
*   1/2 Cup Monterey Jack Cheese, Shredded
Directions:
1.   Start your Grill on "smoke" with the lid open until a fire is established in the burn pot (3-7 minutes). Preheat to 350F.
2.   Place the bacon on the bacon rack and place on the grill. Cook until crispy, about 15 minutes.
3.   Once slightly cooled, crumble the strips into small pieces and set it aside.
4.   Grill the frozen French fries based on the package instructions, cooking on a pan in the instead of the oven.
5.   Once fries are golden brown, sprinkle cheese and bacon on top of the fries, and return the pan to the grill and barbecue at 450°F for 1 minute. Remove from grill and enjoy!

Beer Braised Bbq Pork Butt

Servings: 6-8
Cooking Time: 300 Minutes
Ingredients:
*   One 12Oz Bottle Dark Beer
*   1/2 Cup Brown Sugar
*   2 Tablespoons Granulated Garlic
*   4 Tablespoons Honey
*   1 Cup Ketchup
*   1 Tablespoon Olive Oil
*   Pit Boss Pulled Pork Rub
*   1 Pork Butt, Boneless
*   2 Tablespoons Worcestershire Sauce
*   4 Tablespoons Yellow Mustard
Directions:
1.   Generously season the pork butt with Pit Boss Pulled Pork Rub, making sure to rub the seasoning in on all surfaces of roast. Place the pork onto a roasting rack inside a 9x13 pan.
2.   Pour about half a bottle of dark beer into the bottom of the pan and save the remaining amount of beer, you'll need this later.
3.   Fire up your Pit Boss grill and set the temperature to high. If you're using a gas or charcoal, set it up for high direct heat. Place the pan in the center of the grill and grill for 30 minutes until the pork roast is dark in color and charred in some spots.
4.   Remove the pork from the grill and decrease the temperature of the grill to 325°F. Set aside and began to make the BBQ sauce.
5.   In a medium sized bowl, add ketchup, brown sugar, yellow mustard, honey, Worcestershire, granulated garlic, half bottle of dark beer, and finally 1 tbsp of Pit Boss Pulled Pork Rub. Mix together thoroughly.

6.   Take the sauce and pour it over the roast, cover with aluminum foil.
7.   Cook the roast for 4 - 6 hours or until the meat is falling apart tender and the bone easily comes away from the meat and reaches an internal temperature of 200°F. Remove the pork from the grill and allow it to rest for 10-15 minutes.
8.   Shred the pork with meat claws or forks, discarding any fat or gristle. Toss the shredded pork with the barbecue sauce and serve immediately.

Leftover Pulled Pork Hash With Eggs

Servings: 4
Cooking Time: 20 Minutes
Ingredients:
*   1 Teaspoon Coarse Black Pepper
*   4 Eggs
*   1 Green Bell Pepper, Diced
*   1 Teaspoon Kosher Salt
*   3 Tablespoons Olive Oil
*   1 Small Onion, Diced
*   1 Tablespoon Pit Boss Hickory Bacon Seasoning
*   2 Cups Of Leftover Pulled Pork
*   1 Red Bell Peppers, Diced
*   1 ½ Pounds Red Potatoes, Diced
Directions:
1.   Start your grill on "smoke". Once it's fired up, set the temperature to 350°F.
2.   In a large bowl, toss the potatoes with 2 tablespoons of olive oil and Hickory Bacon seasoning. You want to get the potatoes coated well and evenly with the oil and seasoning.
3.   Add the potatoes to the skillet and cook on the grill for 15 minutes or until they're cooked all the way through and browned. Remove from the pan and set aside.
4.   Add 1 more tablespoon of olive to the pan and cook the peppers and onion for 2-3 minutes or until soft. Remove from the pan and set aside.
5.   Add the pork to the pan and cook until warmed through. Because the pork is already cooked this should only be 1-2 minutes so the meat stays moist.
6.   Add the potatoes, peppers and onions back to the pan, then give everything in the skillet a quick mix, so the hash is evenly blended.
7.   Crack the 4 eggs on top of the hash. Try to space them evenly around. Sprinkle the teaspoons of salt and pepper on top of the eggs, then place the lid on top of the pan and allow the eggs to cook for 5-6 minutes, or until the whites are firm and the yolks are still runny.
8.   Remove from the grill and serve immediately.

Smoked Ground Pork Burgers

Servings: 4
Cooking Time: 25 Minutes
Ingredients:
*   1 Avocado, Sliced
*   1/2 Cup Bacon Bits
*   1 Tbsp Cilantro, Chopped (For Mayo)
*   2 Tbsp Cilantro, Chopped (For Salsa)
*   1 Piece Green Leaf Lettuce
*   2 Lbs Ground Pork
*   4 Hamburger Buns
*   To Taste, Hickory Bacon Rub Seasoning

1 Jalapeño, Minced
1/2 Lime, Zest And Juice (For Mayo)
1/2 Lime, Zest And Juice (For Salsa)
1/3 Cup Mayonnaise
2 Nectarines, Diced
1/2 Red Onion, Minced

ections:

Fire up your Pit Boss Platinum Series KC Combo and set it moke. If using a gas or charcoal grill, set it up for low, irect heat.

Place ground pork and bacon bits in a mixing bowl, then son with Hickory Bacon. Form into 4 patties, pressing an ent into the middle of each patty. Set aside.

Prepare the salsa: In a mixing bowl, combine the tarines, jalapeño, red onion, lime zest and juice, and ntro. Cover and refrigerate.

Prepare the mayo: In a mixing bowl, combine mayonnaise, e zest and juice, and chopped cilantro. Cover and rigerate.

Transfer the pork patties to the grill, on the rack, over irect heat. Cover and smoke for 30 minutes, then increase temperature to 300° F, and continue cooking for another to 25 minutes, until the internal temperature reaches 150° pen the sear slide and grill for 2 minutes, turning and ping. Remove burgers from the grill and allow to rest for 5 utes before serving warm.

Assemble the burgers: bottom bun, cilantro-lime mayo, uce, smoked pork burger patty, avocado, salsa, top bun.

Smoked Dr. Pepper Ribs

vings: 4
king Time: 300 Minutes
redients:
Aluminum Foil
2 Racks Baby Back Ribs
1 Cup Bbq Sauce
1 Stick Butter, Melted
1/2 Cup Dark Brown Sugar
12 Oz Dr. Pepper Soda
1/4 Cup Pit Boss Sweet Rib Rub
1/4 Cup Yellow Mustard

ections:

Fire up your Pit Boss Platinum Series Lockhart and heat grill to 225°F. If using a gas or charcoal grill, set it up low, indirect heat.

After the grill comes to temp, place the ribs directly on the grates, close the lid, and smoke for 2 hours.

In a glass measuring cup, whisk together butter, brown ar, and 8 ounces of Dr. Pepper.

Pour half of the mixture on a foil-lined sheet tray.

Place ribs, meat-side down, on top of the mixture, then r remaining mixture on the bone-side. Tent the sheet tray h foil, then return to the grill for another 2 hours.

Remove ribs from liquid and set meat-side up directly on grill grate.

Whisk together BBQ sauce and 4 ounces of Dr. Pepper, n brush half of the sauce all over the ribs.

Increase temperature to 275°F and cook an additional 30 0 minutes until ribs are tender, and meat pulls away from bones.

Place ribs on a sheet tray, allow to rest for 10 minutes, n slice and serve with remaining BBQ sauce.

Peppercorn Grilled Pork Chops

Servings: 4
Cooking Time: 30 Minutes
Ingredients:
- 3 Tbsp Black Peppercorns, Ground
- 1 Tbsp Coriander, Seed
- 1/4 Cup Cumin
- 1 - 2 Tsp Dry Rub
- 1 Tsp Olive Oil
- 4 Pork, Chop Bone-In
- 1 1/2 Tsp Salt
- 2 Tbsp Sugar

Directions:
1. Start your grill on smoke with the lid open until a fire is established in the burn pot (3-7 minutes). Preheat to 450F.
2. Combine the cumin seeds, whole black peppercorns, and coriander seeds in a cast iron skillet. Stir over medium heat for about 8 minutes until toasted. Let them cool slightly. Finely grind toasted spices in a blender and transfer to a small bowl, then mix in sugar and salt.
3. Rub the spices into the pork chops on both sides. Place cast iron skillet inside the grill. Once hot, add the olive oil to the skillet and coat the bottom. Sprinkle the pork chops with salt, and then add to the skillet. Make sure that each pork chop has enough space in between one another. Cook the chops for about 30 minutes. Once pork chops are fully cooked, turn off the grill, remove skillet, plate and enjoy!

Healthy Hawaiian Pulled Pork

Servings: 8-10
Cooking Time: 640 Minutes
Ingredients:
- 2 Cups Aloe Leaf Juice
- 1 Tsp Coriander, Ground
- 2 Tsp Cracked Pepper
- 1 Tsp Cumin
- Dash Of Salt
- 4-6 Garlic, Cloves
- 1 (3-Inch) Ginger, Fresh
- 1-2 Limes
- 4 Cups No Sodium Added Chicken Bone Broth
- ¼ Cup Olive Oil
- 4 Tsp Paprika
- 6-8 Lbs Pork Shoulder/Butt
- 1/2 Sweet Onion
- 2 Packets Truvia To Sweeten Above Aloe Juice
- 2 Tbs Or 2 Tbs Swerve Brown Sugar Truvia – Honey Substitute

Directions:
1. Set your grill to "smoke". Once the pot catches turn the grill up to 300°F. Make sure your flame broiler is closed, you want to use indirect heat for this recipe.
2. Add all spices into a bowl (salt, paprika, cumin, coriander, pepper, onion powder if needed). Set bowl aside.
3. Grate the ginger into a separate bowl (wet ingredients bowl).
4. Mince or smash the garlic cloves into the same bowl.
5. Dice onion and add it to the ginger and garlic (if no onion sub onion powder).
6. Juice 1-2 limes and add to the "wet" ingredients bowl.

7.	Add 4 cups chicken bone broth.
8.	Add two cups aloe leaf juice w/lemon and add two packets Truvia to sweeten.
9.	Add 1-2 tbsp Truvia honey substitute. Mix and set bowl aside.
10.	Add the oil to your Pit Boss Cast Iron and coat the bottom and sides. Place the pork in the cast iron roasting pan.
11.	Take your dry rub and coat the pork.
12.	Pour the wet ingredients around the pork, into the Pit Boss Cast Iron Roasting Pan.
13.	Cover the roasting pan with the lid and set it on your grill.
14.	Check the pork every couple hours (basting if you prefer). When internal temperature reaches 195°F (after around 6 – 8 hours of cook time), it should easily start to pull apart. Don't pull apart the whole shoulder yet.
15.	Remove the Pit Boss Roasting Pan from the grill and set aside to allow it to rest for 1 hour. Remove the lid to help speed cooling.
16.	Once cooled, shred the pork into a separate bowl, removing the fat as you go.
17.	If you want to add some of the marinade to the pork for additional flavor, make sure you skim the fat off the top first and discard.
18.	Viola! Pair with fresh grilled veggies, delicious fruit or make tacos or salads! So many options for this type of protein.

Smoked Mac And Cheese Quesadillas

Servings: 4
Cooking Time: 75 Minutes
Ingredients:
- 1/2 Lb Bacon, Sliced And Halved
- 3 Tbsp Butter
- 1 Cup Cheddar Cheese, Shredded
- 1 Cup Cheddar Jack Cheese, Shredded
- 4 Oz Cream Cheese
- 2 Tbsp Flour
- 4 Flour Tortillas
- 1 1/2 Tsp Hickory Bacon Seasoning
- 8 Oz Macaroni, Cooked Al Dente
- 1 Tsp Mustard Powder
- 1/2 Cup Parmesan Cheese, Grated
- 1 2/3 Cups Whole Milk

Directions:
1.	Fire up your Pit Boss Platinum Series KC Combo and with the lid open, set your temperature to SMOKE mode.
2.	Once the fire is lit, preheat to 225° F. If using a gas or charcoal grill, set it up for low, indirect heat.
3.	Set a cast iron skillet on the grill. Melt the butter then whisk in flour until smooth. Cook for 1 minute, then whisk in Hickory Bacon and mustard powder.
4.	Pour in milk and bring to a boil, whisking constantly. When sauce begins to thicken, whisk in the cream cheese until smooth, then add cheddar and parmesan and stir until melted
5.	Add the pasta to the cheese sauce. Close the lid, and smoke for 1 hour.
6.	Fire up your Pit Boss griddle to medium-low flame, and cook bacon, turning occasionally, until desired crispness is reached, about 3 to 5 minutes.
7.	Set bacon aside, then place 4 tortillas on the griddle. Sprinkle cheddar jack cheese on top of the tortilla, a heaping scoop of smoked mac 'n cheese on one side, topped with bacon.
8.	Fold over the tortilla and press down gently with a spatula. Remove from the griddle, rest for 2 minutes, then cut

into wedges, and serve warm with an extra side of smoked mac 'n cheese.

Raspberry Chipotle Pork Ribs

Servings: 4
Cooking Time: 180 Minutes
Ingredients:
- Baby Back Rib
- Pit Boss Original Bbq Sauce
- Pit Boss Raspberry Chipotle Spice Rub

Directions:
1.	Begin by gently rinsing off your ribs in cool water. Pat (and remove the flavor blocker (thin membrane on the underside of the ribs) to allow the seasoning to permeate ri into the meat.
2.	Generously season your ribs with Raspberry Chipotle seasoning and place in the refrigerator for an hour for flavo set in.
3.	Fill your hopper with hickory hardwood pellets for a strong, smoky taste and preheat your grill to 250°F. Place yo seasoned rack of ribs on the grill and let cook for 2 hours. N lather on a thick coating of Original BBQ Sauce, turn up the grill to 300°F and let your ribs roast for another hour. Remc cut and serve for a meal that will surely make its way into tl weekly rotation.

Grilled Rosemary Pork Chops

Servings: 4
Cooking Time: 10 Minutes
Ingredients:
- 6 Tbsp Brown Sugar
- 4 Pork, Chop
- 2 Tbsp Dried Rosemary, Springs
- 1 Cup Soy Sauce
- 1/2 Cup Water, Warm

Directions:
1.	Start your Grill on "smoke" with the lid open until a fir established in the burn pot (3-7 minutes). Preheat to 350°F.
2.	Lightly oil the grate. Remove the pork chops from the marinade, shake off the excess, and discard the marinade.
3.	Grill the pork chops until the pork is no longer pink in t center, while brushing occasionally with the reserved marinade, for about 4-5 minutes on each side, or until done.
4.	Remove the pork chops from the grill and serve.

Raspberry Chipotle Pork Kebabs

Servings: 8
Cooking Time: 15 Minutes
Ingredients:
- 1/8 Cup Vinegar Apple Cider
- 3 Green Bell Pepper, Sliced
- 1 Tbsp Honey
- 1 Tbsp Olive Oil
- 2 Tbsp Pit Boss Raspberry Chipotle Spice Rub
- 1 Lb Pork, Loin (Boneless)
- 1 Red Onion, Chunked
- 8 (12 Inch) Skewers

Directions:

In a medium bowl, whisk together apple cider vinegar,
~spberry Chipotle seasoning, olive oil, and honey. Add the
~ed pork loin to marinade and toss to coast. Cover with
~stic wrap and let marinate for 30 minutes to 1 hour.

Once meat is marinated, remove from marinade and
~ead cubed pork loin onto the skewers, alternating with
~ces of bell pepper and red onion.

Light ceramic charcoal barbecue to 400*F. Grill kebabs
~ectly on the grill, turning often, until all sides of the meat is
~ll browned and vegetables are tender (about 15 minutes).

Serve immediately. Note: If using wood skewers, soak in
~ter for 30-45 minutes prior to use.

Smoked Bratwurst

~vings: 8 – 12
~oking Time: 120 Minutes
~redients:
12 Fresh Bratwurst, Linked
~rections:

Fire up your Pit Boss Vertical Smoker or Pellet Grill and
~eheat to 225°F. If using gas or charcoal grill, set it up for low
~irect heat.

Place metal hooks on shelves about 6" apart. Cut
~atwurst links into pairs and string on metal hooks. If you
~n't have metal hooks, you can place bratwurst directly on
~ll grate, but we recommend brushing the casing lightly in oil
~ensure it doesn't stick during smoking.

Smoke bratwurst for one hour, then increase temperature
~300°F. Cook for one additional hour, or until bratwurst skin
~golden brown and they've wrinkled slightly. If using a
~nperature probe, the brats are finished when internal temp
~ches 160°F.

Remove from smoker and serve immediately. We
~commend with buns and/or caramelized onions and
~erkraut.

Chinese Bbq Pork Tenderloin

~vings: 4
~oking Time: 30 Minutes
~redients:
1/4 Cup Bbq Sauce
2 Garlic Cloves, Minced
1/4 Cup Hoisin Sauce
2 Lbs Pork Tenderloin, Trimmed With Silver Skins
~moved
1 Tbsp Sugar, Granulated
1 Tsp Sweet Rib Rub Seasoning
1/4 Cup Tamari
1/4 Cup White Wine
~rections:

In a glass measuring cup, whisk together the hoisin sauce,
~nari, wine, garlic, sugar, and Sweet Rib Rub.

Place pork tenderloin in a resealable bag, then pour the
~rinade over the pork and allow to marinate in the
~rigerator for 4 to 6 hours.

Fire up your Pit Boss pellet grill on SMOKE mode and let it
~ with lid open for 10 minutes then preheat to 400° F. If
~ng a gas or charcoal grill, preheat to medium-high heat.

Remove the pork from the marinade, then pour the
~rinade into a grill-safe pan.

5. Place the marinade on the grill and bring to a boil for 3
minutes. Add the BBQ sauce and simmer for 2 minutes.
Remove from the grill, and set aside.
6. Place the pork on the grill and cook for 18 to 20 minutes,
until an internal temperature of 145° F. Flip and baste the pork
with the sauce every 3 to 5 minutes.
7. Remove the pork from the grill and allow it to rest on a
cutting board for 10 minutes, prior to serving warm with
additional sauce.

Bacon Wrapped Asparagus

Servings: 4
Cooking Time: 30 Minutes
Ingredients:
- 1 Bunch Asparagus
- 1 Package Bacon
Directions:
1. Set grill to 400°F.
2. Lay one piece of bacon on a clean surface.
3. Starting from the bottom, roll the bacon around one piece
of asparagus. Repeat for all pieces of bacon.
4. Place bacon wrapped asparagus on your grill for about 25
minutes, or until the bacon is cooked. Rotate the asparagus so
that the bacon cooks evenly. Serve hot.

Pulled Pork Carnitas

Servings: 4
Cooking Time: 15 Minutes
Ingredients:
- Cilantro
- Cilantro, Chopped
- 8 Corn Tortillas
- Jalepeno, Sliced
- 1 Lime, Wedges
- 2 Cups Pulled Pork
- Radishes, Sliced
- White Onion, Diced
Directions:
1. Preheat your Pit Boss grill to 350F. Grill the corn tortillas
until they are softened and have charred spots, about 30
seconds.
2. To assemble the carnitas, add the pulled pork to the
tortillas, and top with radishes, diced onion, cilantro, jalepeno
and a squeeze of lime juice, if desired. Serve and enjoy!

Coffee-rubbed Ribs

Servings: 6 - 8
Cooking Time: 360 Minutes
Ingredients:
- 1 Tbsp Ancho Chili Powder
- Ground Black Pepper
- ½ Tsp Cocoa Powder
- 2 Tbsp Coffee
- ½ Tsp Coriander, Ground
- 1 Tbsp Dark Brown Sugar
- 1 Tsp Garlic Powder
- 2 Tbsp Kosher Salt
- 1 Tsp Onion Powder
- 1 Tsp Oregano

- 2 Tbsp Paprika
- 8 Lbs. Pork Spareribs

Directions:

1. Begin by preparing the dry rub. In a mixing bowl, whisk together the coffee, salt, paprika, brown sugar, oregano, garlic powder, onion powder, black pepper, cocoa powder and coriander. Set aside.

2. Remove the membrane from the back of your ribs: Take a butter knife and wedge it just underneath the membrane to loosen it. Using your hands or a paper towel to grip, pull the membrane up and off the bone. Place the ribs on a sheet tray, then rub each rack generously with dry rub. Wrap ribs in foil, then refrigerate overnight.

3. When ready to cook, remove ribs from the refrigerator and let come to room temp. Fire up your Pit Boss and preheat to 225°F. If using a gas or charcoal grill, set it up for low indirect heat.

4. Place foil-wrapped ribs on the grill and close lid. Cook for 4 hours then remove foil from ribs and pour accumulated juices into a glass measuring cup. Pour the sauce over the ribs, then continue to cook for an additional 1 ½ - 2 hours or until tender. Remove from grill, slice and serve.

Bacon Wrapped Onion Rings

Servings: 6
Cooking Time: 120 Minutes
Ingredients:
- 1 Pack Bacon
- 2 White Onions

Directions:

1. Preheat your Pit Boss Grill to 250°F.

2. Peel each onion and cut into thirds, separating the onion slices into rings. Using two slices of bacon, wrap around the onion ring until the ring is fully covered, securing in place with a toothpick. Continue until all the bacon is used up.

3. Place the onion rings on the and smoke until the bacon is cooked, about 120 minutes.

Bbq Pork Chops With Bourbon Glaze

Servings: 4
Cooking Time: 30 Minutes
Ingredients:
- 4 8-To-10-Ounce Bone-In Pork Loin Chops, Trimmed Of Excess Fat
- 1/2 Cup Brown Sugar
- 2 Garlic Clove, Minced
- 2 Tbsp Honey
- 1 Cup Ketchup
- 1/4 Cup Molasses
- Sweet Rib Rub Seasoning
- 2 Tbsp Worcestershire Sauce

Directions:

1. First, place pork chops onto sheet pan lined with butcher paper. Season generously with Sweet Rib Rub, making sure to coat all sides of the chops. Set aside while you make the glaze.

2. In a medium sized mixing bowl, combine the ketchup, brown sugar, molasses, honey, garlic, Worcestershire, and 1 tbsp Sweet Rib Rub. Mix well, add 1 shot of bourbon, mix again until sauce becomes smooth. Transfer sauce into an oven proof sauce pan.

3. Fire up your Pit Boss Grill and set the temperature to 375°F. If you're using a gas or charcoal grill, set it up for medium direct heat.

4. Grill the pork chops for 10-15 minutes per side. Place th saucepan on the grill and allow the sauce to come to a boil. Glaze the chops on both sides and let the glaze caramelize o the chops.

5. Grill the pork chops until they are lightly charred and reach an internal temperature of 145°F - 165°F. Remove the pork chops from the grill and allow them to rest for 5 minut

6. Once the pork chops have finished resting, glaze them again if you choose to. Serve immediately.

Hot And Fast Bbq Spare Ribs

Servings: 6
Cooking Time: 180 Minutes
Ingredients:
- 1/2 Tsp Black Pepper
- 1/4 Cup Brown Sugar
- 2 Garlic Cloves, Peeled And Smashed
- 1 Tbsp Honey
- 1/4 Cup Ketchup
- 1 Tsp Kosher Salt
- 1 Tbsp Paprika
- 1 Tbsp Parsley, Chopped
- Pit Boss Pulled Pork Rub
- 2 Red Bell Pepper
- 2 Scallions, Chopped
- 10 Lbs Spare Ribs, Rack
- 2 Tbsp Tamari
- 1 Tbsp Tomato Paste

Directions:

1. Fire up your Pit Boss Platinum Series Lockhart to 325°F and pull both the side knobs out to ensure the smoking cabi maintains a temperature of 200°F.

2. Season ribs on both sides with Pulled Pork Rub, then la on the racks in the smoking cabinet. Smoke for 2 ½ hours.

3. Meanwhile, prepare the sauce: Brush the bell pepper w oil, season with salt, then place directly on the grill grate.

4. Open the sear slide and char over direct flame for 3 minutes, turning often.

5. Remove from the grill, and set aside to cool, then skin a remove seeds.

6. In a food processor, combine peppers, garlic, ketchup, brown sugar, scallions, tamari, honey, tomato paste, parsley, paprika, salt, and pepper.

7. Process for 3 minutes, scraping down sides once or twi Transfer to a jar and set aside.

8. Lay out 4 large pieces of aluminum foil on a sheet tray. Remove ribs from the smoking cabinet, then lay each rack o overlapping pieces of foil. Spoon sauce over each rack, then tightly close foil around the ribs.

9. Lower temperature to 275°F. Transfer to the lower gril then cook ribs another 1 to 1 ½ hours, rotating racks half wa through cooking.

10. Carefully open foil, place racks directly on grates, and cook for another 10 minutes.

11. Remove ribs from the grill, then rest for 15 minutes, before slicing. Serve warm.

Pit Boss Stuffed Pork Tenderloin

vings: 4
king Time: 180 Minutes
redients:

1 Tbsp Brown Sugar
1 Tbsp Chilli, Powder
1/8 Tbsp Cinnamon, Ground
3 Tbsp Honey
1 Tsp Paprika, Smoked
1 Pork, Tenderloin
1 Jar Salsa

ections:

Start your Pit Boss Grill on Smoke with the lid open until a
is established in the burn pot (3-7 minutes). Then set the
l to 225°F. Allow it to come to temp.

Arrange salsa down center of pork tenderloin. Fold in
es and roll tenderloin carefully to distribute salsa evenly.

Using butcher's twine or 2, 1-inch strips of aluminum foil,
ap tenderloin at both ends to secure.

In a bowl, combine the chili powder, brown sugar,
oked paprika, and ground cinnamon. Mix well.

Brush the pork tenderloin with the warmed honey.
inkle the rub over the entire tenderloin. When the pork is
y coated place on the grill.

Smoke the tenderloin for 2 ½ to 3 hours, or until the
ernal temperature of pork has reached 145°F internal
perature. Slice and serve immediately.

Pork Belly Banh Mi

vings: 4
king Time: 420 Minutes
redients:

2 Carrots, Sliced
1 Tbsp Cilantro, Minced
1 Tbsp Honey
2 Kirby Cucumbers, Sliced Thin
1 Lime, Zest & Juice
2 Tbsp Pickling Spice
1 Tbsp Ponzu
2 Lbs Pork Belly
1 Cup Rice Wine Vinegar
2 Tbsp Salt
4 Sandwich Buns
1 Small Daikon Radish, Sliced Thin
To Taste, Smoky Salt & Cracked Pepper Rub
2 Tbsp Soy Sauce
1/2 Cup Sriracha Hot Sauce
4 Cloves Star Anise
1/2 Cup Sugar
1 Cup Water

ections:

30 minutes before you plan to put the belly on the smoker
son liberally with the Pit Boss Smoky Salt and Cracked
per rub.

Fire up your Pit Boss Platinum Series Brunswick on
OKE mode and let it run with lid open for 10 minutes then
heat to 240° F. If using a gas or charcoal grill, set it up for
, indirect heat.

Place the belly on the smoker with a tin pan underneath
meat to catch the drippings. Smoke for 7 hours or until you
ch an internal temp of 195 degrees. Remove the pork and
est for 30 minutes.

4. Make the homemade pickles: Place pickling spice and star
anise in a small sauce pan and toast. Once fragrant add vinegar
and bring to a boil, cook for 3 minutes. Add the water, sugar,
and salt and return to a boil, cook for 5 minutes. Strain the
liquid and immediately pour over the vegetables, making sure
the vegetables are submerged. Set in the fridge once cool.
5. Make the Sriracha Lime Sauce: Combine the sriracha, lime,
soy sauce, honey, cilantro and ponzu in a mixing bowl and
whisk until combined.
6. Assemble the sandwiches, placing sliced pork belly and
homemade pickles on a roll before topping it with the sriracha
lime sauce.

Baked Beans (the Best)

Servings: 12
Cooking Time: 180 Minutes
Ingredients:

- 1 Pack Bacon
- 1/2 Cup Brown Sugar
- 1 Coca Cola, Can
- 2 Cans Mixed Beans
- 1/3 Cup Molasses
- 4 Cans Pork And Beans
- 1 Red Onion, Chopped
- 1/3 Cup Yellow Mustard

Directions:
1. Preheat you to 275 degrees F.
2. Combine all the ingredients and stir until combined.
3. Smoked for 2.5 hours covered. For the last 30 minutes,
smoke uncovered.
4. Serve hot. Enjoy!

Cheesy Potato Stuffed Pork Chops

Servings: 4
Cooking Time: 45 Minutes
Ingredients:

- 4 Bone-In Pork Chops
- 1 Package Frozen Shredded Hash Browns, Thawed
- 1 Tbsp Parsley, Minced Fresh
- Pulled Pork Seasoning
- 1 Cup Shredded Cheddar Cheese
- ¼ Cup Sour Cream
- White Onion, Diced

Directions:
1. Place the pork chops on a flat work surface. Using a sharp
knife, cut a pocket into the side of each pork chop, being
careful not to cut all the way through the sides of the chop.
Season the pork chops generously on both sides with Pulled
Pork Seasoning.
2. In a large mixing bowl, mix together the hash browns,
shredded cheddar, sour cream, diced onion, parsley, and 1
tablespoon of Pulled Pork seasoning. Stuff each pork chop with
about ¼ cup of the potato filling. Use a toothpick to securely
close the chop if needed.
3. Fire up your Pit Boss and set the temperature to 350°F. If
you're using a gas or charcoal grill, set it up for medium heat.
Insert a temperature probe into the thickest part of one of the
chops and place the meat on the grill. Grill the chops on one
side for 10-15 minutes, then flip and grill for another 10-15, or
until the internal temperature of the chops reach 145°F.

Remove the chops from the grill, take the toothpicks out of the meat, and serve immediately.

Hawaiian Pork Butt

Servings: 8 - 10
Cooking Time: 720 Minutes
Ingredients:
- 6 - 8 Pineapple Rings
- 2 Cups Pineapple, Juice
- 1 8-10Lb Pork Butt Roast, Bone-In
- ¼ Cup Sweet Heat Rub

Directions:
1. Fire up your Pit Boss Smoker and set the temperature to 225°F. If not using a pellet smoker, set up the smoker for indirect smoking.
2. Remove the pork butt from its packaging and drain any excess liquid from the pork butt. Pat the pork butt dry with paper towels and discard the paper towels.
3. Generously season the pork butt with the Sweet Heat seasoning, making sure that the roast is coated on all sides.
4. Place the pineapple rings evenly over the pork shoulder, fat side up, and pin with toothpicks. Place the pork butt into the 9x13 pan and pour the pineapple juice over the top.
5. Set the pan into the smoker. Make sure that the pork butt is placed as close to the center of the rack as possible for even cooking.
6. Place a temperature probe into the thickest part of the pork butt, and smoke the pork until it reaches an internal temperature of 201°F. The pork should be deeply browned and smell very porky.
7. Once the pork butt reaches its internal temperature, remove the pork butt from the grill and wrap it tightly in foil. Allow the roast to rest for at least 1 hour before shredding.
8. After the roast has rested for an hour, shred the pork with your meat claws, discarding any large chunks of fat. Serve immediately.

Smoked Bone-in Pork Chops

Servings: 4
Cooking Time: 90 Minutes
Ingredients:
- 1/2 Cup Apple Cider Vinegar
- 4 Pork Butt Roast, Bone-In
- 2 Tbsp Salt
- 1 Tbsp Sugar
- 4 Tablespoons Tennessee Apple Butter Seasoning
- 1/4 Cup Vinegar, Red Wine
- 1/4 Cup Water

Directions:
1. Start up your Pit Boss Grill. Once it's fired up, set the temperature to 250°F.
2. In a large mixing bowl, combine the sugar, red wine vinegar, salt, 2 tablespoons of Tennessee Apple Butter and water to create a brine for the pork chops. Whisk the brine well until the sugar, salt and Tennessee Apple Butter have dissolved.
3. Generously rub the pork chops on all sides with olive oil and season on all sides with the Tennessee Apple Butter. Make sure the meat is coated on all sides.
4. Place the pork chops in the smoker, insert a temperature probe into the thickest part of one of the pork chops, and

smoke until the internal temperature reaches 145°F, or abo 1 hour 30 minutes. The pork chops should have developed good color and be juicy, but no longer be pink in the center.
5. Remove the pork chops from the smoker and allow the to rest for 5-10 minutes under tented aluminum foil, then s along the grain and serve.

Pork Belly Chili Con Carne

Servings: 4
Cooking Time: 120 Minutes
Ingredients:
- Avocado, Diced
- 2 Bay Leaves
- 1 Lbs Beef Stew Meat
- 12 Oz Beef Stock
- 12 Oz Beer, Bottle
- 15 Oz Black Beans, Rinsed And Drained
- 3 Tbsp Chili Powder
- Cilantro, Chopped
- 1 Tsp Coriander, Ground
- 2 Tsp Cumin, Ground
- 1 Tbsp Flour
- 4 Garlic Cloves, Minced
- 2 Tsp Mexican Oregano, Dried
- 2 Tbsp Olive Oil
- 2 Oz Pancetta, Diced
- Pork Belly, Cut Into 1 Inch Chunks
- 2 Red Onion, Chopped
- Rice, Cooked
- To Taste, Salt & Pepper
- Scallion, Sliced Thin
- 1/4 Cup Tomato Purée

Directions:
1. Fire up your Pit Boss pellet grill on SMOKE mode and le run with lid open for 10 minutes then preheat to 425°F. If using a gas or charcoal grill, set it up for medium-high heat. Place Dutch oven on grill and allow to preheat.
2. Heat the olive oil in the Dutch oven, then sauté the pancetta until crisp. Add the onions and sauté for 3 minutes then add the garlic and sauté 1 minute, until fragrant. Remo mixture with a slotted spoon and set aside.
3. Add the pork belly and beef to the pot to brown, then a the chili powder, cumin, oregano, and coriander. Add the flc and cook for 2 minutes, stirring constantly.
4. Add the beer, beef stock, and tomato purée. Stir well, th return the pancetta mixture to the pot. Add the black beans and bay leaves, then season with salt and pepper.
5. Bring chili to a simmer, then reduce temperature to 32 and simmer, uncovered, for 2 hours, stirring occasionally, u meat is tender, and sauce has thickened.
6. Remove the chili from the grill, then serve warm with cooked rice, avocado, fresh cilantro, and scallions.

Hanging St. Louis-style Ribs

Servings: 4
Cooking Time: 270 Minutes
Ingredients:
- 1 1/3 Cup Apple Juice
- 1 2/3 Cup Bbq Sauce, Divided
- Tt Pit Boss Pulled Pork Rub
- 4 Half Racks Spare Ribs, St. Louis Style

rections:

Fire up your Pit Boss Platinum Series Lockhart and
heat to 250° F. If using a gas or charcoal grill, set it up for
w, indirect heat.

Using a sharp knife, remove the back membrane from the
racks and pat dry with paper towel. Cut rib racks in half,
n season generously with Pulled Pork Rub.

Insert a hanging hook under the top rib, then transfer
cks to the smoking cabinet. Smoke for 2 ½ hours.

Remove ribs from the smoking cabinet and set on heavy
ty foil. Mix together ⅔ cup BBQ sauce and ⅓ cup apple juice,
n brush thinned BBQ sauce on both sides of ribs. Pour ¼
of apple juice around each of the ribs. Fold over foil, then
nsfer to the grill, meat side down. Increase temperature to
0° F and continue cooking for an additional 2 hours.

Remove ribs from the grill, baste with BBQ, then return to
grill and cook for another 10 to 15 minutes. Allow to rest
15 minutes, then slice and serve hot.

ulled Pork Queso Dip By James Brown Of Grill Nation

rvings: 8
oking Time: 180 Minutes
gredients:

1/2 Bunch Cilantro, Chopped
3 Ears Corn, Grilled And Removed From The Cobb
1/2 Block Cream Cheese, Room Temperature
3 Tbsp Cumin
3 Grilled Jalapenos, Diced And Seeded
2 Tbsp Lime Zest
1 Lime, Juiced
16 Ounces Mexican Cheese, Shredded
16 Ounces Pepper Jack Cheese, 1" Cubes
Tt Pit Boss Pulled Pork Rub
4 Lbs Pork Shoulder, Bone In
1/2 Yellow Onion, Diced

rections:

Turn on your Pit Boss Grill and set to SMOKE Mode. With
lid open, let the grill run for 10 minutes.

While the grill is heating up, set your Pork shoulder out
d bring to room temp.

Score the fat cap and remove silver skin.

Coat with mustard and season every inch with Pit Boss
lled Pork Rub.

Set your grill temp to 250°F.

Place the pork shoulder on the grill and smoke until it
ches an internal temperature of 165°F. (About 2 - 3 hours)

Remove and wrap in peach butcher paper. Place back in
ir Pit Boss and bump temp up to 275°F. Smoke until
ernal temp of 205°F. Pull and rest for thirty mins.

During the resting period prepare your Queso dip.

Chop all cheese into 1" cubes and pre your veggies &
bs for Queso.

Shred the pork.

Place all Queso ingredients in aluminum pan (2-3 inch
ep pan). Keep the pork warm but do not add yet.

Place in the Boss at 250°F and smoke for 10-15 mins.
ke sure to watch and when the cheese starts to melt into a
ley substance mix everything together. Pull it once
npletely melted and have a cast iron skillet and pork
iting.

Place pulled pork (about 1 pound) on bottom of the cast
n with a light coat of olive oil or butter.

14. Pour gooey Queso onto the pulled pork in the cast iron.
Quickly add 3/4 bag of Mexican cheese.
15. Place back in the Pit Boss at 250°F until cheese is melted
on top.
16. Carefully remove the cast iron skillet and grab a few bags
of chips to enjoy!

Bangers & Mash

Servings: 6 - 8
Cooking Time: 135 Minutes
Ingredients:
- Bbq Sauce
- ¼ Cup Butter
- 3 Garlic, Cloves
- 1 Onion, Chopped
- 8 Red Potatoes, Medium
- 8 Sausages, Pork
- ½ Cup Milk

Directions:
1. Using a fork, poke holes all over every red potato.
2. Cut a whole bulb of garlic in half and set aside.
3. Turn on your Pit Boss Grill and set on smoke. After the
pellets ignite, set grill temp to 300°F.
4. Set the halved garlic bulb and red potatoes on the grill.
Cook the garlic for 30 minutes and the potatoes for 75 minutes.
5. Turn your Pit Boss down to 250°F and allow it to settle to
that temperature.
6. Peel and mash the potatoes and garlic with butter and
milk until the desired smoothness is achieved.
7. Set the sausages on the grill and smoke for 1 hour.
8. Sauté sliced onions in a pan with butter and barbecue
sauce to taste.
9. After 1 hour, remove the sausages and turn off the grill.
Place the onions on top of the mash potatoes and the sausage
on top of the onions. Add more BBQ sauce if you wish.

Smoked Pork And Green Chili Tamales

Servings: 6-8
Cooking Time: 60 Minutes
Ingredients:
- 1 Boneless, Netted Pork Roast
- 1 Cup, Fresh Cilantro, Chopped
- 3 Cloves Garlic, Peeled
- 20 Dried Cornhusks
- 1 Tbsp Lime Juice
- ¼ Cup Olive Oil
- 1 Onion, Quartered
- 4 - 6 Cups Prepared Masa Harina Tamale Dough
- 3 – 4 Serrano Peppers, Deseeded
- 1 Tbsp Sweet Heat Rub
- 1 Lb. Tomatillos, Husked And Washed

Directions:
1. Began by soaking the corn husks in a pan filled with water.
Soak for 2 – 4 hours, or if needed, overnight.
2. Unwrap the tomatillos from their shell and place all of
them into a grill basket followed by a few Serranos, deseeded,
garlic cloves and 1 onion cut into quarters.
3. Fire up your Pit Boss grill and set the temperature to
400°F. If you're using a gas or charcoal grill, set it up for
medium low heat, and use smoke chips to fill your grill with
smoke for 15 minutes. Place the grill basket filled with your

vegetables and roast them over an open flame on your Pit Boss until vegetables have become charred.

4.   Place tomatillos, peppers, garlic and onions in a bowl, cover with plastic wrap, and let stand until cool enough to handle, 10 to 15 minutes.

5.   Season the pork roast generously with Sweet Heat Rub and grill at 350°F for 1 hour until the roast has a nice crust on the outside.

6.   While the pork roast is cooking, add a handful of cilantro, charred vegetables, 1 tbsp of Sweet Heat Rub, 1 tbsp lime juice, and ¼ cup of olive oil to a food processor. Pulse in food processor until mixture is consistent. Set aside

7.   After the pork roast has been grilled for an hour, turn heat down to 275°F. Put roast in pan with about a cup of water, cover with aluminum foil and cook for another 4 hours or until the roast can be shredded. Pour chile verde sauce over shredded pork and toss to combine.

8.   To being assembling tamales, place a corn husk on a work surface. Place 2-3 tablespoons of tamale dough on larger end of husk and spread into a rectangle, about ¼" thick, leaving a small border along the edge. Place large tablespoon of chili and pork filling on top of dough. Fold over sides of husk so dough surrounds filling, then fold bottom of husk up and secure closed by tying a thin strip of husk around tamale.

9.   To cook tamales, place them in a large metal colander over a large stockpot filled with water. Cover and let steam for 1 hour. After the tamales have been steamed, take them off and grill them at 350°F for about 10-20 minutes until corn husks have charred marks.

Smoked Lasagna With Cold Smoked Mozzarella

Servings: 8-12
Cooking Time: 70 Minutes
Ingredients:
- 15 Oz. Ricotta Cheese
- 3 Cups Cold-Smoked Mozzarella, Grated Divided
- 2 Eggs
- 6 Garlic Cloves, Chopped
- 1 Tsp Garlic Powder
- 1 Cup Grated Parmesan Cheese, Divided
- 1 Lb. Italian Sausage
- 1 Tbsp Italian Seasoning
- 1 Pkg."No-Bake" Lasagna Noodles
- 48 Oz. Marinara Sauce
- 1 Lb. Mozzarella Block
- 1 Tbsp Olive Oil
- 1 Tbsp Chopped Oregano
- ¼ Cup Italian Parsley, Chopped
- 1 Yellow Onion, Chopped

Directions:
1.   In a glass bowl, mix together the eggs, Italian seasoning, garlic powder, ricotta cheese, ½ cup parmesan cheese, and 1 cup of smoked mozzarella, and 2 tablespoons of parsley. Cover and refrigerate for 1 hour.

2.   Fire up your Pit Boss Lockhart Grill and preheat to 400°F. If using a gas or charcoal grill, set it up for medium-high heat. Place a cast iron skillet on the grill grates and allow to preheat.

3.   Heat olive oil in skillet, then add Italian sausage and cook for 5 minutes, then add in onion and garlic, and cook an additional 3 minutes. Remove from heat and stir in 1 tablespoon of parsley and dried oregano. Set aside and reduce grill temperature to 350° F.

4.   To assemble, begin by covering the bottom of a 9x13 pa with 1 cup of sauce. For the first layer, place a single layer of uncooked noodles over the sauce, followed by ⅓ of the ricot cheese mixture, half of the Italian sausage, 1 cup of mozzarel cheese, and 1 cup of sauce. Repeat for layer two with a singl layer of uncooked lasagna noodles, ⅓ of the ricotta cheese mixture, and 1 ½ cups of sauce. Repeat for layer three with a layer of uncooked lasagna noodles, remaining ricotta mixtur remaining Italian sausage, 1 cup of sauce. For the final layer, add a layer of uncooked lasagna noodles, remaining sauce, a remaining 1 cup mozzarella plus ½ cup parmesan.

5.   Transfer lasagna to grill and cook, covered with foil, for 35 minutes. Remove foil and continue cooking for 10 minute sprinkle with additional parmesan and parsley, if desired. Remove from grill and let stand 15 minutes before serving.

Hickory Smoked Pork Shoulder With Apple Cid Vinegar

Servings: 7
Cooking Time: 420 Minutes
Ingredients:
- 1 Cup Apple Cider Vinegar
- 2 Tbsp Pit Boss Hickory Bacon Seasoning
- 5 - 6 Lbs Pork Shoulder, Bone In
- 1 Tbsp Sugar

Directions:
1.   Fire up your Pit Boss and set the temperature to 225°F. you're using a gas or charcoal, set up your grill for low, indir heat.

2.   Rinse the pork shoulder (aka pork butt) under cold running water and make sure to pat dry the entire surface, including any small cracks and crevices.

3.   Place the pork shoulder in the aluminum pan, fat side u and sprinkle a liberal amount of Pit Boss Hickory Bacon seasoning over the top. You want to be very generous with t outer layer of seasoning here, making sure to coat the meat from end to end.

4.   In a large bowl, pour the 1 cup of apple cider vinegar, th 2 tablespoons of Hickory Bacon, and 1 tablespoon of sugar. Mix until the sugars are completely dissolved.

5.   Fill your marinade injector with the marinade and injec deep into the meat. For even flavor, inject the marinade all over the pork shoulder at one-inch intervals. Pressing the syringe slowly will help avoid the marinade squirting out.

6.   Tightly wrap aluminum foil over the top of the pan, set on your grill, and close the lid.

7.   Smoke the pork shoulder for 6-8 hours, or until the mea is tender and the internal temperature is 195°F to 200°F.

8.   Remove from the grill and let it rest on a cutting board 20-30 minutes with the aluminum foil loosely tented over th top.

9.   When you're ready to serve, shred the pork shoulder, discarding any large pieces of fat.

Hawaiian Pulled Pork Sliders

Servings: 6 - 8
Cooking Time: 5 Minutes
Ingredients:
- ½ Cup Apple Cider Vinegar
- 1 Package Of Cabbage
- 2 Tbsp Minced Cilantro

1/3 Cup Green Onions, Diced
1 Tbsp Mango Magic
1 ½ Cup Mayonnaise
1 Cup Pineapple, Diced
1 Lbs Pulled Pork
8 Hawaiian Rolls

ections:

In a large bowl mix together all of the coleslaw
redients and let set in refrigerator for at least 2 hours.

Reheat the pulled pork in a microwave or grill.

Serve over the pulled pork on the Hawaiian rolls.

Pulled Pork Sandwich With Pretzel Bun

vings: 4

king Time: 300 Minutes

redients:

⅓ Cup Apple Cider Vinegar
1 ½ Cups Bbq Sauce, Divided
1 Qt. Chicken Stock
⅓ Cup Ketchup
3 Tbsp Pit Boss Pulled Pork Rub, Divided
1, 4 Lb. Pork Shoulder, Bone In
4 Pretzel Buns

ections:

Fire up your Pit Boss and preheat to 400°F. If using a gas
charcoal grill, set it up for medium-high heat. In a bowl,
mbine the apple cider vinegar, chicken stock, ketchup, and 1
blespoon of Pit Boss Pulled Pork Rub. Whisk well to combine
d set aside.

Season the pork shoulder with the remaining 2
blespoons of Pulled Pork Seasoning on all sides of the pork
oulder, then place on the grill and sear on all sides until
den brown, about 10 minutes.

Remove the pork shoulder from the grill and place in the
posable aluminum pan. Pour the sauce over the pork
ulder. It should come about 1/3 to ½ way up the side of the
k shoulder. Cover the top of the pan tightly with aluminum

Reduce the temperature of your Pit Boss grill to 250°F.
ce the foil pan on the grill and cook for 4 to 5 hours, or until
pork is tender and falling off the bone.

Remove the pork from the grill and allow to rest for 15
utes. Drain the liquid from the pan, reserving about a cup,
n shred the pork and cover with the reserved liquid. Set 3
o 4 cups of pulled pork aside for sandwiches, and save the
aining for future use.

While pork is resting, place 1 cup of BBQ sauce in a skillet
heat to simmer. Toss in reserved shredded pork. Divide
k among 4 pretzel buns, spoon additional BBQ sauce over
top and dig in!

Cuban Pork Sandwich

vings: 4

king Time: 270 Minutes

redients:

1 Tbsp Butter
3 Cups Chicken Stock
4 Ciabatta Bread Or Torta Rolls, Halved
1/4 Cup Dijon Mustard
4 Dill Pickle, Slice
1 Lb Ham Or Prosciutto

- 1/4 Cup Mayonnaise
- Pit Boss Pulled Pork Rub
- 3 1/2 Lbs Pork Shoulder
- 8 Oz Swiss Cheese, Sliced
- 1 Tbsp Vegetable Oil
- 1 White Onion, Sliced

Directions:

1. Fire up your Pit Boss Platinum Series KC Combo and preheat to 250° F. If using a gas or charcoal grill, set it up for low, indirect heat.
2. Generously season pork shoulder with Pulled Pork Rub, then transfer to the grill grate. Smoke for 1 hour, then flip pork and smoke for an additional hour.
3. Place onion and chicken stock in a deep cast iron skillet, or metal grill pan. Transfer the pork to the skillet, then cover with a shallow cast iron skillet, or aluminum foil. Braise for 2 hours, then increase grill temperature to 300° F, and braise for 1 more hour.
4. Remove the cover then pull pork with tongs while still on the grill. The stock will have reduced, so be sure and toss the pork in the reduced, seasoned stock and onions. Remove from the grill and set aside.
5. Preheat the griddle to medium-low flame. If using a different grill, preheat a clean cast iron skillet on medium low heat.
6. Heat butter and oil on the griddle, then toast rolls, pressing down by hand or with a metal spatula. Combine mustard and mayonnaise, then spread onto both sides of rolls. Set aside.
7. Divide pork into 4 portions, and place on the griddle, along with the sliced ham. Cook for 2 to 3 minutes, rotating ham and pork. Layer pork, ham, cheese, and pickles. Cover for 1 minute to allow cheese to melt. Return rolls to the griddle, cut each portion of filling in half, then stack 2 per prepared rolls. Press each sandwich down with the bottom of a metal spatula. Carefully flip, and press down again.
8. Remove sandwiches from the griddle and serve warm.

Bourbon Chile Glazed Ham By Chef Shaun O'neale

Servings: 8 – 10

Cooking Time: 90 Minutes

Ingredients:

- ¼ Cup Apple Cider Vinegar
- 2 Cups Bourbon
- 1 Cup Brown Sugar
- 2 Canned Chipotle Chiles In Adobo Sauce
- 2 Cups Chicken Stock
- 2 Dried Ancho Chiles
- 1 Dried Arbol Chile
- 2 Dried Guajillo Chiles
- 2 Tbsp Extra Virgin Olive Oil
- 4 Fresh Garlic, Roughly Chopped
- 4 Cloves Roasted Garlic
- Salt
- 2 Shallots, Roughly Chopped
- 1 Spiral Cut Ham

Directions:

1. Heat your Pit Boss Pellet grill to 450°F with the heat shield open.
2. In a large, heavy-bottomed skillet, heat the oil over medium-high heat. Add the shallots and cook for 5 minutes, or until softened.

3. Add the roasted and fresh garlic and cook, stirring occasionally, for 3 to 4 minutes, until the garlic is browned.
4. Remove the skillet from the heat and add the bourbon.
5. Return the skillet to medium-high heat, add the vinegar, and cook until the liquid is reduced by one third, about 10 minutes.
6. Add the ancho, guajillo, árbol, and chipotle chiles and the brown sugar, then add the chicken stock and continue to cook until the mixture reduces by two thirds, about 15 minutes.
7. Strain the reduction through a fine-mesh strainer into a bowl, then pour it into a small saucepan.
8. Return to the heat over medium and reduce until the glaze coats the back off a spoon. Taste and add salt if needed.

Candied Bacon

Servings: 4
Cooking Time: 60 Minutes
Ingredients:

- 1 Pack Bacon, Thick Cut
- 1/2 Cup Brown Sugar
- 1/2 Cup Maple Syrup
- Pit Boss Mandarin Habanero Seasoning

Directions:
1. Place the bacon in a deep dish. Add the maple syrup, cover and refrigerate 2 - 3 hours or overnight.
2. Start your Grill on "smoke" with the lid open until a fire established in the burn pot (3-7 minutes). Preheat to 225°F.
3. When the grill has preheated, place the bacon directly on the cooking grids and sprinkle with brown sugar and Mandarin Habanero. Check every 15-20. After 30 minutes, flip and rotate bacon and baste with syrup. Allow to hot smoke another 20 to 30 minutes or until the bacon is done to your desired liking.
4. Allow to cool on a rack and serve.
5. Can be refrigerated in an airtight container.

Grilled Lobster Tails

vings: 3
oking Time: 10 Minutes
gredients:

Tt Black Pepper
3/4 Stick Butter, Room Temp
2 Tablespoons Chives, Chopped
1 Clove Garlic, Minced
Lemon, Sliced
3 (7-Ounce) Lobster, Tail
Tt Salt, Kosher

rections:

Start your Grill on "SMOKE" with the lid open until a fire
established in the burn pot (3-7 minutes).
Preheat grill to 350°F.
Blend butter, chives, minced garlic, and black pepper in a
all bowl. Cover with plastic wrap and set aside.
Butterfly the tails down the middle of the softer underside
the shell. Don't cut entirely through the center of the meat.
ush the tails with olive oil and season with salt, to your
ng.
Grill lobsters cut side down about 5 minutes until the
ells are bright red in color. Flip the tails over and top with a
nerous tablespoon of herb butter. Grill for another 4
nutes, or until the lobster meat is an opaque white color.
Remove from the grill and serve with more herb butter
d lemon wedges.

Seared Ahi Tuna Steak

vings: 2
oking Time: 60 Minutes
gredients:

1/2 Cup Gluten Free Soy Sauce
1 Large Sushi Grade Ahi Tuna Steak, Patted Dry
1/4 Cup Lime Juice
2 Tablespoons Rice Wine Vinegar
2 Tablespoons Sesame Oil, Divided
2 Tablespoons Sriracha Sauce
4 Tablespoons Sweet Heat Rub
2 Cups Water

rections:

Start up your Pit Boss. Once it's fired up, set the
mperature to 400°F. If using gas or charcoal, set it up for
h heat over direct heat.
In the glass baking dish, pour in the water, soy sauce, lime
ce, rice wine vinegar, 1 tablespoon sesame oil, sriracha
ice, and mirin. Whisk the marinade together with the whisk
til everything is well combine. Place the ahi steak into the
rinade and place the glass baking dish with the ahi steak in
refrigerator for 30 minutes. After 30 minutes, flip the ahi
ak over so that the ahi has the chance to fully marinate on
sides, and allow to marinate for 30 more minutes.
After the tuna steak has finished marinating, drain off the
rinade and pat the steak dry with paper towels on all sides.
ur the Sweet Heat Rub onto the plate and rub the remaining
lespoon of sesame oil generously on all sides of the tuna
ak, and then gently place the tuna steak into the seasoning
the plate, turning on all sides to coat evenly.
Insert a temperature probe into the thickest part of the
steak and place the steak on the hottest part of the grill.

Grill the ahi tuna steak for 45 seconds on each side, or just
until the outside is opaque and has grill marks. Flip the steak
and allow it to grill for another 45 seconds until the outside is
just cooked through. The ahi tuna steak's internal temperature
should be just at 115°F.
5.   Remove the steak from the grill once it reaches 115°F, and
immediately slice and serve. The inside of the steak should still
be cool and ruby pink.

Bacon Wrapped Shrimp

Servings: 4
Cooking Time: 11 Minutes
Ingredients:

- 8 Bacon, Strip
- 1/4 Cup Butter Style Shortening (Melted)
- 1 Clove Garlic, Minced
- 1 Tsp Lemon, Juice
- Pepper
- Salt
- 16 (Peeled And Veined) Shrimp, Jumbo

Directions:
1.   Start your Grill on "smoke" with the lid open until a fire is
established in the burn pot (3-7 minutes). Preheat to 450°F.
2.   Take one slice of bacon, and wrap it around each piece of
shrimp, and lock it in place with a wooden toothpick.
3.   Place the shortening into a mixing bowl and whisk in the
garlic and lemon juice. Brush each shrimp with the sauce on
both sides.
4.   Place on the grill, and barbecue for 11 minutes.
5.   Turn the grill off, remove the shrimp, serve and enjoy!

Lemon Smoked Salmon

Servings: 4
Cooking Time: 60 Minutes
Ingredients:

- Dill, Fresh
- 1 Lemon, Sliced
- 1 1/2 - 2 Lbs Salmon, Fresh

Directions:
1.   Preheat your Grill to 225°F.
2.   Place the salmon on a cedar plank. Lay the lemon slices
along the top of the salmon. Smoke in your Grill for about 60
minutes.
3.   Top with fresh dill and serve.

Grilled Mango Shrimp

Servings: 4
Cooking Time: 5 Minutes
Ingredients:

- 2 Tablespoon Olive Oil
- 1 Pound Raw Tail-On, Thawed And Deveined Shrimp,
Uncooked

Directions:
1.   Preheat your Pit Boss Grill to 425F. Rinse shrimp off in
sink with cold water. Place in bowl and season generously
with Mango Magic seasoning and olive oil. Toss well in bowl.

2. Thread several shrimp onto a skewer, so that they are all just touching each other. Repeat with other skewers and remaining shrimp.
3. Grill shrimp for 2 - 3 minutes on each side, or until pink and opaque all the way through. Remove from grill and serve immediately.

Grilled Spicy Lime Shrimp

Servings: 4
Cooking Time: 10 Minutes
Ingredients:
- 2 Tsp Chili Paste
- 1/2 Tsp Cumin
- 2 Cloves Garlic, Minced
- 1 Large Lime, Juiced
- 1/4 Tsp Paprika, Powder
- 1/4 Tsp Red Flakes Pepper
- 1/2 Tsp Salt

Directions:
1. In a bowl, whisk together the lime juice, olive oil, garlic, chili powder, cumin, paprika, salt, pepper, and red pepper flakes.
2. Then pour it into a resealable bag, add the shrimp, toss the coat, let it marinate for 30 minutes.
3. Start your Grill on "smoke" with the lid open until a fire is established in the burn pot (3-7 minutes). Preheat to 400F.
4. Next place the shrimp on skewers, place on the grill, and grill each side for about two minutes until it's done. One finished, remove the shrimp from the grill and enjoy!

Scallops Wrapped In Bacon

Servings: 4
Cooking Time: 20 Minutes
Ingredients:
- 3 Tbsp Lemon, Juice
- Pepper
- 12 Scallop

Directions:
1. Start your grill on smoke with the lid open until a fire is established in the burn pot (3-7 minutes).
2. Preheat to 400F.Cut the bacon rashers in half, wrap each half around a scallop and use a toothpick to keep it in place.
3. Next drizzle the lemon juice over the scallops, and then place them on a baking tray.
4. Place in the grill, and grill for about 15-20 minutes, or until the bacon is crisp, remove from the grill, then serve.

Blackened Salmon

Servings: 4
Cooking Time: 10 Minutes
Ingredients:
- 1 Tablespoon, Optional Cayenne Pepper
- 2 Cloves Garlic, Minced
- 2 Tablespoons Olive Oil
- 4 Tablespoons Pit Boss Sweet Rib Rub
- 2 Pound Salmon, Fillet, Scaled And Deboned

Directions:
1. Start up your Pit Boss Grill. Once it's fired up, set the temperature to 350°F.

2. Remove the skin from the salmon and discard. Brush the salmon on both sides with olive oil, then rub the salmon fillet with the minced garlic, cayenne pepper and Sweet Rib Rub.
3. Grill the salmon for 5 minutes on one side. Flip the salmon and then grill for another 5 minutes, or until the salmon reaches an internal temperature of 145°F. Remove from the grill and serve.

Crab Stuffed Mushrooms

Servings: 4-6
Cooking Time: 15 Minutes
Ingredients:
- 1 Package Cream Cheese, Softened
- 1/2 (2 Oz) Package Imitation Crab, Chopped
- 1 Tablespoon Lemon, Juice
- 2 Teaspoon Lemon, Zest
- 3/4 Cup Panko Japanese Bread Crumbs
- 1/2 Cup Divided Parmesan Cheese, Shredded
- 2 Tablespoon Parsley, Fresh
- 1 Teaspoon Pit Boss Chop House Steak Rub
- 12 Porcini Mushroom Caps, Cleaned And Destemmed

Directions:
1. In a large bowl, combine the cream cheese, imitation crab, breadcrumbs, ¼ cup of the parmesan cheese, lemon zest, lemon juice, parsley and Pit Boss Chophouse Steak seasoning. Mix until completely combined.
2. Using a spoon, stuff a large rounded tablespoon of the filling into the mushroom caps and gently pack it into the mushroom. Once all the mushrooms are stuffed, top with the remaining ¼ cup of parmesan cheese.
3. Preheat your Pit Boss grill to 350F. Place the mushroom onto a grill basket and grill for 5 minutes until the cheese is bubbly and golden and the mushrooms are tender.
4. Serve while hot and enjoy!

Cedar Plank Salmon

Servings: 4
Cooking Time: 20 Minutes
Ingredients:
- 1/4 Cup Brown Sugar
- 1/2 Tablespoon Olive Oil
- Pit Boss Competition Smoked Seasoning
- 4 Salmon Fillets, Skin Off

Directions:
1. Soak the untreated cedar plank in water for 24 hours before grilling. When ready to grill, remove and wipe down.
2. Start up your grill. Then, set the temperature to 350°F.
3. In a small bowl, mix the brown sugar, oil, and Lemon Pepper, Garlic, and Herb seasoning. Rub generously over the salmon fillets.
4. Place the plank over indirect heat, then lay the salmon on the plank and grill for 15-20 minutes, or until the salmon is cooked through and flakes easily with a fork. Remove from the heat and serve immediately.

Smoked Salmon Dip With Grilled Artichoke And Cheese

Servings: 12
Cooking Time: 270 Minutes

redients:
28 Oz Artichoke Hearts, Whole, Canned
1/2 Cup Breadcrumbs
1/2 Cup Brown Sugar
8 Oz Cream Cheese
1 Tbsp Garlic Powder
1 Cup Italian Cheese Blend, Shredded
1/4 Cup Kosher Salt
1 Cup Mayonnaise
2 Tsp Olive Oil
1 Tbsp Onion Powder
1/2 Cup Parmesan Cheese
2 Tbsp Parsley, Chopped
Tt Pit Boss Blackened Sriracha Rub
1 1/4 Lbs Salmon, Fillet, Scaled And Deboned
Sour Cream
1/2 Tsp White Pepper, Ground

rections:
In a small mixing bowl, whisk together the brown sugar, , garlic powder, onion powder, and white pepper. This will ke twice the cure needed, so be sure and place the aining half in a resealable plastic bag and save for smoking at a later date.

Lay a sheet of plastic wrap on a sheet tray and sprinkle a layer of the cure on it. Place the salmon skin-side down on of the cure, then sprinkle a couple tablespoons of cure on . Gently press the cure on top of the salmon flesh, then p in plastic wrap.

Refrigerate for 8 hours, or overnight.

Remove salmon from the refrigerator and wash off the e in the sink, under cold water.

Blot salmon with a paper towel, then set salmon skin side a wire rack. Dry at room temperature for two hours, or il a yellowish shimmer appears on the salmon.

Fire up your Pit Boss Platinum Series Lockhart to 250°F. If ng a gas, charcoal or other grill, set it to low, indirect heat.

Place the salmon in the upper cabinet. Smoke for 2 hours, n increase the grill temperature to 350° F to maintain a inet temperature of 225°F and smoke another 1 to 2 hours, il salmon reaches an internal temperature of 145° F.

Remove salmon from the cabinet and set aside to rest for minutes, then flake apart. Reserve ½ cup to top dip after ling.

While the salmon is resting, drain the artichokes, then wer onto metal skewers (if using wooden skewers, make e to soak in water for 1 hour prior to grilling, or you can use ill basket as well).

Season with Blackened Sriracha, then set on the grill. Grill 2 to 3 minutes, until lightly browned.

Remove from the grill, cool slightly, then roughly chop. Set le.

In a mixing bowl, combine shredded Italian cheese, grated mesan, breadcrumbs and parsley. Set aside.

Place cream cheese, mayonnaise, and sour cream in a cast skillet. Stir frequently, with a wooden spoon, for about 5 utes, until the mixture is smooth.

Carefully fold in flaked salmon and grilled artichoke rts, then spread breadcrumb mixture over dip.

Drizzle with olive oil, then close the grill lid and bake for to 30 minutes, until dip begins to bubble around the edges, cheese begins to caramelize on top.

Remove dip from the grill, top with reserved salmon and a ch of parsley. Serve warm with bagel chips, crackers, or sty bread.

Shrimp Scampi

Servings: 3
Cooking Time: 10 Minutes
Ingredients:
- 2 Tsp Blackened Sriracha Rub Seasoning
- 1/2 Cup Butter, Cubed, Divided
- 1/2 Tsp Chili Pepper Flakes
- 3 Garlic Cloves, Minced
- To Taste, Lemon Wedges, For Serving
- 1 Lemon, Juice & Zest
- Linguine, Cooked
- 3 Tbsp Parsley, Chopped
- 1 1/2 Lbs Shrimp, Peeled & Deveined
- Toasted Baguette, For Serving

Directions:
1. Fire up your Pit Boss griddle and preheat to medium-high flame. If using a gas or charcoal grill, set it up for medium-high heat.
2. Add half of the butter to the griddle, then sauté the garlic, Blackened Sriracha, and chili flakes for 1 minute, until fragrant.
3. Add the shrimp, turning occasionally for 2 minutes, until opaque.
4. Add the remaining butter, parsley, lemon zest and juice. Toss the shrimp to coat in lemon butter, then remove from the griddle, and transfer to a serving bowl.
5. Serve immediately, with fresh lemon wedges, and toasted baguette. Serve over linguine, spaghetti or zucchini noodles, if desired.

Salmon Cakes And Homemade Tartar Sauce

Servings: 4
Cooking Time: 15 Minutes
Ingredients:
- 1 1/2 Cups Breadcrumb, Dry
- 1/2 Tablespoon Capers, Diced
- 1/4 Cup Dill Pickle Relish
- 2 Eggs
- 1 1/4 Cup Mayonnaise, Divided
- 1 Tablespoon Mustard, Grainy
- 1/2 Tablespoon Olive Oil
- 1/2 Red Pepper, Diced Finely
- 1/2 Tablespoon Pit Boss Sweet Rib Rub
- 1 Cup Cooked Salmon, Flaked

Directions:
1. In a large bowl, mix together the salmon, eggs, ¼ cup mayonnaise, breadcrumbs, red bell pepper, Sweet Rib Rub, and mustard. Allow the mixture to sit for 15 minutes to hydrate the breadcrumbs.
2. Start your Pit Boss on "smoke". Once it's fired up, set the temperature to 350°F.
3. In a small bowl, mix together the remaining mayonnaise, dill pickle relish, and diced capers. Set aside.
4. Place the baking sheet on the grill to preheat. Once the baking sheet is hot, drizzle the olive oil over the pan and drop rounded tablespoons of the salmon mixture onto the sheet pan. Press the mixture down into a flat patty with a spatula. Allow to grill for 3 to 5 minutes, then flip and grill for 1 to 2 more minutes. Remove from the grill and serve with the reserved tartar sauce.

Garlic Shrimp Pesto Bruschetta

Servings: 12
Cooking Time: 15 Minutes
Ingredients:
- 12 Slices Bread, Baguette
- 1/2 Tsp Chili Pepper Flakes
- 1/2 Tsp Garlic Powder
- 4 Cloves Garlic, Minced
- 2 Tbsp Olive Oil
- 1/2 Tsp Paprika, Smoked
- 1/4 Tsp Parsley, Leaves
- Pepper
- Pesto
- Salt
- 12 Shrimp, Jumbo

Directions:
1. Start your Grill on "smoke" with the lid open until a fire is established in the burn pot (3-7 minutes). Preheat to 350F. Place the baguette slices on a baking sheet lined with foil. Stir together the olive oil, and minced garlic, then brush both sides of the baguette slices with the mix. Place the pan inside the grill, and bake for about 10-15 minutes.
2. In a skillet, add a splash of olive oil, shrimp, chili powder, garlic powder, smoked paprika, salt pepper, and grill on medium-high heat for about 5 minutes (until the shrimp is pink). Be sure to stir often. Once pink, remove pan from heat. Once the baguettes are toasted, let them cool for 5 minutes, then spread a layer of pesto onto each one, then top with a shrimp, and serve.

New England Lobster Rolls

Servings: 4
Cooking Time: 35 Minutes
Ingredients:
- 1/2 Cup Butter
- 4 Hot Dog Bun(S)
- 1 Lemon, Whole
- 4 Lobster, Tail
- 1/4 Cup Mayo
- Pepper

Directions:
1. Start your Grill on "smoke" with the lid open until a fire is established in the burn pot (3-7 minutes). Preheat to 300F.
2. Using kitchen shears, cut the shell of the tail and crack in half so that the meat is exposed. Pour in butter and season with pepper. Place the tails meat side up on the grill and cook until the shell has turned red and the meat is white, about 35 minutes.
3. Remove from the grill and separate the shell from the meat. Place the meat in a bowl with mayo, lemon juice and rind and season with pepper. Stir to combine and evenly distribute into the hot dog buns.

Mango Thai Shrimp

Servings: 4
Cooking Time: 15 Minutes
Ingredients:
- 2 Tablespoons Brown Sugar
- 2 Tablespoons Pit Boss Mango Magic Seasoning
- 1 Pinch (Optional) Red Pepper Flakes
- 1/2 Tablespoons Rice Wine Vinegar
- 1 Pound Raw Tail-On, Thaw And Deveined Shrimp, Uncooked
- 2 Tablespoons Soy Sauce
- 1 Teaspoon Sriracha Hot Sauce
- 1/2 Cup Sweet Chili Sauce

Directions:
1. Preheat your Pit Boss Grill to 425F. Rinse shrimp off in sink with cold water. Place in bowl and put in all of the ingredients listed above. Let marinade for 2 - 4 hours.
2. Thread several shrimp onto a skewer, so that they are just touching each other. Repeat with other skewers and remaining shrimp.
3. Grill shrimp for 2 - 3 minutes on each side, or until pink and opaque all the way through. Remove from grill and serve immediately.

Cedar Smoked Salmon

Servings: 6
Cooking Time: 60 Minutes
Ingredients:
- 1 Tsp Black Pepper
- 3 Cedar Plank, Untreated
- 1 Tsp Garlic, Minced
- 1/3 Cup Olive Oil
- 1 Tsp Onion, Salt
- 1 Tsp Parsley, Minced Fresh
- 1 1/2 Tbsp Rice Vinegar
- 2 Salmon, Fillets (Skin Removed)
- 1 Tsp Sesame Oil
- 1/3 Cup Soy Sauce

Directions:
1. Soak the cedar planks in warm water for an hour or more
2. In a bowl, mix together the olive oil, rice vinegar, sesame oil, soy sauce, and minced garlic.
3. Add in the salmon and let it marinate for about 30 minutes.
4. Start your grill on smoke with the lid open until a fire is established in the burn pot (3-7 minutes).
5. Preheat grill to 225°F.
6. Place the planks on the grate. Once the boards start to smoke and crackle a little, it's ready for the fish.
7. Remove the fish from the marinade, season it with the onion powder, parsley and black pepper, then discard the marinade.
8. Place the salmon on the planks and grill until it reaches 140°F internal temperature (start checking temp after the salmon has been on the grill for 30 minutes).
9. Remove from the grill, let it rest for 10 mins, then serve

Shrimp Tacos With Lime Crema

Servings: 4
Cooking Time: 10 Minutes
Ingredients:
- 1/4 Cabbage, Shredded
- 2 Tsp Cilantro, Chopped
- Corn Tortillas
- 1/2 Lime, Wedges
- 1/4 Cup Mayonnaise

Pit Boss Blackened Sriracha Rub
1/4 Red Bell Pepper, Chopped
1 Lb Shrimp, Peeled & Deveined
1/4 Cup Sour Cream
2 Tsp Vegetable Oil
1/2 White Onion, Chopped

Directions:

Place shrimp In a medium bowl. Season with Pit Boss Blackened Sriracha Rub, then drizzle with vegetable oil. Toss hand to coat well then set aside.

In a small mixing bowl, stir together mayonnaise, sour cream, and fresh lime juice. Season to taste with Blackened Sriracha. Set aside.

In a small mixing bowl, combine jalapeño, onion, red bell pepper, and cilantro. Set aside.

Fire up your Pit Boss Portable Griddle and preheat over medium flame. If using a grill, preheat a cast iron skillet over medium-heat.

Place tortillas on the griddle to warm each side, then turn the burner below.

Transfer shrimp to the hot griddle, and cook for 4 to 6 minutes, tossing occasionally, until opaque. For spicier shrimp, season with additional Blackened Sriracha.

Assemble tacos: shredded cabbage, shrimp, pepper mixture, then drizzle with sauce. Serve warm with fresh lime wedges.

Honey-soy Glazed Salmon

Servings: 4
Cooking Time: 6 Minutes
Ingredients:
1 Tsp Chili Paste
Chives, Chopped
2 Grate Garlic, Cloves
2 Tbsp Minced Ginger, Fresh
1 Tsp Honey
2 Tbsp Lemon, Juice
4 Salmon, Fillets (Skin Removed)
1 Tsp Sesame Oil

- 2 Tbsp Soy Sauce, Low Sodium

Directions:
1. Start your grill on smoke with the lid open until a fire is established in the burn pot (3-7 minutes). Preheat to 400F.
2. Take the salmon and place it in a large resealable plastic bag, and then top with all remaining ingredients, except the chives. Seal the plastic bag and toss evenly to coat the salmon. Marinade in the refrigerator for 20 minutes.
3. After the salmon has been marinading for 20 minutes, place salmon on a flat pan or right on the grates and grill for about 3 minutes, and then flip and grill on the second side for about 3 minutes. Turn off the Grill, remove the pan from grill, plate, garnish with chives, and enjoy!

Fish Tacos

Servings: 12
Cooking Time: 10 Minutes
Ingredients:
- 1 Tsp Black Pepper
- 1/4 Tsp Cayenne Pepper
- 1 1/2 Lbs Cod Fish
- 1/2 Tsp Cumin
- 1 Tsp Garlic Powder
- 1 Tsp Oregano
- 1 1/2 Tsp Paprika, Smoked
- 1/2 Tsp Salt

Directions:
1. Preheat your to 350 degrees.
2. Mix together paprika, garlic powder, oregano, cumin, cayenne, salt and pepper. Sprinkle over cod.
3. Place the cod on your preheated for about 5 minutes per side. Toast tortillas over heat, if desired.
4. Break the cod into pieces, smash the avocado, slice the tomatoes in half and place evenly among the tortillas. Top with red onion, lettuce, jalapenos, sour cream, and cilantro. Spritz with lime juice and enjoy!

TURKEY RECIPES

Pepper And Onion Turkey Burger Sliders

Servings: 5
Cooking Time: 30 Minutes
Ingredients:
- 1 Sweet Onion, Chopped
- 1 Pepper, Anaheim
- Pit Boss Bacon Cheddar Burger Seasoning
- Spinach
- 16 Oz Turkey, Ground

Directions:
1. Turn your grill onto smoke until the flame catches, then turn it to 400°F.
2. Put the ground turkey into a bowl and generously add the Pit Boss Bacon Cheddar Burger seasoning to the mixture.
3. Dice the Anaheim pepper and add it to the bowl as well.
4. Dice about 1/3 of the sweet onion and add it to the bowl.
5. Mix with your hands until the meat looks evenly coated in seasoning and the veggies are evenly mixed.
6. Separate the meat out into 3oz balls, disperse or toss the remnants.
7. Use the Pit Boss 3-in-1 Burger press to create the perfect patty! Place the patties on the grill and cook for 15-20 minutes depending on their thickness. Flip every 5ish minutes.
8. Add the buns to the grill if you'd like them toasted!
9. Remove the turkey sliders (and the buns) from the grill, add spinach, and whatever you think will taste good!
10. Caution: they're delicious :)

Brie Stuffed Turkey Burgers

Servings: 9
Cooking Time: 25 Minutes
Ingredients:
- Blueberry Jalapeno Spread
- 7Oz Bar Brie Cheese
- Burger Buns
- Pit Boss Sweet Onion Burger Seasoning
- 1 Or 2 Red Bell Peppers
- Spinach
- 3 Lbs Turkey, Ground

Directions:
1. Slice the brie into pieces, roughly about 1/2in Wx1in H. (It's ok if they aren't all even, you can puzzle piece them together in the burger as needed, so don't go crazy with measuring this!)
2. Put the 3lbs of ground turkey into a mixing bowl, generously cover with Sweet Onion Burger Seasoning (seasoning amount to preference). Mix the seasoning into the turkey, add additional seasoning if desired.
3. Once the seasoning is mixed into the ground turkey, portion the meat out into 1/3lb balls. Using the Burger Press, add half of the burger patty into the bottom of the press, then add about 3 pieces of cheese to the center of the meat. Place the remaining half of the burger patty on top of the cheese.

Press the burger a couple times using the Burger Press and voil. Flip the press to remove your burger! (repeat)
4. Note: you don't want to see a bunch of the cheese sticki out of the burger patty, make sure it is mostly covered by th meat, in the center, so it doesn't get cooked off on the grill.
5. Remove the burgers from the grill and make your creation! The sweet and spicy jam adds a lot of flavor to the burger, but whatever kind of preserve you want to add is yo call, Boss.

Bbq Smoked Turkey Jerky

Servings: 4 - 6
Cooking Time: 120 Minutes
Ingredients:
- 2 Tablespoons Apple Cider Vinegar
- 2 Tablespoons (Any Kind) Barbecue Sauce
- 1 Tablespoon Quick Curing Salt
- ½ Cup Soy Sauce
- 4 Tablespoons Sweet Sweet Rib Rub
- 2 Pounds Boneless Skinless Turkey Breast
- ¼ Cup Water

Directions:
1. In a large bowl, combine the soy sauce, water, barbecue sauce, apple cider vinegar, quick curing salt, and 2 tablespoc of the Sweet Rib Rub. Whisk together until well combined ar pour into a large, resealable plastic bag.
2. Using a sharp knife, slice the turkey into ¼ inch slices with the grain (this is easier if the meat is partially frozen). Trim off any fat, skin or connective tissue and discard.
3. Place the turkey slices into the plastic bag, seal, and massage the marinade into the turkey. Refrigerate for 24 hours.
4. Once the jerky is ready to go, remove the turkey from tl refrigerator, drain the marinade and discard. Pat the turkey dry with paper towels and sprinkle all sides generously with the remaining Sweet Rib Rub.
5. Fire up your Pit Boss Smoker and set the temperature t 180°F. If you're using a sawdust or charcoal smoker, set it u for medium low heat.
6. Place the turkey slices directly onto the smoker grates and smoke for 2-4 hours, or until the jerky is chewy but still bends slightly.
7. Transfer the jerky to a resealable plastic bag while the jerky is still warm and allow it to sit at room temperature fo hour. Squeeze any air from the bag and place in the refrigerator. It will keep for several weeks.

Smoked Turkey Tamale Pie

Servings: 6
Cooking Time: 240 Minutes
Ingredients:
- 1 Avocado, Diced (For Topping)
- 15 Oz Black Beans, Drained (For Filling)
- To Taste, Blackened Sriracha Rub Seasoning

2 Tsp Blackened Sriracha Rub Seasoning (For Filling)
To Taste, Blackened Sriracha Rub Seasoning (For Polenta)
2 Tbsp Butter (For Polenta)
2 Tbsp Cilantro, Chopped (For Topping)
1 Cup Corn Kernels (For Filling)
2 Cups Enchilada Sauce (For Filling)
1/2 Jalapeño, Minced (For Topping)
2 Cups Milk Or Water (For Polenta)
1 Cup Polenta, Or Fine Cornmeal (For Polenta)
2 Scallions, Sliced (For Topping)
2 Cups Smoked Turkey Breast, Shredded (For Filling)
2 1/2 Lbs Split Turkey Breast , Bone-In
2 Cups Turkey Stock (For Polenta)
4 Oz White Cheddar, Shredded (For Polenta)
4 Oz White Cheddar, Shredded (For Topping)

ections:

Fire up your Pit Boss Platinum Series KC Combo on
OKE mode and let it run with lid open for 10 minutes then
heat to 225° F. If using a gas or charcoal grill, set it up for
, indirect heat.

Season the turkey breast with Blackened Sriracha, then
nsfer to the grill, on a rack, over indirect heat.

Smoke the turkey breast for 2 ½ to 3 hours, until an
ernal temperature of 160° F. Remove the turkey from the
l, allow to rest for 20 minutes, then shred with 2 forks.

While the turkey is resting, prepare the polenta:

Place a deep, cast iron skillet on the grill, then increase
temperature to 375° F. Add chicken broth and milk to a
let and bring to a boil.

Whisk in the polenta, then reduce the heat to a simmer,
ring often for 5 minutes. Season with Blackened Sriracha,
n stir in cheese and butter. Remove the skillet from the grill
smooth out the polenta in an even layer.

In a large glass measuring cup or mixing bowl, combine
turkey, enchilada sauce, black beans, corn and Blackened
acha.

Spoon the turkey mixture over the polenta, then top with
unces of shredded cheese. Place on the grill, over indirect
t and bake for 20 to 25 minutes, until the filling is bubbling
ng the edge and the cheese is melted.

Remove the skillet from the grill and allow it to rest for 10
utes. Serve warm, garnished with avocado, scallions,
peño, and fresh cilantro.

Bacon Lattice Turkey

vings: 7
king Time: 180 Minutes
redients:
2 Apples
Bacon
2 Celery, Stick
(Parsley, Rosemary, Thyme) Herb Mix
1 Onion, Sliced
Pepper
Pit Boss Grills Champion Chicken Seasoning
1 Brined Turkey

Directions:
1. Preheat grill to 300°F.
2. Be sure all the innards and giblets of the turkey have been removed.
3. Wash the external and internal parts of the turkey and pat the surface dry with a paper towel.
4. Slice fruit and veggies into large chunks and stuff inside turkey.
5. Liberally season the whole Turkey with Champion Chicken Seasoning.
6. Prep bacon into lattice design on a flexible cutting board. Flip onto top of turkey, covering the breasts.
7. Season with more Champion Chicken and black pepper
8. Season with more Champion Chicken and black pepper
9. Let the turkey rest for 30 minutes.

Smoked Turkey Legs

Servings: 4
Cooking Time: 150 Minutes
Ingredients:
- 1 Cup Chicken Stock
- 2 Tbsp Pit Boss Blackened Sriracha Rub
- 4 Turkey Legs (Drumsticks)

Directions:
1. Fire up your Pit Boss pellet grill on SMOKE mode. With the lid open, let it run for 10 minutes.
2. Preheat grill to 225°F. If using a gas or charcoal grill, set it up for low, indirect heat.
3. Combine turkey stock with 2 teaspoons of Pit Boss Blackened Sriracha Rub.
4. Place turkey legs on a sheet tray, then inject each with seasoned stock. Season the outside of the legs with remaining Blackened Sriracha.
5. Place turkey legs directly on the grate of the smoking cabinet, and cook for 1 ½ hours.
6. Increase temperature to 325°F, then transfer turkey legs to the bottom grill and cook for another 45 to 60 minutes, until the internal temperature reaches 170°F.
7. Remove turkey from the grill, allow to rest for 10 minutes, then serve warm.

Texas Style Turkey

Servings: 6
Cooking Time: 240 Minutes
Ingredients:
- 1/2 Cup Coarse Black Pepper
- 1Lb Butter
- 1/2 Cup Salt, Kosher
- 1 Brined Turkey

Directions:
1. Preheat Grill to 300°F
2. Liberally season Turkey with equal parts kosher salt and coarse black pepper.
3. Cook on grill until Internal temp reaches approximately 145°F or the skin has darkened to your liking.

4. Place turkey in a roasting pan topped with a pound of chopped butter and cover.
5. Return to the grill until internal temp of the thigh and breast reaches 165°F
6. Let rest for 30 minutes, carve and serve.

Boneless Stuffed Turkey Breast

Servings: 6
Cooking Time: 90 Minutes
Ingredients:
- 1 Bay Leaf
- 1/2 Tsp Black Pepper
- 3 Tbsp Butter, Divided
- 1 Celery Rib, Chopped
- To Taste, Cracked Black Pepper
- 4 Oz Cremini Mushrooms
- 1/2 Cup Dried Cranberries
- 2 Garlic Cloves, Minced
- 1 Package, Approx 2Lbs Honeysuckle White® Turkey Breast, Boneless
- 1/2 Cup Marsala Wine
- 1 Tbsp Olive Oil
- 1 Rosemary Sprigs
- 1/2 Tsp Rubbed Sage
- 1/2 Tsp Salt
- To Taste, Sea Salt
- 6 Oz Stuffing Mix
- 1 1/4 Cup Turkey Stock, Divided
- 1 Yellow Onion, Chopped

Directions:
1. Fire up your Pit Boss Platinum Series Lockhart Grill on SMOKE mode and let it run with lid open for 10 minutes then preheat to 325°F. If using a gas or charcoal grill, set it up for medium-low heat.
2. Melt the butter 1 tablespoon of butter and olive oil in a large skillet over medium heat. Add the onions and celery and cook, stirring frequently, until soft, 3 minutes.
3. Add the garlic and mushrooms and continue to cook for 5 minutes, until the mushrooms are slightly browned.
4. Deglaze with marsala wine, using a wooden spoon to scrape up any browned bits from the bottom of the pan.
5. Add the dried cranberries, black pepper, sage, and salt and simmer for 2 minutes, then remove from the heat.
6. Fold the stuffing into the vegetable mixture, then slowly pour over turkey stock, until stuffing is moistened.
7. Place the Honeysuckle White® Turkey Breast on a large cutting board, skin-side down, then butterfly it. Season with salt and pepper, then spoon over ⅓ of the stuffing, leaving an inch border.
8. Roll the turkey breast, starting at the side with less skin. Use butcher's twine to truss the turkey breast and secure the stuffing. Place in a cast iron skillet, top remaining butter, season with salt and pepper. Place a sprig of rosemary on top, add remaining ¼ cup of stock around the turkey, along with 1 bay leaf. Transfer to the grill.
9. Cook the turkey for 1 to 1 ½ hours, until an internal temperature of 165°F is reached.

10. Remove stuffed turkey breast from the grill, rest for 15 minutes, then slice and serve warm, with remaining stuffing

Bbq Dry Rubbed Turkey Drumsticks

Servings: 6
Cooking Time: 120 Minutes
Ingredients:
- 1/2 Tbsp Black Pepper
- 1 Tbsp Brown Sugar
- 1/2 Tsp Cayenne Pepper
- 1/2 Tbsp Coriander, Ground
- 1/2 Tbsp Granulated Garlic
- 1 Package, Approx 4 Lbs Honeysuckle White® Turkey Drumsticks
- 1 Tbsp Kosher Salt
- 2 Tbsp Olive Oil

Directions:
1. Fire up your Pit Boss pellet grill on SMOKE mode and l run with lid open for 10 minutes then preheat to 225°F. If using a gas or charcoal grill, set it up for low, indirect heat.
2. Place Honeysuckle White® Turkey Legs on a sheet tray coat with olive oil, then season with a blend of salt pepper, cayenne, brown sugar, granulated garlic, and ground corian
3. Place turkey legs in the smoking cabinet and smoke for ½ hours, checking the internal temperature after 1 hour.
4. Increase the temperature to 325°F, transfer the turkey legs to the bottom grill grate and cook for another 25 to 30 minutes, until the internal temperature reaches 170°F.
5. Remove turkey drumsticks from the grill, allow to rest 10 minutes, then serve warm.

Hot Turkey Sandwich

Servings: 4
Cooking Time: 10 Minutes
Ingredients:
- 8 Slices Bread, Sliced
- 1 Cup Gravy, Prepared
- 2 Cups Leftover Turkey, Shredded

Directions:
1. Open the flame broiler of your Grill. Start your grill on "smoke" with the lid open until a fire is established in the b pot (3-7 minutes). Preheat to 400F.
2. Place the BBQ Grill Mat on the grates of your preheated grill and lay the shredded turkey evenly across the mat to reheat for about 10 minutes.
3. Prepare or reheat the gravy. You''ll want to have the gravy warmed and ready as soon as the turkey is reheated a the bread is toasted.
4. Hold each slice of bread over the flame broiler to toast your liking.
5. When all of your ingredients are hot, scoop 1/2 cup of shredded turkey onto a piece of bread, generously cover wi gravy and top with another piece of toasted bread. Serve immediately.

Bourbon Glazed Smoked Turkey Breast

Servings: 6
Cooking Time: 240 Minutes
Ingredients:
- 1/2 Tbsp Black Pepper
- 1/2 Cup Bourbon
- 1/2 Tbsp Garlic Powder
- 1 1/2 Tbsp Kosher Salt
- 1/4 Cup Maple Syrup
- 2 Tbsp Olive Oil
- 1/2 Tbsp Onion Powder
- 1/4 Cup Orange Juice
- 9 Lbs Shady Brook Farms® Turkey Breast, Whole, Bone-
- 1 Sweet Potato, Halved
- 2 Tbsp Tamari
- 1/2 Tbsp Thyme, Dried
- 1 Yellow Onion, Halved

Directions:

Rinse turkey thoroughly under cold water, then blot dry with paper towels.

Rub turkey with olive oil, then season inside and outside the cavity with a blend of kosher salt, black pepper, garlic powder, onion powder, and dried thyme. Place in a cast-iron skillet, and prop up on either side with onion and potato. Set aside.

Fire up your Pit Boss pellet grill on SMOKE mode and let it run with lid open for 10 minutes then preheat to 250° F. If using a gas or charcoal grill, set it up for low, indirect heat.

Transfer turkey to the grill and smoke for 3 to 3 ½ hours, until an internal temperature of 165 F is reached, rotating after 1 ½ hours.

Meanwhile, prepare the glaze: melt the butter in a small saucepan, over medium heat.

Whisk in the bourbon, maple syrup, orange juice, and soy sauce. Bring to a boil, then reduce to a simmer.

Simmer for 10 minutes, until sauce begins to reduce and slightly thicken. Set aside.

Baste turkey with the glaze every 20 to 30 minutes, after rotating the turkey.

Remove the turkey from the grill and allow it to rest for minutes before slicing, and serving warm.

Smoked Turketta (bacon Wrapped Turkey Breast)

Servings: 6
Cooking Time: 180 Minutes
Ingredients:
- 1 Shady Brook Farms® Turketta
Directions:

Fire up your Pit Boss pellet grill on SMOKE mode and let it run with lid open for 10 minutes then preheat to 250°F. If using a gas or charcoal grill, set it up for low, indirect heat.

Place the Turketta directly on the grill grate and smoke 2½ to 3 hours, or until an internal temperature of 165°F is reached.

Bbq Breakfast Sausage Not So Fatty

Servings: 4 - 6
Cooking Time: 35 Minutes
Ingredients:
- 1/4 Cup Bbq Sauce
- 1 Tbsp Brown Sugar
- 4 Oz Cheddar Cheese, Cut Into Sticks
- To Taste, Cracked Black Pepper
- 6 Eggs, Scrambled
- 4 Oz Ham, Diced
- 1 Package, Approx 1 Lb Shady Brook Farms Ground Turkey Sausage
- 10 Oz Turkey Bacon

Directions:
1. Fire up your Pit Boss pellet grill on SMOKE mode and let it run with lid open for 10 minutes then preheat to 375°F. If using a gas or charcoal grill, set it up for medium-high heat.
2. Lay out a piece of plastic wrap then make a bacon weave using your favorite turkey bacon. Top with the Shady Brooks Farms Turkey Sausage and spread out into an even layer with your fingers.
3. Spoon the scrambled eggs into the center of the sausage, then place half of the cheese sticks in the middle, followed by ham, then remaining cheese.
4. Gently lift up one end of the plastic wrap and begin rolling the "not so fatty." Once the roll is completed, remove the plastic wrap and secure the ends of the bacon together with toothpicks, if needed.
5. Set in a cast iron skillet, sprinkle with brown sugar, and season with cracked pepper. Transfer to the grill and cook for 30 minutes, until an internal temperature of 155°F.
6. Baste with BBQ sauce and cook for an additional 5 minutes until the sauce is set and the internal temperature increased to 165°F.
7. Remove from the grill and rest for 5 minutes before slicing and serving warm.

Hot And Fast Bbq Turkey

Servings: 8
Cooking Time: 120 Minutes
Ingredients:
- 1 Bay Leaf
- 1/2 Tsp Black Peppercorns, Ground
- Pinch Chili Flakes
- 4 Garlic Cloves, Peeled And Smashed
- 1/4 Cup Honey
- 3/4 Cup Honey Chipotle Bbq Sauce
- 1 Honeysuckle White® Turkey, Thawed
- 1 Tsp Kosher Salt
- 1/4 Cup Olive Oil
- 3 Thyme Sprigs
- 1 Cup Turkey Stock
- 3 Cups Water
- 2 Tbsp Worcestershire Sauce

Directions:

1. Rinse Honeysuckle White® turkey thoroughly under cold water, then blot dry with paper towels. Place on a greased rack of a roasting pan. Set aside.

2. Prepare the injection solution: in a saucepot, whisk together the turkey stock, honey, olive oil, smashed garlic, Worcestershire sauce, salt, pepper, and chili flakes. Add in the thyme sprigs and bay leaf. Bring mixture to a boil, then simmer for 5 minutes. Remove from heat, cool for 30 minutes, then strain.

3. Using an injection needle, inject the solution throughout the turkey. Rub 1 tablespoon of solution over the top of the turkey. Add water to the bottom of the roasting pan. Set aside.

4. Fire up your Pit Boss pellet grill on SMOKE mode and let it run with lid open for 10 minutes then preheat to 450° F. If using a gas or charcoal grill, set it up for high heat.

5. Transfer the turkey to the grill and roast for 100 to 120 minutes, until an internal temperature of 165° F is reached, rotating every 30 minutes. Tent with foil after 30 minutes, then brush all over with BBQ sauce during the final 10 minutes of roasting time.

6. Remove from the grill, and allow the turkey to rest for 3 minutes, then carve and serve warm.

Sweet Heat Cajun Spatchcock Turkey

Servings: 7
Cooking Time: 180 Minutes
Ingredients:
- 16 Oz Cajun Butter
- Pit Boss Sweet Heat Rub
- 1 Brined Turkey

Directions:

1. Preheat Pit Boss Grill to 300°F

2. Inject the Turkey with Cajun butter and season liberally with Pit Boss Sweet Heat Rub.

3. Place on the grill and cook until thighs and breasts reach 165°.

4. Let rest for 30 minutes and serve.

VEGGIES RECIPES

Parmesan Crusted Smashed Potatoes

vings: 4

king Time: 10 Minutes

redients:

3 Tbsp Butter, Melted

To Taste Cracked Black Pepper

1/4 Tsp Garlic, Granulated

1/3 Cup Parmesan Cheese

1 Tbsp Parsley, Leaves

2 Lbs, Yukon Gold Potatoes

To Taste Salt

2 Tbsp Vegetable Oil

ections:

Fire up your Pit Boss Platinum Series KC Combo and heat the griddle to medium-low flame. If using a gas or rcoal grill, preheat a large cast iron skillet over medium- heat.

Evenly distribute the cooled potatoes on a metal sheet , drizzle with olive oil, and use a potato masher or small tal bowl to gently smash each potato to a height of about ¼ ½ inch (thinner potatoes will be crispier).

Mix together the butter and garlic. Brush the mixture over h potato, then season with salt and pepper.

Pour vegetable oil on griddle, then add flattened potatoes. k for 3 minutes, then flip and sprinkle with half of mesan. Cook for 3 minutes, then flip, sprinkle with aining Parmesan, and cook 1 minute.

Transfer to a pan, sprinkle with parsley and serve hot.

Braised Collard Greens

vings: 4

king Time: 45 Minutes

redients:

2 Quarts Broth, Chicken

3 Lbs, Woody Stems Removed And Cut Into Thick Ribbons ard Greens

4 Peeled Garlic, Cloves

3 Smoked Ham Hock

For Serving Hot Pepper Vinegar

2 Whole Yellow Onion, Sliced

To Taste Salt And Pepper

2 Tbsp Sweet Heat Rub

ections:

In a large stock pot, combine the chicken broth, Sweet t Rub, sliced onions, garlic and ham hocks. Cover and mer for 2-3 hours, or until the ham hocks are tender. Allow ool.

Remove the meat from the ham hocks and chop. Add the ard greens to the broth, fully submerged, and simmer for 45 minutes, or until the greens are tender.

Season to taste, add vinegar if desired, and enjoy!

ussels Sprout Slaw With Apple Butter Dressing

vings: 6-8

king Time: 10 Minutes

redients:

1/4 Cup (For Apple Butter Dressing) Apple Butter

- 2 Tablespoon (For Apple Butter Dressing) Apple Cider Vinegar
- 8 (For The Slaw) Bacon, Strip
- 2 Lbs (For The Slaw) Brussels Sprouts, Rinsed And Trimmed
- 1/2 Teaspoon (For Apple Butter Dressing) Chipotle Pepper, Ground
- 1 Teaspoon (For Apple Butter Dressing) Cinnamon, Ground
- 1/2 Teaspoon (For Apple Butter Dressing) Coriander, Ground
- 1 Cup (For Apple Butter Dressing) Olive Oil
- 1 (For Apple Butter Dressing) Orange, Zest
- 1/2 Cup (For The Slaw) Parmesan Cheese, Shredded
- 1/2 Cup (For The Slaw) Pecans, Toasted
- 1 Teaspoon (For Apple Butter Dressing) Pit Boss Applewood Smoked Bacon Seasoning
- 1/4 Cup (For The Slaw) Pomegranate Arils
- 1 (For The Slaw) Yellow Onion
- Yellow Onion, Sliced

Directions:

1. For the slaw: in a food processor, fit the bowl with a medium grating blade. Shred the brussels sprouts and set aside.
2. Place the bacon and yellow on a grill basket and season both sides with Pit Boss Applewood Smoked Bacon Seasoning. Turn your Pit Boss Grill to 350F and grill for 5-10 minutes, or until bacon is crispy and the yellow onion is soft. Remove from grill and chop into ¼ inch pieces. Set aside.
3. For the dressing: in a large bowl, whisk together the oil, apple butter, coriander, chipotle pepper, cinnamon, vinegar, orange zest and Applewood Smoked Bacon seasoning. Whisk to combine.
4. To assemble the salad: in a large salad bowl, stir together the shredded brussels sprouts, chopped pecans, chopped bacon, parmesan cheese, pomegranate arils and dressing. Serve and enjoy!

Corn On The Cob

Servings: 6

Cooking Time: 20 Minutes

Ingredients:

- 1/2 Cup Butter, Melted
- 6 Corn, Cob
- Salt

Directions:

1. Preheat your Grill to 400 degrees F.
2. Husk the corn and be sure to remove all the silk. Brush with melted butter and sprinkle with salt.
3. Place the corn on the grates of your grill, and rotate every 5 minutes until your desired level of golden brown is achieved. Brush with butter halfway through (or as much as you feel - the more the better).
4. Serve warm. Enjoy!

Hickory Smoked Chive And Cheese Twice Baked Sweet Potatoes

Servings: 6

Cooking Time: 60 Minutes

Ingredients:
- 3 Pieces Brown Sugar Bacon
- Chives, Chopped
- 1 Cup Colby Jack Cheese, Shredded
- 2 Tbs Olive Oil
- Pit Boss Hickory Smoked Finishing Salt
- 3 Potato, Sweet
- 2 Tbs Sour Cream

Directions:
1. Turn your grill to smoke, once the fire pot catches - preheat your grill to 400° F.
2. Washing sweet potatoes and rub olive oil on the skins. Poke holes in the potatoes with a fork.
3. Once grill is heated add bacon rack with brown Sugar bacon – cook 10-15 minutes
4. Place sweet potatoes on indirect flame/heat and cook for about 50 minutes.
5. Remove sweet potatoes and let cool.
6. Reduce the heat to 350° F (for when you put the potatoes back on the grill).
7. While cooling add the sour cream, cheese, 2 tbs(ish) of diced chives, and crumbled bacon into a mixing bowl.
8. Once the potatoes have cooled enough to touch, cut them in half lengthwise.
9. Scoop out the insides with a spoon and add them to the mixing bowl, leaving enough potato to create a boat-like shell.
10. Mix the ingredients together, sprinkle with Pit Boss Grill Hickory Smoked Salt, and add them back into the potato skins.
11. Top with additional shredded cheese or chives if desired.
12. Place the potatoes on a backing sheet, covered with parchment paper (to help prevent burning).
13. Bake for 15-20 minutes, or until the cheese is melted and the tops slightly brown.
14. Remove from the grill and let cool briefly. Top with additional sour cream, some butter, or bacon if desired! Eat up!!

Simply Bossin' Tortilla Chips

Servings: 4
Cooking Time: 15 Minutes
Ingredients:
- Olive Oil
- Pit Boss Cilantro Lime Seasoning
- 8 Flour Tortilla

Directions:
1. Preheat your Grill to 350F.
2. Drizzle olive oil over each flour tortilla. Sprinkle with Cilantro Lime Seasoning and cut into triangles. Place on a prepared baking sheet and grill for 15 minutes. Serve with salsa or your favorite hot dip!

Chili Verde Sauce

Servings: 4
Cooking Time: 10 Minutes
Ingredients:
- 1 Cup Cilantro
- 3 Cloves Garlic, Peeled
- 1 Medium Onion, Peeled And Quartered
- ¼ Cup Olive Oil
- 3-4 Serrano Chili Pepper, Halved And Seeded
- 1 Tbsp Sweet Heat Rub

- 1 Lb. Tomatillos, Husks Removed

Directions:
1. Fire up your pellet grill and set the temperature to 350 If you're using a gas or charcoal grill, set it up for medium hi heat. In a bowl, toss the tomatillos, onion, garlic, and pepper with the oil and toss to coat evenly.
2. Grill vegetables until slight charred and bubbling on all sides, about 10 – 20 minutes. Remove from grill and allow to cool slightly.
3. Transfer grilled vegetables to a blender and add the cilantro, lime juice, olive oil, and Sweet Heat Rub. Pulse the ingredients until they have a consistent texture to them.

Sweet Potato Medley

Servings: 6-8
Cooking Time: 45 Minutes
Ingredients:
- 8-10 Brussels Sprouts
- 2-3 Tablespoons Olive Oil
- 1/2 Sweet White Softball Sized White Onion
- 1 Red Bell Pepper
- Pit Boss Lemon Pepper Garlic Seasoning
- 2 Sweet Potatoes, Scrubbed

Directions:
1. Slice the sweet potatoes, and then cut them into quarte Slice the onion, Anaheim pepper and bell pepper. Be sure to make these slices big enough that they won't fall though the holes in your Pit Boss Grilling Basket. Cut the brussels sprou vertically, stems at the bottom, in 1/2 or 1/3's depending or their size.
2. Add the sweet potatoes to your grilling basket. Drizzle olive oil, enough to cover the potatoes, but not enough to drown them. Sprinkle with Pit Boss Lemon Pepper Garlic seasoning (to taste), and toss again.
3. Toss or mix the additional vegetables in a bowl, and drizzle olive oil over these as well so they are evenly covere with the olive oil. Set aside.
4. Preheat your grill to 450F.
5. Place the sweet potatoes on the grill, (indirect flame heating). Your Medley will take 45-50 minutes depending o the thickness of your potatoes.
6. Every 15 minutes, go out to your Pit Boss Grill and toss/mix the potatoes. After 30 minutes, add the rest of the vegetables to the potatoes and toss - so that the Medley coo evenly.
7. When finished, remove the vegetables from the grill, ar add them to a serving bowl. Serve hot, and chow down!

Cinnamon Twice Baked Sweet Potatoes

Servings: 6
Cooking Time: 60 Minutes
Ingredients:
- 3 Pieces Brown Sugar Bacon
- 3 Tbs Butter
- 1 Tsp Cinnamon, Ground
- (Optional) Marshmallow, Mini
- 1/2 Tsp Nutmeg, Ground
- 2 Tbs Olive Oil
- 3 Potato, Sweet

Directions:

Turn your grill to smoke, once the fire pot catches - heat your grill to 400° F.

Washing sweet potatoes and rub olive oil on the skins. ke holes in the potatoes with a fork.

Once grill is heated add bacon rack with brown Sugar con – cook 10-15 minutes

Place sweet potatoes on indirect flame/heat and cook for ut 50 minutes.

Remove sweet potatoes and let cool.

Reduce the heat to 350° F (for when you put the potatoes ck on the grill).

While cooling add the cinnamon, nutmeg, and softened tter into a mixing bowl.

Once the potatoes have cooled enough to touch, cut them half lengthwise.

Scoop out the insides with a spoon and add them to the xing bowl, leaving enough potato to create a boat-like shell.

Mix the ingredients together and add them back into the tato skins.

Top with bacon pieces or mini marshmallows if desired!

Place the potatoes on a backing sheet, covered with rchment paper (to help prevent burning).

Bake for 15-20 minutes, or until the tops of the rshmellows have browned.

Remove from the grill and let cool briefly.

Dig in!

Southern Green Beans

vings: 6
oking Time: 60 Minutes
gredients:

1 Tablespoon Butter, Unsalted
2 Cups Chicken Broth
2 Pounds Green Beans, Ends Snapped Off And Longer ans Snapped In Half
Hickory Bacon Seasoning
4 Slices Bacon, Raw
2 Cups Water

rections:

Fire up your Pit Boss grill and set the temperature to 0°F. If you're using a gas or charcoal grill, set it up for dium heat. Place a cast iron pan on the grill to preheat. Once pan finishes preheating, place the 4 slices of bacon in the n and cook for 15 minutes until the bacon has rendered and rispy.

Remove the bacon from the pan and reserve for later. ave the pan and drippings on the grill, and add the green ans, chicken broth, water, and Hickory Bacon seasoning to te. Close the lid on the grill and cook for an hour, or until beans are tender.

Chop the bacon on a cutting board and mix into the beans ch the butter. Allow the beans to cook for another minute, n remove from the heat and serve.

Hasselback Potato Bites

vings: 4
king Time: 40 Minutes
redients:

Cheese, Sliced
Olive Oil
1 Lb Potato, Baby

- Salt, Kosher

Directions:
1. Start your Grill on "smoke" with the lid open until a fire is established in the burn pot (3-7 minutes).
2. Preheat to 400F.
3. Place all ingredients in a bowl, combine them and stir well.
4. Shape the mixture into 30 meatballs (1 ½ inches in width).
5. Spray a broiler pan with cooking spray, place on the grill, and bake for 15 minutes until fully cooked and browned.
6. Remove from grill, cool for 5 minutes, and serve.

Grilled Potato Salad With Smoked Hard Boiled Eggs

Servings: 6
Cooking Time: 60 Minutes
Ingredients:
- 1/2 Cup Bacon Bits
- 8 Peeled Egg, Boiled
- 1 Cup Mayonnaise
- 1 Tbsp Olive Oil
- 1/4 Cup Parsley, Chopped
- Tt Pit Boss Hickory Bacon Rub
- 3 Scallions, Chopped
- 1 Cup Sour Cream
- 2 Tbsp Spicy Brown Mustard
- 2 Lbs Yukon Gold Potatoes

Directions:
1. Fire up your Pit Boss Platinum Series Lockhart and preheat to 275°F. If using a gas or charcoal grill, set it up for low, indirect heat.
2. Drizzle olive oil over potatoes. Season both potatoes and eggs with Hickory Bacon.
3. Place potatoes over indirect heat on the grill grate. Place eggs in the smoking cabinet, directly on grates. Remove after 1 hour.
4. Allow potatoes to cool for 10 minutes, then cut in half and return to grill and place flesh side down over direct flame for 1 minute. Remove from grill and cool.
5. Meanwhile, prepare dressing in a mixing bowl by whisking together mayonnaise, sour cream, mustard, bacon bits, parsley, and scallions.
6. Quarter potatoes and cut eggs in half then quarter. Gently mix potatoes and eggs into dressing. Refrigerate for 1 hour, then serve.

Grilled Sweet Potato Casserole

Servings: 4
Cooking Time: 90 Minutes
Ingredients:
- 1/4 Cup Brown Sugar
- Butter, Softened
- 4 Oz Chopped Pecans
- ½ Tsp Cinnamon
- 6 Oz. Mini Marshmallows
- 2 Tsp Pit Boss Tennessee Apple Butter Rub
- 4 Sweet Potatoes

Directions:
1. Fire up your Pit Boss and preheat to 400° F. If using a gas or charcoal grill, set it for medium-high heat.
2. Wash and scrub potatoes then pat dry with paper towel.

3. Coat outside of potatoes generously in softened butter then set butter aside. Place the sweet potatoes directly on the grill grate and smoke until soft, 1 to 1 ½ hours depending on the size of your sweet potatoes.
4. Once sweet potatoes are soft remove from the grill. Coat with more butter and cover with brown sugar and Tennessee Apple Butter. Slice the center of the sweet potato and press on the sides to create an opening. Stuff each sweet potato with a layer of butter, brown sugar, cinnamon, chopped pecans, and marshmallows.
5. Return to the grill and cook, covered, for five minutes, or until marshmallows are lightly browned. Remove from grill and serve warm.

Roasted Pineapple Salsa

Servings: 4
Cooking Time: 30 Minutes
Ingredients:
- Cilantro
- 1 Large Onion, Diced
- 1 Pineapple, Chopped
- 1 Tbsp Pit Boss Mandarin Habanero Spice
- 1 Red Bell Peppers
- 5 Tomato, Roma
- 1 Bag Tortilla Chip

Directions:
1. Set your Grill to 250°F and roast the vegetables whole for 30 minutes. Use Hickory Pellets for your wood pellet grill, to give it a 100% hardwood smoke.
2. While the vegetables are roasting on your Grill, split a whole Pineapple and make a bowl out of one side. Remove the core and place the leftover diced pineapple in a bowl along with some freshly diced cilantro.
3. Once the vegetables are done roasting, peel the tomatoes. Dice the roasted onions, red peppers, and tomatoes. Place in bowl.
4. Add a tablespoon of Mandarin Habanero and process with a hand blender to a chunky consistency.
5. Make some Guacamole with the extra roasted tomatoes and onions.
6. Serve with Nachos!

Scalloped Potatoes

Servings: 10
Cooking Time: 90 Minutes
Ingredients:
- 1 L Heavy Cream
- 2 Cups Mozzarella Cheese, Shredded
- 1 Onion, Sliced
- 8 Red Potatoes, Sliced

Directions:
1. Preheat your Grill to 350F.
2. In a large cast iron pan, layer potatoes and onion. Pour in heavy cream until all potatoes are covered except the top layer. Sprinkle on cheese.
3. Bake in your uncovered for about 1 ½ hour, with the lid closed. The cheese should be golden brown and potatoes soft. Serve hot. Enjoy!

Lemon Garlic Green Beans

Servings: 6
Cooking Time: 20 Minutes
Ingredients:
- 3 - 5 Tbs Butter
- 3 Garlic, Cloves
- 1 Lb Green Bean, Whole
- Pepper
- Pit Boss Lemon Pepper Garlic Seasoning
- Salt

Directions:
1. Turn your grill to smoke, once the fire pot catches - preheat your grill to 350° F.
2. Melt the butter in a ramekin.
3. While your grill is heating, line the grilling basket with tinfoil. Add the green beans and melted butter.
4. Add salt, pepper, and Pit Boss Grills Lemon Pepper Garlic Seasoning to taste
5. Add 2-3 cloves of minced garlic.
6. Toss all ingredients until evenly mixed.
7. Place basket on the grill and cook for 15-20 minutes. Toss the basket half way through the cook time.
8. Once your lemon garlic green beans are finished, remove them and add them to a serving dish – contents are hot! Caution as the butter may boil, splatter a bit.

Grilled Garlic Potatoes

Servings: 6
Cooking Time: 30 Minutes
Ingredients:
- 3 Tbsp Butter
- 3 Sliced Garlic, Cloves
- 1 Large Onion, Sliced
- 1 Tsp Chopped Parsley, Leaves
- Red Potato, Baby
- 1 Cup Shredded Cheddar Cheese

Directions:
1. Preheat the grill then increase the temperature to 400°.
2. Cut and arrange potato slices, separated by onion and butter slices, on a large piece of commercial grade aluminum foil. If commercial grade aluminum foil is unavailable, layer aluminum foil until it is strong, or use a baking sheet.
3. Top potatoes with garlic, and season with parsley, salt, and pepper. Place potatoes on the aluminum foil.
4. Place on the preheated grill and cook for 30-40 minutes or until potatoes are tender. Serve hot.
5. an option, you can sprinkle potatoes with shredded cheddar cheese, reseal foil packets, and continue cooking 5 minutes, or until cheese is melted.

Mexican Street Corn Salad

Servings: 4
Cooking Time: 10 Minutes
Ingredients:
- 1 Tablespoon Of Chopped Cilantro
- 4 Corn, Cob
- 1/2 Cup Crumbled Feta Cheese
- 1 Lime, Juiced
- 2 Tablespoon Mayo
- 1 Teaspoon Paprika, Smoked

1 Tablespoon Pit Boss Champion Chicken Seasoning
1/4 Cup Sour Cream

ections:

Preheat your Pit Boss Grill to 350F. Grill the corn cobs
il slightly charred on all sides, about 10 minutes. Remove
m the grill and allow to cool.

Remove the kernels of corn from the cob and set aside. In
parate bowl, mix together the sour cream, mayonnaise,
e juice, Champion Chicken seasoning, smoked paprika, and
ntro until smooth. Mix with the corn and feta cheese, then
ve immediately.

Gluten Free Mashed Potato Cakes

vings: 6
king Time: 10 Minutes
redients:

1/2 Cup Bacon Bits
2 Tbsp Butter
1 Cup Cheddar Jack Cheese, Shredded
1 Egg, Whisked
1/3 Cup Flour, Gluten Free
3 Cups Mashed Potatoes, Prepared
1 Tsp Pit Boss Hickory Bacon Rub
4 Scallions, Minced
2 Tsp Spicy Mustard

ections:

In a mixing bowl, combine mashed potatoes, bacon bits,
llions, mustard, cheddar jack cheese, and beaten egg. In a
arate bowl, whisk together flour, and teaspoon of Pit Boss
kory Bacon Rub. Incorporate dry into wet ingredients.
er and refrigerate for 30 minutes.

Remove mixture from the refrigerator, then divide into 12
ls (about 2 ½ inches in diameter), and set on a greased
et tray. Use the bottom of a bowl to press down each potato
 to form a ½ inch thick patty. Season with additional
inkling of Hickory Bacon and set aside. Fire up your Pit
s Platinum Series KC Combo or Pit Boss Griddle and
heat the griddle to medium-low flame. If using a gas or
rcoal grill, preheat a cast iron skillet over medium-low heat.

Add butter and oil to griddle to melt, then place mashed
ato cakes on the griddle. Cook for 2 to 3 minutes per side,
il golden brown.

Remove from the griddle. Serve warm with sour cream,
erved bacon bits and scallions.

Smoked Scalloped Potatoes

vings: 4-6
king Time: 60 Minutes
redients:

1 Stick Of Butter
Cast Iron Skillet Or Pan

- 1/2 Chedder Jack Or Colby Jack Cheese, Shredded
- Medium Yellow Onion
- Pit Boss Bacon Cheddar Seasoning
- 6-8 Potatoes
- Salt And Pepper
- Smoked Guoda Cheese, Sliced

Directions:
1. Preheat Grill to 350°F.
2. Peel 6-8 potatoes and slice into 1/4 round slices, cover
with water in pot and bring to boil, allow to boil for 2-3
minutes.
3. In the cast iron skillet, start to layer the potatoes and
cheese. Starting by using a slotted spoon to remove potatoes
from water. You will want some of the water from the boiling
process to make it into the skillet, but not an excessive amount.
Using a slotted spoon but not shaking the potatoes dry works
perfectly.
4. Once you have a base layer of potatoes, add a layer of
sliced onion (approx. ½ of a medium yellow onion), salt,
pepper, Pit Boss Bacon Cheddar Burger Seasoning, a drizzle of
sweet condensed milk, half a stick of butter cut into pats, and a
layer of sliced smoked gouda cheese.
5. Repeat on the 2nd layer. Top with grated cheddar jack or
Colby jack cheese.
6. Cook at 325°F-350°F for approx. 1 hour or until the
potatoes are tender.
7. For crustier cheese on top, turn the grill up to 425°F for
the last 10 to 15 minutes or until the cheese is golden brown.

Green Chile Mashed Potatoes

Servings: 4
Cooking Time: 40 Minutes
Ingredients:
- 1 Stick Butter, Unsalted
- 1 Can Green Chiles, Drained
- 1/4 - 1/2 Warm Milk, Whole
- Pit Boss Competition Smoked Rub
- 2 Tablespoon Pit Boss Competition Smoked Seasoning
- 3 Lbs Russet Potatoes, Peeled And Cut (Large Chunks)

Directions:
1. For the mashed potatoes: add the potatoes to a large pot
and add enough cold water to cover the potatoes. Bring to a
simmer over medium heat until the potatoes are tender
enough to be pierced with a fork, about 30-35 minutes. Drain
the potatoes.
2. Add the potatoes to a large mixing bowl. Add the butter,
Competition Smoked Seasoning, drained green chiles and ¼
cup of warm milk. Mash until smooth and lump free. If
potatoes are too thick, add more milk, a tablespoon at a time,
until you reach your desired consistency.
3. Serve and enjoy!

OTHER FAVORITE RECIPES

Baby Bok Choy With Lime-miso Vinaigrette

Servings: 4
Cooking Time: 25 Minutes
Ingredients:
- ¼ cup good-quality vegetable oil
- Grated zest of 1 lime
- 2 tablespoons fresh lime juice
- 2 tablespoons white or light miso
- 1 tablespoon rice vinegar
- Salt and pepper
- 1½ pounds baby bok choy

Directions:
1. Start the coals or heat a gas grill for medium direct cooking. Make sure the grates are clean.
2. Whisk the oil, lime zest and juice, miso, and vinegar together in a small bowl until combined and thickened. Taste and adjust the seasoning with salt and pepper.
3. Trim the bottoms from the bok choy and cut into halves or quarters as needed. Pour half the vinaigrette into a large baking dish. Add the bok choy and turn in the vinaigrette until completely coated.
4. Put the bok choy on the grill directly over the fire. Close the lid and cook, turning once, until the leaves brown, and you can insert a knife through the core with no resistance, 5 to 10 minutes per side, depending on their size. Transfer to a platter, drizzle with the reserved vinaigrette and serve warm or at room temperature.

Seared Venison Chops With Marsala

Servings: 6
Cooking Time: 1 Hour 10 Minutes
Ingredients:
- 1 cup marsala wine
- Venison chops
- 3 Tbsp unsalted butter
- 2 Tbsp olive oil
- 1 cup of beef stock
- 1 tsp fresh sage, finely chopped
- 1 cup of beef stock
- Salt and pepper to taste
- peeled shallot

Directions:
1. Set the wood pellet smoker-grill to direct cooking at 300F
2. Rinse the venison and pat dry with a paper towel. Season with salt and pepper.
3. Grill both sides of venison for 30 minutes, then set aside and increase the temperature of the grill to High.
4. Place a skillet over cooking grates, add oil and sear venison for 4 minutes per side. Set aside.
5. Place a small pot over cooking grates, melt 1 tbsp of butter and sauté the shallot for 5 minutes, or until they are brown.
6. Add the stock, marsala, and sage and allow it to simmer for 15-20 minutes. Add the remaining butter, season with salt and pepper.
7. Serve with the venison.

Rosemary-smoked Lamb Chops

Servings: 4
Cooking Time: 2 Hours, 5 Minutes
Ingredients:
- 4½ pounds bone-in lamb chops
- 2 tablespoons olive oil
- Salt
- Freshly ground black pepper
- 1 bunch fresh rosemary

Directions:
1. Supply your smoker with wood pellets and follow the manufacturer's specific start-up procedure. Preheat the grill with the lid closed, to 180°F.
2. Rub the lamb chops all over with olive oil and season o both sides with salt and pepper.
3. Spread the rosemary directly on the grill grate, creating surface area large enough for all the chops to rest on. Place chops on the rosemary and smoke until they reach an intern temperature of 135°F.
4. Increase the grill's temperature to 450°F, remove the rosemary, and continue to cook the chops until their interna temperature reaches 145°F.
5. Remove the chops from the grill and let them rest for 5 minutes before serving.

Alder-smoked Salt

Servings: 1
Cooking Time: 4 Hours
Ingredients:
- 1 pound coarse sea salt

Directions:
1. Supply your smoker with wood pellets and follow the manufacturer's specific start-up procedure. Preheat the gril with the lid closed, to 120°F.
2. Pour the salt onto a rimmed baking sheet and smoke fo hours, stirring every hour.
3. Remove the salt from the smoker, let it cool, and store i an airtight container.

Lamb Burger Spiced With Curry

Servings: 4
Cooking Time: 20 Minutes
Ingredients:
- 1/2 tsp of turmeric
- 1 tsp of ground coriander
- 1 fresh chili should be seeded and minced, preferably jalapenos chili
- 1 tsp of ground cumin
- 1-1/2 pound of boneless lamb, preferably shoulder.
- Salt and black pepper, shredded carrot
- Red onion with scallion
- Red ball pepper, diced mango

Directions:
1. Set the grill for direct cooking at 300°F. Use maple pelle for a spicy, smoky taste.
2. Pulse the lamb and onions in a food processor and obta a coarse texture.

Add the cumin, jalapenos chili, pepper, coriander, salt, and ʾmeric to a bowl. Mix thoroughly, then add the blended lamb. ʾr gently.

Form 4 patties with the lamb mixture.

Grill lamb patties for 10 minutes, then flip and grill the ʾer side for another 10 minutes

Serve immediately with mango, onion, and shredded ʾrot.

Dinner Rolls

ʾvings: 12
ʾoking Time: 10 Minutes
ʾgredients:

2 tablespoon active dry yeast
1/3 cup vegetable oil
1 1/10 cup warm water (115 degrees F)
1/4 cup sugar
1 egg, beaten
Pinch salt
3 1/2 cups all-purpose flour
Cooking spray

ʾections:

Set the Pit Boss wood pellet grill to 400 degrees F.
Preheat for 15 minutes while the lid is closed.
Use a stand mixer to mix dry yeast, oil, warm water, and ʾar.
Let it rest for 10 minutes.
Stir in the egg, salt, and flour.
Spray cast iron pan with oil.
Knead the dough and shape into 12 balls.
Place the balls on the pan.
Let rest for 10 minutes.
Bake in the wood pellet grill for 10 minutes.

Crusty Artisan Dough Bread

ʾvings: 6
ʾoking Time: 2 Hours
ʾgredients:

3 cups all-purpose flour
1/2 tsp Yeast
1-1/2 cups of warm water
1-1/2 tsp salt

ʾections:

In a large bowl, combine all your ingredients and mix ʾtil it is sticky and has a shaggy texture. Cover with plastic ʾap and allow to rest for 12 hours

After 12 hours, set the wood pellet smoker-grill to ʾirect cooking at 425F, using any pellet. Preheat the Dutch ʾn.

Transfer prepared mixture to a dry, floured surface and ʾld into a ball. Open the Dutch oven and place the dough in ʾ middle—cover and bake for 30 minutes.

Remove the lid and bake for an additional 20 minutes.
Remove and allow to cool.

Pork Rack Roasted With Romesco Sauce In Spanish-style

ʾvings: 6
ʾoking Time: 85 Minutes

Ingredients:
- 2 Tbsp of olive oil
- 4 piquillo pepper, whole
- 2 Tbsp of minced garlic
- 1 Tbsp of salt
- 1 Tbsp of paprika, Spanish
- 1 cup of spanish sherry, dry
- 2 tsp of black pepper, dried
- 1 of 7-bone of pork rib loin roast
- 1/4 cup of olive oil
- 1/4 cup of bread crumb
- 6 cloves of already sliced garlic
- 1 Tbsp of marjoram
- 1/2 cup of almond, roasted
- 2 tsp of garlic, minced
- 1 peeled Roma tomato, halved and seeded

Directions:
1. Preheat the grill for direct cooking at 300°F. Use maple wood pellets.
2. Mix all the ingredients in a small bowl, then brush it over the pork roast. Place the pork roast in the roasting pan and roast for about 15 minutes.
3. Get a baking dish and pour the garlic, pepper, tomato, oil in it. Put the pork inside it and roast for another 30 minutes. Check if it is done to your taste. If not, keep roasting until you are satisfied.
4. Remove roast from cooking grid and allow to rest.
5. Separate the oil in the roasting pan, then add the tomato, roasted pepper, sherry, and already processed almond from the food processor. Mix until it forms a paste. Add season with pepper and salt.
6. Serve the pork with the prepared sauce.

Greek Leg Of Lamb

Servings: 12 To 16
Cooking Time: 20 To 25 Minutes
Ingredients:
- 2 tablespoons finely chopped fresh rosemary
- 1 tablespoon ground thyme
- 5 garlic cloves, minced
- 2 tablespoons sea salt
- 1 tablespoon freshly ground black pepper
- Butcher's string
- 1 whole boneless (6- to 8-pound) leg of lamb
- ¼ cup extra-virgin olive oil
- 1 cup red wine vinegar
- ½ cup canola oil

Directions:
1. In a small bowl, combine the rosemary, thyme, garlic, salt, and pepper; set aside.
2. Using butcher's string, tie the leg of lamb into the shape of a roast. Your butcher should also be happy to truss the leg for you.
3. Rub the lamb generously with the olive oil and season with the spice mixture. Transfer to a plate, cover with plastic wrap, and refrigerate for 4 hours.
4. Remove the lamb from the refrigerator but do not rinse.
5. Supply your smoker with wood pellets and follow the manufacturer's specific start-up procedure. Preheat, with the lid closed, to 325°F.
6. In a small bowl, combine the red wine vinegar and canola oil for basting.

7. Place the lamb directly on the grill, close the lid, and smoke for 20 to 25 minutes per pound (depending on desired doneness), basting with the oil and vinegar mixture every 30 minutes. Lamb is generally served medium-rare to medium, so it will be done when a meat thermometer inserted in the thickest part reads 140°F to 145°F.

8. Let the lamb rest for about 15 minutes before slicing to serve.

Salt-seared Prawn

Servings: 4
Cooking Time: 1 Hour 20 Minutes
Ingredients:
- 2 lb. Prawns, head intact
- 2 lb. Salt rock
- 1 lime, cut into 8 wedges
- Pinch of crushed red pepper flakes
- 12 black peppercorn, smashed
- 4-star anise pod, pieced
- cinnamon stick, broken to pieces

Directions:
1. Preheat the wood pellet smoker-grill for indirect cooking at 300F using any pellet.
2. Mix the cinnamon, peppercorns, pepper flakes, anise, then bake for 40 minutes.
3. Place the salt block on the pellet smoker-grill and heat for 10 minutes, then increase the temperature to 450F (High), and heat for another 10 minutes.
4. Sear the prawn for 4 minutes per side. Serve the prawn with the lime wedges.

Chicken Rub

Servings: 1/4 Cup
Cooking Time:5 Minutes
Ingredients:
- 2 tablespoons packed light brown sugar
- 1½ teaspoons coarse kosher salt
- 1¼ teaspoons garlic powder
- ½ teaspoon onion powder
- ½ teaspoon freshly ground black pepper
- ½ teaspoon ground chipotle chile pepper
- ½ teaspoon smoked paprika
- ¼ teaspoon dried oregano leaves
- ¼ teaspoon mustard powder
- ¼ teaspoon cayenne pepper

Directions:
1. In a small airtight container or zip-top bag, combine the brown sugar, salt, garlic powder, onion powder, black pepper, chipotle pepper, paprika, oregano, mustard, and cayenne.
2. Close the container and shake to mix. Unused rub will keep in an airtight container for months.

Smoked Cheese Dip

Servings: 8
Cooking Time: 1 Hour And 15 Minutes
Ingredients:
- Ice cubes
- 1 block cheddar cheese
- 8 tablespoons butter
- ½ cup carrots, chopped
- 1 onion, chopped
- 1 cup heavy cream
- 3/4 cup flour
- Hot sauce
- 1 teaspoon Worcestershire sauce

Directions:
1. Preheat your Pit Boss wood pellet grill to 180 degrees F for 15 minutes while the lid is closed.
2. Add ice cubes to a pan.
3. Place a cooling rack on top.
4. Put the cheese block on the rack.
5. Put this on top of the grill.
6. Smoke for 30 minutes.
7. Transfer the cheese to your freezer.
8. In a pan over medium heat, add the butter and let it melt.
9. Cook the onion and carrots for 15 minutes.
10. Stir in the rest of the ingredients.
11. Reduce heat and simmer for 15 minutes.
12. Take the cheese out of the freezer and shred.
13. Put the shredded cheese into the mixture.
14. Stir while cooking until cheese has melted.

Pork Carnitas

Servings: 6
Cooking Time: 3 Hours
Ingredients:
- Lime wedges
- 3 jalapeno pepper, minced
- A handful of cilantro, chopped
- 1 cup of chicken broth
- 2 Tbsp olive oil
- Corn tortilla
- 3lb pork shoulder, cut into cubes
- Queso Fresco, crumbled
- 2 Tbsp pork rubs

Directions:
1. Preheat wood pellet smoker-grill to 300⁰F.
2. Mop the rub over the pork shoulder. Place pork shoulder in a cast-iron Dutch oven and pour in chicken broth. Transfer pot to grill grate and cook 2½ hours, until fork tender.
3. Remove the cover, bring to a boil then reduce the liquid pot by half. All this happens within 15 minutes.
4. Place a tablespoon of bacon fat on the skillet and fry the pork for about 10 minutes, until crisp.
5. Take out pork and serve with cilantro, jalapeno, lime, queso fresco, and corn tortillas.

Summer Treat Corn

Servings: 6
Cooking Time: 20 Minutes
Ingredients:
- 6 fresh whole corn on the cob
- ½ C. butter
- Salt, to taste

Directions:
1. Set the temperature of Pit Boss Grill to 400 degrees F and preheat with closed lid for 15 minutes.
2. Husk the corn and remove all the silk.
3. Brush each corn with melted butter and sprinkle with salt

Place the corn onto the grill and cook for about 20
nutes, rotating after every 5 minutes and brushing with
ter once halfway through.

Serve warm.

Corned Beef Hash

vings: 4

)king Time: 4 Hours

redients:

2 lb. corned beef brisket

Pepper to taste

2 cups chicken broth

1 lb. potatoes, peeled

6 slices bacon, chopped

1 red bell pepper, chopped

1 onion, chopped

1 teaspoon thyme, chopped

1-1/2 teaspoon hickory bacon rub

2 tablespoons parsley, chopped

ections:

Season the corned beef with the seasoning packet from its
*kage and with the pepper.

Let it rest for 30 minutes.

Set your wood pellet grill to smoke setting for 10 to 15
iutes.

Set it to 225 degrees F.

Place the corned beef on top of the grills.

Smoke for 3 hours.

Transfer the corned beef to a baking pan.

Add the chicken broth and potatoes to the pan.

Cover the pan with foil.

Cook for 30 minutes.

Let the corned beef and potatoes cool.

Refrigerate for 1 hour.

Slice the potatoes and corned beef.

Add a cast iron pan to the pellet grill.

Preheat it to 400 degrees F.

Cook the bacon until golden and crispy.

Transfer to a plate lined with a paper towel.

Add the red bell pepper and onion to the pan.

Cook for 3 minutes.

Stir in the corned beef.

Add the rest of the ingredients.

Serve while hot.

Beets And Greens With Lemon-dill Vinaigrette

vings:4

)king Time: 1 Hour

redients:

1½ pounds small beets, with fresh-looking greens still
iched if possible

½ cup plus 2 tablespoons good-quality olive oil

Salt and pepper

3 tablespoons fresh lemon juice

2 tablespoons minced fresh dill

ections:

Start the coals or heat a gas grill for medium to medium-
direct cooking. Make sure the grates are clean.

Cut the greens off the beets. Throw away any wilted or
colored leaves; rinse the remainder thoroughly to remove
grit and drain. Trim the root ends of the beets and scrub

well under running water. Pat the leaves and beets dry. Toss
the beets with 2 tablespoons of the oil and a sprinkle of salt
until evenly coated.

3. Put the beets on the grill directly over the fire. (No need to
wash the bowl.) Close the lid and cook, turning them every 5 to
10 minutes, until a knife inserted in the center goes through
with no resistance, 30 to 40 minutes total. Transfer to a plate
and let sit until cool enough to handle.

4. Toss the beet greens in the reserved bowl to coat in oil.
Put the greens on the grill directly over the fire. Close the lid
and cook, tossing once or twice, until they're bright green and
browned in spots, 2 to 5 minutes total. Keep a close eye on
them; if they're on too long, they'll crisp up to the point where
they'll shatter. Transfer to a plate.

5. Put the remaining ½ cup oil and the lemon juice in a
serving bowl and whisk until thickened. Stir in the dill and
some salt and pepper. Peel the skin from the beets and cut into
halves or quarters. Cut the stems from the leaves in 1-inch
lengths; cut the leaves across into ribbons. Put the beets,
leaves, and stems in the bowl and toss with the vinaigrette
until coated. Serve warm or at room temperature. Or makeup
to several hours ahead, cover, and refrigerate to serve chilled.

Sausage Pepper Skewers

Servings: 6 To 8

Cooking Time: 10 Minutes

Ingredients:

- 12 Ounce andouille sausage, cut into 2 inch slices
- 1/2 Whole red onion, sliced
- 1 Whole Green Bell Pepper, Sliced
- 1 Whole Yellow Bell Pepper, sliced
- To Taste olive oil
- To Taste Cajun Shake
- 1/2 Cup Minced Tomatoes
- 1/2 Tablespoon Minced Chipotle in Adobo Sauce
- 1/4 Teaspoon cracked black pepper
- 1 Teaspoon honey
- 1/4 Teaspoon ancho chile powder
- 1/4 Teaspoon garlic powder
- 1/4 Teaspoon onion powder
- 1/4 Teaspoon Kosher Sea Salt

Directions:

1. If using wooden skewers, soak skewers in water for about
30 minutes prior to cooking.

2. Start the Pit Boss on High heat, lid closed, for 10 to 15
minutes.

3. Cut pepper, onion and sausage into chunks. Thread
skewer alternating between meat and vegetables.

4. Drizzle each of the skewers with olive oil and season on
all sides with the Pit Boss Cajun Rub.

5. Put skewers directly on grill grate and cook for about 5
minutes. Flip skewers over and cook for an additional 5
minutes.

6. Spicy Ketchup Dipping: Mix together sauce ingredients
and transfer to a small serving bowl.

7. Pull skewers off grill and serve with spicy dipping sauce.
Enjoy!

All-purpose California Beef Rub

Servings: 1/3 Cup

Cooking Time:5 Minutes

Ingredients:
- 2 tablespoons finely ground coffee
- 1 ½ tablespoons kosher salt
- 1 ½ tablespoons granulated garlic
- 1 heaping teaspoon black pepper
- 1 tablespoon brown sugar
- ¼ teaspoon cayenne pepper
- ¼ teaspoon ground cloves
- ¼ teaspoon cinnamon

Directions:
1. Combine all ingredients in a bowl and mix well with a fork to break up the sugar and combine the spices. Mixture will keep in an airtight container, out of the light, for a few months.

Lemon And Thyme Roasted With Bistro Chicken

Servings: 4
Cooking Time: 25 Hours
Ingredients:
- 1 4pounds chicken
- 3 Tbsp of unsalted butter, melted
- 1 lemon
- 1 Tbsp of thyme, fresh and chopped.
- Salt and ground black pepper, to taste

Directions:
1. Season chicken with salt and pepper as desired. Make sure to rub seasoning all over, including the inner cavities. Refrigerate seasoned chicken, uncovered, for 24 hours.
2. Preheat the grill for direct cooking at 420°F (High). Use mesquite wood pellets for a distinctive, strong woody taste.
3. Put the lemon zest, chopped thyme, and butter in a bowl, then mix. Rub the mixture all over the chicken, and put half lemon in the chicken.
4. Place the chicken in a roasting pan and roast for about 35 minutes. Turn it to the other side and roast for 15 minutes or until internal temperature reads 160°F.
5. Cool for 10 minutes before slicing and serving.

Roasted Almonds

Servings: 6
Cooking Time: 1 Hour And 30 Minutes
Ingredients:
- 1 egg white
- Salt to taste
- 1 tablespoon ground cinnamon
- 1 cup granulated sugar
- 1 lb. almonds

Directions:
1. Beat the egg white in a bowl until frothy.
2. Stir in salt, cinnamon and sugar.
3. Coat the almonds with this mixture.
4. Spread almonds on a baking pan.
5. Set your Pit Boss wood pellet grill to 225 degrees F.
6. Preheat for 15 minutes while the lid is closed.
7. Roast the almonds for 90 minutes, stirring every 10 minutes.
8. Tips: Store in an airtight container with lid for up to 1 week.

Grilled Scallion Salad

Servings: 4-6
Cooking Time: 20 Minutes
Ingredients:
- 1/3 cup of rice vinegar
- 2 tsp of sugar
- 1 Tbsp of sesame oil
- 1 Tbsp of gochugaru
- 1 pound of scallion, untrimmed
- 1 Tbsp of sesame seeds

Directions:
1. Set the grill for indirect cooking at 250°F. Use hickory wood pellets to give scallions a robust taste.
2. Brush sesame oil on scallions, then arrange it on the cooking grid. Grill with for about 8 minutes.
3. Remove scallions from heat and rub with sugar, vinega sesame seeds, and vinegar. Serve immediately.

Twice-baked Spaghetti Squash

Servings: 2
Cooking Time:1 Hour 15 Minutes
Ingredients:
- 1 medium spaghetti squash
- 1/2 cup of parmesan cheese (grated and divided)
- 1/2 cup of mozzarella cheese (shredded and divided)
- 1 tsp Salt
- Tbsp Extra-virgin olive oil
- 1/2 tsp Pepper

Directions:
1. Set the wood pellet smoker-grill to indirect cooking at 375F
2. Using a knife, cut the squash into half lengthwise and remove the seed and pulp. Rub the inside of the squash with olive oil, salt, and pepper. Place on the hot grill with the ope part facing up and bake for 45 minutes or until the squash c be easily pierced with a fork. Remove and allow to cool.
3. Place on a cutting board. Using a fork, scrape across the surface in a lengthwise direction to remove the flesh-in stra (to look like spaghetti). Transfer to a bowl, add parmesan a mozzarella cheese, then stir well. Stuff back into the shell, sprinkle cheese on the toppings.
4. Increase the pellet smoker-grill to 425F, place the stuff squash on the hot grill and bake for 15 minutes or until che starts to brown.
5. Remove and allow to cool, serve.

Amazing Irish Soda Bread

Servings: 10
Cooking Time: 1½ Hours
Ingredients:
- 4 C. flour
- 1 C. raisins
- ½ C. sugar
- 1 tbsp. caraway seeds
- 2 tsp. baking powder
- 1 tsp. baking soda
- ¾ tsp. salt
- 1¼ C. buttermilk
- 1 C. sour cream
- 2 eggs

rections:

Set the temperature of Pit Boss Grill to 350 degrees F and heat with closed lid for 15 minutes.

Grease a 9-inch round cake pan.

Reserve 1 tbsp. of flour in a bowl.

In a large bowl, mix together remaining flour, raisins, gar, caraway seeds, baking powder, baking soda and salt.

In another small bowl, add buttermilk, sour cream and gs and beat until well combined.

Add egg mixture into flour mixture and mix until just istened.

With your hands, knead the dough until sticky.

Place the dough into the prepared pan evenly and cut a ¾-inch deep slit in the top.

Dust the top with reserved flour.

Place the pan onto the grill and cook for about 1½ hours until a toothpick inserted in the center comes out clean.

Remove from grill and place the pan onto a wire rack to ol for about 10 minutes.

Carefully, invert the bread onto the wire rack to cool mpletely before slicing.

Cut the bread into desired-sized slices and sere.

Curried Chicken Roast With Tarragon And Custard

vings: 4

oking Time: 1 Hour 45 Minutes

gredients:

3 Tbsp of olive oil

1 Tbsp of salt, kosher

1 4pounds chicken

1/2 cup of grain mustard, whole

3 Tbsp of tarragon, freshly chopped

1 tsp of black pepper, freshly ground

1 Tbsp of curry powder

rections:

Preheat the grill for direct cooking at 420°F (High). Use kory wood pellets for a robust taste.

Mix the salt, olive oil, mustard, tarragon, pepper, and rry powder in a bowl. Coat the prepared rub all over the cken with a grill brush. Put the chicken inside a Ziploc bag d refrigerate for an hour.

Roast the chicken on the preheated grill for 35 minutes.

th a tong, flip the chicken and roast for another 15 minutes, until the internal temperature of the thigh reads between 8-169F.

Allow cooling for about 10 minutes before slicing and ving.

Bacon-wrapped Chicken Tenders

vings: 6

oking Time: 30 Minutes

gredients:

1/2 tbsp Italian seasoning

1/2 tbsp salt

1/2 tbsp black pepper

1 tbsp paprika

1 tbsp garlic powder

1 tbsp onion powder

1lb chicken tenders

10 strips bacon

- 1/3 cup brown sugar
- 1 tbsp chili powder

Directions:

1. Preheat your Pit Boss to 450F.
2. In a small mixing bowl, mix seasoning, salt, pepper, paprika, garlic powder, and onion powder.
3. Sprinkle the mixture over all sides of the chicken tenders until well coated.
4. Wrap the bacon around the chicken tenders and tuck in the ends.
5. Mix sugar and chili powder in a bowl and sprinkle over the bacon-wrapped chicken.
6. Place the chicken on the grill and cook for 30 minutes or until chicken and bacon are cooked through.
7. Broil the chicken in a broiler for a few minutes to crisp up the bacon if you desire.
8. Serve and enjoy.

Beer-braised Pork Shank

Servings:6

Cooking Time: 23 Minutes

Ingredients:

- 2 Tbsp Flour
- Kosher salt
- Ground black pepper
- 2 Tbsp olive oil
- 2 Tbsp butter
- 1 medium onion, diced
- 2 carrots, trimmed and diced
- 1 Tbsp garlic, minced
- 1 cup dried mushrooms
- 2 cup beef broth
- 2 Tsp chili powder
- 2 thyme sprigs
- 2 Tsp coffee, instant
- 1 Tbsp Worcestershire sauce
- 12 oz dark beer, porter
- 2 dried bay leaves

Directions:

1. Preheat wood pellet smoker-grill to 300°F with the cover of the grill closed for 10 minutes.
2. Hold pork shank together with a butcher string and sprinkle pepper and salt over it.
3. Place a Dutch oven on the cooking grid. Add oil and pork shanks. Cook shank until brown on both sides.
4. Remove shanks from heat and transfer to a plate.
5. Sauté onions, carrots, and garlic in Dutch oven until tender, about 8 minutes.
6. Mix in beef broth, beer, and Worcestershire sauce to the sautéed vegetables. Increase the temperature and bring to boil. Allow simmering at Medium temperature until one-third of the liquid is gone.
7. Add tomato paste, coffee, thyme, chili powder, and bay leaves.
8. Transfer pork shanks from the plate into the Dutch oven and scoop sauce atop it.
9. Cook shanks until tender, about 3 hours.
10. Combine in a bowl, butter, and flour. Add the flour mixture in the last hour to thicken the sauce.
11. Take out bay leaves and thyme springs. Cut out butcher's string. Serve pork shank with gravy atop it and garnish with parsley.

Cinnamon Almond Shortbread

Servings: 5
Cooking Time: 20 Minutes
Ingredients:
- 2tsp cinnamon
- ½ cup unsalted butter (softened)
- 1large egg (beaten)
- ½ tsp salt or to taste
- 2cups almond flour
- ¼ cup sugar
- 1tsp ginger (optional)

Directions:
1. Preheat the grill to 300°F with the lid closed for 5 minutes.
2. Grease a cookie sheet with oil.
3. In a large bowl, combine the cinnamon, almond flour, sugar, ginger, and salt. Mix thoroughly to combine.
4. In another mixing bowl, whisk the egg and softened butter together.
5. Pour the egg mixture into the flour mixture and mix until the mixture forms a smooth batter.
6. Use a tablespoon to measure out equal amounts of the mixture and roll into balls.
7. Arrange the balls into the cookie sheet in a single layer.
8. Now, use the flat bottom of a clean glass cup to press each ball into a flat round cookie. Grease the bottom of the cup before using it to press the balls.
9. Place the cookie sheet on the grill and bake until browned. This will take about 20 to 25 minutes.
10. Remove the cookie sheet from the grill and let the shortbreads cool for a few minutes.
11. Serve and enjoy.

Sweetbread Skewers With Lemon

Servings: 8
Cooking Time: 1 Hour 30 Minutes
Ingredients:
- 1½ pounds veal or lamb sweetbreads
- 1tablespoon salt
- 1tablespoon black peppercorns
- 2lemons, 1 halved and 1 cut into small wedges
- 2tablespoons good-quality olive oil

Directions:
1. Put the sweetbreads in a large bowl and cover with cold water. Soak in the refrigerator for at least 2 hours or overnight, changing the water several times to remove any blood. Drain and rinse.
2. Prepare an ice bath in a large bowl. In a large pot, combine 8 cups water, the salt, and the peppercorns. Squeeze the juice from the lemon halves into the water and add the reamed-out shells as well. Bring to a boil, reduce the heat to a very gentle simmer (bubbles just barely breaking the surface), and add the sweetbreads. Poach just until firm, 6 to 10 minutes. Drain and transfer to the ice water to stop the cooking.
3. When the sweetbreads have cooled, using your fingers, pull away as much of the membrane as you can, along with any fat, gristle, and hard bits. Break the sweetbreads into 1- to 2-inch pieces. (They will largely come apart on their own.) Toss with the oil. (You can prepare them to this point up to a day before cooking; cover and refrigerate.)

4. If you're using bamboo or wooden skewers, soak them water for 30 minutes. Meanwhile, start the coals or heat a ga grill for medium direct cooking. Make sure the grates are cle
5. Alternate 2 or 3 pieces of sweetbreads per skewer, depending on their size, with a wedge of lemon. Put the skewers on the grill directly over the fire. Close the lid and cook, turning several times, until the sweetbreads are crisp the outside and heated through, 8 to 15 minutes total, depending on the size of the pieces. Serve hot or warm for th best flavor.

Hot Sauce With Cilantro

Servings: 4
Cooking Time: 10 Minutes
Ingredients:
- ½ tsp coriander
- ½ tsp cumin seeds
- ¼ tsp black pepper
- 2 green cardamom pods
- 2 garlic cloves
- 1 tsp salt
- 1 oz. parsley
- 2 tablespoons olive oil

Directions:
1. In a blender place all ingredients and blend until smoot
2. Pour sauce in a bowl and serve

Bbq Elk Short Ribs

Servings: 6
Cooking Time: 1 Hour
Ingredients:
- 1/2 pound green beans
- 3 pounds elk short ribs
- 1/2 pound chanterelle mushrooms
- 6 ounces rib rub
- Salt as needed
- Ground black pepper as needed
- 4 tablespoons unsalted butter

Directions:
1. Switch on the Pit Boss grill, fill the grill hopper with cherry flavored wood pellets, power the grill on by using the control panel, select 'smoke' on the temperature dial, or set t temperature to 275 degrees F and let it preheat for a minim of 15 minutes.
2. Meanwhile, prepare the ribs, and for this, season them with salt and rib rub until well coated.
3. When the grill has preheated, open the lid, place ribs or the grill grate rib-side down, shut the grill and smoke for 30 minutes.
4. Then wrap ribs in foil in the double layer, return to the grill grate and continue smoking 15 minutes or until the internal temperature reaches 125 degrees.
5. When done, transfer ribs to a dish and let them rest unt required.
6. Change the smoking temperature to 450 degrees F, shu with lid, and let it preheat for 15 minutes.
7. Then place a skillet pan on the grill grate and when hot, add butter and when it melts, add mushrooms and beans, to until mixed, shut with lid, and cook for 15 minutes until vegetables have turned tender and golden brown.
8. Serve grilled vegetables with elk ribs.

Pit Boss Apple Cake

vings: 12

king Time: 45 Minutes

redients:

Cake

1/2 cup canola oil

1-1/2 cup brown sugar

1 egg

1 cup sour cream

1 tbsp baking soda

1/2 tbsp baking soda

1/2 tbsp baking powder

1-1/2 tbsp vanilla

2-1/2 cups flour

2 apples, finely diced.

Streusel

1 stick butter

1/2 cup brown sugar

1/2 cup flour

1/2 cup oats

1/2 tbsp cinnamon

Glaze

2 cups powdered sugar

1 tbsp apple cinnamon blend

3 tbsp milk

ections:

Preheat your Pit Boss to 325F.

Add the cake ingredients except for the apples in a nder and pulse until well-combined .fold in the diced apples.

Spread the mixture on a 9x13 baking pan.

Mix the streusel ingredients using hands until crumbly n pour the mixture over the cake mixture.

Place the baking pan at the top rack of your Pit Boss to ate a space between the cake pan and the fire.

Bake for 45 minutes or until the tester comes out with st crumbs only.

Let rest for 10 minutes before serving.

Smoked Rib Eye With Bourbon Butter

vings: 4-6

king Time: 1 Hour And 30 Minutes

redients:

4 Ribeye steaks (1 inch thick).

Fresh ground pepper – 1/2 tsp.

Garlic (minced) – 1-2 cloves.

Green Onion (finely minced) – 1 tbsp.

Parsley (finely minced) – 1 tbsp.

Salt– 1/2 tsp.

Bourbon – 2 tbsp.

Butter – 1/2 cup.

Pit Boss prime rub.

ections:

In a mixing bowl, add butter, parsley, chives, bourbon, lic, salt, and pepper. Stir all of the ingredients with a oden spoon. Put the smoker on.

Until the fire is established, keep the lid open. The fire uld be established in about 4-5 minutes.

Season the rib eye steaks with a prime rub. Arrange the aks on the grill and smoke them for about an hour.

4. Then temporarily remove the steaks from the smoker and set your smoker's temperature up to 450F. Place the steaks back on the grill. Give one side about 6-8 minutes and then turn it over.

5. Keep the other side for the same amount of time. Otherwise, if you like your steak medium rare then keep cooking and turning over until the internal temperature is 135 F.

6. Take the steak out of the smoker after they are cooked to your liking and immediately pat them with the bourbon butter sauce you made earlier.

7. Let the meat rest for about 3 minutes before serving it.

Pellet-grill Flatbread Pizza

Servings: 3

Cooking Time: 20 Minutes

Ingredients:

- Dough
- 2 cups flour
- 1 tbsp salt
- 1 tbsp sugar
- 2 tbsp yeast
- 6 oz warm water
- Toppings
- Green/red bell pepper
- 1/2 garlic
- 1 zucchini
- 1/2 onion
- Olive oil
- 5 bacon strips
- 1 cup halved yellow cherry tomatoes
- Sliced jalapenos
- Sliced green olives
- Sliced kalamata olives
- Goat cheese
- For drizzling: Balsamic vinegar

Directions:

1. Combine all dough ingredients in a stand mixer bowl. Mix until the dough is smooth and elastic. Divide into 3 equal balls.

2. Roll each dough ball with a rolling pin into a thin round enough to fit a 12-inch skillet.

3. Grease the skillet using olive oil.

4. Meanwhile, turn your pellet grill on smoke for about 4-5 minutes with the lid open. Turn to high and preheat for about 10-15 minutes with the lid closed.

5. Once ready, arrange peppers, garlic, zucchini, and onion on the grill grate then drizzle with oil and salt. Check at 10 minutes.

6. Now remove zucchini from the grill and add bacon. Continue to cook for another 10 minutes until bacon is done.

7. Transfer the toppings on a chopping board to cool. Chop tomatoes, jalapenos and olive.

8. Brush your crust with oil and smash garlic with a fork over the crust. Smear carefully not to tear the crust.

9. Add toppings to the crust in the skillet.

10. Place the skillet on the grill and cook for about 20 minutes until brown edges.

11. Repeat for the other crusts.

12. Now drizzle each with vinegar and slice.

13. Serve and enjoy.

Korean Bbq Short Ribs

Servings:4
Cooking Time: 5 Hours 40 Minutes
Ingredients:
- 1 cup beef broth
- 1 Tsp ginger, minced
- 1/2 cup of soy sauce
- 1 Tsp toasted sesame seeds
- 6 beef short ribs, membrane removed
- 2 Tbsp brown sugar
- 1 Tbsp beef rub
- 2 garlic cloves, minced
- 1 Tbsp sriracha sauce

Directions:
1. Preheat wood pellet smoker-grill to 250^{0}F.
2. Combine in a medium bowl, brown sugar, garlic, ginger, beef broth, soy sauce, sriracha, sesame, beef, and brisket rub, and then set aside.
3. Place ribs in a baking dish and add the marinade. Cover and leave to marinate in a refrigerator for about 6-12hours.
4. Transfer marinated short rib to the top of the grill grate. Grill for 4 hours; rub leftover marinade juice on the rib occasionally.
5. Remove rib from the grill and leave to rest on a platter for 15minutes. Serve.

Special Mac And Cheese

Servings: 8
Cooking Time: 1 Hour
Ingredients:
- 4 strips bacon, cooked crispy and chopped
- 2 cups breadcrumbs
- 2 tablespoons fresh parsley, minced
- Salt and pepper to taste
- 2 tablespoons olive oil
- 1 white onion, chopped
- 3 cloves garlic, crushed and minced
- 1/2 cup melted butter
- 5 tablespoons all-purpose flour
- 12 oz. cheddar cheese, shredded
- 4 oz. brie cheese
- 4 oz. mozzarella cheese, shredded
- 12 oz. raclette
- 8 oz. gruyere cheese, grated
- 1 cup heavy cream
- 4 oz. milk
- 8 cups cooked macaroni pasta
- 1 teaspoon freshly grated nutmeg

Directions:
1. In a bowl, mix the bacon bits, breadcrumbs, parsley, salt, and pepper. Set aside.
2. Preheat your wood pellet grill to 350 degrees F with the lid closed.
3. Pour the olive oil into a pan over medium heat.
4. Cook the onion and garlic for 2 minutes.
5. Add the jalapeño and cook for 1 more minute.
6. Stir in the butter and flour.
7. Cook while stirring for 5 minutes.
8. Add all the cheeses along with the cream and milk.
9. Reduce heat to low and cook while stirring for 7 minutes.
10. Add the pasta and stir to coat evenly with the sauce.
11. Season with the salt and pepper.

12. Pour the mixture to a cast-iron pan.
13. Cover with foil.
14. Place on top of the wood pellet grill.
15. Bake for 20 minutes.
16. Sprinkle the breadcrumb mixture on top.
17. Bake for another 20 minutes.

Wood Pellet Smoked Nut Mix

Servings: 8-12
Cooking Time: 20 Minutes
Ingredients:
- 3cups mixed nuts (pecans, peanuts, almonds, etc.)
- 1/2 tbsp brown sugar
- 1tbsp thyme, dried
- 1/4 tbsp mustard powder
- 1tbsp olive oil, extra-virgin

Directions:
1. Preheat your pellet grill to 250F with the lid closed for about 15 minutes.
2. Combine all ingredients in a bowl, large, then transfer i a cookie sheet lined with parchment paper.
3. Place the cookie sheet on a grill and grill for about 20 minutes.
4. Remove the nuts from the grill and let cool.
5. Serve and enjoy.

Grilled Homemade Croutons

Servings: 6
Cooking Time: 30 Minutes
Ingredients:
- 2 tbsp Mediterranean Blend Seasoning
- 1/4 cup olive oil
- 6 cups cubed bread

Directions:
1. Preheat your wood pellet grill to 250F.
2. Combine seasoning and oil in a bowl then drizzle the mixture over the bread cubes. Toss to evenly coat.
3. Layer the bread cubes on a cookie sheet, large, and plac on the grill.
4. Bake for about 30 minutes. Stir at intervals of 5 minute for browning evenly.
5. Once dried out and golden brown, remove from the gri
6. Serve and enjoy!

Carne Asada Marinade

Servings: 5
Cooking Time: 2hours
Ingredients:
- cloves garlic, chopped
- tsp Lemon juice
- 1/2 cup extra virgin olive oil
- 1/2 tsp Salt
- 1/2 tsp Pepper

Directions:
1. Mix all your ingredients in a bowl.
2. Pour the beef into the bowl and allow to marinate for 2 3hours before grilling.

Butter-braised Springs Onions With Lots Of Chives

rvings:3
oking Time: 25minutes
gredients:
- 1lb spring onions, trimmed
- Kosher salt
- 1/4 tsp chives, chopped
- 4 Tbsp unsalted butter

ections:

In a large skillet, add onions, 1/2 cup water, two
lespoons butter and sprinkle in the salt. Cover skillet and
ng to a boil. Reduce heat and simmer onion until almost
der, about 15 minutes. Remove cover, stir continuously and
ve onions to cook for another 5 minutes, until fork-tender.

Take out onions and place them on a plate. Heat the liquid
skillet until it reduces to about two teaspoons, then add the
maining butter. Transfer onions to the skillet and stir it in
h the sauce. Garnish with chives.

Cinnamon Sugar Donut Holes

rvings: 4
oking Time: 35 Minutes
gredients:
- 1/2 cup flour
- 1tbsp cornstarch
- 1/2 tsp baking powder
- 1/8 tsp baking soda
- 1/8 tsp ground cinnamon
- 1/2 tsp kosher salt
- 1/4 cup buttermilk
- 1/4 cup sugar
- 11/2 tbsp butter, melted
- 1egg
- 1/2 tsp vanilla
- Topping
- 2tbsp sugar
- 1tbsp sugar
- 1tsp ground cinnamon

ections:

Preheat pellet grill to 350°F.

In a medium bowl, combine flour, cornstarch, baking
wder, baking soda, ground cinnamon, and kosher salt.
nisk to combine.

In a separate bowl, combine buttermilk, sugar, melted
tter, egg, and vanilla. Whisk until the egg is thoroughly
nbined.

Pour wet mixture into the flour mixture and stir. Stir just
til combined, careful not to overwork the mixture.

Spray mini muffin tin with cooking spray.

Spoon 1 tbsp of donut mixture into each mini muffin hole.

Place the tin on the pellet grill grate and bake for about 18
nutes, or until a toothpick can come out clean.

Remove muffin tin from the grill and let rest for about 5
nutes.

In a small bowl, combine 1 tbsp sugar and 1 tsp ground
namon.

Melt 2 tbsp of butter in a glass dish. Dip each donut hole
the melted butter, then mix and toss with cinnamon sugar.
ce completed donut holes on a plate to serve.

Pan-seared Pork Tenderloin With Apple Mashed Potatoes

Servings: 6
Cooking Time: 20 Minutes
Ingredients:
- 2 pork tenderloin
- medium potatoes (peeled and sliced)
- 3 Tbsp unsalted butter
- 1/2 cup of heavy cream
- 2 Tbsp Olive oil
- 1-1/2 Tbsp Pepper
- 1-1/2 Tbsp Salt.
- 2 apple (cored and sliced)

Directions:
1. Preheat the wood pellet smoker-grill for direct cooking at 300F using any pellet.
2. Season the pork with salt and pepper, then roast meat for 20 minutes.
3. Increase the temperature of the grill to High, then place an iron skillet on the grates, and add 1 Tbsp butter and oil. Cook until the butter becomes brown, make sure it does not burn.
4. Place the tenderloin and cook for 4 minutes per side or until it is brown, transfer to a baking sheet and bake for 10 minutes.
5. Rearrange the grill for indirect cooking at 300F
6. Place a pot over the cooking grid and fill it with water. Add potatoes and allow to boil, reduce the heat and simmer for 8 minutes or until soft. Drain the water
7. Pour the potatoes into a food processor, add cream and butter. Puree the mixture, add the apples and puree until they are finely chopped. Season with salt and pepper and serve with the pork.

Braised Pork Carnitas

Servings: 6
Cooking Time: 3 Hours
Ingredients:
- 3 lb. pork shoulder, sliced into cubes
- 2 tablespoons pulled pork dry rub
- 1 cup chicken broth
- 2 tablespoons olive oil
- Corn tortillas
- 3 jalapeno pepper, minced
- Cilantro, chopped
- Fresh cheese, crumbled
- Red onion, sliced

Directions:
1. Turn on your wood pellet grill.
2. Set it to 300 degrees F.
3. Sprinkle the pork cubes with the dry rub.
4. Place in a Dutch oven.
5. Pour in the chicken broth.
6. Add the Dutch oven on top of the grill.
7. Open the sear slide.
8. Bring to a boil.
9. Cover the Dutch oven and seal the sear slide.
10. Simmer for 2 hours and 30 minutes.
11. Uncover and open the sear slide.
12. Bring to a boil.
13. Take the Dutch oven off the grill. Set aside.
14. Pour the olive oil into a pan over medium heat.

15. Fry the pork for 10 minutes.
16. Top the corn tortillas with the pork cubes and the rest of the ingredients.

Twice-Baked Potatoes With Smoked Gouda And Grilled Scallions

Servings: 6
Cooking Time: 1hours 15 Minutes
Ingredients:
- 3 large potatoes
- 8 TbspUnsalted butter
- Tbsp Of barbeque rub
- 1-1/2 cup of smoked gouda cheese (grated)
- 1/4 cup of extra-virgin olive oil
- 3/4 cup heavy cream
- Salt and pepper to taste
- 1/4 cup chopped scallions

Directions:
1. Set the wood pellet smoker-grill to indirect cooking at 400F
2. Brush the potatoes with olive oil, make incisions with fork and season with salt. Wrap with aluminum foil paper and bake on grill grates for 30 minutes per side. Transfer to a rimmed sheet and allow to cool.
3. Cut the potatoes lengthwise, scoop out the flesh into a bowl. Add butter and 1 cup of cheese. Set aside. Place a small pot over low-medium heat, add cream, then heat for 1 minute. Add the scallions and the barbeque rub and mix well
4. Add the scallion mixture to the potatoes and cheese in the bowl, combine until it is evenly mixed. Scoop the mixture back into the potato shell and top with cheese.
5. Bake for 5 minutes or until the cheese melts.

Roasted Pork With Strawberry

Servings: 4
Cooking Time: 1 Hour
Ingredients:
- 2 lb. pork tenderloin
- 2 tablespoons dried rosemary
- Salt and pepper to taste
- 2 tablespoons olive oil
- 12 strawberries
- 1 cup balsamic vinegar
- 4 tablespoons sugar

Directions:
1. Preheat your Pit Boss wood pellet grill to 350 degrees F for 15 minutes while the lid is closed.
2. Season the pork tenderloin with rosemary, salt, and pepper.
3. In a pan over high heat, sear the tenderloin for 2 minutes per side.
4. Place the pan in the grill and cook for 20 minutes.
5. Transfer to a cutting board.
6. In another pan, simmer the strawberries in sugar and vinegar for 30 minutes.
7. Slice the pork and pour it with the sauce before serving.

Smoked Bologna

Servings: 4-6

Cooking Time: 4 Hours And 5 Minutes
Ingredients:
- 1 tsp. low sodium Soy sauce
- 1 tbsp. Mustard, yellow
- 1/4 cup of Brown sugar
- 1/8 tsp. Worcestershire
- 1-pound Bologna

Directions:
1. Score the log but don't go too deep.
2. In a bowl combine the Worcestershire, soy sauce, mustard and brown sugar. Stir. Rub the mixture on the bologna.
3. Preheat the grill to 225F with closed lid.
4. Smoke the bologna 3 - 4 hours. Transfer onto a plate to cool down. Once cooled, slice.
5. Assemble a sandwich with your favorite toppings and enjoy!

Bruschetta

Servings: 4
Cooking Time: 25 Minutes
Ingredients:
- 8 1-inch slices baguette or Italian bread
- 1/4 cup good-quality olive oil
- 1or 2 cloves garlic, peeled

Directions:
1. Start the coals or heat a gas grill for medium-high direct cooking. Make sure the grates are clean.
2. Lightly brush both sides of the bread slices with the oil. Put them on the grill directly over the fire. Close the lid and toast, turning once, until the bread develops grill marks, 1 to minutes per side. Transfer the slices to a platter. When the bread has cooled just enough that you can handle it, rub one both sides of the bread with the garlic, and serve.

Classic Apple Pie

Servings: 8
Cooking Time: 2 Hours
Ingredients:
- 2 Tbsp all-purpose flour
- 2 pie dough rounds
- 6 cups of apple, peeled and sliced
- 1 Tbsp lemon juice
- 3/4 cup of sugar
- 1/4 tsp powdered nutmeg
- 1/2 tsp powdered cinnamon
- 1/2 tsp salt

Directions:
1. Set the wood pellet smoker-grill to indirect cooking at 425F
2. In a large bowl, combine all your ingredients (except for the pie dough) and mix well. Gently press one of the pie dough unto a 10-inch pie dough plate. Make sure it is firm and cover the sides.
3. Pour in your apple mixture. Cover the filling with the second pie dough, gently clip the two doughs together. Make crosshatch slit on the top with a knife—transfer dough plate the cooking grid.
4. Bake for 45-60 minutes or until the crust browns. Allow to cool for 1 hour before serving.

Smoked Pork Tenderloin With Mexican Pineapple Sauce

Servings: 6
Cooking Time: 3 Hours And 55 Minutes
Ingredients:

Pineapple Sauce
1 can (11 oz) unsweetened crushed pineapple
1 can (11 oz) roasted tomato or tomatillo
1/2 cup port wine
1/4 cup orange juice
1/4 cup packed brown sugar
1/4 cup lime juice
2 tbsp Worcestershire sauce
1 tsp garlic powder
1/4 tsp cayenne pepper
PORK
2 pork tenderloin (1 pound each)
1 tsp ground cumin
1/2 tsp pepper
1/4 tsp cayenne pepper
2 tbsp lime juice (freshly squeezed)

Directions:

Combine cumin, pepper, cayenne pepper and lime juice and rub over tenderloins.
Smoke grill for 4-5 minutes. Preheat, lid closed for 10-15 minutes
Smoke tenderloin for 2 ½ to 3 hours.
Rest for 5 minutes
For Sauce:
Combine ingredients and boil for 25 minutes
Remove from heat and cool.
Serve pork slices with pineapple sauce and lime wedges.

Smoked Garlic White Sauce

Servings: 2
Cooking Time: 1 Hour
Ingredients:

2 cups hickory wood chips, soaked in water for 30 minutes
3 whole garlic heads
1/2 cup mayonnaise
1/3 cup sour cream
1 juiced lemon
2 tbsp apple cider vinegar
Salt to taste

Directions:

Cut garlic heads to expose the inside and place in a container, microwave-safe, with 2 tbsp water. Microwave for about 5-6 minutes on medium.
Preheat your grill. Place garlic heads on a shallow foil "at" and place it on the grill.
Close the grill and cook for about 20-25 minutes until soft completely. Remove and cool.
Transfer into a blender then add the remaining ingredients. Process until smooth.
Serve immediately or store in a refrigerator for up to 5 s.

Smoked Spicy Pork Medallions

Servings: 6

Cooking Time: 1 Hour And 45 Minutes
Ingredients:
- 2 pounds pork medallions
- 3/4 cup chicken stock
- 1/2 cup tomato sauce (organic)
- 2 Tbs of smoked hot paprika (or to taste)
- 2 Tbsp of fresh basil finely chopped
- 1 Tbsp oregano
- Salt and pepper to taste

Directions:
1. Combine the chicken stock, tomato sauce, paprika, oregano, salt, and pepper.
2. Brush on tenderloin. Smoke grill for 4-5 minutes
3. Temperature must rise to 250 degrees Fahrenheit until 15 to 15 minutes at most
4. Place the pork on the grill grate and smoke until the internal temperature of the pork is at least medium-rare (about 145°F), for 1 1/2 hours.

Turkey Sandwich

Servings: 4
Cooking Time: 20 Minutes
Ingredients:
- 8 bread slices
- 1 cup gravy
- 2 cups turkey, cooked and shredded

Directions:
1. Set your wood pellet grill to smoke.
2. Preheat it to 400 degrees F.
3. Place a grill mat on top of the grates.
4. Add the turkey on top of the mat.
5. Cook for 10 minutes.
6. Toast the bread in the flame broiler.
7. Top the bread with the gravy and shredded turkey.

Beef Pot Roast

Servings: 6
Cooking Time: 3 Hours 10 Minutes
Ingredients:
- 3 cup beef stock
- 1 cup carrots, chopped
- 1 Tbsp garlic, minced
- 1/4 cup softened butter
- 1 Tsp ground black pepper
- 2 red onions, chopped
- 4lb chuck roast
- 1 Tbsp kosher salt
- 1Tbsp sage, chopped
- 1/2 cup red wine

Directions:
1. Preheat Pit Boss Grill & Smoker to 300°F with the cover of the grill closed for 10 minutes.
2. In a stockpot, put in red wine, beef stock, butter, garlic, carrot, red onion, sage, and chuck roast—season with pepper and salt. Stir the contents and cover the pot.
3. Transfer stockpot to the preheated grill; close the grill lid and leave to cook for 3 hours, until the roast reaches an internal temperature of 203°F.
4. Serve.

Smoked Mushroom Sauce

Servings: 4
Cooking Time: 1 Hour
Ingredients:

- 1-quart chef mix mushrooms
- 2 tbsp canola oil
- 1/4 cup julienned shallots
- 2 tbsp chopped garlic
- Salt and pepper to taste
- 1/4 cup alfasi cabernet sauvignon
- 1 cup beef stock
- 2 tbsp margarine

Directions:

1. Crumple four foil sheets into balls. Puncture multiple places in the foil pan then place mushrooms in the foil pan. Smoke in a pellet grill for about 30 minutes. Remove and cool.
2. Heat canola oil in a pan, sauté, add shallots and sauté until translucent.
3. Add mushrooms and cook until supple and rendered down.
4. Add garlic and season with pepper and salt. Cook until fragrant.
5. Add beef stock and wine then cook for about 6-8 minutes over low heat. Adjust seasoning.
6. Add margarine and stir until sauce is thickened and a nice sheen.
7. Serve and enjoy!

Smoked Porterhouse Steak

Servings: 2-4
Cooking Time: 1 Hour
Ingredients:

- 2 porterhouse steaks (1 inch thick) (20 oz. or 1.25 lb.).
- Melted butter – 4 tbsp.
- Worcestershire Sauce – 2 tsp.
- Dijon Mustard – 1 tbsp.
- Coffee rub – 1 tsp.

Directions:

1. Start your wood pellet smoker on grill instructions when you are ready to cook.
2. Set the temperature to smoke setting. Preheat for 5 minutes while keeping the lid closed.
3. Mix the butter, Worcestershire sauce, and mustard until it is smooth. Brush the mixture on both sides of the steaks. Season the porterhouse steaks with coffee rub.
4. Arrange the steaks on the grill grate and smoke them for about 30 minutes. Remove the steaks using tongs.
5. Increase the heat to 450° F. Brush the steaks again with the butter sauce mixture that was prepared earlier.
6. When the grill comes up to the temperature, place the steaks back on the grill grate and cook until it is done according to your choice. Whichever doneness you prefer i.e. rare, medium rare or well done.
7. In case of medium rare, cook until the internal temperature is about 135° F. Before serving, let the steaks rest for 5 minutes.

Mango Bread

Servings: 4
Cooking Time: 1 Hour
Ingredients:

- 2½ cup cubed ripe mangoes
- 2 cups all-purpose flour
- 1 tsp baking powder
- 1 tsp baking soda
- 2 eggs (beaten)
- 1 tsp cinnamon
- 1 tsp vanilla extract
- ½ tsp nutmeg
- ¾ cup olive oil
- ¾ cup of sugar
- 1 tbsp lemon juice
- ½ tsp salt
- ½ cup chopped dates

Directions:

1. Start your grill on smoke mode and leave the lip opened for 5 minutes, or until the fire starts.
2. Close the lid and preheat the grill to 350°F for 15 minutes using alder hardwood pellets.
3. Grease an 8 by 4-inch loaf pan.
4. In a mixing bowl, combine the flour, baking powder, baking soda, cinnamon, salt, and sugar.
5. In another mixing bowl, whisk together the egg, lemon juice, oil, and vanilla.
6. Pour the egg mixture into the flour mixture and mix until you well combined.
7. Fold in the mangoes and dates.
8. Pour the mixture into the loaf pan and place the pan in grill.
9. Place the loaf pan directly on the grill bake for about 50-60 minutes or until a toothpick inserted in the middle of the bread comes out clean.
10. After the baking cycle, remove the loaf pan from the grill and transfer the bread to a wire rack to cool completely.
11. Slice and serve.

Baked Wild Sockeye Salmon

Servings: 6
Cooking Time: 45 Minutes
Ingredients:

- 6 sockeye salmon fillets
- 3/4 tsp Old bay seasoning
- 1/2 tsp Seafood seasoning.

Directions:

1. Set the wood pellet smoker-grill to indirect cooking at 400F
2. Rinse the fillet and pat dry with a paper towel. Add the seasoning, then rub all over the fillets.
3. Arrange fillets in a baking dish with the skin facing down then transfer the dish to the cooking grid. Cover grill and bake for 15-20 minutes or until fillets begin to flake.
4. Serve.

Thai Dipping Sauce

Servings: 4
Cooking Time: 10 Minutes
Ingredients:

- 6 tsp garlic sauce
- 2 tablespoons fish sauce
- 2 tablespoons lime juice
- 1 tablespoon brown sugar
- 1 tsp chili flakes

rections:
In a blender place all ingredients and blend until smooth
Pour sauce in a bowl and serve

Grilled Flank Steak

rvings: 6
oking Time: 2 Hours 15 Minutes
gredients:
1/2 cup of soy sauce
1-1/2 pound of flank steak.
1/2 cup of bourbon
1/2 cup of water
rections:
Set the grill for direct cooking at 300°F. Use hickory wood
llets for a strong taste and aroma.
Pour the soy sauce, 1/2 cup of water, and bourbon in a
wl. Whisk together to make a marinade. Pour the marinade
side a food storage bag and add the steak to the bag. Keep in
e refrigerator for 2 hours to allow flavors to combine and
netrate steak.
Remove from the refrigerator and dry with a paper towel.
Grill the steak for about 30 minutes, flipping every five
nutes to ensure both sides are equally cooked.
Cover the steak with foil paper and allow it to rest for
out 5 minutes.
Serve.

Chile Cheeseburgers

rvings: 4
oking Time: 30 Minutes
gredients:
1 lb ground chuck (80% lean, 20% fat)
4 Monterey Jack cheese slices
1/4 cup yellow onion, finely chopped
4 hamburger buns
2 tbsp hatch chiles, peeled and chopped
6 tbsp hatch chile salsa
1 tsp kosher salt
Mayonnaise, to taste
1 tsp ground black pepper
rections:
In a bowl, combine beef, diced onion, chopped hatch
les, salt, and fresh ground pepper. Once evenly mixed,
ape into 4 burger patties
Preheat pellet grill to 350°FPlace burgers on grill, and
ok for about 6 minutes per side or until both sides of each
rger are slightly crispy
After burger is cooked to desired doneness and both sides
ve light sear, place cheese slices on each burger. Allow to
at for around 45 seconds or until cheese melts
Remove from grill and allow to rest for about 10
nutesSpread a little bit of mayonnaise on both sides of each
n. Place burger patty on bottom side of the bun, then top
ch hatch chile salsa on top to taste

Pizza Dough Roll

rvings: 6
oking Time: 1hour 15 Minutes
gredients:
1 tsp Yeast

- 1 cup of warm water
- 2-1/2 cups of all-purpose flour
- 1 tsp Kosher salt
- Tbsp Virgin olive oil
- 1 tsp Sugar

Directions:
1. Set the wood pellet smoker-grill to indirect cooking at
400F
2. Combine all your ingredients and mix until the mixture is
sticky and has a shaggy texture. Knead the dough for 3-5
minutes, then set aside and cover. Keep for 1 hour at room
temperature or until it doubles in size.
3. Divide the dough into six equal parts and roll into a ball
using a floured hand. Cover the baking pan with a parchment
paper, place the roll on it, then cover and allow to rise for 30
minutes. Transfer the baking pan to the cooking grid, then
cover.
4. Bake for 15-20min or until the rolls are golden brown.
Allow to cool before serving.

Crispy Fish Sticks

Servings: 6
Cooking Time: 5 Minutes
Ingredients:
- Olive oil
- 1 ½ lb. halibut, sliced into strips
- 1/2 cup all-purpose flour
- Salt and pepper to taste
- 2 eggs, beaten
- 1 1/2 cup panko breadcrumbs
- 2 tablespoon dried parsley
- 1 teaspoon dried dill weed

Directions:
1. Preheat the Pit Boss wood pellet grill to high for 15
minutes while the lid is closed.
2. Pour olive oil to a pan.
3. Add pan on top of the grill.
4. Add flour, salt and pepper to a bowl. Mix well.
5. Add the eggs to another bowl.
6. In another bowl, mix the breadcrumbs and herbs.
7. Dip the fish strips in the flour mixture, eggs and
breadcrumb mixture.
8. Place in oil and fry for 5 minutes or until golden.
9. Tips: Beat the egg white first until frothy before stirring in
egg yolk. This makes it easier for breadcrumbs to stick to the
fish.

Smoked Pork Chops Marinated With Tarragon

Servings: 4
Cooking Time: 4-6 Hours
Ingredients:
- 1/2 cup olive oil
- 4 Tbsp of fresh tarragon chopped
- 2 tsp fresh thyme, chopped
- salt and grated black pepper
- 2 tsp apple-cider vinegar
- 4 pork chops or fillets

Directions:
1. Whisk the olive oil, tarragon, thyme, salt, pepper, apple
cider and stir well. Place the pork chops in a container and
pour with tarragon mixture.

2. Refrigerate for 2 hours. Start pellet grill on, lid open, until the fire is established (4-5 minutes).
3. The temperature must rise to 250 degrees Fahrenheit with the lid closed until 15 minutes
4. The temperature must rise up to 250 degrees Fahrenheit and must be preheated for at most 15 minutes. Remove chops from marinade and pat dry on kitchen towel. Arrange pork chops on the grill rack and smoke for about 3 to 4 hours. Transfer chops on a serving platter and let rest 15 minutes before serving.

Cajun Rub

Servings: 3
Cooking Time:5 Minutes
Ingredients:
- 1 teaspoon freshly ground black pepper
- 1 teaspoon onion powder
- 1 teaspoon coarse kosher salt
- 1 teaspoon garlic powder
- 1 teaspoon sweet paprika
- ½ teaspoon cayenne pepper
- ½ teaspoon red pepper flakes
- ½ teaspoon dried oregano leaves
- ½ teaspoon dried thyme
- ½ teaspoon smoked paprika

Directions:
1. In a small airtight container or zip-top bag, combine the black pepper, onion powder, salt, garlic powder, sweet paprika, cayenne, red pepper flakes, oregano, thyme, and smoked paprika.
2. Close the container and shake to mix. Unused rub will keep in an airtight container for months.

Keto Quiche

Servings: 6
Cooking Time: 45 Minutes
Ingredients:
- 12 tbsp unsalted butter (soften)
- 12 large eggs
- 8 ounces grated cheddar cheese (divided)
- 4 ounces cream cheese
- ½ tsp salt or to taste
- ½ tsp ground black pepper or to taste
- 1 yellow onion (diced)
- 1 green bell pepper (chopped)
- 3 cups broccoli florets (chopped)
- 1 tbsp olive oil

Directions:
1. Preheat the grill to 325°F with the lid closed for 15 minutes.
2. Heat up the olive oil in a skillet over high heat.
3. Add the chopped onion, broccoli, and green pepper. Cook for about 8 minutes, stirring constantly.
4. Remove the skillet from heat.
5. Process the egg and cheese in a food processor, adding the melted butter in a bit while processing.
6. Combine 4ounce grated cheddar cheese, salt, and pepper in a quiche pan.
7. Toss the cooked vegetable into the pan and mix.
8. Pour the egg mixture over the ingredients in the quiche pan.

9. Sprinkle the remaining grated cheese over it.
10. Place the pan in the preheated grill and bake for 45 minutes.
11. Remove and transfer the quiche to a rack to cool.
12. Slice and serve.

Bison Burgers

Servings: 6
Cooking Time: 17 To 19 Minutes
Ingredients:
- 2 pounds ground bison
- 2 tablespoons steak seasoning
- 4 tablespoons (½ stick) unsalted butter, cut into pieces
- 1 large onion, finely minced
- 6 slices Swiss cheese
- 6 ciabatta buns, split
- Sweet and Spicy Jalapeño Relish, for serving
- Lettuce and sliced tomatoes, for serving

Directions:
1. Supply your smoker with wood pellets and follow the manufacturer's specific start-up procedure. Preheat, with th lid closed, to 425°F.
2. In a large bowl, combine the ground bison and steak seasoning until well blended.
3. Shape the meat mixture into 6 patties and make a thum indentation in the center of each. Set aside.
4. Place a rimmed baking sheet on the grill and add the butter and onion. Sauté for 5 minutes, or until the onion is translucent. Top with the bison burger patties, indention-sic down.
5. Close the lid and smoke for 6 to 7 minutes, then flip the burgers and smother them in the sautéed onion. Close the li again and continue smoking for 6 to 7 minutes. During the la few minutes of cooking, top each burger with a slice of Swiss cheese. For safe consumption, the internal temperature sho reach between 140°F (medium) and 160°F (well-done).
6. Lightly toast the ciabatta buns, split-side down, on one side of the smoker.
7. Serve the onion-smothered cheeseburgers on the toaste buns with jalapeño relish, lettuce, and tomato—or whatever toppings you like.

Simplest Grilled Asparagus

Servings: 4
Cooking Time: 25 Minutes
Ingredients:
- 1½–2 pounds asparagus
- 1–2 tablespoons good-quality olive oil or melted butter
- Salt

Directions:
1. Start the coals or heat a gas grill for direct hot cooking. Make sure the grates are clean.
2. Cut the tough bottoms from the asparagus. If they're thi trim the ends with a vegetable peeler. Toss with the oil and sprinkle with salt.
3. Put the asparagus on the grill directly over the fire, perpendicular to the grates, so they don't fall through. Close the lid and cook, turning once, until the thick part of the stal can barely be pierced with a skewer or thin knife, 5 to 10 minutes total. Transfer to a platter and serve.

Smoked Chuck Roast

Servings: 6
Cooking Time: 5 Hours
Ingredients:
- 3 lb. chuck roast
- 3 tablespoons sweet and spicy rub
- 3 cups beef stock, divided
- 1 yellow onion, sliced

Directions:
- Add the chuck roast to a baking pan.
- Coat with the sweet, spicy rub.
- Cover with foil. Refrigerate and marinate overnight.
- Set the wood pellet grill to smoke.
- Preheat it to 225 degrees F.
- Add the chuck roast to the grill.
- Close the lid.
- Smoke the chuck roast for 3 hours.
- Brush with 1 cup beef stock every 1 hour.
- Add the onion slices to a baking pan.
- Pour the remaining beef stock.
- Transfer the chuck roast on top of the onions.
- Increase the heat to 250 degrees F.
- Smoke for 3 hours.
- Cover the chuck roast with the foil.
- Smoke for another 2 hours and 30 minutes.
- Let the chuck roast rest for 10 minutes.
- Serving Suggestion: Serve with mashed potatoes.

Smoked Cranberry Sauce

Servings: 2
Cooking Time: 1 Hour
Ingredients:
- 12 oz bag cranberries
- 2 chunks ginger, quartered
- 1 cup apple cider
- 1 tbsp honey whiskey
- 5.5 oz fruit juice
- 1/8 tbsp ground cloves
- 1/8 tbsp cinnamon
- 1/2 orange zest
- 1/2 orange
- 1 tbsp maple syrup
- 1 apple, diced and peeled
- 1/2 cup sugar
- 1/2 brown sugar

Directions:
- Preheat your pellet grill to 375F.
- Place cranberries in a pan then add all other ingredients.
- Place the pan on the grill and cook for about 1 hour until cooked through.
- Remove ginger pieces and squeeze juices from the orange to the sauce.
- Serve and enjoy!

Green Smoothie

Servings: 3 To 4
Cooking Time: 5 Minutes
Ingredients:
- 1/4 cup Baby Spinach
- 1/2 cup Ice

- 1/4 cup Kale
- 1/2 cup Pineapple Chunks
- 1/2 cup Coconut Water
- 1/2 cup mango, diced
- 1/2 banana, diced

Directions:
1. Begin by placing all the ingredients needed to make the smoothie in the blender pitcher.
2. Now, press the 'extract' button.
3. Transfer the smoothie into the serving glass.

White Bbq Sauce

Servings: 3 Cups
Cooking Time: 10 Minutes
Ingredients:
- 1 ½ cups mayonnaise
- ⅓ cup plus 2 tablespoons apple-cider vinegar
- 2 tablespoons lemon juice
- 2 tablespoons prepared horseradish
- 1 teaspoon mustard powder
- Kosher salt and freshly ground black pepper, to taste
- cayenne pepper, to taste

Directions:
1. Combine the mayonnaise, vinegar, lemon juice, horseradish and mustard powder in a medium nonreactive bowl, and whisk until smooth.
2. Add salt, pepper and cayenne to taste. Brush on grilled or roasted chicken during the end of the cooking process, and pass remaining sauce at the table.

Grilled Plantains

Servings: 2
Cooking Time: 6 Minutes
Ingredients:
- 2Plantains, cut and sliced horizontally
- 1tablespoon coconut oil, melted

Directions:
1. Put the grill grate inside the grill and set the timer to 8 minutes at high for preheating.
2. Once, the grill is preheated, open the unit.
3. Brush the plantains with coconut oil and add to the hot grill.
4. Close the unit and cook for 3 minutes at medium.
5. Flip to cook from the other side and cook for an additional 3 minutes.
6. Once done, serve.

Garlic Aioli And Smoked Salmon Sliders

Servings: 12
Cooking Time: 1 Hour And 30 Minutes
Ingredients:
- For Brine:
- Water as needed
- ½ a cup of salt
- 1 tablespoon of dried tarragon
- 1 and a ½ pound of salmon fillets
- For Aioli:
- 1 cup of mayonnaise
- 3 tablespoon of fresh lemon juice

- 3 minced garlic cloves
- 1 and a ½ teaspoon of ground black pepper
- ½ a teaspoon of lemon zest
- Salt as needed
- ½ a cup of apple wood chips
- 12 slide burger buns

Directions:

1. Take a large sized baking dish and add ½ a cup of salt alongside about half water
2. Add tarragon, salmon in the brine mix and keep adding more water
3. Cover up the dish and freeze for 2-12 hours. Take a small bowl and add lemon juice, mayonnaise, pepper, garlic, 1 pinch of salt and lemon zest.
4. Mix and chill for 30 minutes
5. Remove your Salmon from the brine and place it on a wire rack and let it sit for about 30 minutes.
6. Smoke them over low heat for 1 and a ½ to 2 hours. Assemble sliders by dividing the salmon among 12 individual buns.
7. Top each of the pieces with a spoonful of aioli and place another bun on top

Pit Boss Steak Kabobs

Servings: 6
Cooking Time: 10 Minutes
Ingredients:

- 3 lb steak
- 2 small zucchini
- 1 onion
- 2 small yellow squash
- Salt and pepper
- 1 cup teriyaki sauce
- 3 tbsp sesame seeds, toasted

Directions:

1. Preheat your Pit Boss to 400F.
2. Cut the steak and veggies into skewable pieces.
3. Place the meat and veggies on the skewers then sprinkle with salt and pepper.
4. Place the skewers on the grill and cook for 5 minutes per side.
5. Remove the skewers, drizzle teriyaki sauce and top with sesame seeds.
6. Serve when hot. Enjoy.

Texas Barbeque Rub

Servings: 1/2 Cup
Cooking Time: 15 Minutes
Ingredients:

- 1 tsp Sugar
- Tbsp Seasoned salt
- Tbsp Black pepper
- tsp Chilli powder
- Tbsp Powdered onions
- Tbsp Smoked paprika
- 1 tsp Sugar
- Tbsp Powdered garlic

Directions:

1. Pour all the ingredients into a small bowl and mix thoroughly.
2. Keep stored in an airtight jar or container.

Smoked Brisket

Servings: 8
Cooking Time: 12 Hours
Ingredients:

- Salt and pepper to taste
- 2 tablespoons beef rub
- 1 tablespoon Worcestershire sauce
- 6 lb. brisket
- 1 cup beef broth

Directions:

1. Mix salt, pepper, beef rub and Worcestershire sauce in bowl.
2. Rub brisket with this mixture.
3. Preheat your Pit Boss wood pellet grill to 180 degrees for 15 minutes while the lid is closed.
4. Smoke the brisket for 7 hours.
5. Transfer brisket on top of a foil.
6. Pour the broth over the brisket.
7. Wrap it with foil.
8. Smoke for 5 hours.
9. Let rest before slicing.
10. Tips: Slice against the grain.

Satisfying Veggie Casserole

Servings: 10
Cooking Time: 3 Hours
Ingredients:

- 5 tbsp. olive oil, divided
- 6 C. onions, sliced thinly
- 1 tbsp. fresh thyme, chopped and divided
- Salt and freshly ground black pepper, to taste
- 1 tbsp. unsalted butter
- 1¼ lb. Yukon gold potatoes, peeled and 1/8-inch thick slices
- ½ C. heavy cream
- 2¼ lb. tomatoes, cut into ¼-inch thick slices
- ¼ cup black olives, pitted and sliced

Directions:

1. In a large cast iron pan, heat 3 tbsp. of oil and over high heat and cook onions, 1 tsp. of thyme, salt and black pepper about 5 minutes, stirring occasionally.
2. Add the butter and cook over medium heat for about 1 minutes.
3. Reduce the heat to low and cook for about 10 minutes.
4. Set the temperature of Pit Boss Grill to 350 degrees F a preheat with closed lid for 15 minutes.
5. Meanwhile, in a bowl, add potatoes slices, cream, 1 tsp. thyme, salt and black pepper and toss to coat.
6. In another bowl, add tomato slices, salt and black pepp and toss to coat.
7. Transfer half of the caramelized onions into a small bo
8. In the bottom of the cast iron pan, spread the remainin onion slices evenly and top with 1 layer of potatoes and tomatoes.
9. Drizzle with 2 tbsp. of cream from potato mixture and tbsp. of olive oil.
10. Sprinkle with a little salt, black pepper and ½ tsp. of thyme.
11. Spread remaining caramelized onions on top, followed potatoes, tomatoes and olives.

Drizzle with remaining cream from the potatoes and
~~~maining tbsp. of olive oil.
Sprinkle with a little salt, black pepper and remaining ½
~. of thyme.
With a piece of foil, cover the cast iron pan tightly.
Place the pan onto the grill and cook for about 2 hours.
Remove from grill and uncover the cast iron pan.
Now, set the temperature of Pit Boss Grill to 450 degrees

Place the cast iron pan, uncovered onto the grill and cook
about 25-30 minutes.
Remove from grill and serve hot.

Smoked Pot Roast

~vings: 4
~oking Time: 6 Hours
~gredients:
Salt and pepper to taste
1 teaspoon onion powder
1 teaspoon garlic powder
3 lb. chuck roast
2 cups potatoes, sliced in half
2 cups carrots, sliced
2 onions, peeled
1 teaspoon chili powder
1 cup red wine
1 tablespoon fresh rosemary, chopped
1 tablespoon fresh thyme, chopped
2 dried chipotle peppers
2 cups beef stock
~rections:
Mix salt, pepper, onion powder and garlic powder in a
~wl.
Rub chuck roast with this mixture.
Preheat your Pit Boss wood pellet grill to 180 degrees F
~ 15 minutes while the lid is closed.
Smoke the beef for 1 hour.
Increase temperature to 275 degrees F.
Place the beef and the rest of the ingredients in a Dutch
~n.
Seal the Dutch oven and place on the grill.
Braise for 5 hours.
Tips You can also use dried herbs in place of fresh herbs.

Tea Injectable

~vings: 2 Cups
~oking Time:30 Minutes
~gredients:
¼ cup favorite spice rub or shake
2 cups water
~rections:
Place the rub in a standard paper coffee filter and tie it up
~h kitchen string to seal.
In a small pot over high heat, bring the water to a boil.
Drop the filter into the boiling water and remove the pot
~m the heat. Let it steep for 30 minutes.
Remove and discard the filter. Discard any unused tea
~er injecting the meat.

North American Pot Pie

Servings: 10
Cooking Time: 1 Hour 25 Minutes
Ingredients:
- 2 tbsp. cornstarch
- 2 tbsp. water
- 3 C. chicken broth
- 1 C. milk
- 3 tbsp. butter
- 1 tbsp. fresh rosemary, chopped
- 1 tbsp. fresh thyme, chopped
- Salt and freshly ground black pepper, to taste
- 2¾ C. frozen chopped broccoli, thawed
- 3 C. frozen peas, thawed
- 3 C. chopped frozen carrots, thawed
- 1 frozen puff pastry sheet
Directions:
1. Set the temperature of Pit Boss Grill to 375 degrees F and preheat with closed lid for 15 minutes.
2. In a small bowl, dissolve cornstarch in water. Set aside.
3. In a pan, add broth, milk, butter and herbs over medium heat and bring to a boil.
4. Add the cornstarch mixture and stir to combine well.
5. Stir in salt and black pepper and remove from the heat.
6. In a large bowl, add the vegetables and milk sauce and mix well.
7. Transfer mixture into a cast iron skillet.
8. With the puff pastry, cover the mixture and cut excess from edges.
9. Place the skillet onto the grill and cook for about 80 minutes.
10. Remove the pan from grill and set aside for about 15 minutes before serving.
11. Cut the pie into desired-sized portions and serve.

Texas Styled Smoked Flounder

Servings: 6
Cooking Time: 20 Minutes
Ingredients:
- 1 whole flounder
- 1 halved lemon
- Ground black pepper as needed
- 2 tablespoons of chopped up fresh dill
- 1 tablespoon of olive oil
- 1 cup of soaked wood chips
Directions:
1. Preheat your smoker to a temperature of 350 degrees Fahrenheit.
2. Slice half of your lemon and place them into the slices. Rub the fish with a coating of olive oil. Squeeze another half of the lemon all over the fish. Season with some black pepper.
3. Rub 1 tablespoon of dill into the slits and insert the lemon slices firmly. Place the flounder on top of a large piece of aluminum foil and fold the sides all around the fish.
4. Place the fish in your smoker and throw a couple handful of soaked wood chips into the coals. And smoke for 10 minutes Once done, seal up the foil and smoke it until it is fully done. Remove fish and garnish with some extra dill

Smoking Burgers

Servings: 8
Cooking Time: 4o Minutes
Ingredients:
- For the topping:
- 3 apples, peeled and cut into slices
- 75g blueberries
- 25g salted butter
- 2 tablespoons maple syrup
- For the cake:
- 75g butter, cut into cubes
- 75g organic virgin coconut oil, cut into cubes
- 100g cane sugar
- 2 large free-range eggs, beaten
- 75g buckwheat flour
- 75g ground almonds
- ½ teaspoon bicarbonate of soda
- 1 teaspoon baking powder
- 1 teaspoon cinnamon

Directions:
1. Preheat oven to 180°C. Caramelize the apples.
2. Add the blueberries last. Set aside. Place the sugar, butter and coconut oil into a mixing bowl and cream until pale and fluffy.
3. Gradually add the beaten eggs, adding a bit of flour if the mixture begins to curdle. Continue to beat the mixture until fluffy. Fold in the remaining flour, ground almonds, baking powder and cinnamon.
4. Transfer the apple and blueberry mixture into the bottom of a greased Bundt cake mold, leveling well with the back of a spoon. Then pour the cake mixture over the top. Bake for about 40 minutes or until a skewer comes out clean. Leave to cool. Delicious served with Greek yogurt.

Rosemary Chicken Glazed With Balsamic With Bacon Pearl Onions

Servings:4
Cooking Time: 50 Minutes
Ingredients:
- 2 Tbsp of unsalted butter
- 1 Tbsp of brown sugar, light
- 1 4pounds chicken
- 2 Tbsp of balsamic vinegar
- 1/4 pound of bacon
- 1 Tbsp of thyme, fresh
- 3/4 of pearl onions, frozen

Directions:
1. Rub black pepper and salt all over the chicken, including cavities. Put the chicken on a rack and keep inside the refrigerator for 24 hours.
2. Preheat the grill for direct cooking at 420°F (High). Use mesquite wood pellets for a distinctive, strong woody taste.
3. Mix the vinegar, butter, brown sugar, and thyme in a bowl, then rub it on the chicken with a brush.
4. Put the pearl onion, balsamic mixture, and bacon under the chicken in the roasting pan.
5. Roast the chicken on the preheated grill for 35 minutes. Flip the chicken with a tong and roast for another 15 minutes, or until the internal temperature of the thigh reads 165-170F.
6. Rest for 5 minutes, then serve the chicken with the bacon and the onion.

Venison Steaks

Servings: 4
Cooking Time: 1 Hour 20 Minutes
Ingredients:
- 4 (8-ounce) venison steaks
- 2 tablespoons extra-virgin olive oil
- 4 garlic cloves, minced
- 1 tablespoon ground sage
- 2 teaspoons sea salt
- 2 teaspoons freshly ground black pepper

Directions:
1. Supply your smoker with wood pellets and follow the manufacturer's specific start-up procedure. Preheat, with th lid closed, to 225°F.
2. Rub the venison steaks well with the olive oil and seaso with the garlic, sage, salt, and pepper.
3. Arrange the venison steaks directly on the grill grate, close the lid, and smoke for 1 hour and 20 minutes, or until a meat thermometer inserted in the center reads 130°F to 140 depending on desired doneness. If you want a better sear, remove the steaks from the grill at an internal temperature 125°F, crank up the heat to 450°F, or the "High" setting, and cook the steaks on each side for an additional 2 to 3 minutes

Grilled Pineapple With Chocolate Sauce

Servings: 6 To 8
Cooking Time: 25 Minutes
Ingredients:
- 1pineapple
- 8 oz bittersweet chocolate chips
- 1/2 cup spiced rum
- 1/2 cup whipping cream
- 2tbsp light brown sugar

Directions:
1. Preheat pellet grill to 400°F.
2. De-skin the pineapple and slice pineapple into 1 in cube
3. In a saucepan, combine chocolate chips. When chips be to melt, add rum to the saucepan. Continue to stir until combined, then add a splash of the pineapple's juice.
4. Add in whipping cream and continue to stir the mixture Once the sauce is smooth and thickening, lower heat to simmer to keep warm.
5. Thread pineapple cubes onto skewers. Sprinkle skewer with brown sugar.
6. Place skewers on the grill grate. Grill for about 5 minute per side, or until grill marks begin to develop.
7. Remove skewers from grill and allow to rest on a plate about 5 minutes. Serve alongside warm chocolate sauce for dipping.

Soy Dipping Sauce

Servings: 4
Cooking Time: 10 Minutes
Ingredients:
- ¼ cup soy sauce
- ¼ cup sugar
- ¼ cup rice vinegar
- ½ cup scallions

½ cup cilantro

ections:
In a blender place all ingredients and blend until smooth
Pour sauce in a bowl and serve

Tofu Smoothie

vings: 2
oking Time: 5 Minutes
redients:
1 Banana, sliced and frozen
3/4 cup Almond Milk
2 tbsp. Peanut Butter
1/2 cup Yoghurt, plain and low-fat
1/2 cup Tofu, soft and silken
1/3 cup Dates, chopped
ections:
First, place tofu, banana, dates, yogurt, peanut butter, and
ond milk in the blender pitcher.
After that, press the 'smoothie' button.
Finally, transfer to serving glass and enjoy it.

Smoke Pork Side Ribs With Chives

vings: 6
king Time: 3-4 Hours
redients:
1/3 cup of olive oil (or garlic-infused olive oil)
3 Tbsp of ketchup
3 Tbsp chives finely chopped
3 pounds of pork side ribs
Salt and black pepper to taste
ections:
Stir together olive oil, finely chopped chives, ketchup, and
salt and pepper.
Cut pork and coat with chives mixture. Start and smoke
l
The temperature must be 250 degrees Fahrenheit until 15
utes
Arrange pork chops on the grill rack and smoke for about
4 hours.
Allow resting 15 minutes before serving.

Salt-seared Kobe Beef With Tarragon Shallot Butter

vings: 4
king Time: 40 Minutes
redients:
1 (8-inch) square salt block
3 Tbsp Unsalted butter
2 finely chopped shallot
12 oz. Kobe beef, boneless, trimmed, then boiled
Grounded black pepper to taste
1/4 cup of dry vermouth
Finely chopped tarragon leaves (1 sprig)
ections:
Preheat the wood pellet smoker-grill for direct cooking at
F using any pellet
Heat the salt block on the smoker-grill for 10 minutes,
ease the temperature to 450F (High), and heat for another

10 minutes. While the salt is heating, transfer your beef to a
freezer for 10-15 minutes. Do not allow to freeze.
3.   Place a medium skillet on the cooking grate, then add the
vermouth and shallot. Stir occasionally to prevent the shallot
from boiling dry. Boil until 1 tbsp of shallot remains in the
skillet, stir in the pepper and tarragon. Allow to cool and mix
with butter.
4.   Remove the beef and slice to about 1/4 -inch-thickness.
Sear for 5 minutes per side on the salt block. Serve with
shallot-tarragon butter.

Smoked Pheasant

Servings: 4 To 6
Cooking Time: 3 To 4 Hours
Ingredients:
- 1 gallon hot water
- 1 cup salt
- 1 cup packed brown sugar
- 2 (2- to 3-pound) whole pheasants, cleaned and plucked
- ¼ cup extra-virgin olive oil
- 2 tablespoons onion powder
- 2 tablespoons freshly ground black pepper
- 2 tablespoons cayenne pepper
- 1 tablespoon minced garlic
- 2 teaspoons smoked paprika
- 1 cup molasses

Directions:
1.   In a large container with a lid, combine the hot water, salt,
and brown sugar, stirring to dissolve the salt and sugar. Let
cool to room temperature, then submerge the pheasants in the
brine, cover, and refrigerate for 8 to 12 hours.
2.   Remove the pheasants from the brine, then rinse them
and pat dry. Discard the brine.
3.   Supply your smoker with wood pellets and follow the
manufacturer's specific start-up procedure. Preheat, with the
lid closed, to 250°F.
4.   In a small bowl, combine the olive oil, black pepper,
cayenne pepper, onion powder, garlic, and paprika to form a
paste.
5.   Rub the pheasants with the paste and place breast-side up
on the grill grate. Close the lid and smoke for 1 hour.
6.   Open the smoker and baste the pheasants with some of
the molasses. Close the lid and continue smoking for 2 to 3
hours, basting with the molasses every 30 minutes, until a
meat thermometer inserted into the thigh reads 160°F.
7.   Remove the pheasants from the grill and let rest for 20
minutes before serving warm or cold.

Smoked Beef Tenderloin

Servings: 8
Cooking Time: 3 Hours
Ingredients:
- Black pepper, freshly ground
- Vegetable oil
- 4 pound of beef tenderloin
- Kosher or sea salt
- 2 Tbsp of olive oil
- Horseradish sauce

Directions:
1.   Preheat the grill for 15 minutes at 250°F. Use cherry
wood pellets.

2. Season tenderloin with salt and black pepper. Place it on the baking sheet and brush all the sides of the tenderloin with olive oil.

3. Place the tenderloin in the preheated grill and smoke for 3 hours or until internal temperature reads 160°F.

4. Remove from grill when it is done and allow it to rest for 10 minutes.

5. Serve the tenderloin.

Pork Dry Rub

Servings: 1
Cooking Time: 15 Minutes
Ingredients:
- Tbsp Kosher salt
- 2 Tbsp Powered onions
- Tbsp Cayenne pepper
- 1tsp Dried mustard
- 1/4 cup brown sugar
- Tbsp Powdered garlic
- Tbsp Powdered chili pepper
- 1/4 cup smoked paprika
- 2 Tbsp Black pepper

Directions:
1. Combine all the ingredients in a small bowl.
2. Transfer to an airtight jar or container.
3. Keep stored in a cool, dry place.

Texas-style Brisket Rub

Servings: 1
Cooking Time: 15 Minutes
Ingredients:
- 2 tsp Sugar
- 2 Tbsp Kosher salt
- 2 tsp Chilli powder
- 2 Tbsp Black pepper
- Tbsp Cayenne pepper
- Tbsp Powdered garlic
- tsp Grounded cumin
- 2 Tbsp Powdered onion
- 1/4 cup paprika, smoked

Directions:
1. Mix all the ingredients in a small bowl until it is well blended.
2. Transfer to an airtight jar or container. Store in a cool place.

Berry Cobbler

Servings: 8
Cooking Time: 35 Minutes
Ingredients:
- Fruit Filling
- 3 cups berries, mixed(blueberries, blackberries, raspberries)
- 1 cup brown sugar
- 1 lemon juice
- 1 tbsp lemon zest
- 1 tbsp vanilla extract
- 1 pinch salt
- Cobbler Topping

- 1-1/2 cups flour, all-purpose
- 3 tbsp granulated sugar
- 1-1/2 tbsp baking powder
- 1/2 tbsp salt
- 8 tbsp cold butter
- 1/2 cup sour cream
- 2 tbsp sugar

Directions:
1. Fire up the Pit Boss to smoke setting for 5 minutes with the lid open or until the fire has been established, then preh it to 350F with the lid closed

2. Combine berries, sugar, juice, zest, vanilla, and salt in a mixing bowl until the fruits are well coated.

3. Place the fruit mixture in an 8x8 aluminum pan. Make cobbler topping by mixing all-purpose flour, brown sugar, baking powder, and salt in a mixing bowl. Cut the butter in t flour into pea-size pieces.

4. Stir in sour cream until the dough starts to come togeth Pinch the dough into small pieces placing them on top of the fruits until well covered.

5. Top with sugar if you desire.

6. Put the grill pan on the grill grate and cook for 35 minu or until the top is golden brown.

7. Carefully remove the pan from the Pit Boss and let rest a few minutes to Serve.

Yummy Gyro

Servings: 4
Cooking Time: 40 Minutes
Ingredients:
- 1 pound ground lamb
- 2 teaspoons salt
- 1 teaspoon freshly ground black pepper
- 2 tablespoons chopped fresh oregano
- 1 tablespoon minced garlic
- 1 tablespoon onion powder
- 4 to 6 pocketless pitas
- Tzatziki sauce, for serving
- 1 tomato, chopped, for serving
- 1 small onion, thinly sliced, for serving

Directions:
1. In a medium bowl, combine the lamb, salt, pepper, oregano, garlic, and onion powder; mix well. Cover with pla wrap and refrigerate overnight.

2. Supply your smoker with wood pellets and follow the manufacturer's specific start-up procedure. Preheat, with tl lid closed, to 300°F.

3. Remove the meat mixture from the refrigerator and, or Frogmat or a piece of heavy-duty aluminum foil, roll and sh it into a rectangular loaf about 8 inches long by 5 inches wic

4. Place the loaf directly on the grill, close the lid, and sm for 35 minutes, or until a meat thermometer inserted in the center reads 155°F.

5. Remove the loaf from the heat and increase the temperature to 450°F.

6. Cut the loaf into ⅛-inch slices and place on a Frogmat piece of heavy-duty foil.

7. Return the meat (still on the Frogmat or foil) to the smoker, close the lid, and continue cooking for 2 to 4 minut or until the edges are crispy.

8. Warm the pitas in the smoker for a few minutes and se with the lamb, tzatziki sauce, chopped tomato, and sliced onion.

Pan-seared Ribeye Steak With Parsley Potatoes

Servings: 6
Cooking Time: 60 Minutes
Ingredients:
- 2 pork tenderloin
- medium potatoes (peeled and sliced)
- 3 tbsps extra-virgin olive oil
- 2 Tbsp Fresh parsley (chopped)
- Salt and pepper to taste.

Directions:
Preheat the wood pellet smoker-grill for direct cooking at 0F using any pellets
Rinse the meat and pat dry, then season with salt and pper.
Grill pork for 20 minutes, then set aside and increase the mperature of the grill to High.
Place an iron skillet on grill grates, add the oil and heat for ninute. Sear the meat for 3 minutes per side or until brown. ow it to rest before serving.
Rearrange the grill for indirect cooking at 300F
Place a pot on grates and fill with water, add the potatoes d allow to boil, reduce the heat and simmer for 15 minutes until the potatoes become soft. Drain the water. Transfer to owl, add parsley, and olive oil.
Serve with pork.

Spatchcocked Quail With Smoked Fruit

Servings: 4
Cooking Time: 1 Hour
Ingredients:
- 4 quail, spatchcocked
- 2 teaspoons salt
- 2 teaspoons freshly ground black pepper
- 2 teaspoons garlic powder
- 4 ripe peaches or pears
- 4 tablespoons (½ stick) salted butter, softened
- 1 tablespoon sugar
- 1 teaspoon ground cinnamon

Directions:
Supply your smoker with wood pellets and follow the nufacturer's specific start-up procedure. Preheat, with the closed, to 225°F.
Season the quail all over with the salt, pepper, and garlic wder.
Cut the peaches (or pears) in half and remove the pits (or e cores).
In a small bowl, combine the butter, sugar, and cinnamon; aside.
Arrange the quail on the grill grate, close the lid, and oke for about 1 hour, or until a meat thermometer inserted he thickest part reads 145°F.
After the quail has been cooking for about 15 minutes, d the peaches (or pears) to the grill, flesh-side down, and oke for 30 to 40 minutes.
Top the cooked peaches (or pears) with the cinnamon tter and serve alongside the quail.

Dill Seafood Rub

Servings: 5
Cooking Time:5 Minutes
Ingredients:
- 2 tablespoons coarse kosher salt
- 2 tablespoons dried dill weed
- 1 tablespoon garlic powder
- 1½ teaspoons lemon pepper

Directions:
1. In a small airtight container or zip-top bag, combine the salt, dill, garlic powder, and lemon pepper.
2. Close the container and shake to mix. Unused rub will keep in an airtight container for months.

Baked Apple Crisp

Servings: 7
Cooking Time: 30 Minutes
Ingredients:
- Butter for greasing
- 1/2 cup flour
- 1/2 cup rolled oats
- 1 stick butter, sliced into cubes
- 1 cup brown sugar
- 1 1/2 teaspoon ground cinnamon
- 1/4 cup walnuts, chopped
- 3 lb. apples, sliced thinly
- ½ cup dried cranberries
- 2 1/2 tablespoons bourbon
- 1/2 cup brown sugar
- 1 tablespoon lemon juice
- 1/4 cup honey
- 1 teaspoon vanilla
- 1 1/2 teaspoons ground cinnamon
- Pinch salt

Directions:
1. Grease cast iron pan with butter.
2. Add flour, oats, butter cubes, 1 cup sugar, cinnamon and walnuts to a food processor. Pulse until crumbly.
3. In a bowl, mix the apples with the rest of the ingredients.
4. Pour apple mixture into the greased pan.
5. Spread flour mixture on top.
6. Bake in the Pit Boss wood pellet grill at 350 degrees F for 1 hour.
7. Tips: Use freshly squeezed lemon juice.

Easy Grilled Corn

Servings: 6
Cooking Time: 40 Minutes
Ingredients:
- 6 fresh corn ears, still in the husk
- Pepper, salt and butter

Directions:
1. Preheat your wood pellet grill to 375-400F.
2. Cut off the large silk ball from the corn top and any hanging or loose husk pieces.
3. Place the corn on your grill grate directly and do not peel off the husk.
4. Grill for about 30-40 minutes. Flip a few times to grill evenly all round.

5. Transfer the corn on a platter, serve, and let guests peel their own.
6. Now top with pepper, salt, and butter.
7. Enjoy!

Baked Asparagus & Bacon

Servings: 8
Cooking Time: 20 Minutes
Ingredients:
- 3 eggs
- 1 cup heavy cream
- 1 tablespoon chopped fresh chives
- 1/4 cup goat cheese
- 4 tablespoons Parmesan cheese
- 8 oz. fresh asparagus, trimmed
- 8 oz. bacon, cooked crispy and chopped
- ¼ teaspoon lemon zest

Directions:
1. Preheat the Pit Boss wood pellet grill to 375 degrees F for 15 minutes while the lid is closed.
2. In a bowl, beat the eggs and stir in cream, chives, goat cheese and Parmesan cheese.
3. Arrange the asparagus in a baking pan.
4. Spread cream mixture on top.
5. Sprinkle bacon bits and lemon zest on top.
6. Bake for 20 minutes.
7. Tips: You can also use this recipe for other vegetables like broccoli.

Grilled Watermelon

Servings: 2-3
Cooking Time: 2 Minutes
Ingredients:
- 6watermelon slices, each measuring 3 inches across and 1-inch thick
- 2tablespoons honey

Directions:
1. Put the grill grate inside the hood and close the unit.
2. Set temperature to the max and set the timer to 2 minutes.
3. Stop the unit as it is preheated.
4. Now brush the watermelon slices with honey.
5. Grease the grill grate with oil spray.
6. Place the watermelon slices on the grill grate.
7. Close the hood and grill for 2 minutes without flipping it.
8. Once done, take out watermelon slices and serve immediately.

Decadent Chocolate Cheesecake

Servings: 8
Cooking Time: 1 Hour 10 Minutes
Ingredients:
- For Base:
- 1 C. chocolate wafer crumbs
- 2 tbsp. butter, melted
- For Filling:
- 4 oz. unsweetened baking chocolate, chopped
- 16 oz. cream cheese, softened
- ¾ C. white sugar
- 2 eggs

- 1 tsp. vanilla extract
- For Topping:
- ¼ C. heavy cream
- 2 oz. unsweetened baking chocolate, chopped finely
- ¼ C. white sugar
- 1 tbsp. unsalted butter

Directions:
1. Set the temperature of Pit Boss Grill to 325 degrees F and preheat with closed lid for 15 minutes.
2. For base: in a bowl, mix together wafer crumbs and melted butter.
3. Line an 8-inch springform pan with parchment paper.
4. Place the crumb mixture in the bottom of prepared springform pan and gently, press to fit.
5. Place the pan onto the grill and cook for about 10 minutes.
6. Remove the pan from grill and set aside to cool.
7. For filling: in a microwave-safe bowl, add chocolate and microwave on High for about 1-2 minutes or until melted, stirring after every 30 seconds.
8. Remove from microwave and set aside to cool slightly.
9. In another bowl, add cream cheese and sugar and beat until light and fluffy.
10. Add the eggs, one at a time, beating well after each addition.
11. Add melted chocolate and vanilla extract and mix well.
12. Place filling mixture over cooled base evenly and cook onto the grill for about 45-50 minutes.
13. Remove the cheesecake from grill and place onto a wire rack to cool.
14. For topping: in a heavy-bottomed pan, place heavy cream over medium-low heat and cook until heated through.
15. Add chocolate, sugar and butter and cook until sugar dissolves, stirring continuously.
16. Remove the pan from heat and set aside to cool slightly.
17. Pour chocolate mixture over the cooled cheesecake evenly.
18. Refrigerate for at least 4 hours before serving.

Pit Boss Marinated Chicken Kabobs

Servings: 6
Cooking Time: 12 Minutes
Ingredients:
- Marinade
- 1/2 cup olive oi
- 2 tbsp white vinegar
- 1 tbsp lemon juice
- 1-1/2 tbsp salt
- 1/2 tbsp ground pepper
- 2 tbsp fresh chives, chopped
- 1-1/2 tbsp thyme, chopped
- 2 tbsp Italian parsley, chopped
- 1 tbsp minced garlic
- Kabobs
- 1-1/2 lb chicken breast
- 12 crimini mushrooms
- 1 each orange, red and yellow bell pepper
- Serve with
- Naan bread

Directions:
1. Mix all the marinade ingredients then toss the chicken and mushrooms until well coated.
2. Place in the fridge to marinate for 30 minutes.

Meanwhile, soak the skewers in water. And preheat your Boss to 450F.

Assemble the kabobs and grill for 6 minutes on each side. aside.

Heat up the naan bread on the grill for 2 minutes .serve enjoy.

Barbecue Bacon Bites

vings: 4

king Time: 30 Minutes

redients:

1 tablespoon ground fennel

Salt and pepper to taste

1/2 cup brown sugar

1 lb. pork belly, sliced into cubes

ections:

Preheat your Pit Boss wood pellet grill to 350 degrees F. 15 minutes while the lid is closed.

In a bowl, mix the ground fennel, salt, pepper and brown ar.

Coat the bacon cubes with this mixture.

Grill for 30 minutes.

Tips: It's also a good idea to use a foil for cooking the on to catch the bacon drippings and reserve for later use.

The Ultimate Bbq Sauce

vings: 3 Cups

king Time: 30 Minutes

redients:

1 small onion, finely chopped

2 garlic cloves, finely minced

2 cups ketchup

1 cup water

½ cup molasses

½ cup apple cider vinegar

5 tablespoons granulated sugar

5 tablespoons light brown sugar

1 tablespoon Worcestershire sauce

1 tablespoon freshly squeezed lemon juice

2 teaspoons liquid smoke

1½ teaspoons freshly ground black pepper

1 tablespoon yellow mustard

ections:

On the stovetop, in a saucepan over medium heat, nbine the onion, garlic, ketchup, water, molasses, apple er vinegar, granulated sugar, brown sugar, Worcestershire ce, lemon juice, liquid smoke, black pepper, and mustard. ng to a boil, then reduce the heat to low and simmer for 30 nutes, straining out any bigger chunks, if desired.

Let the sauce cool completely, then transfer to an airtight tainer and refrigerate for up to 2 weeks, or use a canning cess to store for longer.

Smoked Cheddar Cheese

vings: 2

king Time: 5 Hour

redients:

2, 8-oz, cheddar cheese blocks

ections:

1. Preheat and set your pellet grill to 90F.
2. Place the cheese blocks directly on the grill grate and smoke for about 4 hours.
3. Remove and transfer into a plastic bag, resealable. Refrigerate for about 2 weeks to allow flavor from smoke to permeate your cheese.
4. Now enjoy!

Basil Pesto Sauce

Servings: 4

Cooking Time: 10 Minutes

Ingredients:
- 2 cloves garlic
- 2 oz. basil leaves
- 1 tablespoon pine nuts
- 1 oz. parmesan cheese
- ½ cup olive oil

Directions:
1. In a blender place all ingredients and blend until smooth
2. Pour sauce in a bowl and serve

Berry Smoothie

Servings: 1

Cooking Time: 1 Minutes

Ingredients:
- 2 scoops Protein Powder
- 2 cups Almond Milk
- 4 cups Mixed Berry
- 2 cups Yoghurt

Directions:
1. First, place mixed berry, protein powder, yogurt, and almond milk in the blender pitcher.
2. Then, select the 'smoothie' button.
3. Finally, pour the smoothie to the serving glass.

Smoked Teriyaki Tuna

Servings: 4

Cooking Time: 2 Hours

Ingredients:
- Tuna steaks, 1 oz.
- 2 c. marinade, teriyaki
- Alder wood chips soaked in water

Directions:
1. Slice tuna into thick slices of 2 inch. Place your tuna slices and marinade then set in your fridge for about 3 hours
2. After 3 hours, remove the tuna from the marinade and pat dry. Let the tuna air dry in your fridge for 2-4 hours. Preheat your smoker to 180 degrees Fahrenheit
3. Place the Tuna on a Teflon-coated fiberglass and place them directly on your grill grates. Smoke the Tuna for about an hour until the internal temperature reaches 145 degrees Fahrenheit.
4. Remove the tuna from your grill and let them rest for 10 minutes. Serve!

Grilled Clam With Lemon-cayenne Butter

Servings: 2

Cooking Time: 15 Minutes

Ingredients:
- 2 tsp of lemon juice, preferably fresh
- Large pinch of salt (kosher)
- 2 dozen of littleneck clams
- 1 large clove of garlic
- Chives, freshly chopped
- 4 Tbsp of unsalted butter, already melted
- Pinch of cayenne pepper

Directions:
1. Set the grill for direct cooking at 300°F. Use alder wood pellets for mild taste and aroma.
2. Mash garlic and salt with a mortar and pestle to form a paste.
3. Scoop the paste into a small bowl and add cayenne pepper, butter, and lemon.
4. Grill clam over the preheated cooking grid for 5 minutes. When clam is ready, it will open. Carefully transfer opened clam to the bowl containing lemon-cayenne butter. Do not spill the clam-juice when transporting.
5. Gently mix the clam and butter until it is well-combined.
6. Serve immediately with chives.

Smoked Up Salmon And Dungeness Crab Chowder

Servings: 6
Cooking Time: 45 Minutes
Ingredients:
- 4 gallons of water
- 3 fresh Dungeness crabs
- 1 cup of rock salt
- 3 cups of Cold-Hot Smoked Salmon
- 3 cups of ocean clam juice
- 5 diced celery stalks
- 1 yellow diced onion
- 2 peeled and diced large sized russet potatoes
- 14 ounces of sweet corn
- 12 ounce of clam chowder dry soup mix
- 4 bacon slices crumbled and cooked

Directions:
1. Bring 4 gallons of water and rock salt to a boil. Add the Dungeness crab and boil for 20 minutes
2. Remove the crabs , let it cool and clean the crabs and pick out crab meat. Place it over high heat.
3. Add clam juice, 5 cups of water, diced potatoes, diced celery, and onion. Bring the mix to a boil as well. Add corn to the liquid and boil.
4. Whisk in the clam chowder and keep mixing everything. Simmer on low for about 15 minutes and add the crumbled bacon. Add bacon, garnish with ½ cup flaked smoked salmon and ½ cup Dungeness crabmeat. Serve!

Crunchy Potato Wedges

Servings: 5
Cooking Time: 16 Minutes
Ingredients:
- 4 Yukon gold potatoes
- 2 tbsp. olive oil
- 1 tbsp. garlic, minced
- 2 tsp. onion powder
- ½ tsp. red pepper flakes, crushed
- Salt and freshly ground black pepper, to taste

Directions:

1. Set the temperature of Pit Boss Grill to 500 degrees F a preheat with closed lid for 15 minutes.
2. Cut each potato into 8 equal-sized wedges.
3. In a large bowl, add potato wedges and remaining ingredients and toss to coat well.
4. Arrange the potato wedges onto the grill and cook for about 8 minutes per side.
5. Remove from grill and serve hot.

Low Carb Almond Flour Bread

Servings: 24
Cooking Time: 1 Hour 15 Minutes
Ingredients:
- 1tsp sea salt or to taste
- 1tbsp apple cider vinegar
- ½ cup of warm water
- ¼ cup of coconut oil
- 4large eggs (beaten)
- 1tbsp gluten-free baking powder
- 2cup blanched almond flour
- ¼ cup Psyllium husk powder
- 1tsp ginger (optional)

Directions:
1. Preheat the grill to 350°F with the lid closed for 15 minutes.
2. Line a 9 by 5 inch loaf pan with parchment paper. Set aside.
3. Combine the ginger, Psyllium husk powder, almond flo salt, baking powder in a large mixing bowl.
4. In another mixing bowl, mix the coconut oil, apple cide vinegar, eggs and warm water. Mix thoroughly.
5. Gradually pour the flour mixture into the egg mixture, stirring as you pour. Stir until it forms a smooth batter.
6. Fill the lined loaf pan with the batter and cover the bat with aluminum foil.
7. Place the loaf pan directly on the grill and bake for abo 1 hour or until a toothpick or knife inserted in the middle o the bread comes out clean.

Smoked Potatoes

Servings: 6
Cooking Time: 1 Hour
Ingredients:
- 2 tablespoon butter
- 1/2 cup milk
- 1 cup heavy cream
- 2 cloves garlic, crushed and minced
- 2 tablespoons flour
- 4 potatoes, sliced thinly
- Salt and pepper to taste
- 1 cup cheddar cheese, grated

Directions:
1. Preheat your Pit Boss wood pellet grill to 375 degrees for 15 minutes while the lid is closed.
2. Add butter to your cast iron pan.
3. In a bowl, mix the milk, cream, garlic and flour.
4. Arrange some of the potatoes in a pan.
5. Season with salt and pepper.
6. Pour some of the sauce over the potatoes.
7. Repeat layers until ingredients have been used.
8. Grill for 50 minutes.

Sprinkle cheese on top and cook for 10 minutes.
Tips: Soak the potatoes in water to avoid discoloration.

Smoked Garlic Sauce

Servings: 2
Cooking Time: 30 Minutes
Ingredients:
- 3 whole garlic heads
- 1/2 cup mayonnaise
- 1/4 cup sour cream
- 2 tbsp lemon juice
- 2 tbsp cider vinegar
- Salt to taste

Directions:
Cut the garlic heads off then place in a microwave-safe bowl, add 2 tbsp water and cover. Microwave for about 5-6 minutes on medium.
Heat your grill on medium.
Place the garlic heads in a shallow 'boat' foil and smoke about 20-25 minutes until soft.
Transfer the garlic heads into a blender. Process for a few minutes until smooth.
Add remaining ingredients and process until everything is combined.
Enjoy!

Bourbon Braised Beef Short Ribs

Servings: 6
Cooking Time: 3 Hours 15 Minutes
Ingredients:
- 2 Tbsp Worcestershire sauce
- 3 Tbsp soy sauce
- 2 Tbsp bourbon
- 1/2 cup Dijon mustard
- 1 cup beef stock
- 12 beef short ribs

Directions:
Preheat wood pellet smoker-grill to 250^{0}F, with the lid closed for about 15 minutes
Mix the Worcestershire sauce, mustard, and molasses. Brush sauce on each side of the rib.
Prepare the mop sauce by mixing the soy sauce, beef stock, and bourbon in a food-safe plastic spray bottle.
Arrange the ribs directly on the grill and braise for 2 hours, until an internal temperature of 165^{0}F is reached. Spray the mop sauce over the rib occasionally for tender perfection.
Remove rib from the grill and place on an aluminum foil. Pour remaining mop sauce over the ribs and wrap the foil over the ribs.
Transfer foil enclosed rib for direct cooking to the grill grate. Braise the ribs until the Instant read thermometer reads temperature of 195^{0}F, about one hour.
Remove foil enclosed rib from grill and place on a platter rest for 15 minutes
Take out ribs from foil and serve.

Bradley Maple Cure Smoked Salmon

Servings: 6
Cooking Time: 1 Hour And 30 Minutes
Ingredients:

- 1 large sized salmon fillet
- 1 quart of water
- ½ a cup of pickling and canning salt
- ½ a cup of maple syrup
- ¼ cup of dark rum
- ¼ cup of lemon juice
- 10 whole cloves
- 10 whole allspice berries
- 1 bay leaf

Directions:
1. Take a medium sized bowl and add the brine ingredients. Mix them well. Place the salmon fillet in a cover with brine. Cover it up and let it refrigerate for about 2 hours. Remove the Salmon and pat dry then air dry for 1 hour. Preheat your smoker to a temperature of 180 degrees Fahrenheit and add Bradley Maple-Flavored briquettes. Smoke the salmon for about 1 and a ½ hour.

Smoked Soy Sauce

Servings: 1
Cooking Time: 1 Hour
Ingredients:
- 100ml soy sauce
- Bradley flavor bisquettes cherry

Directions:
1. Put soy sauce in a heat-resistant bowl, large-mouth.
2. Smoke in a smoker at 158-176F for about 1 hour. Stir a few times.
3. Remove and cool then put in a bottle. Let sit for one day.
4. Serve and enjoy!

Barbecue Pork Belly

Servings: 6
Cooking Time: 3 Hours
Ingredients:
- 3 lb. pork belly
- Salt and pepper to taste
- Barbecue dry rub

Directions:
1. Preheat your Pit Boss wood pellet grill to 275 degrees F for 15 minutes while the lid is closed.
2. Sprinkle all sides of pork belly with salt, pepper and dry rub.
3. Cook for 3 hours.
4. Let rest for 10 minutes before slicing and serving.
5. Tips: You can also coat with barbecue sauce before serving.

Ancho-dusted Jícama Sticks With Lime

Servings: 8
Cooking Time: 30 Minutes
Ingredients:
- 1/2-pound jícama, trimmed and peeled
- 2 tablespoons good-quality olive oil
- 2 teaspoons ancho chile powder
- Salt
- 1 lime, cut into wedges

Directions:

1. Start the coals or heat the gas grill for medium-high direct cooking. Make sure the grates are clean.
2. Cut the jícama into ½-inch slices. Brush the slices on both sides with the olive oil. Put the slices on the grill directly over the fire. Close the lid and cook, turning once, until they develop grill marks, 7 to 10 minutes per side.
3. Transfer the jícama to a cutting board and cut the slices into ½-inch-wide sticks. Put on a serving platter and sprinkle with the ancho powder and salt to taste, turning them to coat evenly. Squeeze the lime wedges over them, again turning to coat evenly, and serve.

Grapefruit Juice Marinade

Servings: 3
Cooking Time: 1hours 10 Minutes
Ingredients:
- 1/2 reduced-sodium soy sauce
- cups grapefruit juice, unsweetened
- 1-1/2 lb. Chicken, bone and skin removed
- 1/4 brown sugar

Directions:
1. Thoroughly mix all your ingredients in a large bowl.
2. Add the chicken and allow it to marinate for 2-3 hours before grilling.

Lamb Shanks, Smoke-braised

Servings: 2
Cooking Time: 5 Hours 20 Minutes
Ingredients:
- 1/2 cup of brown sugar
- 2 cups of water
- 4 strips of orange
- 2 cinnamon sticks
- 3 whole of star anise
- 1/2 cup of soy sauce
- 2 shank of lamb
- 1/2 cup of rice wine
- 3 Tbsp of sesame oil, Asian

Directions:
1. Put the lamb shank on an aluminum foil paper.
2. In a bowl, mix the sesame oil, water, soy sauce, and brown sugar in a bowl until the sugar dissolves. Add the cinnamon stick, orange zest, and star anise to the bowl. Pour the mixture on the lamb.
3. Preheat the grill for 15 minutes at 250°F. Use alder wood pellets
4. Place the lamb shank on the cooking grates with the foil. Smoke the lamb for 5 hours, until it is brown.
5. Remove the lamb from the smoker and place it on a board to trim off excess fat. Serve immediately.

Grilled Eggplant With Pine Nuts

Servings: 8
Cooking Time: 20 Minutes
Ingredients:
- 1/3 cup of fresh lemon juice
- 1/4 cup of pine nuts
- 2 medium of eggplants
- 2 cloves of garlic
- 3 Tbsp of fresh parsley, chopped
- 2 tomatoes
- 1-1/2 tsp of salt
- Squares of flatbread
- Freshly ground black pepper to taste
- 1/2 cup of olive oil
- 1/4 cup of chopped scallion

Directions:
1. Set the grill for direct cooking at 250°F. Use cherry woo pellets for a sweet fruity flavor.
2. Perforate eggplants with a fork and place it on hot cooking grates. Flip periodically to ensure both sides are grilled. Do this for 10 minutes.
3. Wrap scorched eggplants in aluminum foil and place the on the cooking grids. Cook until eggplants become soft.
4. Pierce tomatoes with a skewer and arrange on the grate Grill until skin wrinkles.
5. Peel off the scorched skin of the eggplants and put then a bowl. Add the grilled tomatoes to the bowl and mash together with a fork
6. To the bowl containing the mashed eggplant and tomat add the pepper, salt, pine nuts, lemon juice, oil, and garlic. M ingredients thoroughly.
7. Sprinkle scallions and parsley over the mixture. Serve i immediately with flatbread.

Baked Breakfast Casserole

Servings: 8
Cooking Time: 1 Hour
Ingredients:
- 6 bread slices, cut into cubes
- 6 eggs
- 3/4 teaspoon ground mustard
- 1 cup milk
- Salt and pepper to taste
- 1 onion, chopped
- 1 bell pepper, chopped
- 6 ounces chorizo
- 6 ounces ground turkey
- 1 cup baby spinach
- 4 slices bacon, cooked crispy and chopped into bits
- 1 cup Swiss cheese, grated
- 2 cups cheddar cheese, grated

Directions:
1. Set the Pit Boss wood pellet grill to 350 degrees F.
2. Preheat for 15 minutes while the lid is closed.
3. Spray your baking pan with oil.
4. Arrange the bread cubes in the baking pan.
5. Beat the eggs in a bowl.
6. Stir in the mustard, milk, salt and pepper.
7. Spray your pan with oil.
8. Place the pan over medium heat.
9. Cook the onion, bell pepper, ground turkey and chorizo
10. Stir in the spinach.
11. Cook for 1 minute.
12. Place the meat mixture on top of the bread.
13. Pour egg mixture on top.
14. Sprinkle cheeses on top.
15. Repeat layers.
16. Cover the baking pan with foil.
17. Bake in the wood pellet grill for 40 minutes.
18. Remove cover and bake for another 10 minutes.

Tips: You can also cook ground turkey and chorizo in ⌐ance to less preparation time.

Wood-fired Burger Seasoning

▸vings: 2
▸king Time:5 Minutes
▸redients:
  1 teaspoon coarse kosher salt
  1 teaspoon garlic powder
  1 teaspoon dried minced onion
  1 teaspoon onion powder
  1 teaspoon freshly ground black pepper
  ½ teaspoon sweet paprika
  ¼ teaspoon mustard powder
  ¼ teaspoon celery seed
▸ections:
  In a small airtight container or zip-top bag, combine the ⌐, garlic powder, minced onion, onion powder, black pepper, ⌐et paprika, mustard powder, and celery seed.
  Close the container and shake to mix. Unused burger ⌐ke will keep in an airtight container for months.

⌐ Roast And Yorkshire Pudding With Bacon And Rosemary Jus

▸vings: 10
▸king Time: 45 Minutes
▸redients:
  1 Tbsp of black pepper
  1 bacon with rosemary jus
  3 Tbsp of thyme, preferably fresh leaves
  6 cloves of garlic, already peeled
  2-1/2 Tbsp of salt
  2-1/2 Tbsp of olive oil
  1 of 5-bone of rib-eye roast, standing
  1 scallion with parmesan Yorkshire pudding
▸ections:
  Put garlic inside a running food processor. Scrape it into a ▸vl, mix with pepper, salt, thyme, and oil until a paste is ⌐ned.
  Preheat the grill for direct cooking at 350°F. Use mesquite ⌐od pellets for a distinctive, strong woody taste.
  Press the herb mixture into the sliced ribs. Put the ribs in ⌐ roasting pan and roast both sides for 20 minutes or until ⌐ernal temperature reads 145°F.
  Allow the ribs to rest for 10 minutes before serving. After ⌐n, serve with Yorkshire pudding.

All-purpose Dry Rub

▸vings: 2 And ½ Cups
▸king Time:5 Minutes
▸redients:
  ½ cup paprika, or 1/3 cup smoked paprika
  ¼ cup kosher salt
  ¼ cup freshly ground black pepper
  ¼ cup brown sugar
  ¼ cup chile powder
  3 tablespoons ground cumin
  2 tablespoons ground coriander
  1 tablespoon cayenne pepper, or to taste

Directions:
1.   Combine all ingredients in a bowl and mix well with a fork to break up the sugar and combine the spices. Mixture will keep in an airtight container, out of the light, for a few months.

Grilled Chicken With Lemon & Cumin

Servings: 4
Cooking Time: 10 Minutes
Ingredients:
- 4 chicken breast fillets
- 2 teaspoons olive oil
- 4 teaspoons ground cumin
- 2 tablespoons lemon juice
- 1 tablespoon lime juice
- Salt and pepper to taste

Directions:
1.   Coat the chicken breast with oil.
2.   In a bowl, mix the rest of the ingredients.
3.   Brush the chicken breast with the lemon and cumin mixture.
4.   Cover and marinate in the refrigerator for 3 hours.
5.   Set your Pit Boss wood pellet grill to 350 degrees F.
6.   Preheat for 15 minutes while the lid is closed.
7.   Grill the chicken for 5 minutes per side.
8.   Let rest for 5 minutes before serving.
9.   Tips: You can also pound the chicken breast with a meat mallet before preparing it.

Grilled Cocoa Steak

Servings: 8
Cooking Time: 10 Minutes
Ingredients:
- 1 tablespoon cocoa powder
- 1 1/2 tablespoons brown sugar
- 1 teaspoon chipotle chili powder
- 2 teaspoons chili powder
- 1/2 teaspoon onion powder
- 1/2 teaspoon garlic powder
- 1 tablespoon smoked paprika
- 1 tablespoon ground cumin
- Salt and pepper to taste
- 2 lb. flank steak
- Olive oil

Directions:
1.   Make the dry rub by mixing the cocoa powder, sugar, spices, salt and pepper.
2.   Coat the flank steak with olive oil.
3.   Sprinkle dry rub on both sides.
4.   Preheat your Pit Boss wood pellet grill to high for 15 minutes while the lid is closed.
5.   Grill the steak for 5 minutes per side.
6.   Let rest for 10 minutes before slicing and serving.
7.   Tips: Slice against the grain after a few minutes of resting.

Smoked Deviled Eggs

Servings: 12
Cooking Time: 45 Minutes
Ingredients:
- 12 hard-boiled eggs, peeled and sliced in half

- 2 jalapeño peppers
- 2 slices bacon, cooked crisp and chopped
- 1/2 cup mayonnaise
- 2 teaspoon white vinegar
- 2 teaspoon mustard
- 1/2 teaspoon chili powder
- 1/2 teaspoon paprika
- Salt to taste
- Pinch paprika
- Chopped chives

Directions:
1. Set the Pit Boss wood pellet grill to 180 degrees F.
2. Preheat for 15 minutes while the lid is closed.
3. Smoke the eggs and peppers for 45 minutes.
4. Transfer to a plate.
5. Scoop out the egg yolks and place in a bowl.
6. Stir in the rest of the ingredients.
7. Mash the eggs and mix well.
8. Scoop the egg mixture on top of the egg whites.
9. Serve with the roasted peppers.
10. Tips: Add vinegar to your water when boiling the eggs to make them easier to peel.

Slum Dunk Brisket

Servings: 9
Cooking Time: 9 Hours
Ingredients:
- 1/4 cup of pickle juice, dill
- kosher or sea salt
- barbecue sauce
- 1/4 cup of mustard, Dijon
- 6 pounds of brisket
- 6 strips of bacon, artisanal
- Black pepper

Directions:
1. Preheat the grill for 15 minutes at 250°F. Use apple wood pellets for a distinctive, strong woody taste.
2. Mix the pickle juice and mustard in a bowl. Trim off the fats on the brisket, then rub the mustard mixture on it—season with salt and pepper. Put bacon on the brisket.
3. Place the coated brisket and bacon directly on the grates, close the steel construction, and smoke for 9 hours or until internal temperature reads 160°F.
4. Remove the brisket from the grill when it ready. Allow it to rest for an hour before carving and slicing.

Sweet Sensation Pork Meat

Servings: 3
Cooking Time: 3 Hours
Ingredients:
- 2 tsp of nutmeg, ground
- 1/4 cup of allspice
- 2 tsp of thyme, dried
- 1/4 cup of brown sugar
- 2 pounds of pork
- 2 tsp of cinnamon, ground
- 2 Tbsp of salt, kosher or sea

Directions:
1. Preheat the grill for 15 minutes at 225°F. Use hickory wood pellets

2. Combine all the ingredients (except pork) in a bowl. Mi thoroughly.
3. Slice the sides of the pork meat in 4-5 places. Put some the ingredients into the slices and rub the rest over the pork
4. Place the pork on the preheated grill and smoke for 3 hours or until internal temperature reads 145°F.
5. Allow it to rest before serving.

Smoked Bacon

Servings: 6
Cooking Time: 30 Minutes
Ingredients:
- 1-pound thick cut bacon

Directions:
1. Preheat your wood pellet grill to 375 degrees.
2. Line a huge baking sheet. Place a single layer of thick-c bacon on it.
3. Bake for 20 minutes and then flip it to the other side.
4. Cook for another 10 minutes or until the bacon is crisp
5. Take it out and enjoy your tasty grilled bacon.

Grilled Venison Kebab

Servings: 4
Cooking Time: 15 Minutes
Ingredients:
- 1 venison, sliced into cubes
- 2 red onions, sliced into wedges
- 2 red bell pepper, sliced into 2
- 2 yellow bell pepper, sliced into 2
- Olive oil
- Salt and pepper to taste
- 2 tablespoons lemon juice
- 1 1/2 tablespoons fresh mint leaves, chopped
- 1 1/2 tablespoons parsley, chopped

Directions:
1. Add the venison chunks, onion and bell peppers in a bo
2. Coat with olive oil and season with salt and pepper.
3. Thread onto skewers alternately.
4. In another bowl, mix lemon juice, mint leaves and pars Set aside.
5. Set the Pit Boss wood pellet grill to high.
6. Preheat while the lid is closed for 10 minutes.
7. Grill the kebabs for 7 to 8 minutes per side.
8. Brush with the lemon mixture in the last minute of cooking.
9. Tips: If using wooden skewers, soak first in water befo using.

Roasted Lamb

Servings: 8
Cooking Time: 1 Hour And 30 Minutes
Ingredients:
- 1 leg of lamb
- 8 cloves garlic, minced
- 1 sprig oregano, chopped
- 2 sprigs rosemary, chopped
- 6 tablespoons olive oil
- 2 tablespoons lemon juice
- Salt and pepper to taste

rections:

Make slits on the lamb leg.
Combine the garlic and herbs.
Mash to form a paste.
Stuff mixture inside the slits.
Add the lamb leg to a roasting pan.
Drizzle it with olive oil and lemon juice.
Cover with foil and refrigerate for 10 hours.
When ready to cook, sprinkle lamb with salt and pepper.
Set the Pit Boss wood pellet grill to 400 degrees F.
Preheat for 15 minutes while the lid is closed.
Open the lid and let it establish fire for 5 minutes.
Roast the leg of lamb for 30 minutes.
Reduce temperature to 350 degrees F and cook for 1 hour.
Let rest before slicing and serving.
Tips: You can also use a food processor to create a paste
m the garlic and herbs.

Ginger Dipping Sauce

vings: 4
king Time: 10 Minutes
gredients:

6 tablespoons ponzu sauce
2 tablespoons scallions
2 tsp ginger
2 tsp mirin
1 tsp sesame oil
¼ tsp salt

rections:

In a blender place all ingredients and blend until smooth
Pour sauce in a bowl and serve

Compound Butter

vings: 1/2 Cup
king Time:10 Minutes
gredients:

8 tablespoons unsalted butter
1 tablespoon herb leaves, minced
1 small shallot, peeled and minced
2 teaspoons freshly squeezed lemon or lime juice
Splash Champagne or white-wine vinegar

rections:

Put the butter on a cutting board and, using a fork, cut the
er ingredients into it until the butter is creamy and smooth.
ape the butter together with a chef's knife, and form it into
ugh log. If making ahead of time, roll it tightly in a sheet of
stic wrap and refrigerate or freeze until ready to use.

Smoked Chicken With Perfect Poultry Rub

vings: 2
king Time: 3 Hours 15 Minutes
gredients:

2 Tbsp of onion, powder
1/4 cup of black pepper, freshly ground
2 Tbsp of dry mustard
3/4 cup of paprika
4pound chicken
3 lemon
2 tsp of cayenne

- 1/4 cup of sugar
- 1/4 cup of celery salt

Directions:
1. In a bowl, mix the onion powder, paprika, black pepper, dry mustard, cayenne, sugar, celery, salt, and 2 lemons.
2. Add your chicken to the rub and slice some parts so that the ingredients will find their way in.
3. Preheat the grill for 15 minutes at 225°F. Use apple wood pellets for a distinctive, strong woody taste.
4. Place the coated chicken on the preheated grill and smoke for 3 hours or until internal temperature reads 160°F.
5. Allow chicken to cool, then serve.

Barbecue Pulled Pork

Servings: 12
Cooking Time: 8 Hours
Ingredients:
- 2 tablespoons mayonnaise
- 2 tablespoons mustard
- 1 tablespoon ketchup
- 1/2 teaspoon brown sugar
- 2 teaspoons pickle relish
- 10 lb. pork shoulder
- 6 oz. spicy dry rub
- 8 oz. barbecue sauce

Directions:
1. Set the Pit Boss wood pellet grill to smoke.
2. Preheat it for 10 minutes while the lid is closed.
3. Mix the mayo, mustard, ketchup, sugar, and pickles in a bowl and set aside.
4. Sprinkle all sides of the pork shoulder with the dry rub.
5. Marinate for 45 minutes.
6. Open the lid of the wood pellet grill and let fire establish for 5 minutes.
7. Set it to 225 degrees F.
8. Add the pork shoulder and smoke for 3 hours.
9. Increase temperature to 275 degrees F.
10. Roast for 5 hours.
11. Use a fork to shred the meat off.
12. Transfer to a bowl and stir in the reserved sauce and barbecue sauce.
13. Tips: Use a foil pan for smoking the pork shoulder.

Mutton Barbecued And Black Dip

Servings:7
Cooking Time: 7 Hours 20 Minutes
Ingredients:
- Kosher or sea salt
- 7 hamburger buns
- 2 Tbsp of butter
- Sliced dill pickle
- 6 pounds of lamb shoulder
- Black dip

Directions:
1. Season lamb with salt and pepper
2. Preheat the grill for 15 minutes at 250°F. Use pecan wood pellets.
3. Put the lamb inside black dip, then transfer it to the smoking rack. Smoke the lamb for 7 hours.
4. Put the already smoked lamb on a dish or board. Allow it to rest for 10 minutes. Remove the fat lumps.

5. Put butter on the buns, pile the lamb on the buns, and add pickle slices.
6. Serve it with black dip.

Fire And Ice Smoked Salmon

Servings: 7
Cooking Time: 50 Minutes
Ingredients:
- ½ a cup of brown sugar
- 2 tablespoons of salt
- 2 tablespoon of crushed red pepper flakes
- Mint leaves
- ¼ cup of brandy
- 1 (4 pounds) salmon side with bones removed
- 2 cups of alder wood chips, soaked up in water

Directions:
1. Take a medium bowl and mix in the brown sugar, crushed red pepper flakes, salt, mint leaves and brandy until a paste form. Coat the paste on all sides of the salmon and wrap the Salmon up in plastic wrap.
2. Let it refrigerate for at least 4 hours or overnight. Preheat your smoker to high heat and oil up the grate. Add soaked alder chips to your heat box and wait until smoke starts to appear.
3. Turn the heat to your lowest setting and place the salmon on the grate. Lock up the lid and let your Salmon smoke for about 45 minutes.

Smoked Turkey

Servings: 6
Cooking Time: 4 Hours And 30 Minutes
Ingredients:
- 2 gallons of water, divided
- 2 cups of sugar
- 2 cups salt
- Ice cubes
- 1 whole turkey
- ½ cup kosher salt
- ½ cup black pepper
- 3 sticks butter, sliced

Directions:
1. Add one-quart water to a pot over medium heat.
2. Stir in the 2 cups each of sugar and salt.
3. Bring to a boil.
4. Remove from heat and let cool.
5. Add ice and the remaining water.
6. Stir to cool.
7. Add the turkey to the brine.
8. Cover and refrigerate for 24 hours.
9. Rinse the turkey and dry with paper towels.
10. Season with salt and pepper.
11. Preheat the Pit Boss wood pellet grill to 180 degrees F for 15 minutes while the lid is closed.
12. Smoke the turkey for 2 hours.
13. Increase temperature to 225 degrees. Smoke for another 1 hour.
14. Increase temperature to 325 degrees. Smoke for 30 minutes.
15. Place the turkey on top of a foil sheet.
16. Add butter on top of the turkey.
17. Cover the turkey with foil.
18. Reduce temperature to 165 degrees F.
19. Cook on the grill for 1 hour.

Fall Season Apple Pie

Servings: 8
Cooking Time: 1 Hour
Ingredients:
- 8 C. apples, peeled, cored and sliced thinly
- ¾ C. sugar
- 1 tbsp. fresh lemon juice
- 1 tsp. ground cinnamon
- ¼ tsp. ground nutmeg
- 2 whole frozen pie crusts, thawed
- ¼ C. apple jelly
- 2 tbsp. apple juice
- 2 tbsp. heavy whipping cream

Directions:
1. Set the temperature of Pit Boss Grill to 375 degrees F a preheat with closed lid for 15 minutes.
2. In a bowl, add the apples, sugar, lemon juice, flour, cinnamon, and nutmeg and mix well.
3. Roll the pie crust dough into two (11-inch) circles.
4. Arrange 1 dough circle into a 9-inch pie plate.
5. Spread the apple jelly over dough evenly and top with apple mixture.
6. Dampen the edges of dough crust with apple juice.
7. Cover with the top crust, pressing the edges together to seal.
8. Trim the pastry, and flute the edges.
9. With a sparing knife, make several small slits in the top crust.
10. Brush the top of the pie with the cream.
11. Place the pie pan onto the grill and cook for about 50-60 minutes.
12. Remove from the grill and place the pie onto a wire rack to cool slightly.
13. Serve warm.

Roasted Korean Short Ribs

Servings: 4
Cooking Time: 8 Hours
Ingredients:
- 1 cup beef stock
- 1/2 cup soy sauce
- 3 cloves garlic, peeled
- 1 tablespoon ginger, minced
- 1 tablespoon beef and brisket dry rub
- 2 tablespoons brown sugar
- 1 tablespoon hot sauce
- 4 beef short ribs

Directions:
1. In a bowl, mix all the ingredients except the short ribs.
2. Add the ribs to a baking pan.
3. Pour the mixture on top of the ribs.
4. Cover and marinate in the refrigerator for 4 hours.
5. Set your wood pellet grill to 250 degrees F.
6. Roast the ribs for 4 hours.

Barbecue Hot Dog

vings: 6

king Time: 10 Minutes

redients:

    6 hot dogs
    ½ cup barbecue sauce
    6 hot dog buns
    1 onion, chopped
    ½ cup cheddar cheese, shredded

ections:

Set the Pit Boss grill to 450 degrees F.

Preheat while the lid is closed for 10 minutes.

Grill the hot dogs for 5 minutes per side.

Brush the hot dogs with the barbecue sauce.

Serve in the hot dog buns topped with the onion and ese.

Tips: Use whole-wheat hot dog buns.

Smoked Tomato Cream Sauce

vings: 1

king Time: 1 Hour 20 Minutes

redients:

    1 lb beefsteak tomatoes, fresh and quartered
    1-1/2 tbsp olive oil
    Black pepper, freshly ground
    Salt, kosher
    1/2 cup yellow onions, chopped
    1 tbsp tomato paste
    2 tbsp minced garlic
    Pinch cayenne
    1/2 cup chicken stock
    1/2 cup heavy cream

ections:

Prepare your smoker using directions from the nufacturer.

Toss tomatoes and 1 tbsp oil in a bowl, mixing, then son with pepper and salt.

Smoke the tomatoes placed on a smoker rack for about 30 utes. Remove and set aside reserving tomato juices.

Heat 1/2 tbsp oil in a saucepan over high-medium heat.

Add onion and cook for about 3-4 minutes. Add tomato te and garlic then cook for an additional 1 minute.

Add smoked tomatoes, cayenne, tomato juices, pepper, salt then cook for about 3-4 minutes. Stir often.

Add chicken stock and boil for about 25-30 minutes under ntle simmer. Stir often.

Place the mixture in a blender and puree until smooth.

w squeeze the mixture through a sieve, fine-mesh, to :ard solids and release the juices,

Transfer the sauce in a saucepan, small, and add the am.

Simmer for close to 6 minutes over low-medium heat il thickened slightly. Season with pepper and salt.

Serve warm with risotto cakes.

Smoked Rack Of Lamb

vings: 6

king Time: 4 To 6 Hours

redients:

    1 (2-pound) rack of lamb
    1 batch Rosemary-Garlic Lamb Seasoning

Directions:

1. Supply your smoker with wood pellets and follow the manufacturer's specific start-up procedure. Preheat the grill, with the lid closed, to 225°F.

2. Using a boning knife, score the bottom fat portion of the rib meat.

3. Using your hands, rub the rack of lamb all over with the seasoning, making sure it penetrates into the scored fat.

4. Place the rack directly on the grill grate, fat-side up, and smoke until its internal temperature reaches 145°F.

5. Remove the rack from the grill and let it rest for 20 to 30 minutes, before slicing it into individual ribs to serve.

Cherry Smoked Strip Steak

Servings: 3

Cooking Time: 70 Minutes

Ingredients:

- Kosher or sea salt
- Olive oil
- Black pepper
- 1-1/2 pound of rib steak

Directions:

1. Preheat the grill for 15 minutes at 225°F. Use maple wood pellets.

2. Season the steak with salt and black pepper.

3. Place the seasoned steak directly on the grates and smoke for 2 hours or until internal temperature reads 160°F.

4. After smoking, rub olive oil on the steak then return it to the grates of the grill. Increase the temperature to 300°F and grill it for another 10 minutes.

5. Serve it hot.

Carrot Strawberry Smoothie

Servings: 2

Cooking Time: 5 Minutes

Ingredients:

- 1/3 cup Bell Pepper, diced
- 1 cup Carrot Juice, chilled
- 1 cup mango, diced
- 1 cup Strawberries, unsweetened and frozen

Directions:

1. To start with, place strawberries, bell pepper, and mango in the blender pitcher.

2. After that, pulse it a few times.

3. Next, pour the carrot juice into it.

4. Finally, press the 'smoothie' button.

Monster Smoked Pork Chops

Servings: 4

Cooking Time: 2 Hours 30 Minutes

Ingredients:

- 1/3 cup of sugar
- 4 tsp of pink curing salt
- Vegetable oil
- 1 cup of kosher or sea salt
- 1-1/4 pound pork chops
- 1/4 hot water
- 1/4 cold water

Directions:

1. Put the pork on a big baking pan. Mix the salt, curing salt, sugar, and hot water in a bowl. Add the pork to the mixture, and refrigerate for 12 hours.
2. Preheat the grill for 15 minutes at 250°F. Use pecan wood pellets
3. Bring the pork out and remove the brine from the pork.
4. Smoke the pork for about two and a half hours until it is done or until the internal temperature reads 145°F.
5. Brush olive oil all over the sides of the pork. Then increase the temperature of the cooker to 300°F and grill the pork chop for another 5 minutes until it is done.

Mushroom With Fennel Dressed With Roasted Chicken

Servings: 4
Cooking Time: 22 Hours 50 Minutes
Ingredients:
- 8 sun-dried tomatoes, oil-packed
- 4pound chicken
- Salt with black pepper
- 1-1/2 Tbsp of thyme
- 10 ounces of mushroom, preferably white button
- 1/2 pound of crusty bread
- 4 cloves of garlic, preferably smashed
- 1 Tbsp of balsamic vinegar
- 2 Tbsp of butter without salt.
- 1 fennel bulb

Directions:
1. Rub black pepper and salt all over the chicken, including cavities. Keep in the refrigerator for 22 hours.
2. Remove chicken from the refrigerator and rub with butter. In a big bowl, mix sun-dried tomato, mushroom, fennel, garlic, thyme, salt, and pepper. Then put the mixture into the roasting pan along with the chicken.
3. Roast the chicken on the preheated grill for 35 minutes. Flip the chicken with a tong and roast for another 15 minutes, or until the internal temperature of the thigh reads between 165-170F.

Cajun Shrimp

Servings: 4
Cooking Time: 10 Minutes
Ingredients:
- 4 tablespoon olive oil
- 1 tablespoon lemon juice
- 2 cloves garlic, minced
- 1 tablespoon Cajun rub
- Salt to taste
- 2 lb. shrimp, peeled and deveined

Directions:
1. Mix all the ingredients in a bowl.
2. Cover the bowl and refrigerate for 3 hours.
3. Set the Pit Boss grill to high and preheat for 15 minutes while the lid is closed.
4. Thread the shrimp onto skewers.
5. Grill the shrimp for 4 minutes per side.
6. Tips: If using wooden skewers, soak first in water for 15 minutes before using.

Wood Pellet Spicy Brisket

Servings: 10
Cooking Time: 9 Hours
Ingredients:
- 2 tbsp garlic powder
- 2 tbsp onion powder
- 2 tbsp paprika
- 2 tbsp chili powder
- 1/3 cup salt
- 1/3 cup black pepper
- 12 lb whole packer brisket, trimmed
- 1-1/2 cup beef broth

Directions:
1. Set your wood pellet temperature to 225°F. Let prehea for 15 minutes with the lid closed.
2. Meanwhile, mix garlic, onion, paprika, chili, salt, and pepper in a mixing bowl.
3. the brisket generously on all sides.
4. Place the meat on the grill with the fat side down and le cool until the internal temperature reaches 160°F.
5. Remove the meat from the grill and double wrap it wit foil. Return it to the grill and cook until the internal temperature reaches 204°F.
6. Remove from grill, unwrap the brisket and let rest for 1 minutes.
7. Slice and serve.

Savory Applesauce On The Grill

Servings: 2
Cooking Time: 45 Minutes
Ingredients:
- 1½ pounds whole apples
- Salt

Directions:
1. Start the coals or heat a gas grill for medium direct cooking. Make sure the grates are clean.
2. Put the apples on the grill directly over the fire. Close t lid and cook until the fruit feels soft when gently squeezed with tongs, 10 to 20 minutes total, depending on their size. Transfer to a cutting board and let sit until cool enough to touch.
3. Cut the flesh from around the core of each apple; disca the cores. Put the chunks in a blender or food processor and process until smooth, or put them in a bowl and purée with immersion blender until as chunky or smooth as you like. A a generous pinch of salt, then taste and adjust the seasoning Serve or refrigerate in an airtight container for up to 3 days

Grilled Bacon Dog

Servings: 4 To 6
Cooking Time: 25 Minutes
Ingredients:
- 16 Hot Dogs
- 16 Slices Bacon, sliced
- 2 Onion, sliced
- 16 hot dog buns
- As Needed The Ultimate BBQ Sauce
- As Needed Cheese

Directions:
1. When ready to cook, set the Pit Boss to 375°F and preh lid closed for 15 minutes.

Wrap bacon strips around the hot dogs, and grill directly the grill grate for 10 minutes each side. Grill onions at the me time as the hot dogs, and cook for 10 -15 minutes.

Open hot dog buns and spread BBQ sauce, the grilled hot gs, cheese sauce and grilled onions. Top with vegetables. ve, enjoy!

Fennel And Almonds Sauce

vings: 4
king Time: 10 Minutes
redients:
- 1 cup fennel bulb
- 1 cup olive oil
- 1 cup almonds
- 1 cup fennel fronds

rections:
- In a blender place all ingredients and blend until smooth
- Pour sauce in a bowl and serve

Roasted Mustard Steak

vings: 8
king Time: 4 Hours
redients:
- 1 cup mustard
- 2 tablespoon garlic, crushed
- Salt and pepper to taste
- 1 prime rib roast

rections:
- In a bowl, mix the mustard, garlic, salt, and pepper.
- Rub the roast with this mixture.
- Preheat your wooden pellet grill.
- Set it to 400 degrees F.
- Add the roast on the grill.
- Seal the lid.
- Roast for 45 minutes.
- Reduce temperature to 325 degrees F.
- Cook for 2 hours and 30 minutes.
- Let rest for 15 minutes before slicing and serving.

Roast Chicken With Caramelized Shallots And Fingerling Potatoes

vings: 4
king Time: 50 Minutes
redients:
- 4 peeled shallots
- 2 Tbsp of unsalted butter
- 1-1/2 of fingerling potatoes
- 1 Tbsp of sherry vinegar
- 1 of 4 pounds of chicken
- 2 Tbsp of rosemary, fresh
- Kosher salt and black pepper

rections:
Rub black pepper and salt all over the chicken, including ities. Put the chicken on a rack and keep inside the rigerator for 24 hours. However, if the chicken has been ned, you can skip this step and move on to the roasting.

Preheat the grill for direct cooking at 420°F (High). Use ple wood pellets for a strong, woody taste.

3. Mix the butter, and 1 Tbsp of rosemary inside a bowl. Rub the mixture all over the chicken. In another bowl, mix the pepper, rosemary, potato, and shallots. Pour the mixture into the roasting pan and place the chicken on it.
4. Roast the chicken on the preheated grill for 35 minutes. Flip the chicken and roast for another 15 minutes, or until the internal temperature of the thigh reads between 165-170F.
5. Serve after cooling for 10 minutes.

Take And Bake Pepperoni Pizza

Servings: 4
Cooking Time: 15 Minutes
Ingredients:
- Take and bake pizza bread
- Pepperoni toppings of your choice

Directions:
1. Set the wood pellet smoker-grill to indirect cooking at 400F
2. If refrigerated, remove pizza bread from the refrigerator 20-30 minutes before baking. Add the toppings and place the bread directly on the cooking grates for a crispier crust.
3. Bake for 10-15 minutes. Remove pizza with a pizza paddle, and allow to cool before cutting into sclices and serving.

Smoked Cherry Bbq Sauce

Servings: 2
Cooking Time: 1 Hour
Ingredients:
- 2 lb dark sweet cherries, pitted
- 1 large chopped onion
- 1/2 tbsp red pepper flakes, crushed
- 1 tbsp kosher salt or to taste
- 1/2 tbsp ginger, ground
- 1/2 tbsp black pepper
- 1/2 tbsp cumin
- 1/2 tbsp cayenne pepper
- 1 tbsp onion powder
- 1 tbsp garlic powder
- 1 tbsp smoked paprika
- 2 chopped garlic cloves
- 1/2 cup pinot noir
- 2 tbsp yellow mustard
- 1-1/2 cups ketchup
- 2 tbsp balsamic vinegar
- 1/3 cup apple cider vinegar
- 2 tbsp dark soy sauce
- 1 tbsp liquid smoke
- 1/4 cup Worcestershire sauce
- 1 tbsp hatch chile powder
- 3 tbsp honey
- 1 cup brown sugar
- 3 tbsp molasses

Directions:
1. Preheat your smoker to 250F.
2. Place cherries in a baking dish, medium, and smoke for about 2 hours.
3. Saute onions and red pepper flakes in a pot, large, with 2 tbsp oil for about 4 minutes until softened.
4. Add salt and cook for an additional 1 minute.

5. Add ginger, black pepper, cumin, onion powder, garlic powder, and paprika then drizzle with oil and cook for about 1 minute until fragrant and spices bloom.
6. Stir in garlic and cook for about 30 seconds.
7. Pour in pinot noir scraping up for 1 minute for any bits stuck to your pan bottom.
8. Add yellow mustard, ketchup, balsamic vinegar, apple cider vinegar, dark soy sauce, liquid smoke, and Worcestershire sauce. Stir to combine.
9. Add cherries and simmer for about 10 minutes.
10. Add honey, brown sugar, and molasses and stir until combined. Simmer for about 30-45 minutes over low heat until your own liking.
11. Place everything into a blender and process until a smooth sauce.
12. Enjoy with favorite veggies or protein. You can refrigerate in jars for up to a month.

Smoked Pork Shoulder

Servings: 8
Cooking Time: 7 Hours
Ingredients:
- 2 tsp of garlic powder
- 4 tsp of salt, either sea and kosher
- 2 tsp of onion powder
- 4 tsp of black pepper
- 2 tsp of garlic
- 6 pounds of pork shoulder
- 1 tsp of cayenne pepper
- Carolina vinegar sauce
- 11 sesame seed buns, already split
- 3 Tbsp of melted butter.

Directions:
1. Preheat the grill for 15 minutes at 245°F. Use apple wood pellets for a distinctive, strong woody taste.
2. Mix onion powder, pepper, garlic powder, cayenne, salt, and black pepper in a bowl. Use your fingers to rub the mixture on the meat.
3. Place the pork shoulder inside the grill and smoke for 7 hours.
4. Slice the pork, and the bones will remove effortlessly.
5. Put the shredded pork in a plate, add sauce and stir it together
6. Serve it with butter and toasted buns.

Smoked Tuna

Servings: 6
Cooking Time: 3 Hours
Ingredients:
- 2 cups water
- 1 cup brown sugar
- 1 cup salt
- 1 tablespoon lemon zest
- 6 tuna fillets

Directions:
1. Mix water, brown sugar, salt and lemon zest in a bowl.
2. Coat the tuna fillets with the mixture.
3. Refrigerate for 6 hours.
4. Rinse the tuna and pat dry with paper towels.
5. Preheat the Pit Boss wood pellet grill to 180 degrees F for 15 minutes while the lid is closed.
6. Smoke the tuna for 3 hours.
7. Tips: You can also soak tuna in the brine for 24 hours.

Smoked Burgers

Servings: 4
Cooking Time: 45 Minutes
Ingredients:
- 1 pound ground beef
- 1 egg
- Wood-Fired Burger Seasoning

Directions:
1. Supply your Pit Boss with wood pellets and follow the start-up procedure. Preheat the grill, with the lid closed, to 180°F.
2. In a medium bowl, thoroughly mix together the ground beef and egg. Divide the meat into 4 portions and shape each into a patty. Season the patties with the burger shake.
3. Place the burgers directly on the grill grate and smoke f 30 minutes.
4. Increase the grill's temperature to 400°F and continue t cook the burgers until their internal temperature reaches 145°F. Remove the burgers from the grill and serve as you li

Cumin Salt

Servings: 1/4 Cup
Cooking Time: 5 Minutes
Ingredients:
- 1 teaspoon cumin seeds
- ¼ cup medium-coarse or flaky sea salt
- Pinch red pepper flakes (optional)
- Pinch cayenne or hot paprika (optional)

Directions:
1. Toast cumin seeds in a dry skillet over medium-high he until fragrant and lightly colored, about 1 minute.
2. Grind very coarsely in a mortar or spice mill.
3. Combine in a bowl with salt and stir together.
4. Add red pepper flakes or cayenne, if using.

Turkey Meatballs

Servings: 8
Cooking Time: 40 Minutes
Ingredients:
- 1 1/4 lb. ground turkey
- 1/2 cup breadcrumbs
- 1 egg, beaten
- 1/4 cup milk
- 1 teaspoon onion powder
- 1/4 cup Worcestershire sauce
- Pinch garlic salt
- Salt and pepper to taste
- 1 cup cranberry jam
- 1/2 cup orange marmalade
- 1/2 cup chicken broth

Directions:
1. In a large bowl, mix the ground turkey, breadcrumbs, e milk, onion powder, Worcestershire sauce, garlic salt, salt a pepper.
2. Form meatballs from the mixture.

Preheat the Pit Boss wood pellet grill to 350 degrees F for ⌐minutes while the lid is closed.
Add the turkey meatballs to a baking pan.
Place the baking pan on the grill.
Cook for 20 minutes.
In a pan over medium heat, simmer the rest of the ⌐redients for 10 minutes.
Add the grilled meatballs to the pan.
Coat with the mixture.
Cook for 10 minutes.

Smoked Corn On The Cob

⌐vings: 4
⌐king Time: 1 Hour
⌐redients:
4 corn ears, husk removed
4 tbsp olive oil
Pepper and salt to taste
⌐ections:
Preheat your smoker to 225F.
Meanwhile, brush your corn with olive oil. Season with ⌐per and salt.
Place the corn on a smoker and smoke for about 1 hour ⌐minutes.
Remove from the smoker and serve.
Enjoy!

Sweet And Spicy Cinnamon Rub

⌐vings: 1/4 Cup
⌐king Time:5 Minutes
⌐redients:
2 tablespoons light brown sugar
1 teaspoon coarse kosher salt
1 teaspoon garlic powder
1 teaspoon onion powder
1 teaspoon sweet paprika
½ teaspoon freshly ground black pepper
½ teaspoon cayenne pepper
½ teaspoon dried oregano leaves
½ teaspoon ground ginger
½ teaspoon ground cumin
¼ teaspoon smoked paprika
¼ teaspoon ground cinnamon
¼ teaspoon ground coriander
¼ teaspoon chili powder
⌐ections:
In a small airtight container or zip-top bag, combine the ⌐wn sugar, salt, garlic powder, onion powder, sweet paprika, ⌐k pepper, cayenne, oregano, ginger, cumin, smoked ⌐rika, cinnamon, coriander, and chili powder.
Close the container and shake to mix. Unused rub will ⌐p in an airtight container for months.

Succulent Lamb Chops

⌐vings: 4 To 6
⌐king Time: 10 To 20 Minutes
⌐redients:
½ cup rice wine vinegar
1 teaspoon liquid smoke

- 2 tablespoons extra-virgin olive oil
- 2 tablespoons dried minced onion
- 1 tablespoon chopped fresh mint
- 8 (4-ounce) lamb chops
- ½ cup hot pepper jelly
- 1 tablespoon Sriracha
- 1 teaspoon salt
- 1 teaspoon freshly ground black pepper

Directions:
1. In a small bowl, whisk together the rice wine vinegar, liquid smoke, olive oil, minced onion, and mint. Place the lamb chops in an aluminum roasting pan. Pour the marinade over the meat, turning to coat thoroughly. Cover with plastic wrap and marinate in the refrigerator for 2 hours.
2. Supply your smoker with wood pellets and follow the manufacturer's specific start-up procedure. Preheat, with the lid closed, to 165°F, or the "Smoke" setting.
3. On the stove top, in a small saucepan over low heat, combine the hot pepper jelly and Sriracha and keep warm.
4. When ready to cook the chops, remove them from the marinade and pat dry. Discard the marinade.
5. Season the chops with the salt and pepper, then place them directly on the grill grate, close the lid, and smoke for 5 minutes to "breathe" some smoke into them.
6. Remove the chops from the grill. Increase the pellet cooker temperature to 450°F, or the "High" setting. Once the grill is up to temperature, place the chops on the grill and sear, cooking for 2 minutes per side to achieve medium-rare chops. A meat thermometer inserted in the thickest part of the meat should read 145°F. Continue grilling, if necessary, to your desired doneness.
7. Serve the chops with the warm Sriracha pepper jelly on the side.

Lobster Butter

Servings: 1/2 Cup
Cooking Time: 40 Minutes
Ingredients:
- Shells of cooked lobsters, crushed into small pieces
- 8 tablespoons (1 stick) unsalted butter per lobster

Directions:
1. Heat grill to 300 degrees. Put lobster shells on the largest sheet pan you can fit in the oven, and allow them to dry and roast, about 15 to 20 minutes. Remove and set aside.
2. Meanwhile, melt 1 stick butter per lobster in a large bowl or double boiler set over simmering water, making sure bowl does not touch the surface of water. Add lobster shells to the melted butter and simmer gently, without boiling, for about 20 minutes.
3. Strain the melted butter through a cheesecloth-lined sieve into another bowl, then set that bowl into ice to chill. Cover bowl and refrigerate to set, then skim off the top and discard any liquids. Use within a few days, or freeze for up to a few weeks.

Lemon Butter Mop For Seafood

Servings: 1 And 1/2 Cups
Cooking Time:5 Minutes
Ingredients:
- 8 tablespoons (1 stick) butter
- Juice of 1 small lemon

- 1 tablespoon fine salt
- 1½ teaspoons garlic powder
- 1½ teaspoons dried dill weed

Directions:
1. In a small skillet over medium heat, melt the butter.
2. Stir in the lemon juice, salt, garlic powder, and dill, stirring until well mixed. Use immediately.

Pan-seared Lamb Chops

Servings: 6
Cooking Time: 40 Minutes
Ingredients:
- 12 fresh lamb chops
- 2 Tbsp Olive oil
- 1/2 Tbsp Pepper
- 1/2 Tbsp Salt.

Directions:
1. Preheat the wood pellet smoker-grill for direct cooking at 300F using any pellet.
2. Rinse the lamb chops and pat dry with a paper towel, season with salt and pepper.
3. Grill both sides of lamb chops for 20 minutes, then increase the temperature of the grill to High.
4. Place an iron skillet over the cooking grid, add olive oil, and sear the chops for 3 minutes per side or until it is golden brown.
5. Place on the baking sheet and roast for 10 minutes or until the internal temperature is 125F.

Roast Bison Sirloin

Servings: 7
Cooking Time: 3 Hours
Ingredients:
- 3 Tbsp of spice rub
- 1 6pounds bison sirloin roast, boneless
- 2 Tbsp of herbs, either fennel or thyme or sage or rosemary
- 3 Tbsp of olive oil

Directions:
1. Remove roast from refrigerator and allow to thaw until temperature reads between 50-55 °F.
2. Preheat the grill for indirect cooking at 200°F. Use alder wood pellets.
3. Rub the surface of the meat with oil, then season with salt and pepper. Place bison in a skillet and Place on the cooking grid. Add the herbs and spices rub.
4. Roast for about 2 ½ hours or until internal temperature reads 120-125°F.
5. After removing the roast from the oven, allow it to rest for 15 minutes before carving and serving.

Grilled Tuna Burger With Ginger Mayonnaise

Servings: 4
Cooking Time: 20 Minutes
Ingredients:
- 1 Tbsp of sesame oil, optional
- 4 Tbsp of ginger, optional
- 4 hamburger buns
- Black pepper, freshly ground

- 2 Tbsp and 1 tsp of soy sauce
- 4 of 5 ounces of tuna steak
- Natural oil
- 1/2 cup of mayonnaise

Directions:
1. Set the grill for direct cooking at 300°F. Use maple pelle for a robust woody taste.
2. Rub soy sauce on the tuna steak and season with peppe
3. In another bowl, prepare a rub by mixing the ginger, mayonnaise, 1 tsp of soy sauce, and sesame oil.
4. With a brush, apply the rub on the tuna steak then grill 10 minutes before flipping. Grill the other side for another 1 minutes.
5. Serve immediately with fish between buns. Add mayonnaise and ginger as layers.

Banana Walnut Bread

Servings: 1
Cooking Time: 1 Hour 15 Minutes
Ingredients:
- 2-1/2 cup of all-purpose flour
- 1 cup of sugar
- 2 eggs
- 1 cup ripe banana, mashed
- 1/4 cup whole milk
- 1/4 cup walnut, finely chopped
- 1 tsp salt
- 3 Tbsp of Vegetable oil
- 3 tsp baking powder

Directions:
1. Set the wood pellet smoker-grill for indirect cooking at 350F.
2. Combine all the ingredients in a large bowl. Using a mix (electric or manual), mix the ingredients. Grease and flour t loaf pan. Pour the mixture into the loaf pan.
3. Transfer loaf pan to the grill and cover with steel construction. Bake for 60-75 minutes. Remove and allow to cool.

Roasted Tri-tip With Spanish Adobo Rub

Servings: 5
Cooking Time: 2 Hours 45 Minutes
Ingredients:
- 1 Tbsp of olive oil
- 2 tsp of salt
- 3 cloves of garlic, already peeled
- 1 tsp of black pepper
- 2 tsp of marjoram, preferably freshly chopped
- 3 Tbsp of paprika, Spanish
- 1/4 cup of vinegar, sherry
- 1 of 2pound of tri-tip roast

Directions:
1. Preheat the grill for direct grilling at 420°F (High). Use hickory wood pellets for a robust woody taste.
2. Prepare the rub by pulsing garlic, paprika, marjoram, a vinegar in a food processor. Rub the mixture produced all o the meat. Allow meat to marinate for 2 hours.
3. Place the meat on the cooking grid and sear for 2 minu per side.

Reduce the temperature of the grill to 350°F and roast the
at for 45 minutes or until the internal temperature reads
0- 145°F.

Allow to rest for 10 minutes before serving.

Smoked Brisket Pie

rvings: 8
oking Time: 45 Minutes
gredients:

1 cup Onions, peeled and blanched (pearl)
½ cup Peas, frozen
1 Garlic clove, minced
1 Onion, chopped (yellow)
2 Carrots, chopped (peeled)
2 tbsp. of Butter
2 cups chopped Leftover Brisket
1 Egg
1 Sheet Pastry dough, frozen
2 cups of Beef Stock

rections:

In a pot add the butter. Place it over medium - high heat.
ce the butter is melted sauté the carrots for 10 minutes.
Add the onion. Cook 7 minutes and then add the garlic.
ok 30 seconds.
Add in the brisket, peas, and stock. Let it simmer until
ck so that it coats the spoon. In case it doesn't thickens
ke a slurry from cornstarch and add it. Add black pepper
d salt to season
Place mixture inside baking dish and cover with dough.
In a bowl whisk the egg and brush the pastry.
Preheat the grill to 350F with closed lid. Once heated
ce the baking dish on the grate and let it bake 45 minutes.
aside.
Cool down for 10 minutes and serve. Enjoy!

Red Wine Beef Stew

rvings: 8
oking Time: 3 Hours 30 Minutes
gredients:

1-1/2 tsp kosher salt
4lb chuck roast, cut into 2-inch pieces
1 Tsp ground black pepper
1/4 cup tomato paste
1 Tsp olive oil
2 cups dry red wine
2 bay leaves
4 spring's fresh thyme
2 lb carrots, peeled and chopped
1lb red potatoes, cut into half
4 cups chicken broth
3 Tsp all-purpose flour

rections:

Preheat wood pellet smoker-grill to 325⁰F, with the lid
sed for about 15 minutes
Place meat in a bowl and sprinkle in salt, pepper, and
ur. Toss together until meat is adequately seasoned.
Heat oil in a cast-iron Dutch oven and cook the meat at
dium for about 8 minutes, until brown.
Remove meat and place on a plate. Add wine, broth,
nato paste, thyme, bay leaves, and 1/4 of carrots into the
tch oven and bring to a boil. Transfer meat to Dutch oven

and place on the grill grate for direct cooking. Cook meat for
about 2 hours.
5.   Remove cooked vegetables from Dutch oven and add
remaining carrots and potatoes. Cook until meat is fork-tender,
about 1 hour.
6.   Serve.

Grilled Pizza

Servings: 4
Cooking Time: 10 Minutes
Ingredients:
•   2tablespoons all-purpose flour, plus more as needed
•   6-8 ounces of pizza dough
•   1tablespoon canola oil, divided
•   1/2 cup Alfredo sauce
•   1cup mozzarella cheese, shredded
•   1/2 cup ricotta cheese, pieces
•   14pepperoni slices
•   1/2 teaspoon of dried oregano for serving, optional
Directions:
1.   Place the grill grate inside the unit and close the hood.
2.   Set temperatures to Max and let it preheat for 8 minutes.
3.   Meanwhile, spread flour on a clean flat surface, roll the
dough onto surface, and use a rolling pin
4.   Roll the dough and then cut in rod shape that it fits inside
the grill grate.
5.   Brush the dough evenly with canola oil and flip to coat the
dough form another side as well.
6.   Poke the dough with the fork.
7.   Place it on the grill grate and close the hood.
8.   Cook for 4 minutes and then flip to cook from another
side by opening the hood.
9.   Cook for 4 more minutes.
10.   Now open the unit and spread sauce, cheeses, and
pepperoni on top.
11.   Close the hood and let it cook for 3 minutes.
12.   Once it's done, serve with a sprinkle of oregano.

Pizza Bianca

Servings: 2
Cooking Time: 3 Hours
Ingredients:
•   3cups all-purpose or bread flour, plus more as needed
•   2teaspoons instant yeast
•   2teaspoons kosher or coarse sea salt, plus more for
sprinkling
•   2tablespoons good-quality olive oil, plus more for
drizzling
•   1tablespoon or more chopped fresh rosemary
Directions:
1.   Whisk the flour, yeast, and salt together in a large bowl.
Add the oil and 1 cup water and mix with a heavy spoon.
Continue to add water, 1 tablespoon at a time, until the dough
forms a ball and is slightly sticky to the touch. In the unlikely
event that the mixture gets too sticky, add flour 1 tablespoon
at a time until you have the right consistency.
2.   Lightly flour a work surface and turn out the dough onto
it. Knead by hand for a minute until smooth, then form into a
round ball. Put the dough in a bowl and cover with plastic
wrap; let rise in a warm spot until it doubles in size, 1 to 2
hours. You can cut this rising time short if you're in a hurry, or

you can let the dough rise more slowly, in the refrigerator, for up to 8 hours. You can freeze the dough at this point for up to a month: Wrap it tightly in plastic wrap or put in a zipper bag. Thaw in the refrigerator; bring to room temperature before shaping.

3. To shape, divide the dough into 2 or more pieces; roll each piece into a round ball. Put each ball on a lightly floured work surface, sprinkle lightly with flour, and cover with plastic wrap or a towel. Let rest until slightly puffed, 25 to 30 minutes.

4. Start the coals or heat a gas grill for medium direct cooking. Make sure the grates are clean.

5. Roll or lightly press each ball into a flat, round disk, lightly flouring the work surface and the dough as necessary to keep it from sticking (use only as much flour as you need). To stretch the dough, push down at the center and outward to the edge, turning the round as you do. Continue pushing down and out and turning the dough until the round is the size you want; if you're making 2 pizzas, aim for rounds 10 to 12 inches in diameter. Sprinkle the tops evenly with the rosemary and a pinch or so coarse salt, then drizzle with olive oil.

6. Put the crusts on the grill directly over the fire. Close the lid and cook until the bottoms firm up and brown and the tops are cooked through, 5 to 10 minutes, depending on how hot the fire is; the top side of the dough will bubble up from the heat underneath but likely won't take on much color. Transfer to a cutting board and use a pizza cutter to slice into wedges or small pieces and serve.

Barbecue Kebabs

Servings: 8
Cooking Time: 1 Hour
Ingredients:
- 1 tablespoon olive oil
- 1/8 cup apple cider vinegar
- 1 tablespoon honey
- 2 tablespoons raspberry chipotle rub
- 1 lb. pork loin, sliced into cubes
- 1 red onion, sliced
- 3 green bell peppers, sliced
- 1/2 cup barbecue sauce

Directions:
1. In a bowl, mix the oil, vinegar, honey, and rub.
2. Marinate the pork slices in this mixture.
3. Cover with foil and marinate in the refrigerator for 1 hour.
4. Thread the pork cubes into skewers alternating with the red onion and green bell pepper.
5. Set the wood pellet grill to 400 degrees F.
6. Grill the kebabs for 15 to 20 minutes, rotating every 5 minutes.
7. Brush with barbecue sauce.

Pork And Portobello Burgers

Servings: 4
Cooking Time: 30 Minutes
Ingredients:
- 1 pound ground pork
- 1 tablespoon minced garlic
- 1 teaspoon minced fresh rosemary, fennel seed or parsley
- Salt and ground black pepper
- 4 large portobello mushroom caps, stems removed
- Olive oil

- 4 burger buns
- Any burger fixings you like

Directions:
1. Combine the ground pork, garlic, rosemary and a sprinkle of salt and pepper. Use a spoon to lightly scrape away the gills of the mushrooms and hollow them slightly. Drizzle the mushrooms (inside and out) with olive oil and sprinkle with salt and pepper. Press 1/4 of the mixture into each of the hollow sides of the mushrooms; you want the meat to spread all the way across the width of the mushrooms. They should look like burgers.
2. Grill the burgers, meat side down, until the pork is well browned, 4 to 6 minutes. Flip and cook until the top side of the mushrooms are browned and the mushrooms are tender, another 6 to 8 minutes. If you like, use an instant-read thermometer to check the interior temperature of the pork, which should be a minimum of 145 degrees.
3. Serve the burgers on buns (toasted, if you like) with any fixings you like.

Smoked Sriracha Sauce

Servings: 2
Cooking Time: 1 Hour
Ingredients:
- 1 lb Fresno chiles, stems pulled off and seeds removed
- 1/2 cup rice vinegar
- 1/2 cup red wine vinegar
- 1 carrot, medium and cut into rounds, 1/4 inch
- 1-1/2 tbsp sugar, dark-brown
- 4 garlic cloves, peeled
- 1 tbsp olive oil
- 1 tbsp kosher salt
- 1/2 cup water

Directions:
1. Smoke chiles in a smoker for about 15 minutes.
2. Bring to boil both vinegars then add carrots, sugar, and garlic. Simmer for about 15 minutes while covered. Cool for minutes.
3. Place the chiles, olive oil, vinegar-vegetable mixture, salt and 1/4 cup water into a blender.
4. Blend for about 1-2 minutes on high. Add remaining water and blend again. You can add another 1/4 cup water if you want your sauce thinner.
5. Pour the sauce into jars and place in a refrigerator.
6. Serve.

Rosemary Cheese Bread

Servings: 30
Cooking Time: 12 Minutes
Ingredients:
- 1½ cup sunflower seeds
- ½ tsp sea salt
- 1egg
- 1tsp fresh rosemary (finely chopped)
- 2tsp xanthan gum
- 2tbsp cream cheese
- 2cups grated mozzarella

Directions:
1. Preheat the grill to 400°F with the lid closed for 15 minutes.

Toss the sunflower seeds into a powerful blender and nd until it smooth and flour-like.

Transfer the sunflower seed flour into a mixing bowl and l the rosemary and xanthan gum. Mix and set aside.

Melt the cheese in a microwave. To do this, combine the am cheese and mozzarella cheese in a microwave-safe dish.

Place the microwave-safe dish in the grill and heat the ese on high for 1 minute.

Bring out the dish and stir. Place the dish in the grill and t for 30 seconds. Bring out the dish and stir until smooth.

Pour the melted cheese into a large mixing bowl.

Add the sunflower flour mixture to the melted cheese and the ingredients are well combined.

Add the salt and egg and mix thoroughly to form a smooth gh.

Measure out equal pieces of the dough and roll into sticks.

Grease a baking sheet with oil and arrange the adsticks into the baking sheet in a single layer.

Use the back of a knife or metal spoon to make lines on breadsticks.

Place the baking sheet on the grill and make for about 12 utes or until the breadsticks turn golden brown.

Remove the baking sheet from the grill and let the adsticks cool for a few minutes.

Serve.

Nectarine And Nutella Sundae

vings: 4
king Time: 25 Minutes
redients:
2nectarines, halved and pitted
2tsp honey
4tbsp Nutella
4scoops vanilla ice cream
1/4 cup pecans, chopped
Whipped cream, to top
4cherries, to top
ections:
Preheat pellet grill to 400°F.
Slice nectarines in half and remove the pits.
Brush the inside (cut side) of each nectarine half with ey.
Place nectarines directly on the grill grate, cut side down. k for 5-6 minutes, or until grill marks develop.
Flip nectarines and cook on the other side for about 2 utes.
Remove nectarines from the grill and allow it to cool.
Fill the pit cavity on each nectarine half with 1 tbsp ella.
Place 1 scoop of ice cream on top of Nutella. Top with pped cream, cherries, and sprinkle chopped pecans. Serve enjoy!

Smoked Vegetables

vings: 4
king Time: 20 Minutes
redients:
1head of broccoli
4 carrots
16 oz snow peas
1tbsp olive oil

- 1cup mushrooms, chopped
- 1-1/2 tbsp pepper
- 1tbsp garlic powder

Directions:
1. Cut broccoli and carrots into bite-size pieces. Add snow peas and combine them.
2. Toss the veggies with oil and seasoning.
3. Now cover a pan, sheet, with parchment paper. Place veggies on top.
4. Meanwhile, set your wood pellet smoker to 180F.
5. Place the pan into the smoker. Smoke for about 5 minutes.
6. Adjust smoker temperature to 400F and continue cooking for another 10-15 minutes until slightly brown broccoli tips.
7. Remove, serve, and enjoy.

Smoked Mac And Cheese

Servings: 8
Cooking Time: 1 Hour
Ingredients:
- 1/2 cup butter, salted
- 1/3 cup flour
- 1/2 tbsp salt
- 6 cups whole milk
- Dash of Worcestershire
- 1/2 tbsp dry mustard
- 1 lb small cooked shells, al dente in well-salted water
- 2 cups white cheddar, smoked
- 2 cups cheddar jack cheese
- 1 cup crushed ritz

Directions:
1. Set your grill on "smoke" and run for about 5-10 minutes with the lid open until fire establishes. Now turn your grill to 325 F then close the lid.
2. Melt butter in a saucepan, medium, over low--medium heat then whisk in flour.
3. Cook while whisking for about 5-6 minutes over low heat until light tan color.
4. Whisk in salt, milk, Worcestershire, and mustard over low-medium heat stirring frequently until a thickened sauce.
5. Stir noodles, small shells, white sauce, and 1 cup cheddar cheese in a large baking dish, 10x3" high-sided, coated with butter.
6. Top with 1 cup cheddar cheese and ritz.
7. Place on the grill and bake for about 25-30 minutes until a bubbly mixture and cheese melts.
8. Serve immediately. Enjoy!

Red Wine Braised Short Ribs

Servings: 12
Cooking Time: 9 Hours
Ingredients:
- Kosher salt
- 1/2 cup onion, thinly sliced
- 4 garlic cloves, smashed
- 5lb brisket, flat-cut
- 2 Tbsp olive oil
- 2 bay leaves
- 6 spring's thyme
- 28 oz of canned whole tomatoes
- 4 medium carrots cut lengthwise
- 750ml red wine

- 1 Tbsp tomato paste

Directions:
1. Preheat wood pellet smoker-grill to 350°F.
2. Place brisket on a flat surface and sprinkle pepper and salt on it.
3. Pour oil into a large ovenproof pot and cook the brisket in it for about 10 minutes or until meat browns. Remove brisket and place on a plate, then discard fat in the pot.
4. Add onions, garlic, thyme, bay leaves, tomatoes, wine, tomato paste, celery, salt, and pepper in a large pot. Return brisket to pot, fat side up, and then cover the pot. Braise brisket on the grill for about 3hours, until fork tender.
5. Place carrot on brisket, then cook until carrot is tender and braising liquid in the pot is concentrated. It will take about 30 minutes.
6. Remove fat from the sauce—transfer brisket and braising liquid to a bowl. Cover and leave to rest for at least 4 hours.
7. When ready to serve, preheat grill to 325°F. Heat braising liquid and brisket for about 1 hour.

Pan-seared Lamb Loins With Horseradish Potato Gratin

Servings: 6
Cooking Time: 2hours
Ingredients:
- 2 lamb loins
- 2 Tbsp Olive oil
- 1-1/2 Tbsp Pepper
- 1-1/2 Tbsp Salt.
- 2 Tbsp prepared horseradish
- Tbsp Unsalted butter
- 1/2 cup of crumbled goat cheese
- 1 cup of whipped cream
- potatoes, peeled and sliced
- 1/2 cup of parmesan cheese

Directions:
1. Preheat the wood pellet smoker-grill for direct cooking at 300F using any pellet.
2. Rinse the lamb chops and pat dry with a paper towel, season with salt and pepper.
3. Grill the lamb loins for 15 minutes, then set the temperature of the grill to High
4. Place an iron skillet on the cooking grid, add olive oil, then sear the lamb for 10 minutes until brown on all sides. Perform this action carefully to prevent the lamb from burning; it will develop a bitter taste.
5. Allow it to rest before slicing.
6. Grease a large baking dish with butter. In a large bowl, combine the cream, parmesan cheese, goat cheese, horseradish, salt, and pepper. Whisk together and drop the sliced potatoes into the mixture.
7. Arrange the potatoes in the baking dish and cover with plastic wrap, then add a layer of aluminum foil and bake for 1 hour. Remove the cover and bake for another 30 minutes.
8. Serve with the lamb.

Grilled Brussels Sprouts

Servings: 8
Cooking Time: 20 Minutes
Ingredients:
- 1/2 lb bacon, grease reserved

- 1 b Brussels Sprouts
- 1/2 tbsp pepper
- 1/2 tbsp salt

Directions:
1. Cook bacon until crispy on a stovetop, reserve its grease then chop into small pieces.
2. Meanwhile, wash the Brussels sprouts, trim off the dry end and remove dried leaves, if any. Half them and set aside
3. Place 1/4 cup reserved grease in a pan, cast-iron, over medium-high heat.
4. Season the Brussels sprouts with pepper and salt.
5. Brown the sprouts on the pan with the cut side down for about 3-4 minutes.
6. In the meantime, preheat your pellet grill to 350-375F.
7. Place bacon pieces and browned sprouts into your grill safe pan.
8. Cook for about 20 minutes.
9. Serve immediately.

Native Southern Cornbread

Servings: 8
Cooking Time: 20 Minutes
Ingredients:
- 2 tbsp. butter
- 1½ C. all-purpose flour
- 1½ C. yellow cornmeal
- 2 tbsp. sugar
- 3 tsp. baking powder
- ¾ tsp. baking soda
- ¾ tsp. salt
- 1 C. whole milk
- 1 C. buttermilk
- 3 large eggs
- 3 tbsp. butter, melted

Directions:
1. Set the temperature of Pit Boss Grill to 400 degrees F a preheat with closed lid for 15 minutes.
2. In a 13x9-inch baking dish, place 2 tbsp. of butter.
3. Place the baking dish onto grill to melt butter and heat the pan.
4. In a large bowl, mix together flour, cornmeal, sugar, baking powder, baking soda and salt.
5. In another bowl, add milk, buttermilk, eggs and melted butter and beat until well combined.
6. Add the egg mixture into flour mixture and mix until just moistened.
7. Carefully, remove the heated baking dish from grill.
8. Place the bread mixture into heated baking dish evenly
9. Place the pan onto the grill and cook for about 20 minu or until a toothpick inserted in the center comes out clean.
10. Remove from grill and place the pan onto a wire rack to cool for about 10 minutes.
11. Carefully, invert the bread onto the wire rack to cool completely before slicing.
12. Cut the bread into desired-sized slices and sere.

French Onion Burgers

Servings: 4
Cooking Time: 20 To 25 Minutes
Ingredients:
- 1 pound lean ground beef

1 tablespoon minced garlic
1 teaspoon Better Than Bouillon Beef Base
1 teaspoon dried chives
1 teaspoon freshly ground black pepper
8 slices Gruyère cheese, divided
½ cup soy sauce
1 tablespoon extra-virgin olive oil
1 teaspoon liquid smoke
3 medium onions, cut into thick slices (do not separate
rings)
1 loaf French bread, cut into 8 slices
4 slices provolone cheese

rections:

In a large bowl, mix together the ground beef, minced
lic, beef base, chives, and pepper until well blended
Divide the meat mixture and shape into 8 thin burger
tties
Top each of 4 patties with one slice of Gruyère, then top
th the remaining 4 patties to create 4 stuffed burgers
Supply your smoker with wood pellets and follow the
nufacturer's specific start-up procedure. Preheat, with the
closed, to 425°FArrange the burgers directly on one side of
e grill, close the lid, and smoke for 10 minutes. Flip and
oke with the lid closed for 10 to 15 minutes more, or until a
at thermometer inserted in the burgers reads 160°F. Add
other Gruyère slice to the burgers during the last 5 minutes
smoking to melt.
Meanwhile, in a small bowl, combine the soy sauce, olive
, and liquid smoke
Arrange the onion slices on the grill and baste on both
es with the soy sauce mixture. Smoke with the lid closed for
minutes, flipping halfway through
Lightly toast the French bread slices on the grill. Layer
th of 4 slices with a burger patty, a slice of provolone cheese,
d some of the smoked onions. Top each with another slice of
sted French bread. Serve immediately

Smoked Christmas Crown Roast Of Lamb

rvings: 4
oking Time: 1 To 2 Hours
gredients:

2 racks of lamb, trimmed, frenched, and tied into a crown
1¼ cups extra-virgin olive oil, divided
2 tablespoons chopped fresh basil
2 tablespoons chopped fresh rosemary
2 tablespoons ground sage
2 tablespoons ground thyme
8 garlic cloves, minced
2 teaspoons salt
2 teaspoons freshly ground black pepper

rections:

Set the lamb out on the counter to take the chill off, about
hour.
In a small bowl, combine 1 cup of olive oil, the basil,
emary, sage, thyme, garlic, salt, and pepper.
Baste the entire crown with the herbed olive oil and wrap
e exposed frenched bones in aluminum foil.
Supply your smoker with wood pellets and follow the
nufacturer's specific start-up procedure. Preheat, with the
closed, to 275°F.

5. Put the lamb directly on the grill, close the lid, and smoke
for 1 hour 30 minutes to 2 hours, or until a meat thermometer
inserted in the thickest part reads 140°F.
6. Remove the lamb from the heat, tent with foil, and let rest
for about 15 minutes before serving. The temperature will rise
about 5°F during the rest period, for a finished temperature of
145°F.

Strip Steak Smoked And Seared

Servings: 4
Cooking Time: 3 Hours
Ingredients:
- Strip streaks – 2 (At least 1" thick)
- Olive oil – 2 teaspoons
- Kosher salt to taste
- Freshly ground pepper to taste

Directions:
1. Use a teaspoon of olive oil to brush strip steaks on both
sides the season with freshly ground black pepper and salt.
2. Repeat the same process with the other strip steak then
set aside. Place the steaks over the lower rack of wood pellet
grill then set the temperature to about 225F.
3. Smoke the steaks for about an hour or until the internal
temperature reaches 100F Remove from the grill when ready
then let them stay warm as you preheat the wood pellet grill to
700F.
4. Once the grill is heated, switch it to open flame cooking
mode then remove the lower racks and replace with direct
flame insert. Place back the grates on the grill at the lower
position.
5. Sear the steaks as you use tongs to turn them until it
develops a nice crust on the outside. Once cooked, transfer the
steak strips to a cutting board then allow to rest for about 5
minutes.
6. Add kosher salt to your liking before serving

Smoked Hot Paprika Pork Tenderloin

Servings: 6
Cooking Time: 2 ½ To 3 Hours
Ingredients:
- 2-pound pork tenderloin
- 3/4 cup chicken stock
- 1/2 cup tomato-basil sauce
- 2 tbsp smoked hot paprika (or to taste)
- 1 tbsp oregano
- Salt and pepper to taste

Directions:
1. In a bowl, combine the chicken stock, tomato-basil sauce,
paprika, oregano, salt, and pepper together.
2. Brush over tenderloin.
3. Smoke grill for 4-5 minutes. Pre head, lid closed for 10-14
minutes
4. Place pork for 2 ½ to 3 hours.
5. Rest for 10 minutes.

Venison Rib Roast

Servings: 6
Cooking Time: 25 Minutes
Ingredients:
- 2 pounds venison roast, about 8 ribs

- Rib rub as needed
- 1 tablespoon olive oil

Directions:
1. Switch on the Pit Boss grill, fill the grill hopper with hickory flavored wood pellets, power the grill on by using the control panel, select 'smoke' on the temperature dial, or set the temperature to 375 degrees F and let it preheat for a minimum of 5 minutes.
2. Meanwhile, brush roast with oil and then season with rib rub until well coated.
3. When the grill has preheated, open the lid, place food on the grill grate, shut the grill, and smoke for 25 minutes until the internal temperature reaches 125 degrees F.
4. When done, transfer roast to a cutting board, let it rest for 10 minutes, then cut into slices and serve.

Reverse-seared Tilapia

Servings: 4
Cooking Time: 20 Minutes
Ingredients:
- tilapia fillets
- 2 Tbsp melted butter (unsalted)
- 1/2 cup of all-purpose flour
- Salt and pepper to taste

Directions:
1. Preheat the wood pellet smoker-grill for direct cooking at 350F using any pellet
2. Rinse the fillets and pat dry with a paper towel. Season with salt and pepper, coat with the flour.
3. Transfer Tilapia fillets to cooking grate and grill for 20 minutes or until internal temperature measure 150F. Then set fillets aside and increase the temperature of the grill to 450F
4. Sear the tilapia for 4 minutes per side or until it flakes. Brush melted butter on the tilapia.
5. Serve.

Venison Meatloaf

Servings: 6
Cooking Time: 1 Hour And 15 Minutes
Ingredients:
- For the Meatloaf:
- 1 medium white onion, peeled, diced
- 2 pounds ground venison
- 1 cup bread crumbs
- 1 teaspoon salt
- 1 tablespoon Worcestershire sauce
- ½ teaspoon ground black pepper
- 2 tablespoons onion soup mix
- 1 egg, beaten
- 1 cup milk, unsweetened
- For the Glaze:
- 1/4 cup brown sugar
- 1/4 cup ketchup
- 1/4 cup apple cider vinegar

Directions:
1. Switch on the Pit Boss grill, fill the grill hopper with big game blend wood pellets, power the grill on by using the control panel, select 'smoke' on the temperature dial, or set the temperature to 350 degrees F and let it preheat for a minimum of 15 minutes.

2. Meanwhile, take a large bowl, place all the ingredients f the meatloaf in it, and stir until just combined; don't overmix
3. Take a loaf pan, grease it with oil, place meatloaf mixtur in it, and spread evenly.
4. Prepare the glaze and for this, take a small bowl, place a of its ingredients in it, stir until combined, and then spread evenly on top of meatloaf.
5. When the grill has preheated, open the lid, place loaf pa on the grill grate, shut the grill and smoke for 1 hour and 15 minutes until the internal temperature reaches 165 degrees
6. Serve straight away.

Smoked Bananas Foster Bread Pudding

Servings: 8 To 10
Cooking Time: 2 Hours 15 Minutes
Ingredients:
- 1loaf (about 4 cups) brioche or challah, cubed to 1 inch cubes
- 3eggs, lightly beaten
- 2cups of milk
- 2/3 cups sugar
- 2large bananas, peeled and smashed
- 1tbsp vanilla extract
- 1tbsp cinnamon
- 1/4 tsp nutmeg
- 1/2 cup pecans
- Rum Sauce Ingredients:
- 1/2 cup spiced rum
- 1/4 cup unsalted butter
- 1cup dark brown sugar
- 1tsp cinnamon
- 5large bananas, peeled and quartered

Directions:
1. Place pecans on a skillet over medium heat and lightly toast for about 5 minutes, until you can smell them.
2. Remove from heat and allow to cool. Once cooled, chop pecans.
3. Lightly butter a 9" x 13" baking dish and evenly layer bread cubes in the dish.
4. In a large bowl, whisk eggs, milk, sugar, mashed banana vanilla extract, cinnamon, and nutmeg until combined.
5. Pour egg mixture over the bread in the baking dish eve Sprinkle with chopped pecans. Cover with aluminum foil an refrigerate for about 30 minutes.
6. Preheat pellet grill to 180°F. Turn your smoke setting t high, if applicable.
7. Remove foil from dish and place on the smoker for 5 minutes with the lid closed, allowing bread to absorb smoky flavor.
8. Remove dish from the grill and cover with foil again. Increase your pellet grill's temperature to 350°F.
9. Place dish on the grill grate and cook for 50-60 minutes until everything is cooked through and the bread pudding is bubbling.
10. In a saucepan, while pudding cooks heat up butter for rum sauce over medium heat. When the butter begins to me add the brown sugar, cinnamon, and bananas. Sauté until bananas begin to soften.
11. Add rum and watch. When the liquid begins to bubble, light a match, and tilt the pan. Slowly and carefully move the match towards the liquid until the sauce lights. When the flames go away, remove skillet from heat.

If you're uncomfortable lighting the liquid with a match, cook it for 3-4 minutes over medium heat after the rum been added.

Keep rum sauce on a simmer or reheat once it's time to ve.

Remove bread pudding from the grill and allow it to cool about 5 minutes.

Cut into squares, put each square on a plate and add a ce of banana then drizzle rum sauce over the top. Serve on own or a la mode and enjoy it!

Pit Boss Smoked Sausage

vings: 4 To 6
king Time: 3 Hours
redients:
- 3 Pound ground pork
- 1/2 Tablespoon ground mustard
- 1 Tablespoon onion powder
- 1 Tablespoon garlic powder
- 1 Teaspoon pink curing salt
- 1 Tablespoon salt
- 4 Teaspoon black pepper
- 1/2 Cup ice water
- Hog casings, soaked and rinsed in cold water

ections:
In a medium bowl, combine the meat and seasonings, mix l.

Add ice water to meat and mix with hands working ckly until everything is incorporated.

Place mixture in a sausage stuffer and follow nufacturer's instructions for operating. Use caution not to rstuff or the casing might burst.

Once all the meat is stuffed, determine your desired link gth and pinch and twist a couple of times or tie it off. peat for each link.

When ready to cook, set Pit Boss temperature to 225℉ preheat, lid closed for 15 minutes. For optimal flavor, use er Smoke if available.

Place links directly on the grill grate and cook for 1 to 2 rs or until the internal temperature registers 155℉. Let sage rest a few minutes before slicing. Enjoy!

Potluck Favorite Baked Beans

vings: 10
king Time: 3 Hours 5 Minutes
redients:
- 1 tbsp. butter
- ½ of red bell pepper, seeded and chopped
- ½ of medium onion, chopped
- 2 jalapeño peppers, chopped
- 2 (28-oz.) cans baked beans, rinsed and drained
- 8 oz. pineapple chunks, drained
- 1 C. BBQ sauce
- 1 C. brown sugar
- 1 tbsp. ground mustard

ections:
Set the temperature of Pit Boss Grill to 220-250 degrees F preheat with closed lid for 15 minutes.

In a non-stick skillet, melt butter over medium heat and té the bell peppers, onion and jalapeño peppers for about minutes.

3. Remove from heat and transfer the pepper mixture into a bowl.
4. Add remaining ingredients and stir to combine.
5. Transfer the mixture into a Dutch oven.
6. Place the Dutch oven onto the grill and cook for about 2½-3 hours.
7. Remove from grill and serve hot.

Smoky Caramelized Onions On The Pellet Grill

Servings: 4
Cooking Time: 1 Hour
Ingredients:
- 5 large sliced onions
- 1/2 cup fat of your choice
- Pinch of Sea salt

Directions:
1. Place all the ingredients into a pan. For a deep rich brown caramelized onion, cook them off for about 1hour on a stovetop.
2. Keep the grill temperatures not higher than 250 - 275F.
3. Now transfer the pan into the grill.
4. Cook for about 1-1½ hours until brown. Check and stir with a spoon, wooden, after every 15 minutes. Make sure not to run out of pellets.
5. Now remove from the grill and season with more salt if necessary.
6. Serve immediately or place in a refrigerator for up to 1 week.

Seasoned Potatoes On Smoker

Servings: 6
Cooking Time: 45 Minutes
Ingredients:
- 1-1/2 lb creamer potatoes
- 2 tbsp olive oil
- 1tbsp garlic powder
- 1/4 tbsp oregano
- 1/2 tbsp thyme, dried
- 1/2 tbsp parsley, dried

Directions:
1. Preheat your pellet grill to 350F.
2. Spray an 8x8 inch foil pan using non-stick spray.
3. Mix all ingredients in the pan and place it into the grill.
4. Cook for about 45 minutes until potatoes are done. Stir after every 15 minutes.
5. Serve and enjoy!

Smoked Beef Ribs

Servings: 8
Cooking Time: 4o Minutes
Ingredients:
- For the topping:
- 3 apples, peeled and cut into slices
- 75g blueberries
- 25g salted butter
- 2 tablespoons maple syrup
- For the cake:
- 75g butter, cut into cubes
- 75g organic virgin coconut oil, cut into cubes

- 100g cane sugar
- 2 large free-range eggs, beaten
- 75g buckwheat flour
- 75g ground almonds
- ½ teaspoon bicarbonate of soda
- 1 teaspoon baking powder
- 1 teaspoon cinnamon

Directions:
1. Preheat the oven to 180°C. Caramelize the apples in a little water, adding the butter and maple syrup once softened.
2. Add the blueberries last. Set aside. Place the sugar, butter and coconut oil into a mixing bowl and cream until pale and fluffy.
3. Gradually add the beaten eggs, adding a bit of flour if the mixture begins to curdle. Continue to beat the mixture until fluffy. Fold in the remaining flour, ground almonds, baking powder and cinnamon.
4. Transfer the apple and blueberry mixture into the bottom of a greased Bundt cake mold (We use a silicon one), leveling well with the back of a spoon. Then pour the cake mixture over the top.
5. Bake for about 40 minutes or until a skewer comes out clean. Leave to cool. Delicious served with Greek yogurt.

Bearnaise Sauce With Marinated London Broil

Servings: 4
Cooking Time: 50 Minutes
Ingredients:
- 2 cups of Rory's marinade
- 1-1/2 cups of béarnaise sauce
- 2-1/2 pound of London broil

Directions:
1. Place London broil in a big baking dish, pour marinade over the steak, then refrigerate it over the night.
2. Set the grill for direct cooking at 300°F. Use maple pellets for a robust woody taste.
3. Remove London broil from the marinade the following morning. Place it on the preheated grill and cook for 15 minutes before flipping and grilling the other side for 10 minutes. Serve immediately with béarnaise sauce.

Buttered Green Peas

Servings: 1-2
Cooking Time: 30 Minutes
Ingredients:
- 1/2 cup butter, melted
- Kosher salt
- 24 oz green beans, trimmed
- 1/4 cup veggie rub

Directions:
1. Preheat the wood pellet smoker-grill to 345°F using pellets of your choice
2. Pour the beans into a baking pan lined with parchment sheets and rub melted butter over the beans. Season with salt. Place the baking pan on the cooking grid.
3. Arrange the beans on the pan with a tong and pour the veggie rub over it.
4. Braise the beans until tender and lightly browned. Flip after 20 minutes.
5. Serve.

Scrambled Eggs

Servings: 3 To 4
Cooking Time: 10 Minutes
Ingredients:
- 1/4 cup Cheddar and Monterey Cheese Blend, shredded
- Sea Salt and Black Pepper, as needed
- 1 tbsp. Butter
- 6 Eggs
- 3 tbsp. Nut Milk or milk of your choice
- Green onion or fresh herbs of your choice, for garnish

Directions:
1. First, place eggs, milk, cheese blend, pepper, and salt in the blender pitcher.
2. Next, press the 'medium' button and blend the mixture 25 to 30 seconds or until everything comes together and is frothy.
3. Then, heat the butter in a medium-sized saucepan over medium-low heat.
4. Once the skillet becomes hot and the butter has melted swirl the pan so that the butter coats all the sides.
5. Pour the egg mixture into it and allow it to sit for 20 seconds.
6. With a spatula, break it down and continue cooking until the egg is set and cooked. Garnish with green onion.
7. Serve it along with toasted bread.

Roasted Steak

Servings: 5
Cooking Time: 12 Hours 30 Minutes
Ingredients:
- 2 Tbsp of rosemary, preferably freshly chopped
- 2 tsp of salt
- 1 Tbsp of thyme, preferably fresh leaves
- 1/2 cup of olive oil
- 1-1/2 tsp of black pepper
- 1 of 3-inch steak
- 5 cloves of garlic, preferably thinly sliced

Directions:
1. Make the marinade by cooking garlic until it is soft, then add rosemary and thyme. Cook for about 1 minute.
2. Rub black pepper and salt all over the steak, then put it inside a Ziploc bag with the garlic mixture. Keep in the refrigerator overnight.
3. Remove steak from the refrigerator the next morning, discard the garlic marinade. Roast the steak on the preheated grill for 30 minutes or until the internal temperature reads 160°F.
4. Serve the steak and season with salt and black pepper before eating.

Polish Kielbasa

Servings: 8
Cooking Time: 1 To 2 Hours
Ingredients:
- 4 pounds ground pork
- ½ cup water
- 2 garlic cloves, minced
- 4 teaspoons salt
- 1 teaspoon freshly ground black pepper
- 1 teaspoon dried marjoram

½ teaspoon ground allspice

14 feet natural hog casings, medium size

rections:

In a large bowl, combine the pork, water, garlic, salt, pper, marjoram, and allspice.

Stuff the casings according to the instructions on your sage stuffing device, or use a funnel (see Tip).

Twist the casings according to your desired length and ck each with a pin in several places so the kielbasa won't rst.

Transfer the kielbasa to a plate, cover with plastic wrap, d refrigerate for at least 8 hours or overnight.

Remove from the refrigerator and allow the links to come room temperature.

Supply your smoker with wood pellets and follow the nufacturer's specific start-up procedure. Preheat, with the closed, to 225°F.

Place the kielbasa directly on the grill grate, close the lid, d smoke for 1 hour 30 minutes to 2 hours, or until a meat rmometer inserted in each link reads 155°F. (The internal nperature will rise about 5°F when resting, for a finished np of 160°F.)

Serve with buns and condiments of your choosing, or cut the kielbasa and serve with smoked cabbage

Veal Paprikash

vings: 6

oking Time: 1 Hour 25 Minutes

gredients:

3lb Veal, cut into 1-inch piece

1 yellow onion, chopped

1 tsp cayenne pepper

1 small red pepper, finely chopped

Kosher salt

1 cup regular sour cream

1 Tsp all-purpose flour

1 medium ripe tomato

1 Tsp paprika

2 Tbsp vegetable oil

2 Tbsp butter

ections:

Preheat wood pellet smoker-grill to 350⁰F, with the lid sed for about 15 minutes

Heat oil and melt butter in a Dutch oven, add the onion d cook until tender, about 3 minutes.

Add veal, and then season onion with paprika and enne pepper. Cover the lid of the Dutch oven and allow the at to cook for about 10 minutes.

Add tomato, bell pepper, and season with salt. Stir and ve to cook for 45 minutes, until tender.

Combine the flour and sour cream in a small bowl. Stir in flour mixture into the Dutch oven and cook for another 10 utes.

Remove pot from the cooking grid and enjoy the dish.

eafaring Seafood Rub With Smoked Swordfish

vings: 6-8

oking Time: 2 Hours 15 Minutes

redients:

4 tsp of garlic, ground

2 tsp of paprika

- 1 tsp of nutmeg, ground
- 1/2 tsp of allspice, ground
- 4 tsp of ginger, ground
- 1 tsp of cayenne
- 2 Tbsp of celery seed
- 1/4 cup of sea salt
- 4 tsp of black pepper, freshly ground
- 2 pounds of swordfish
- 2 tsp of brown sugar

Directions:

1. Preheat the grill for 15 minutes at 225°F. Use oak wood pellets for a distinctive, strong woody taste.
2. Combine all the ingredients (except swordfish) in a bowl. Mix thoroughly.
3. Add the swordfish to the bowl and gently coat it with the mixture. Do not allow the swordfish to break.
4. Place the coated swordfish directly on the preheated grate and smoke for 2 hours or until fish turns opaque and flakes.
5. Serve immediately.

Honey Dipping Sauce

Servings: 4

Cooking Time: 10 Minutes

Ingredients:

- 5 tablespoons unsalted butter
- 8 tablespoons kimchi paste
- 2 tablespoons honey
- 1 tsp sesame seeds

Directions:

1. In a blender place all ingredients and blend until smooth
2. Pour sauce in a bowl and serve

Cowboy Steak

Servings: 4

Cooking Time: 1 Hour

Ingredients:

- 2.5 lb. cowboy cut steaks
- Salt to taste
- Beef rub
- 1/4 cup olive oil
- 2 tablespoons fresh mint leaves, chopped
- ½ cup parsley, chopped
- 1 clove garlic, crushed and minced
- 1 tablespoon lemon juice
- 1 tablespoon lemon zest
- Salt and pepper to taste

Directions:

1. Season the steak with the salt and dry rub.
2. Preheat the Pit Boss wood pellet grill to 225 degrees F for 10 minutes while the lid is closed.
3. Grill the steaks for 45 minutes, flipping once or twice.
4. Increase temperature to 450 degrees F.
5. Put the steaks back to the grill. Cook for 5 minutes per side.
6. In a bowl, mix the remaining ingredients.
7. Serve steaks with the parsley mixture.

Avocado With Lemon

Servings: 4
Cooking Time: 20 Minutes
Ingredients:
- 2 ripe avocados
- Good-quality olive oil for brushing
- 1 lemon, halved
- Salt and pepper

Directions:
1. Start the coals or heat a gas grill for medium direct cooking. Make sure the grates are clean.
2. Cut the avocados in half lengthwise. Carefully strike a chef's knife into the pit, then wiggle it a bit to lift and remove it. Insert a spoon underneath the flesh against the skin and run it all the way around to separate the entire half of the avocado. Repeat with the other avocado. Brush with oil, then squeeze one of the lemon halves over them thoroughly on both sides, so they don't discolor. Cut the other lemon half into 4 wedges.
3. Put the avocados on the grill directly over the fire, cut side down. Close the lid and cook, turning once, until browned in places, 5 to 10 minutes total. Serve the halved avocados as is, or slice and fan them for a prettier presentation. Sprinkle with salt and pepper and garnish with the lemon wedges.

Pellet Grill Funeral Potatoes

Servings: 8
Cooking Time: 1 Hour
Ingredients:
- 1, 32 oz, package frozen hash browns
- 1/2 cup cheddar cheese, grated
- 1 can cream of chicken soup
- 1 cup sour cream
- 1 cup Mayonnaise
- 3 cups corn flakes, whole or crushed
- 1/4 cup melted butter

Directions:
1. Preheat your pellet grill to 350F.
2. Spray a 13 x 9 baking pan, aluminum, using a cooking spray, non-stick.
3. Mix together hash browns, cheddar cheese, chicken soup cream, sour cream, and mayonnaise in a bowl, large.
4. Spoon the mixture into a baking pan gently.
5. Mix corn flakes and melted butter then sprinkle over the casserole.
6. Grill for about 1-1/2 hours until potatoes become tender. If the top browns too much, cover using a foil until potatoes are done.
7. Remove from the grill and serve hot.

Smoked Brats

Servings: 12 To 15
Cooking Time: 1 To 2 Hours
Ingredients:
- 4 (12-ounce) cans of beer
- 2 onions, sliced into rings
- 2 green bell peppers, sliced into rings
- 2 tablespoons unsalted butter, plus more for the rolls
- 2 tablespoons red pepper flakes
- 10 brats, uncooked
- 10 hoagie rolls, split
- Mustard, for serving

Directions:
1. On your kitchen stove top, in a large saucepan over high heat, bring the beer, onions, peppers, butter, and red pepper flakes to a boil.
2. Supply your smoker with wood pellets and follow the manufacturer's specific start-up procedure. Preheat, with the lid closed, to 225°F.
3. Place a disposable pan on one side of grill, and pour the warmed beer mixture into it, creating a "brat tub" (see Tip below).
4. Place the brats on the other side of the grill, directly on the grate, and close the lid and smoke for 1 hour, turning 2 c 3 times.
5. Add the brats to the pan with the onions and peppers, cover tightly with aluminum foil, and continue smoking with the lid closed for 30 minutes to 1 hour, or until a meat thermometer inserted in the brats reads 160°F.
6. Butter the cut sides of the hoagie rolls and toast cut-side down on the grill.
7. Using a slotted spoon, remove the brats, onions, and peppers from the cooking liquid and discard the liquid.
8. Serve the brats on the toasted buns, topped with the onions and peppers and mustard (ketchup optional).

Red Chile And Lime Shortbread Cookies

Servings: 8
Cooking Time: 30 Minutes
Ingredients:
- 2 tsp lime zest
- 8 Tbsp unsalted butter
- 1 cup of all-purpose flour
- 1/2 tsp Salt
- 1 tsp Red Chile rub
- 1/4 cup of sugar

Directions:
1. Set the wood pellet smoker-grill to indirect cooking at 300F
2. In a large bowl, combine all the ingredients (except flou Mix thoroughly until the butter is creamy but not smooth. Gradually add the flour until it forms a ball.
3. Transfer the dough onto a floured surface, roll until abo 1/4-inches thick. Cut into eight equal parts, but do not cut through.
4. Arrange in a cake pan, bake for 10 minutes. Allow to co before serving.

Smoked Sausage & Potatoes

Servings: 4 To 6
Cooking Time: 50 Minutes
Ingredients:
- 2 Pound Hot Sausage Links
- 2 Pound Potatoes, fingerling
- 1 Tablespoon fresh thyme
- 4 Tablespoon butter

Directions:
1. When ready to cook, set the Pit Boss to 375°F and preh lid closed for 15 minutes.
2. Put your sausage links on the grill to get some color. Th should take about 3 minutes on each side.

While sausage is cooking, cut the potatoes into bite size ces all about the same size so they cook evenly. Chop the me and butter, then combine all the ingredients into a Pit ss cast iron skillet.

Pull your sausage off the grill, slice into bite size pieces add to your cast iron.

Turn grill down to 275°F and put the cast iron in the grill 45 minutes to an hour or until the potatoes are fully ked.

After 45 minutes, use a butter knife to test your potatoes cutting into one to see if its done. To speed up cook time can cover cast iron will a lid or foil. Serve. Enjoy!

Sweet Tooth Carving Rhubarb Crunch

vings: 8
king Time: 1 Hour
redients:
- 1 C. oatmeal
- 1 C. flour
- 1 C. brown sugar
- ½ C. butter, melted
- ¼ tsp. salt
- 4 C. raw rhubarb, chopped finely
- 1 C. white sugar
- 2 tbsp. cornstarch
- 1 C. cold water
- 1 tsp. vanilla extract

ections:
Set the temperature of Pit Boss Grill to 350 degrees F and heat with closed lid for 15 minutes.

In a bowl, add oatmeal, flour, brown sugar, butter and salt mix until well combined.

In a pan, add white sugar, cornstarch, cold water and illa extract and cook until sugar is dissolves, stirring tinuously.

Place half of the four mixture into a 9x12-inch pan and top h chopped rhubarb evenly.

Place sugar mixture over rhubarb evenly and top with aining flour mixture.

Place the pan onto the grill and cook for about 1 hour.

Remove from grill and place the crunch onto a wire rack ool in the pan for about 10 minutes.

Cut into desired-sized slices and serve warm.

Bison Slider

vings: 8
king Time: 8 Minutes
redients:
- 1 pound ground buffalo meat
- 1 tablespoon minced garlic
- 1 teaspoon salt
- 1 teaspoon ground black pepper
- 2 tablespoons Worcestershire sauce

ections:
Switch on the Pit Boss grill, fill the grill hopper with ored wood pellets, power the grill on by using the control el, select 'smoke' on the temperature dial, or set the perature to 450 degrees F and let it preheat for a minimum minutes.

2. Meanwhile, take a medium bowl, place all the ingredients in it, stir until well combined, and then shape the mixture into eight patties.
3. When the grill has preheated, open the lid, place patties on the grill grate, shut the grill and smoke for 4 minutes per side until thoroughly cooked.
4. Serve patties with toasted buns and favorite toppings.

Chipotle Honey Smoked Beef Roast

Servings: 10
Cooking Time: 4 Hours And 20 Minutes
Ingredients:
- Beef roast (5-lbs., 2.3-kg.)
- The Rub Vegetable oil – 2 tablespoons
- Black pepper – 1 ½ tablespoons
- Salt – 1 ½ tablespoons
- Brown sugar – ¾ tablespoon
- Onion powder – ¾ tablespoon
- Mustard – 1 teaspoon
- Garlic powder – 1 ½ teaspoons
- Chipotle powder – 1 ½ teaspoons
- The Glaze Honey – ½ cup
- Water – 2 tablespoons
- Minced garlic – 1 ½ tablespoons

Directions:
1. Place the rub ingredients—vegetable oil, black pepper, salt, brown sugar, onion powder, mustard, garlic powder, and chipotle powder in a bowl then mix until combined.
2. Rub the beef roast with the spice mixture then set aside. Plug the wood pellet smoker and place wood pellet inside the hopper.
3. Turn the switch on. Set the "Smoke" setting and prepare the wood pellet smoker for indirect heat.
4. Wait until the smoke is ready and adjust the temperature to 275°F (135°C). Once the wood pellet smoker has reached the desired temperature, place the seasoned beef roast directly on the grate inside the wood pellet smoker and smoke for 2 hours.
5. In the meantime, combine honey, water, and minced garlic in a bowl then stir until incorporated. After 2 hours, take the beef roast out of the wood pellet smoker and place on as sheet of aluminum foil.
6. Leave the wood pellet smoker on and adjust the temperature to 300°F (149°C). Baste the beef roast with the glaze mixture then wrap it with the aluminum foil. Return the wrapped beef roast to the wood pellet smoker then smoke for another 2 hours.
7. Once the internal temperature of the smoked beef roast has reached 165°F (74°C), remove it from the wood pellet smoker.
8. Let the smoked beef roast rest for about 10 minutes then unwrap it. Transfer the smoked beef roast to a serving dish then serve. Enjoy!

Wood Pellet Grill Chicken Flatbread

Servings: 6
Cooking Time: 30 Minutes
Ingredients:
- 6 mini breads
- 1-1/2 cups divided buffalo sauce
- 4 cups cooked and cubed chicken breasts

- For drizzling: mozzarella cheese

Directions:
1. Preheat your pellet grill to 375 - 400F.
2. Place the breads on a surface, flat, then evenly spread 1/2 cup buffalo sauce on all breads.
3. Toss together chicken breasts and 1 cup buffalo sauce then top over all the breads evenly.
4. Top each with mozzarella cheese.
5. Place the breads directly on the grill but over indirect heat. Close the lid.
6. Cook for about 5-7 minutes until slightly toasty edges, cheese is melted and fully hated chicken.
7. Remove and drizzle with ranch or blue cheese.
8. Enjoy!

Twice Grilled Potatoes

Servings: 6
Cooking Time: 4 Hours
Ingredients:
- 6 russet potatoes
- 2 tbsp. olive oil
- Salt, to taste
- 8 cooked bacon slices, crumbled
- ½ C. heavy whipping cream
- 4 oz. cream cheese, softened
- 4 tbsp. butter, softened
- 4 jalapeño peppers, seeded and chopped
- 1 tsp. seasoned salt
- 2 C. Monterrey Jack cheese, grated and divided

Directions:
1. Set the temperature of Pit Boss Grill to 225 degrees F and preheat with closed lid for 15 minutes.
2. With paper towels, pat dry the washed potatoes completely.
3. Coat the potatoes with olive oil sprinkle with some salt.
4. Arrange potatoes onto the grill and cook for about 3-3½ hours.
5. Remove the potatoes from grill and cut them in half lengthwise.
6. With a large spoon carefully, scoop out the potato flesh from skins, leaving a little potato layer.
7. In a large bowl, add potato flesh and mash it slightly.
8. Add bacon, cream, cream cheese, butter, jalapeno, seasoned salt and 1 C. of Monterrey Jack cheese and gently, stir to combine.
9. Stuff the potato skins with bacon mixture and top with remaining Monterrey Jack cheese.
10. Arrange the stuffed potatoes onto a baking sheet.
11. Place the baking sheet in grill and cook for about 30 minutes.
12. Serve hot.

Italian Marinade

Servings: 1 Cup
Cooking Time:5 Minutes
Ingredients:
- 1 cup extra-virgin olive oil
- ¾ cup red wine vinegar
- Zest of 1 lemon
- ¼ cup freshly squeezed lemon juice (about 2 lemons)
- 4 cloves garlic, peeled, smashed and roughly chopped

- 1 bay leaf
- 1 tablespoon thyme leaves
- 1 tablespoon oregano leaves
- 1 tablespoon basil leaves, rolled and chopped into chiffonade
- 1 teaspoon granulated sugar
- 1 teaspoon kosher salt
- 1 teaspoon freshly cracked black pepper
- 1 teaspoon red pepper flakes, or to taste

Directions:
1. Whisk together all the ingredients in a large bowl. Refrigerate any unused marinade in an airtight container fo or 3 days.

Coconut Dipping Sauce

Servings: 4
Cooking Time: 10 Minutes
Ingredients:
- 4 tablespoons coconut milk
- 1 tablespoon curry paste
- 2 tablespoons lime juice
- 2 tsp soy sauce
- 1 oz. parsley
- 2 tablespoons olive oil

Directions:
1. In a blender place all ingredients and blend until smoo
2. Pour sauce in a bowl and serve

Barbeque Sauce

Servings: 2
Cooking Time: 15 Minutes
Ingredients:
- 1/4 cup of water
- 1/4 cup red wine vinegar
- Tbsp Worcestershire sauce
- 1 tsp Paprika
- 1 tsp Salt
- Tbsp Dried mustard
- 1 tsp black pepper
- 1 cup ketchup
- 1 cup brown sugar

Directions:
1. Pour all the ingredients into a food processor, one afte the other.
2. Process until they are evenly mixed.
3. Transfer sauce to a close lid jar. Store in the refridgera

Espresso Brisket Rub

Servings: 1/2 Cup
Cooking Time:5 Minutes
Ingredients:
- 3 tablespoons coarse kosher salt
- 2 tablespoons ground espresso coffee
- 2 tablespoons freshly ground black pepper
- 1 tablespoon garlic powder
- 1 tablespoon light brown sugar
- 1½ teaspoons dried minced onion
- 1 teaspoon ground cumin

Directions:

In a small airtight container or zip-top bag, combine the
t, espresso, black pepper, garlic powder, brown sugar,
nced onion, and cumin.

Close the container and shake to mix. Unused rub will
ep in an airtight container for months.

Steak Sauce

rvings: ½ Cup
oking Time: 25 Minutes
gredients:

Tbsp Malt vinegar
1/2 tsp Salt
1/2 tsp black pepper
Tbsp Tomato sauce
2 Tbsp brown sugar
1 tsp hot pepper sauce
2 Tbsp Worcestershire sauce
2 Tbsp Raspberry jam.
ections:

Preheat your grill for indirect cooking at 150°F
Place a saucepan over grates, add all your ingredients,
l allow to boil.
Reduce the temperature to Smoke and allow the sauce to
mer for 10 minutes or until sauce is thick.

Rosemary-garlic Lamb Seasoning

rvings: 2
oking Time:5 Minutes
gredients:

2 teaspoons dried rosemary leaves
2 teaspoons coarse kosher salt
1 teaspoon garlic powder
1 teaspoon freshly ground black pepper
½ teaspoon onion powder
½ teaspoon dried minced onion
ections:

In a small airtight container or zip-top bag, combine the
emary, salt, garlic powder, black pepper, onion powder,
l minced onion.
Close the container and shake to mix. Unused seasoning
l keep in an airtight container for months.

Banana Nut Oatmeal

rvings: 2
oking Time: 5 Minutes
gredients:

1/2 tbsp. Maple Syrup
1/4 cup Hemp Seeds
1/2 cup Steel Cut Oats
Dash of Sea Salt
1 tsp. Vanilla Extract
1/2 cup Water
1/2 tsp. Cinnamon
1 tsp. Nutmeg
1/3 cup Milk
1 Banana, medium, sliced and divided
ections:

First, keep half of the banana, salt, oats, vanilla, cinnamon,
nond milk, nutmeg, and maple syrup in the blender pitcher.

2.   After that, press the 'cook' button and then the 'high'
button.
3.   Cook for 5 minutes.
4.   Once done, divide the oatmeal among the serving bowls
and top it with the remaining sliced banana and hempseeds.

Ranch Burgers

Servings: 4
Cooking Time: 30 Minutes
Ingredients:
- 1 lb ground beef (preferably 80% lean 20% fat ground chuck)
- 1/2 yellow onion, chopped
- 1 package ranch dressing mix (1 oz)
- 1 cup cheddar cheese, shredded
- 1 egg, beaten
- 4 buns, toasted (optional)
- 3/4 cup bread crumbs
- 3/4 cup mayonnaise
- 1/4 cup relish
- 1/4 cup ketchup
- 2 tbsp Worcestershire sauce

Directions:
1.   Mix ground beef, cheese, ranch dressing mix, egg, bread
crumbs, and onion in a bowl until evenly combined.
2.   Form burger mixture into 1/4 pound circular patties.
3.   Preheat pellet grill to 350°F.
4.   Lightly oil grill grate and place burger patties on the grill.
5.   Cook burgers until they reach an internal temperature of
155°F (typically cooks for about 6 minutes per side).
6.   Remove burgers once done and let rest at room
temperature for 15 minutes.
7.   Combine sauce ingredients in a bowl and whisk well.
8.   Place burger patties on buns and top with desired
toppings, including homemade sauce.

Grilled Peaches And Cream

Servings: 8
Cooking Time: 8 Minutes
Ingredients:
- 4halved and pitted peaches
- 1tbsp vegetable oil
- 2tbsp clover honey
- 1cup cream cheese, soft with honey and nuts

Directions:
1.   Preheat your pellet grill to medium-high heat.
2.   Coat the peaches lightly with oil and place on the grill pit
side down.
3.   Grill for about 5 minutes until nice grill marks on the
surfaces.
4.   Turn over the peaches then drizzle with honey.
5.   Spread and cream cheese dollop where the pit was and
grill for additional 2-3 minutes until the filling becomes warm.
6.   Serve immediately.

Pit Boss Smoked Mac And Cheese

Servings: 8
Cooking Time: 1 Hour
Ingredients:

- 1/2 cup salted butter
- 1/3 cup flour
- 6 cups whole milk
- 1/2 tbsp salt
- 1/2 tbsp dry mustard
- A dash of Worcestershire
- White sauce
- noodles
- 1 lb small shells, cooked in saltwater
- 2 cups cheddar jack cheese
- 2 cups white cheddar, smoked
- 1 cup ritz, crushed

Directions:
1. Startup the Pit Boss and set it to smoke with the lid open. Let it run for 10 minutes then turn the grill up to 325F with the lid closed.
2. Meanwhile, melt butter in a saucepan over medium heat. Whisk in flour, reduce heat and continue whisking for 6 minutes or until it turns into light tan color.
3. Stir in milk, salt, dry mustard, and Worcestershire. increase the heat to medium and cook while stirring until the sauce has thickened.
4. Stir in white sauce, noodles, small shells, and all cheeses in 1 cup in a baking dish sprayed with cooking spray.
5. Top with ritz and the remaining cheese. Place the baking dish in the Pit Boss and bake for 30 minutes.

Cold Hot Smoked Salmon

Servings: 4
Cooking Time: 8 Hours
Ingredients:
- 5 pound of fresh sockeye (red) salmon fillets
- For trout Brine
- 4 cups of filtered water
- 1 cup of soy sauce
- ½ a cup of pickling kosher salt
- ½ a cup of brown sugar
- 2 tablespoon of garlic powder
- 2 tablespoon of onion powder
- 1 teaspoon of cayenne pepper

Directions:
1. Combine all of the ingredients listed under trout brine in two different 1-gallon bags. Store it in your fridge. Cut up the Salmon fillets into 3-4-inch pieces. Place your salmon pieces into your 1-gallon container of trout brine and let it keep in your fridge for 8 hours.
2. Rotate the Salmon and pat them dry using a kitchen towel for 8 hours
3. Configure your pellet smoker for indirect cooking. Remove your salmon pieces of from your fridge Preheat your smoker to a temperature of 180 degrees Fahrenheit
4. Once a cold smoke at 70 degrees Fahrenheit starts smoke your fillets
5. Keep smoking it until the internal temperature reaches 145 degrees Fahrenheit.
6. Remove the Salmon from your smoker and let it rest for 10 minutes

Veal Kidney On Skewer

Servings: 4
Cooking Time: 30 Minutes
Ingredients:
- Salt with ground pepper, preferably fresh
- 8 slices of bacon
- Bearnaise Sauce
- 2 veal of kidney, fat removed
- 2 Tbsp of peanuts or vegetable oil

Directions:
1. Set the grill for direct cooking at 300°F. Use hickory wo pellets to give scallions a robust taste.
2. Dice kidney to obtain about 46 pieces. Also, cut the bacc into 2-inch pieces
3. Arrange kidney and bacon on a skewer. Prepare as man shewer as possible with the materials available, then brush skewers with oil.
4. Carefully arrange the skewers on the preheated grill an let it cook for about 10 minutes. Flip, season with salt and pepper on it, then cook for another 10 minutes.
5. Serve immediately with béarnaise sauce if available.

Shepherd's Pie With Steak

Servings: 4
Cooking Time: 45 Minutes
Ingredients:
- 2 tablespoons flour
- 2 tablespoons butter
- 1 cup beef broth
- 2 tablespoons steak seasoning
- 2 cups of mixed frozen vegetables
- 2 cups steak, cooked and diced
- 1 cup cooked mashed potatoes

Directions:
1. Preheat your wood pellet grill to 350 degrees F.
2. In a pan over medium heat, add the flour and butter.
3. Cook for 1 minute, stirring.
4. Pour in the beef broth.
5. Cook for 5 to 6 minutes.
6. Stir in the steak seasoning. Set aside.
7. Add the vegetables and diced steak into the mixture.
8. Pour this mixture into a baking pan.
9. Spread the mashed potatoes on top.
10. Grill the pie for 15 minutes.

Chicken Marinade

Servings: 3
Cooking Time: 35 Minutes
Ingredients:
- halved chicken breast (bone and skin removed)
- Tbsp Spicy brown mustard
- 2/3 cup of soy sauce
- tsp Powdered garlic
- 2 Tbsp Liquid smoke flavoring
- 2/3 cup extra virgin olive oil
- 2/3 cup lemon juice
- 2 tsp Black pepper

Directions:
1. Mix all the ingredients in a large bowl.
2. Pour the chicken into the bowl and allow it to marinate for about 3-4hours in the refrigerator. Remove the chicken, then smoke, grill, or roast the chicken.

Apple Pie Grill

Servings: 4
Cooking Time: 30 Minutes
Ingredients:

¼ cup of sugar
4 apples, sliced
1 tablespoon cornstarch
1 teaspoon cinnamon, ground
1 pie crust, refrigerator, soften in according to the directions on the box
½ cup peach, preserves

Directions:

Preheat your smoker to 375 degrees F, the closed lid
Take a bowl and add cinnamon, cornstarch, apples and keep it on the side
Place piecrust in pie pan and spread preserves, place apples
Fold crust slightly
Place pan on your smoker (upside down), smoke for 30-minutes
Once done, let it rest
Serve and enjoy!

Smoked Mushrooms

Servings: 4
Cooking Time: 45 Minutes
Ingredients:

4 cups Portobello mushrooms
1 tablespoon oil
1 teaspoon onion powder
1 teaspoon granulated garlic
Salt and pepper to taste

Directions:

Add all the ingredients in a large bowl.
Mix well.
Preheat your Pit Boss wood pellet grill to 180 degrees F.
Smoke the mushrooms for 30 minutes.
Increase temperature to 200 degrees F and smoke for other 15 minutes.
Tips: You can also use other types of mushrooms for this recipe.

Pit Boss Apple Crisp

Servings: 15
Cooking Time: 1 Hour
Ingredients:

Apple
10 apples, washed, peeled and cored
1/2 cup four
1 cup dark brown sugar
1/2 tbsp cinnamon
1/2 cup butter
Crisp
3 cups oatmeal, old fashioned
1-1/2 cups flour
1-1/2 cups salted butter
1-1/2 tbsp cinnamon
Cups brown sugar

Directions:

Preheat your Pit Boss to 350F.

2. Slice the apples into cubes then toss with flour, sugar, and cinnamon
3. Spray cooking spray on a 10x12 foil grill pan, then place the apples in it. place the butter randomly on the apples.
4. In a mixing bowl, mix the crisp ingredients until well combined. Place the mixture over the apples.
5. Place the grill pan at the hottest part of the Pit Boss and cook while checking every 20 minutes.
6. Remove the pan from the Pit Boss when the edges are bubbly, the topping is golden brown and the apples are tender.
7. Let rest for 25 minutes before serving.

Alder Wood Smoked Bony Trout

Servings: 4
Cooking Time: 2 Hours
Ingredients:

- 4 fresh boned whole trout with their skin on
- For trout Brine
- 4 cups of filtered water
- 1 cup of soy sauce
- ½ a cup of pickling kosher salt
- ½ a cup of brown sugar
- 2 tablespoon of garlic powder
- 2 tablespoon of onion powder
- 1 teaspoon of cayenne pepper

Directions:

1. Combine all of the ingredients listed under trout brine in two different 1-gallon bags.
2. Store it in your fridge.
3. Place your trout in the sealable bag with trout brine and place the bag in a shallow dish.
4. Let it refrigerate for about 2 hours, making sure to rotate it after 30 minutes.
5. Remove them from your brine and pat them dry using kitchen towels.
6. Air Dry your brine trout in your fridge uncovered for about 2 hours.
7. Preheat your smoker to a temperature of 180 degrees Fahrenheit using alder pellets.
8. The pit temperature of should be 180 degrees Fahrenheit and the cold smoke should be 70 degrees Fahrenheit.
9. Cold smoke your prepared trout for 90 minutes.
10. After 90 minutes transfer the cold smoked boned trout pellets to your smoker grill are and increase the smoker temperature to 225 degrees Fahrenheit.
11. Keep cooking until the internal temperature reaches 145 degrees Fahrenheit in the thickest parts.
12. Remove the trout from the grill and let them rest for 5 minutes.
13. Serve!

Delicious Donuts On A Grill

Servings: 6
Cooking Time: 10 Minutes
Ingredients:

- 1-1/2 cups sugar, powdered
- 1/3 cup whole milk
- 1/2 teaspoon vanilla extract
- 16 ounces of biscuit dough, prepared
- Oil spray, for greasing
- 1 cup chocolate sprinkles, for sprinkling

Directions:
1. Take a medium bowl and mix sugar, milk, and vanilla extract.
2. Combine well to create a glaze.
3. Set the glaze aside for further use.
4. Place the dough onto the flat, clean surface.
5. Flat the dough with a rolling pin.
6. Use a ring mold, about an inch, and cut the hole in the center of each round dough.
7. Place the dough on a plate and refrigerate for 10 minutes.
8. Open the grill and install the grill grate inside it.
9. Close the hood.
10. Now, select the grill from the menu, and set the temperature to medium.
11. Set the time to 6 minutes.
12. Select start and begin preheating.
13. Remove the dough from the refrigerator and coat it with cooking spray from both sides.
14. When the unit beeps, the grill is preheated; place the adjustable amount of dough on the grill grate.
15. Close the hood, and cook for 3 minutes.
16. After 3 minutes, remove donuts and place the remaining dough inside.
17. Cook for 3 minutes.
18. Once all the donuts are ready, sprinkle chocolate sprinkles on top.
19. Enjoy.

Beef Tartare Burger

Servings: 4
Cooking Time: 30 Minutes
Ingredients:
- 1 Tbsp of capers
- 1 shallot, already peeled
- Salt with pepper
- 1 medium of clove garlic
- 1-1/2 pound of fatty chuck
- 2 anchovy fillets, optional
- 1 medium-cooked egg, chopped
- 2 tsp of Worcestershire sauce
- 1/2 cup of parsley, preferably freshly chopped
- 1/2 tsp of tabasco sauce
- White onion and peeled lemon slices

Directions:
1. Set the grill for direct cooking at 300°F. Use maple pellets for a strong, woody taste.
2. Pour garlic, beef, anchovies, shallot, and capers inside a food processor. Pulse until it is has a coarse texture (soother than chopped, but not by much).
3. Mix the parsley, Worcestershire sauce, salt, pepper, and tabasco in a bowl. Stir together with blended beef. Mold the mixture to form 4 patties.
4. Grill the meat for about 3-4 minutes (rare). Flip and grill until the other side is done.
5. Serve immediately with caper, onion, parsley with egg, lemon.

Smoked Ribs

Servings: 8
Cooking Time: 6 Hours
Ingredients:

- 4 baby back ribs
- 1 cup pork rub
- 1 cup barbecue sauce

Directions:
1. Preheat your grill to 180 degrees F for 15 minutes while the lid is closed.
2. Sprinkle baby back ribs with pork rub.
3. Smoke the ribs for 5 hours.
4. Brush the ribs with barbecue sauce.
5. Wrap the ribs with foil.
6. Put the ribs back to the grill.
7. Increase temperature to 350 degrees F.
8. Cook for 45 minutes to 1 hour.
9. Let rest before slicing and serving.
10. Tips: Trim excess fat from the baby back ribs before cooking.

Sandwich With Roasted Beef

Servings: 4
Cooking Time: 25 Minutes
Ingredients:
- Butter
- Barbecue sauce
- 1 pound of beef roast
- 4 hamburger buns

Directions:
1. Set the grill for direct cooking at 300°F. Use hickory pellets.
2. Roast the beef on the grill for 20 minutes or until intern temperature reads 135°F.
3. Lightly rub butter on the hamburger buns, then arrang the roasted beef between the buttered buns. You can also p the barbecue sauce well on the meat.
4. Serve immediately.

Grilled Pepper Steak With Mushroom Sauce

Servings: 4
Cooking Time: 30 Minutes
Ingredients:
- 2 cloves garlic, minced
- 1 tablespoon Worcestershire sauce
- 1/2 cup Dijon mustard
- 2 tablespoons bourbon
- 4 tenderloin steaks
- Salt and tri-color peppercorns to taste
- 1 tablespoon olive oil
- 1 onion, diced
- 1/2 cup white wine
- 1/2 cup chicken broth
- 16 oz. mushrooms, sliced
- ½ cup cream
- Salt and pepper to taste

Directions:
1. In a bowl, mix the garlic, Worcestershire sauce, Dijon mustard, and bourbon.
2. Spread the mixture on both sides of the steak and wrap with foil.
3. Marinate at room temperature for 1 hour.
4. Unwrap and season the steak with salt and peppercorn
5. Press the peppercorns into the steak.

Preheat your Pit Boss wood pellet grill to 180 degrees F 15 minutes while the lid is closed.

Grill the steaks for 30 minutes, flipping once or twice.

Make the mushroom gravy by cooking onion in olive oil in an over medium heat.

Add mushrooms.

Pour in the broth and white wine.

Simmer for 5 minutes.

Stir in the cream.

Season with salt and pepper.

Serve steaks with sauce.

Roasted Ham

Servings: 12
Cooking Time: 6 Hours
Ingredients:

2 quarts water
1/2 cup quick home meat cure
1/2 cup kosher salt
3/4 cup brown sugar
1 tablespoon pork rub
1 teaspoon whole cloves
10 lb. fresh ham
1 teaspoon whole cloves
1/4 cup pure maple syrup
2 cup apple juice

Directions:

In a large container, pour in the water and add the meat cure, salt, sugar, pork rub and whole cloves.

Mix well.

Soak the ham in the brine.

Cover and refrigerate for 1 day.

Rinse ham with water and dry with paper towels.

Score the ham with crosshatch pattern.

Insert remaining cloves into the ham.

Season ham with the pork rub.

Add ham to a roasting pan.

Smoke the ham in the Pit Boss wood pellet grill for 2 hours at 180 degrees F.

Make the glaze by mixing the maple syrup and apple juice.

Brush the ham with this mixture.

Increase heat to 300 degrees F.

Roast for 4 hours.

Tips: You can also inject the brine into the ham.

Breakfast Sausage Casserole

Servings: 6
Cooking Time: 30 Minutes
Ingredients:

1 pound ground sausage
1 tsp ground sage
¼ cup green beans (chopped)
2 tsp yellow mustard
1 tsp cayenne
8 tbsp mayonnaise
1 large onion (diced)
2 cups diced zucchini
2 cups shredded cabbage
1 ½ cup shredded cheddar cheese
Chopped fresh parsley to taste

Directions:

1. Preheat the grill to 360°F and grease a cast iron casserole dish.
2. Heat up a large skillet over medium to high heat.
3. Toss the sausage into the skillet, break it apart and cook until browned, stirring constantly.
4. Add the cabbage, zucchini, green beans, and onion and cook until the vegetables are tender, stirring frequently.
5. Pour the cooked sausage and vegetable into the casserole dish and spread it.
6. Break the eggs into a mixing bowl and add the mustard, cayenne, mayonnaise, and sage. Whish until well combined.
7. Stir in half of the cheddar cheese.
8. Pour the egg mixture over the ingredients in the casserole dish.
9. Sprinkle with the remaining shredded cheese.
10. Place the baking dish on the grill and bake for 30 minutes or until the top of the casserole turns golden brown.
11. Garnish with chopped fresh parsley.

Roasted Buffalo Wings

Servings: 6
Cooking Time: 1 Hour
Ingredients:
- 4 lb. chicken wings
- 1 tablespoon cornstarch
- Salt to taste
- Chicken rub
- 6 tablespoon butter
- 1/2 cup hot sauce
- 1/4 cup spicy mustard

Directions:
1. Preheat the Pit Boss wood pellet grill to 375 degrees F for 15 minutes while the lid is closed.
2. In a bowl, mix the cornstarch, salt and chicken rub.
3. Sprinkle the chicken with this mixture.
4. Roast the chicken for 16 minutes per side.
5. In a pot over medium heat, simmer the rest of the ingredients for 15 minutes.
6. Dip the wings in the butter mixture.
7. Cook for 10 more minutes.
8. Serving Suggestion: Serve with blue cheese dressing.
9. Tips: Pat the chicken wings dry with paper towels before seasoning.

Honey Cured Ham Ribs

Servings: 3
Cooking Time: 5 Hours 20 Minutes
Ingredients:
- 3/4 cup of honey
- 1-1/2 cup of cold water
- 1-1/2 cup of hot water
- 8 cloves
- 1 rack of spareribs
- 3/4 cup of kosher or sea salt
- 1-1/2 tsp of pink curing salt
- 3 bay leaves
- Mustard seed caviar

Directions:
1. Place the ribs on the baking sheet. Mix the hot water, honey, coarse salt, and pink curing salt until the salt and honey dissolve in the water. Allow it to cool to room temperature.

2. Add the rib to the cooled brine and transfer it to a Ziploc bag. Keep in the refrigerator for 3 days.
3. Remove the ribs from the refrigerator and place it on the baking pan.
4. Preheat the grill for 15 minutes at 250°F. Use pecan wood pellets for a spicy, nutty taste.
5. Put the ribs on the grates of the grid and smoke for about 4 hours.
6. Serve immediately with mustard seed caviar.

Smoked Pumpkin Pie

Servings: 8
Cooking Time: 50 Minutes
Ingredients:
- 1tbsp cinnamon
- 1-1/2 tbsp pumpkin pie spice
- 15oz can pumpkin
- 14oz can sweetened condensed milk
- 2beaten eggs
- 1unbaked pie shell
- Topping: whipped cream

Directions:
1. Preheat your smoker to 325F.
2. Place a baking sheet, rimmed, on the smoker upside down, or use a cake pan.
3. Combine all your ingredients in a bowl, large, except the pie shell, then pour the mixture into a pie crust.
4. Place the pie on the baking sheet and smoke for about 50-60 minutes until a knife comes out clean when inserted. Make sure the center is set.
5. Remove and cool for about 2 hours or refrigerate overnight.
6. Serve with a whipped cream dollop and enjoy it!

Empanadas

Servings: 4
Cooking Time: 20 Minutes
Ingredients:
- 3/4 cup + 1 tbsp all-purpose flour
- ½ tsp baking powder
- 1tbsp sugar
- ¼ tsp salt or to taste
- 2tbsp cold water
- 1/3 cups butter
- 1small egg (beaten)
- Filling:
- ½ small onion (chopped)
- 57 g ground beef (1/8 pound)
- 2tbsp marinara sauce
- 1small carrot peeled and diced)
- 1/8 small potato (peeled and diced) 35 grams
- 2tbsp water
- 1garlic clove (minced)
- 1tbsp olive oil
- 1tbsp raisin
- 2tbsp green peas
- ½ tsp salt or taste
- 1/2 tsp ground black pepper or to taste
- 1hard-boiled egg (sliced)

Directions:

1. Start your grill on smoke mode and leave the lid open for 5 minutes, or until fire starts.
2. Close the grill and preheat grill to 400°F with the lid closed for 15 minutes, using hickory hardwood pellets.
3. For the fillet, place a cast iron skillet on the grill and add the oil.
4. Once the oil is hot, add the onion and garlic and sauté until the onion is tender and translucent.
5. Add the ground beef and sauté until it is tender, stirring often.
6. Stir in the marinara, salt, water, and pepper.
7. Bring to a boil and reduce the heat. Cook for 30 seconds.
8. Stir in the carrot, raisin, and potatoes and cook for 3 minutes.
9. Stir in the green peas and sliced egg. Cook for additional minutes, stirring often.
10. Spray a baking dish with a non-stick spray.
11. For the dough, combine the flour, baking powder salt and sugar in a large mixing bowl. Mix until well combined.
12. Add butter and mix until it is well incorporated.
13. Add egg and mix until you form the dough.
14. Put the dough on a floured surface and knead the dough for a few minutes. Add more flour if the dough is not thick enough.
15. Roll the dough flat with a rolling pin. The flat dough should be ¼ inch thick.
16. Cut the flat dough into circles.
17. Add equal amounts of the beef mixture to the middle of each flat circular dough slice. Fold the dough slice and close the edges by pressing with your fingers or a fork.
18. Arrange the empanadas into the baking sheet in a single layer.
19. Place the baking sheet on the grill and bake for 10 minutes.
20. Remove the baking sheet from the grill and flip the empanadas.
21. Bake for another 10 minutes on the grill or until empanadas are golden brown.

Grilled Pound Cake With Fruit Dressing

Servings: 12
Cooking Time: 50 Minutes
Ingredients:
- 1buttermilk pound cake, sliced into 3/4 inch slices
- 1/8 cup butter, melted
- 1.1/2 cup whipped cream
- 1/2 cup blueberries
- 1/2 cup raspberries
- 1/2 cup strawberries, sliced

Directions:
1. Preheat pellet grill to 400°F. Turn your smoke setting to high, if applicable.
2. Brush both sides of each pound cake slice with melted butter.
3. Place directly on the grill grate and cook for 5 minutes per side. Turn 90° halfway through cooking each side of the cake for checkered grill marks.
4. You can cook a couple of minutes longer if you prefer deeper grill marks and smoky flavor.
5. Remove pound cake slices from the grill and allow it to cool on a plate.
6. Top slices with whipped cream, blueberries, raspberries and sliced strawberries as desired. Serve and enjoy!

Avocado Smoothie

vings: 2
king Time: 5 Minutes
redients:
1 cup Coconut Milk, preferably full-fat
1 cup Ice
3 cups Baby Spinach
1 Banana, frozen and quartered
1/2 cup pineapple chunks, frozen
1/2 of 1 Avocado, smooth
ections:
First, place ice, pineapple chunks, pineapple chunks, ana, avocado, baby spinach in the blender pitcher.
Now, press the 'extract' button.
Finally, transfer to a serving glass.

Peach Blueberry Cobbler

vings: 4
king Time: 1hour15 Minutes
redients:
2 cups of peaches, peeled and sliced
1 cup of fresh blueberries
1 cup of all-purpose flour
1 cup of milk
1/2 cup of melted butter, salted
2 tsp Baking powder
1-1/2 cup sugar
1/2 tsp salt
1/2 tsp vanilla extract
ections:
Set the wood pellet smoker-grill to indirect cooking at F
In a bowl, add blueberry, peaches, and ¾ cup sugar. Stir mixture until the blueberry is coated. Set aside.
In another bowl, combine the other ingredients with the aining sugar and mix well. Be careful not to over stir the ture.
Pour into the baking dish, add the blueberry-peach ture on top. Do not stir.
Transfer baking pan to the grill and cover with steel struction. Bake for 45-60 minutes, remove and allow to before serving.

Grilled Carrots

vings: 6
king Time: 20 Minutes
redients:
1 lb carrots, large
1/2 tbsp salt
6 oz butter
1/2 tbsp black pepper
Fresh thyme
ections:
Thoroughly wash the carrots and do not peel. Pat them and coat with olive oil.
Add salt to your carrots.
Meanwhile, preheat a pellet grill to 350F.

4. Now place your carrots directly on the grill or on a raised rack.
5. Close and cook for about 20 minutes.
6. While carrots cook, cook butter in a saucepan, small, over medium heat until browned. Stir constantly to avoid it from burning. Remove from heat.
7. Remove carrots from the grill onto a plate then drizzle with browned butter.
8. Add pepper and splash with thyme.
9. Serve and enjoy.

Smoked Pork Loin In Sweet-beer Marinade

Servings: 6
Cooking Time: 3 Hours
Ingredients:
- Marinade
- 1 onion finely diced
- 1/4 cup honey (preferably a darker honey)
- 1 1/2 cups of dark beer
- 4 Tbs of mustard
- 1 Tbs fresh thyme finely chopped
- Salt and pepper
- Pork 3 1/2 pounds of pork loin

Directions:
1. Combine all ingredients for the marinade in a bowl.
2. Place the pork along with marinade mixture in a container and refrigerate overnight. Remove the pork from marinade and dry on kitchen towel.
3. Prepare the grill on Smoke with the lid open until the fire is established (4 to 5 minutes).
4. The temperature must reach 250 degrees Fahrenheit and preheat, lid closed, for 10 to 15 minutes.
5. Place the pork on the grill rack and smoke until the internal temperature of the pork is at least 145-150 ℉ (medium-rare), 2-1/2 to 3 hours.
6. Remove meat from the smoker and let rest for 15 minutes before slicing.
7. Serve hot or cold.

Worcestershire Mop And Spritz

Servings: 1 Cup
Cooking Time:5 Minutes
Ingredients:
- ½ cup water
- ½ cup Worcestershire sauce
- 2 garlic cloves, sliced

Directions:
1. In a small bowl, stir together the water, Worcestershire sauce, and garlic until mixed.
2. Transfer to a spray bottle for spritzing. Refrigerate any unused spritz for up to 3 days and use for all kinds of meats.

Grilled Fruit And Cream

Servings: 4
Cooking Time: 10 Minutes
Ingredients:
- 2apricots, halved
- 1nectarine, halved
- 2peaches, halved

- ¼ cup blueberries
- ½ cup raspberries
- 2 tablespoons honey
- 1 orange, peel
- 2 cups cream
- ½ cup balsamic vinegar

Directions:
1. Preheat your smoker to 400 degrees F, lid closed
2. Grill peaches, nectarines, apricots for 4 minutes, each side
3. Place pan on the stove and turn on medium heat
4. Add 2 tablespoons honey, vinegar, orange peel
5. Simmer until medium-thick
6. Add honey and cream in a bowl and whip until it reaches a soft form
7. Place fruits on serving plate and sprinkle berries, drizzle balsamic reduction
8. Serve with cream and enjoy!

Smoked Pork Ribs With Fresh Herbs

Servings: 6
Cooking Time: 3 Hours
Ingredients:
- 1/4 cup olive oil
- 1 Tbs garlic minced
- 1 Tbs crushed fennel seeds
- 1 tsp of fresh basil leaves finely chopped
- 1 tsp fresh parsley finely chopped
- 1 tsp fresh rosemary finely chopped
- 1 tsp fresh sage finely chopped
- Salt and ground black pepper to taste
- 3 pounds pork rib roast bone-in

Directions:
1. Combine spices and mix well
2. Coat chop with mixture
3. Start the pellet grill Set temperature to 225 ℉ and preheat, lid closed, for 10 to 15 minutes. Smoke the ribs for 3 hours. Place the ribs to you preferred container and serve while it is hot

Ginger And Chili Grilled Shrimp

Servings: 6
Cooking Time: 1 Hour 15 Minutes
Ingredients:
- 1 tsp of salt, kosher
- 2 mangos, riped, peeled, and chopped
- 1 Tbsp of fresh ginger, grated
- 2 cloves of garlic, crushed
- 1-1/4 pound of jumbo shrimp, deveined and peeled.
- 2 jalapenos, chopped
- 1/2 cup of buttermilk, low-fat
- 1/2 tsp of black pepper, ground
- 1 lime, small and also cut into wedges (6)

Directions:
1. Set the grill for direct cooking at 150°F. Use hickory wood pellets for a robust taste.
2. Pour the ginger into a bowl, add buttermilk, jalapenos, garlic, pepper, and salt. Mix thoroughly.
3. Put shrimps inside the same bowl, and mix well with a wooden spoon. Allow it to marinate in the refrigerator for an hour

4. Arrange 2 mango chops, 3 shrimps on a water-soaked wooden skewer. Do this for the other 5 skewers.
5. Place shrimp skewers on the grates and grill for 10 minutes, or until the shrimps turn opaque. Serve immediate with the lime wedge

Smoked Pork Cutlets In Citrus-herb Marinade

Servings: 4
Cooking Time: 1 Hour And 45 Minutes
Ingredients:
- 4 pork cutlets
- 1 fresh orange juice
- 2 large lemons freshly squeezed
- 10 twigs of coriander chopped
- 2 Tbs of fresh parsley finely chopped
- 3 cloves of garlic minced
- 2 Tbs of olive oil
- Salt and ground black pepper

Directions:
1. Place the pork cutlets in a large container along with al remaining ingredients; toss to cover well.
2. Refrigerate at least 4 hours, or overnight. When ready, remove the pork cutlets from marinade and pat dry on kitch towel. Start pellet grill on, lid open, until the fire is established (4-5 minutes).
3. The temperature must rise up to 250 degrees Fahrenho and preheat until 15 minutes at most. Place pork cutlets on grill grate and smoke for 1 1/2 hours.

Grilled Lime Chicken

Servings: 6
Cooking Time: 45 Minutes
Ingredients:
- 2 teaspoon sugar
- 1 teaspoon chili powder
- 1 1/2 teaspoons granulated garlic
- 1 1/2 teaspoons ground cumin
- Salt and pepper to taste
- 12 chicken thighs, skin removed
- 1 1/2 tablespoons olive oil
- 1 1/2 tablespoons butter
- 4 tablespoons pineapple juice
- 4 tablespoons honey
- 1 1/2 tablespoons lime juice
- 1/4 teaspoon red pepper flakes
- 1 1/2 tablespoons hot sauce

Directions:
1. Set the Pit Boss grill to 375 degrees F.
2. Preheat it for 10 minutes.
3. In a bowl, mix the sugar, chili powder, garlic, cumin, sa and pepper.
4. Coat the chicken with the olive oil and sprinkle with th dry rub.
5. Grill the chicken for 7 minutes per side.
6. In a pan over medium heat, simmer the rest of the ingredients for 10 minutes.
7. Remove from heat and transfer to a bowl.
8. Brush the mixture on both sides of the chicken.
9. Cook for another 7 minutes per side.
10. Tips: Add more hot sauce to the glaze if you want your chicken spicier.

Quick And Easy Teriyaki Marinade

Servings: 1 Cup
Cooking Time:5 Minutes
Ingredients:

- ¼ cup water
- ¼ cup soy sauce
- ¼ cup packed light brown sugar
- ¼ cup Worcestershire sauce
- 2 garlic cloves, sliced

Directions:

In a small bowl, whisk the water, soy sauce, brown sugar, Worcestershire sauce, and garlic until combined. Refrigerate any unused marinade in an airtight container for 2 or 3 days.

Chocolate Pecan Bourbon Pie

Servings: 6
Cooking Time: 60 Minutes
Ingredients:

- 1/4 cup bourbon
- 1 cup semisweet chocolate chips
- 1 cup of dark corn syrup
- Tbsp of melted unsalted butter
- 3 large egg (beaten)
- 1 cup of pecan (chopped)
- 1 cup of brown sugar
- 1 pie shell

Directions:

Set the wood pellet smoker-grill to indirect cooking at   0F

In a bowl, combine the corn syrup, egg, butter, sugar, and bourbon. Then add the chocolate chips and mix well. Pour the filling into the pie shell.

Place the pie plates on the grid and bake for 45 minutes or until fillings turn brown.

Remove and allow to cool. Refrigerate or serve.

Spiced Nuts

Servings: 32
Cooking Time: 20 Minutes
Ingredients:

- 1teaspoon dried rosemary
- 1/8 teaspoon cayenne pepper
- 1/8 teaspoon ground black pepper
- ½ teaspoon salt or to taste
- ½ teaspoon ground cuminutes
- 1tablespoon olive oil
- 2tablespoon maple syrup
- 2/3 cup raw and unsalted cashew nuts
- 2/3 cup raw and unsalted pecans
- 2/3 cup raw and unsalted walnuts

Directions:

Start your grill on smoke mode, leaving the lid open for 5 minutes, until the fire starts.

Close the grill lid and preheat the grill to 350°F.

In a large bowl, combine all the ingredients except the dried rosemary. Mix thoroughly until the ingredients are evenly mixed, and all nuts are coated with spices.

Spread the spiced nuts on a baking sheet.

5. Place the baking sheet on the grill and roast the nuts for 20 to 25 minutes.
6. Remove the nuts from heat.
7. Sprinkle the dried rosemary on the nuts and stir to mix.
8. Leave the nuts to cool for a few minutes.
9. Serve and enjoy.

Thanksgiving Turkey Brine

Servings: 1
Cooking Time:5 Minutes
Ingredients:

- 2 gallons water
- 2 cups coarse kosher salt
- 2 cups packed light brown sugar

Directions:
1. In a clean 5-gallon bucket, stir together the water, salt, and brown sugar until the salt and sugar dissolve completely.

Coffee-chile Rub

Servings: 1 Cup
Cooking Time:5 Minutes
Ingredients:

- ¼ cup finely ground dark-roast coffee
- ¼ cup ancho chile powder
- ¼ cup dark brown sugar, tightly packed
- 2 tablespoons smoked paprika
- 2 tablespoons kosher salt
- 1 tablespoon ground cumin

Directions:
1. In a small bowl, mix all the ingredients thoroughly, massaging the mixture with your fingers to break down the dark brown sugar into fine crystals.
2. Liberally sprinkle a thin layer of the rub onto the steak, then pat it in with your fingers so it adheres.

Pellet Grill Chocolate Chip Cookies

Servings: 12
Cooking Time: 45 Minutes
Ingredients:

- 1cup salted butter, softened
- 1cup of sugar
- 1cup light brown sugar
- 2tsp vanilla extract
- 2large eggs
- 3cups all-purpose flour
- 1tsp baking soda
- 1/2 tsp baking powder
- 1tsp natural sea salt
- 2cups semi-sweet chocolate chips, or chunks

Directions:
1. Preheat pellet grill to 375°F.
2. Line a large baking sheet with parchment paper and set aside.
3. In a medium bowl, mix flour, baking soda, salt, and baking powder. Once combined, set aside.
4. In stand mixer bowl, combine butter, white sugar, and brown sugar until combined. Beat in eggs and vanilla. Beat until fluffy.
5. Mix in dry ingredients, continue to stir until combined.

6. Add chocolate chips and mix thoroughly.
7. Roll 3 tbsp of dough at a time into balls and place them on your cookie sheet. Evenly space them apart, with about 2-3 inches in between each ball.
8. Place cookie sheet directly on the grill grate and bake for 20-25 minutes, until the outside of the cookies is slightly browned.
9. Remove from grill and allow to rest for 10 minutes. Serve and enjoy!

Sweet Brown Sugar Rub

Servings: 1/4 Cup
Cooking Time:5 Minutes
Ingredients:
- 2 tablespoons light brown sugar
- 1 teaspoon coarse kosher salt
- 1 teaspoon garlic powder
- 1 teaspoon onion powder
- 1 teaspoon sweet paprika
- ½ teaspoon freshly ground black pepper
- ½ teaspoon cayenne pepper
- ½ teaspoon dried oregano leaves
- ¼ teaspoon smoked paprika

Directions:
1. In a small airtight container or zip-top bag, combine the brown sugar, salt, garlic powder, onion powder, sweet paprika, black pepper, cayenne, oregano, and smoked paprika.
2. Close the container and shake to mix. Unused rub will keep in an airtight container for months.

Garlic Butter Injectable

Servings: 2 Cups
Cooking Time:5 Minutes
Ingredients:
- 16 tablespoons (2 sticks) salted butter
- 2 tablespoons salt
- 1½ tablespoons garlic powder

Directions:
1. In a small skillet over medium heat, melt the butter.
2. Stir in the salt and garlic powder until well mixed. Use immediately.

Super-addicting Mushrooms

Servings: 4
Cooking Time: 45 Minutes
Ingredients:
- 4 C. fresh whole baby Portobello mushrooms, cleaned
- 1 tbsp. canola oil
- 1 tsp. granulated garlic
- 1 tsp. onion powder
- Salt and freshly ground black pepper, to taste

Directions:
1. Set the temperature of Pit Boss Grill to 180 degrees F and preheat with closed lid for 15 minutes, using charcoal.
2. In a bowl, add all ingredients and mix well.
3. Place the mushrooms onto the grill and cook for about 30 minutes.
4. Remove the mushrooms from grill.

5. Now, preheat the Grill to 400 degrees F and preheat with closed lid for 15 minutes.
6. Place the mushrooms onto the grill and cook for about minutes.
7. Remove the mushrooms from grill and serve warm.

Kahluá Coffee Brownies

Servings: 12
Cooking Time: 60 Minutes
Ingredients:
- 4 oz. pure chocolate, unsweetened
- 1 cup of white chocolate chip
- 1 cup of bittersweet chocolate chip
- 4 eggs
- 1/8 Tsp of salt
- Tbsp instant coffee
- 1-1/2 cup all-purpose flour
- cups of sugar
- 1 cup unsalted butter

Directions:
1. Set the wood pellet smoker-grill to indirect cooking at 350F
2. Place a small pot on the cooking grid, then add the butter and coffee. Stir until it melts completely. Remove the pot from heat and stir in the unsweetened chocolate, stir until it is smooth. Add the eggs one at a time, mix well. While still mixing add the sugar, flour, and salt. Gently fold the white chocolate and bittersweet chocolate into the mixture.
3. Pour the mixture into a baking pan and bake on the grate for 20 minutes or until a toothpick comes out clean.
4. Remove and allow to cool.

Belgian Ale-braised Brisket

Servings: 6
Cooking Time: 3 Hours
Ingredients:
- 1/4 cup Dijon mustard
- 2 bay leaves
- 1/4 cup all-purpose flour
- 1/4 cup dark brown sugar, packed
- 2 Tbsp bacon fat
- 2 medium onion, thinly sliced
- Kosher salt
- 4lb beef brisket, flat cut, untrimmed
- 1 Tbsp grated ginger
- 4 cups beef broth
- 750ml bottle Belgian style tripel ale

Directions:
1. Preheat wood pellet smoker-grill to 400°F.
2. Rub brisket in salt and leave in a reusable plastic bag for hours at room temperature.
3. In a small bowl, mix ginger, brown sugar, and ginger.
4. Remove brisket from the bag, rub mustard over brisket and place on the grill grate. Roast for 40 minutes, until the top is brown.
5. Transfer brisket to a plate and set aside.
6. Reduce the temperature of the grill to 300°F.
7. Heat bacon fat in a cast-iron Dutch oven placed on the grill. Add onions and sprinkle in the salt. Stir continuously and cook until brown, about 10 minutes.

Reduce heat and stir in flour and cook for another 4 〔mi〕nutes. Add ale, bay leaves, and stock, and then allow to 〔si〕mmer. Put in brisket and cover the lid of the Dutch oven.

Braise brisket for 4 hours with the grill cover closed.

Remove bay leaves and place brisket on a platter. Allow 〔res〕ting of brisket for 20 minutes before carving.

Serve brisket with braising liquid.

Bourbon Whiskey Sauce

〔Ser〕vings: 3
〔Coo〕king Time: 45 Minutes
〔Ing〕redients:

〔2〕 cups ketchup
1/4 cup Worcestershire sauce
3/4 cup bourbon whiskey
1/3 cup apple cider vinegar
1/2 onions, minced
1/4 cup of tomato paste
〔2〕 cloves of garlic, minced
1/2 tsp Black pepper
1/2 cup brown sugar
1/2 Tbsp Salt
Hot pepper sauce to taste
〔1〕 Tbsp Liquid smoke flavoring

〔Dir〕ections:

Preheat your grill for indirect cooking at 150°F
Place a saucepan over grates, then add the whiskey, garlic, 〔and〕 onions.
Simmer until the onion is translucent. Then add the other 〔ing〕redients and adjust the temperature to Smoke. Simmer for 〔X 〕minutes. For a smooth sauce, sieve.

Smoked Pork Cutlets With Caraway And Dill

〔Ser〕vings: 4
〔Coo〕king Time: 1 Hour And 45 Minutes
〔Ing〕redients:

4 pork cutlets
2 lemons freshly squeezed
2 Tbs fresh parsley finely chopped
1 Tbsp of ground caraway
3 Tbsp of fresh dill finely chopped
1/4 cup of olive oil
Salt and ground black pepper

〔Dir〕ections:

Place the pork cutlets in a bag along and shake to combine 〔al〕l. Refrigerate for at least 4 hours.
Remove the pork cutlets from marinade and pat dry
Start and smoke pellet grill
Temperature must be 250 degrees Fahrenheit
Arrange pork cutlets on the grill rack and smoke for about 〔1/〕2 hours. Allow cooling on room temperature before 〔ser〕ving.

Hickory Smoked Green Beans

〔Ser〕vings: 10
〔Coo〕king Time: 3 Hours
〔Ing〕redients:

6 cups fresh green beans, halved and ends cut off
2 cups chicken broth

- 1 tbsp pepper, ground
- 1/4 tbsp salt
- 2 tbsp apple cider vinegar
- 1/4 cup diced onion
- 6-8 bite-size bacon slices
- Optional: sliced almonds

Directions:
1. Add green beans to a colander then rinse thoroughly. Set aside.
2. Place chicken broth, pepper, salt, and apple cider in a pan, large. Add green beans.
3. Blanch over medium heat for about 3-4 minutes then remove from heat.
4. Transfer the mixture into an aluminum pan, disposable. Make sure all mixture goes into the pan, so do not drain them.
5. Place bacon slices over the beans and place the pan into the wood pellet smoker,
6. Smoke for about 3 hours uncovered.
7. Remove from the smoker and top with almonds slices.
8. Serve immediately.

Eastern North-carolina Bbq Sauce

Servings: 1 Cup
Cooking Time: 5 Minutes
Ingredients:
- ½ cup white vinegar
- ½ cup cider vinegar
- ½ tablespoon sugar
- ½ tablespoon crushed red pepper flakes
- ½ tablespoon Tabasco sauce
- Salt and freshly cracked black pepper to taste

Directions:
1. Whisk ingredients together in a bowl. Drizzle on barbecued meat. Covered, sauce will keep about 2 months.

Traditional English Mac N' Cheese

Servings: 12
Cooking Time: 1 Hour 20 Minutes
Ingredients:
- 2 lb. elbow macaroni
- ¾ C. butter
- ½ C. flour
- 1 tsp. dry mustard
- 1½ C. milk
- 2 lb. Velveeta cheese, cut into ½-inch cubes
- Salt and freshly ground black pepper, to taste
- 1½ C. cheddar cheese, shredded
- 2 C. plain dry breadcrumbs
- Paprika, to taste

Directions:
1. Set the temperature of Pit Boss Grill to 350 degrees F and preheat with closed lid for 15 minutes.
2. In a large pan of lightly salted boiling water, cook the macaroni for about 7-8 minutes.
3. Drain the macaroni well and transfer into a large bowl.
4. Meanwhile, in a medium pan, melt 8 tbsp. of butter over medium heat.
5. Slowly, add flour and mustard, beating continuously until smooth.
6. Cook for about 2 minutes, beating continuously.
7. Slowly, add milk, beating continuously until smooth.

8. Reduce the heat to medium-low and slowly, stir in Velveeta cheese until melted.
9. Stir in salt and black pepper and remove from heat.
10. Place cheese sauce over cooked macaroni and gently, stir to combine.
11. Place the macaroni mixture into greased casserole dish evenly and sprinkle with cheddar cheese.
12. In a small frying pan, melt remaining 4 tbsp. of butter.
13. Stir in breadcrumbs and remove from heat.
14. Place breadcrumbs mixture over cheddar cheese evenly and sprinkle with paprika lightly.
15. Arrange the casserole dish onto the grill and cook for about 45-60 minutes, rotating the pan once halfway through.
16. Serve hot.

Sweet Potato Spiced Fries

Servings: 4
Cooking Time: 30 Minutes
Ingredients:
- 1 tsp of kosher salt
- 2 Tbsp of olive oil
- 1 tsp of paprika
- 1/2 tsp of cumin, ground
- 2 pounds of sliced sweet potatoes
- 1 tsp of brown sugar, light
- 1 tsp of chili powder
- 1 tsp of garlic powder

Directions:
1. Mix the brown sugar, paprika, garlic powder, chili powder, salt, and cumin in a bowl.
2. Mix the sliced potatoes and oil in a separate bowl, then add the brown sugar mixture and toss well. Pour the coated potatoes into a roasting pan and roast until it is brown and tender. This will take about 15-20 minutes.
3. Serve as soon as possible.

Spicy Tofu Marinade

Servings: 1/2 Cup
Cooking Time:5 Minutes
Ingredients:
- ¼ cup soy sauce
- 1 tablespoon rice vinegar
- 1 teaspoon brown sugar
- 2 tablespoons mirin (sweet Japanese rice wine)
- 1 to 2 garlic cloves, to taste, minced or puréed
- 1 tablespoon minced or grated fresh ginger
- 1 teaspoon Asian chili paste or cayenne to taste
- 2 tablespoons dark sesame oil

Directions:
1. Whisk together all of the ingredients in a bowl. Use as a marinade and/or dipping sauce for pan-seared, grilled or plain tofu.

Salt-seared Calf Liver And Beacon

Servings: 2
Cooking Time: 30 Minutes
Ingredients:
- 1 (8-inch) square salt block
- Tbsp Sherry vinegar

- Tbsp Parsley, fresh and finely chopped
- 1 piece of bacon, thick and quartered
- 12 oz. Calf liver
- Salt and pepper to taste

Directions:
1. Preheat the wood pellet smoker-grill for direct cooking 350F using any pellet.
2. Place the salt block on the pellet smoker-grill and heat 10 minutes, increase the temperature to 450F (High), and h for another 10 minutes. While heating the salt block, season the liver with salt and pepper.
3. Place the bacon on the salt block and heat until crisp, m excess fat dripping from the bacon. Remove and allow to co Place the liver on the salt block and sear for 2 minutes per s
4. Transfer to a plate, add the beacon, and drizzle with vinegar. Sprinkle the parsley.

Grilled Duck Breast

Servings: 6
Cooking Time: 20 Minutes
Ingredients:
- 4 duck breasts, boneless, each about 6 ounces
- 1/4 cup game rub

Directions:
1. Switch on the Pit Boss grill, fill the grill hopper with cherry flavored wood pellets, power the grill on by using th control panel, select 'smoke' on the temperature dial, or set temperature to 450 degrees F and let it preheat for a minim of 15 minutes.
2. Meanwhile, score the skin of the duck breast in the for of the ¼-inch diamond pattern by using a sharp knife and t season with game rub until evenly coated.
3. When the grill has preheated, open the lid, place duck breasts on the grill grate skin-side down, shut the grill and smoke for 20 minutes until cooked and the internal temperature reaches 135 degrees F.
4. When done, transfer duck breasts to a cutting board, le them rest for 10 minutes, then cut into slices and then serve

Pork Fennel Burger

Servings: 4
Cooking Time: 30 Minutes
Ingredients:
- 1 fennel bulb, trimmed and cut into large chunks
- 3 to 4 garlic cloves
- 2 ½ pounds boneless pork shoulder, with some of the f cut into 1-inch cubes
- 1 tablespoon fennel seeds
- 1 teaspoon caraway seeds (optional)
- 1 teaspoon salt
- ½ teaspoon pepper, or more to taste
- Peeled orange slices to garnish (optional)
- Chopped olives to garnish (optional)
- Chopped parsley to garnish (optional)
- Chopped roasted red pepper to garnish (optional)
- Fennel slices, to garnish (optional)

Directions:
1. Put fennel and garlic into a food processor and pulse u just chopped; remove to a large bowl. Put pork fat in proces and grind until just chopped; add to bowl. Working in batch process meat with fennel seeds, caraway, if using and salt a

pper, until meat is just chopped (be careful not to over-ocess). Add to bowl and mix well. Shape mixture into 8 ties.

Supply your smoker with wood pellets and follow the nufacturer's specific start-up procedure. Preheat, with the closed, to 425°FArrange the burgers directly on one side of e grill, close the lid, and smoke for 10 minutes. Flip and oke with the lid closed for 10 to 15 minutes more, or until a at thermometer inserted in the burgers reads 160°F. Add other Gruyère slice to the burgers during the last 5 minutes smoking to melt.

Garnish with peeled orange slices, chopped olives, pped parsley, chopped roasted red pepper and fennel es, to taste.

Pit Boss Stuffed Burgers

vings: 6
king Time: 15 Minutes
gredients:
- 3 lb ground beef
- 1/2 tbsp onion powder
- 1/4 tbsp garlic powder
- 1 tbsp salt
- 1/2 tbsp pepper
- 1-1/2 cups Colby jack cheese, shredded
- Johnny's seasoning salt
- 6 slices Colby Jack cheese

ections:
Preheat your Pit Boss to 375F.
Mix beef, onion powder, garlic powder, salt, and pepper til well combined. Make 12 patties.
Place cheese on the burger patty and cover with another ty then seal the edges.
Season with salt, then place the patties on the grill. Cook patties on the grill grate for 8 minutes, flip the patties and k for additional 5 minutes.
Place a slice of cheese on each patty and grill with the lid sed to melt the cheese.
Remove the patties from the Pit Boss and let rest for 10 utes. Serve and enjoy with a toasted bun.

Maple Syrup Dipping Sauce

vings: 4
king Time: 10 Minutes
gredients:
- 2 tablespoons peanut butter
- 2 tablespoons maple syrup
- 2 tsp olive oil
- 2 tablespoon Korean black bean paste

ections:
In a blender place all ingredients and blend until smooth
Pour sauce in a bowl and serve

Braised Lamb

vings: 4
king Time: 3 Hours And 20 Minutes
gredients:
- 4 lamb shanks
- Prime rib rub

- 1 cup red wine
- 1 cup beef broth
- 2 sprigs thyme
- 2 sprigs rosemary

Directions:
1. Sprinkle all sides of lamb shanks with prime rib rub.
2. Set temperature of the wood pellet grill to high.
3. Preheat it for 15 minutes while the lid is closed.
4. Add the lamb to the grill and cook for 20 minutes.
5. Transfer the lamb to a Dutch oven.
6. Stir in the rest of the ingredients.
7. Transfer back to the grill.
8. Reduce temperature to 325 degrees F.
9. Braise the lamb for 3 hours.

Seafood On Skewers

Servings: 4
Cooking Time: 40 Minutes
Ingredients:
- 2 Tbsp of peanuts or corn oil
- 16 cubes of swordfish
- 8 sea scallops, big
- Salt and ground pepper, fresh
- 16 cubes of monkfish
- 12 jumbo shrimp
- Sauce Bearnaise

Directions:
1. Set the grill for direct cooking at 200°F. Use oak wood pellets for rich, woody taste.
2. Arrange four pieces of alternating swordfish and monkfish pieces, shrimps, and scallops on a metal skewer. Repeat this for the other three skewers. Rub oil on the skewers.
3. Place the skewers on the preheated grill, and cook for 10 minutes. Flip to the other side and season with salt and pepper. Allow the other side to cook for another 10 minutes. Serve it with béarnaise sauce.

Black Bean Dipping Sauce

Servings: 4
Cooking Time: 10 Minutes
Ingredients:
- 2 tablespoons black bean paste
- 2 tablespoons peanut butter
- 1 tablespoon maple syrup
- 2 tablespoons olive oil

Directions:
1. In a blender place all ingredients and blend until smooth
2. Pour sauce in a bowl and serve

Jerk Seasoning

Servings: ¼ Cup
Cooking Time:5 Minutes
Ingredients:
- 1 tablespoon allspice berries
- ¼ teaspoon nutmeg pieces (crack a whole nutmeg with a hammer)
- 1 teaspoon black peppercorns
- 2 teaspoons dried thyme
- 1 teaspoon cayenne, or to taste

- 1 tablespoon paprika
- 1 tablespoon sugar
- 1 tablespoon salt
- 2 teaspoons minced garlic
- 2 teaspoons minced ginger (or 2 teaspoons ground ginger)

Directions:
1. Put allspice, nutmeg, peppercorns and thyme in a spice or coffee grinder and grind to a fine powder.
2. Mix in remaining ingredients and use immediately. To use later, omit garlic and ginger and store in a tightly covered container; add garlic and ginger immediately before using.

Berry Cobbler On A Pellet Grill

Servings: 8
Cooking Time: 35 Minutes
Ingredients:
- For fruit filling
- 3cups frozen mixed berries
- 1lemon juice
- 1cup brown sugar
- 1tbsp vanilla extract
- 1bsp lemon zest, finely grated
- Apinch of salt
- Forcobbler topping
- 1-1/2 cups all-purpose flour
- 1-1/2 tbsp baking powder
- 3tbsp sugar, granulated
- 1/2 tbsp salt
- 8tbsp cold butter
- 1/2 cup sour cream
- 2tbsp raw sugar

Directions:
1. Set your pellet grill on "smoke" for about 4-5 minutes with the lid open until fire establishes, and your grill starts smoking.
2. Preheat your grill to 350 F for about 10-15 minutes with the grill lid closed.
3. Meanwhile, combine frozen mixed berries, Lemon juice, brown sugar, vanilla, lemon zest, and a pinch of salt. Transfer into a skillet and let the fruit sit and thaw.
4. Mix flour, baking powder, sugar, and salt in a bowl, medium. Cut cold butter into peas sizes using a pastry blender then add to the mixture. Stir to mix everything together.
5. Stir in sour cream until dough starts coming together.
6. Pinch small pieces of dough and place over the fruit until fully covered. Splash the top with raw sugar.
7. Now place the skillet directly on the grill grate, close the lid and cook for about 35 minutes until juices bubble, and a golden-brown dough topping.
8. Remove the skillet from the pellet grill and cool for several minutes.
9. Scoop and serve warm.

Rosemary Braised Lamb Shank

Servings:4
Cooking Time: 2 Hours 45 Minutes
Ingredients:
- 2 spring's rosemary
- 2 celery stalk
- 3 garlic clove, minced
- 2 cups red wine
- 2 carrots, diced
- 4 lamb shanks, fat trimmed
- 2 Tbsp olive oil
- 2 Tbsp chophouse steak
- 2 onion, diced

Directions:
1. Preheat wood pellet smoker-grill to 350^{0}F.
2. Brush oil over lamb shanks, arrange on grill and grill on each side until brown, about 2 minutes.
3. Transfer the shanks from grill to a heatproof baking pan, add onions, carrots, garlic, onions, rosemary springs, beef stock, red wine, and Chophouse steaks.
4. Reduce grill temperature to 325^{0}F
5. Cover baking pan with aluminum foil and place on grill.
6. Braise the shanks for 2-1/2 hours on smoker-grill, until tender.

Pit Boss beef Pot Pie

Servings: 8
Cooking Time: 60 Minutes
Ingredients:
- 1 pie crust
- Pot Pie
- 2 cups potatoes, diced
- 3 cups leftover pot roast
- 1 cup corn
- 1 cup carrots
- 1/2 cup peas
- 1/2 cup green beans
- Gravy
- 1/4 cup butter +2 tbsp
- 1/4 cup flour
- 3 cups beef broth
- 1/4 tbsp sherry
- 1/2 tbsp onion powder
- 1/8 tbsp garlic powder
- 1/4 thyme
- Egg Wash
- 1 egg yolk
- 1 tbsp water

Directions:
1. Preheat your Pit Boss to 350F.
2. Take the potatoes and drizzle with some oil then sprinkle with salt. Microwave them for 4 minutes.
3. Place the pot pie ingredients in a cast iron pan.
4. Melt butter in a nonstick skillet, then whisk in flour until there are no lumps.
5. Stir cook the mixture for 7 minutes over medium heat. Whisk in broth, sherry, onion powder, garlic powder, and thyme.
6. Pour the mixture over the meat and vegetables. Top everything with a pie crust and slits for vents.
7. Whisk together the egg wash ingredients and brush the mixture at the top of the bowl.
8. Place the pie in the Pit Boss, close the lid, and cook for 1 hour or until the internal temperature reaches 165F. Cover the pie with a foil if it gets too much dark.
9. Let rest for 10 minutes before serving.

Vegan Pesto

Servings: 4

king Time: 10 Minutes
redients:

- 1 cup cilantro leaves
- 1 cup basil leaves
- 1 cup parsley leaves
- ½ cup mint leaves
- ½ cup walnuts
- 1 tsp miso
- 1 tsp lemon juice
- ¼ cup olive oil

ections:
In a blender place all ingredients and blend until smooth
Pour sauce in a bowl and serve

Pellet Grill Apple Crisp

vings: 15
king Time: 1 Hour
redients:
Apples

- 10 large apples
- 1/2 cup flour
- 1cup sugar, dark brown
- 1/2 tbsp cinnamon
- 1/2 cup butter slices

Crisp

- 3cups oatmeal, old-fashioned
- 1-1/2 cups softened butter, salted
- 1-1/2 tbsp cinnamon
- 2cups brown sugar

ections:
Preheat your grill to 350 F.
Wash, peel, core, and dice the apples into cubes, medium-

Mix flour, dark brown sugar, and cinnamon, then toss
h your apple cubes.
Spray a baking pan, 10x13", with cooking spray then place
les inside. Top with butter slices.
Mix all crisp ingredients in a medium bowl until well
bined. Place the mixture over the apples.
Place on the grill and cook for about 1-hour checking after
ry 15-20 minutes to ensure cooking is even. Do not place it
he hottest grill part.
Remove and let sit for about 20-25 minutes
It's very warm.

Mouthwatering Cauliflower

vings: 8
king Time: 30 Minutes
redients:

- 2 large heads cauliflower head, stem removed and cut
  2-inch florets
- 3 tbsp. olive oil
- Salt and freshly ground black pepper, to taste
- ¼ C. fresh parsley, chopped finely

ections:
Set the temperature of Pit Boss Grill to 500 degrees F and
heat with closed lid for 15 minutes.
In a large bowl, add cauliflower florets, oil, salt and black
per and toss to coat well.
Divide the cauliflower florets onto 2 baking sheets and
ead in an even layer.

4. Place the baking sheets onto the grill and cook for about 20-30 minutes, stirring once after 15 minutes.
5. Remove the vegetables from grill and transfer into a large bowl.
6. Immediately, add the parsley and toss to coat well.
7. Serve immediately.

Prosciutto-wrapped Melon

Servings: 8
Cooking Time: 25 Minutes
Ingredients:

- 1ripe cantaloupe
- Salt and pepper
- 16thin slices prosciutto

Directions:
1. Start the coals or heat a gas grill for medium direct cooking. Make sure the grates are clean.
2. Cut the cantaloupe in half lengthwise and scoop out all the seeds. Cut each half into 8 wedges, then cut away the rind from each wedge. Sprinkle with salt and pepper and wrap each wedge with a slice of prosciutto, covering as much of the cantaloupe as possible.
3. Put the wedges on the grill directly over the fire. Close the lid and cook, turning once, until the prosciutto shrivels, browns, and crisps in places, 2 to 3 minutes per side. Serve hot or at room temperature.

Pit Boss Smoked Italian Meatballs

Servings: 6
Cooking Time: 1 Hour 5 Minutes;
Ingredients:

- 2 lb beef, ground
- 2 slices white bread
- 1/2 cup whole milk
- 1 tbsp salt
- 1/2 tbsp onion powder
- 1/2 tbsp minced garlic
- 2 tbsp Italian seasoning
- 1/4 tbsp black pepper

Directions:
1. In a mixing bowl, mix all the ingredients until well combined using your hands. Turn on your Pit Boss and set it to smoke then line a baking sheet with parchment paper.
2. Roll golf size meatballs using your hands .and place them on the baking dish. Place the baking dish in the Pit Boss and smoke for 35 minutes.
3. Increase the Pit Boss heat to 325F and cook for 30 more minutes or until the internal temperature reaches 160F.
4. Serve when hot

Smoked Peach Parfait

Servings: 4
Cooking Time: 35-45 Minutes
Ingredients:

- 4barely ripe peaches, halved and pitted
- 1tablespoon firmly packed brown sugar
- 1-pint vanilla ice cream
- 3tablespoons honey

Directions:

1. Preheat your smoker to 200 degrees Fahrenheit
2. Sprinkle cut peach halves with brown sugar
3. Transfer them to smoker and smoke for 33-45 minutes
4. Transfer the peach halves to dessert plates and top with vanilla ice cream
5. Drizzle honey and serve!

Avocado Salsa

Servings: 4
Cooking Time: 10 Minutes
Ingredients:
- 2 avocados
- 1 onion
- 1 jalapeno
- 2 garlic cloves
- ¼ cup red wine vinegar
- 1 tablespoon lime juice
- ¼ cup parsley leaves

Directions:
1. In a blender place all ingredients and blend until smooth
2. Pour sauce in a bowl and serve

Smoked Beef Stew

Servings: 6-8
Cooking Time: 4 Hours
Ingredients:
- 2 ½ lbs. Beef Roast, sliced into 1 -inch cubes
- 2 Potatoes for boiling, cut into pieces (peeled)
- 4 Carrots cut into pieces (peeled)
- 1 ½ tsp. Thyme, dried
- 1 - 2 Bay leaves
- 2 tsp. of Worcestershire sauce
- 1 tbsp. of Tomato paste
- 2 Garlic cloves, minced
- 1 onion sliced lengthwise
- 3 cups Beef broth, low sodium
- Optional: ½ cup of Red wine
- 2 tbsp. Oil
- Black pepper and salt
- 2 tbsp. of Flour
- 2 - 3 tbsp. Potato flakes
- For serving: Buttered noodles or Biscuits
- For Garnish: Parsley, chopped

Directions:
1. In a bag add the flour, salt, and black pepper to taste. Add the meat pieces. Toss and coat.
2. Heat the oil in a large pot until hot. Add the meat pieces. Cook until browned. Add the wine, broth and scrape the brown bits using a wooden spoon. Add thyme, bay leaves, Worcestershire, tomato paste, garlic, and onion. Cover the pot.
3. Preheat the grill to 300F with the lid closed.
4. Put pot on grate and cook 2 hours. After 2 hours add the potatoes and carrots. Cook until the veggies and meat are tender, 2 hours more.
5. If you need to thicken the gravy add 2 - 3 tbsp. Potato flakes.
6. Serve garnished with parsley.

Grilled Chili Burger

Servings: 8
Cooking Time: 20 Minutes
Ingredients:
- 1 tsp of chili powder
- 4 tsp of butter
- 2 pounds of round steak, twice-grounded
- 1 clove of garlic
- Salt and ground pepper, preferably freshly ground
- 1/4 cup of bread crumbs

Directions:
1. Set the grill for direct cooking at 300°F. Use maple pelle for a robust and woody taste.
2. Pour the meat inside a bowl and add the rest of the ingredients. Mix until well-combined. Mold the meat mixtur to form 8 patties.
3. Arrange patties on the preheated cooking grid and grill for 10 minutes before flipping and grilling the other side for another 10 minutes.
4. Serve immediately with hamburger buns.

Veggie Lover's Burgers

Servings: 6
Cooking Time: 51 Minutes
Ingredients:
- ¾ C. lentils
- 1 tbsp. ground flaxseed
- 2 tbsp. extra-virgin olive oil
- 1 onion, chopped
- 2 garlic cloves, minced
- Salt and freshly ground black pepper, to taste
- 1 C. walnuts, toasted
- ¾ C. breadcrumbs
- 1 tsp. ground cumin
- 1 tsp. paprika

Directions:
1. In a pan of boiling water, add the lentils and cook for about 15 minutes or until soft.
2. Drain the lentils completely and set aside.
3. In a small bowl, mix together the flaxseed with 4 tbsp. o water. Set aside for about 5 minutes.
4. In a medium skillet, heat the oil over medium heat and sauté the onion for about 4-6 minutes.
5. Add the garlic and a pinch of salt and pepper and sauté about 30 seconds.
6. Remove from the heat and place the onion mixture into food processor.
7. Add the ¾ of the lentils, flaxseed mixture, walnuts, breadcrumbs and spices and pulse until smooth.
8. Transfer the mixture into a bowl and gently, fold in the remaining lentils.
9. Make 6 patties from the mixture.
10. Place the patties onto a parchment paper-lined plate a refrigerate for at least 30 minutes.
11. Set the temperature of Pit Boss Grill to 425 degrees F a preheat with closed lid for 15 minutes, using charcoal.
12. Place the burgers onto the grill and cook for about 8-10 minutes flipping once halfway through.
13. Serve hot.

Breakfast Sausage

vings: 6

king Time: 9 Hours

redients:

20/22 millimeter natural sheep casings, rinsed

Warm water

2 lb. ground pork

Apple butter rub

Pinch dried marjoram

1/2 teaspoon ground cloves

1 tablespoon brown sugar

1/3 cup ice water

Pepper to taste

ections:

Soak the sheep casings in warm water for 1 hour.

In a bowl, mix all the ingredients.

Use a mixer set on low speed to combine the ingredients.

Cover and refrigerate the mixture for 15 minutes.

Insert the casings into the sausage stuffer.

Stuff the casings with the ground pork mixture.

Twist into five links.

Remove bubbles using a pricker.

Put the sausages on a baking pan.

Refrigerate for 24 hours.

Set your wood pellet grill to smoke.

Hang the sausages on hooks and put them in the smoking inet.

Set the temperature to 350 degrees F.

Smoke the sausages for 1 hour.

Increase the temperature to 425 degrees F.

Cook for another 30 minutes.

Kid-friendly Zucchini Bread

vings: 4

king Time: 50 Minutes

redients:

1 ½ cup whole wheat flour

2 eggs

1 tsp salt

1 tsp baking powder

1 tsp baking soda

½ cup maple syrup

4 tbsp butter (melted)

2 tsp cinnamon

2 tsp vanilla extract

1 ½ cups shredded zucchini

2 tbsp lemon juice

1 tsp ground nutmeg

ections:

Start your grill on smoke mode, leave the lip open for 5 nutes, or until the fire starts.

Close the lid and preheat the grill to 350°F for 15 minutes, ng apple hardwood pellets.

Wrap the shredded zucchini with a clean kitchen towel squeeze to remove excess liquid. Set aside.

In a mixing bowl, whisk together the eggs, maple syrup, ter, vanilla extract, and lemon juice.

In a large mixing bowl, mix together the flour, baking soda, ing powder, nutmeg, cinnamon, and salt.

Pour the egg mixture into the flour mixture and mix until ingredients are well combined.

Fold in the shredded zucchini.

8. Pour the batter into the prepared loaf pan and spread it to the edges of the pan.

9. Place the loaf pan directly on the grill and bake for about 50 minutes or until a toothpick inserted in the middle of the bread comes out clean.

10. Remove the loaf pan from the grill and transfer the bread to a wire rack to cool.

11. Serve and enjoy.

Barbecue Sandwich

Servings: 6

Cooking Time: 30 Minutes

Ingredients:

- 3 lb. steak
- ½ cup barbecue sauce
- 6 ciabatta rolls
- 6 slices cheddar cheese

Directions:

1. Preheat your Pit Boss wood pellet grill to 450 degrees F. for 15 minutes while the lid is closed.

2. Grill the steak for 30 minutes.

3. Let rest on a cutting board.

4. Slice thinly.

5. Coat with the barbecue sauce.

6. Stuff in ciabatta rolls with cheese.

7. Tips: You can also smoke the beef before grilling.

Smoked Irish Bacon

Servings: 7

Cooking Time: 3 Hours

Ingredients:

- 1 bay leaf
- 2/4 cup of water
- 2/3 cup of sugar
- 6 star anise, whole
- 1 cup of fresh fennel, preferably bulb and fronds
- 2 spring thyme, fresh
- 1 clove of garlic
- 2 tsp of curing salt
- 2-1/2 pound of pork loin
- 1-1/2 tsp of peppercorns, black
- 1-1/2 tsp of fennel seed

Directions:

1. In a big stockpot, mix the fennel seeds, peppercorn, star anise, and pork roast for about 3 minutes. Also, mix the sugar, water, thyme, garlic, curing salt, coarse salt, and bay leaves in a pot and, boil for 3 minutes until the salt and sugar dissolves.

2. Place the pork loin in a Ziploc bag, seal it, and put it in a roasting pan. Keep refrigerated for 4 days.

3. Preheat the grill for 15 minutes at 250°F. Use pecan wood pellets.

4. Remove the pork from the brine and place on the grates of the grill. Smoke it for 2 hours 30 minutes or until internal temperature reads 145°F.

5. Serves immediately or when it is cool.

Simple Roasted Butternut Squash

Servings: 8

Cooking Time: 25 Minutes

Ingredients:

- 1(2 pounds) butternut squash
- 2garlic cloves (minced)
- 2tablespoon extra olive virgin oil
- 1tsp paprika
- 1tsp oregano
- 1tsp thyme
- Salt and pepper to taste

Directions:

1. Start your grill on smoke mode and leave the grill open for 5 minutes, until fire Preheat the grill to 400°F.
2. Peel the butternut squash.
3. Cut the butternut squash into two (cut lengthwise).
4. Use a spoon to scoop out the seeds.
5. Cut the butternut squash into 1-inch chunks and wash t chunks with water.
6. In a big bowl, combine the butternut squash chunks and other ingredients.
7. Stir until the chunks are coated with the ingredients.
8. Spread the coated chunks on the sheet pan.
9. Place the sheet pan on the grill and bake for 25 minutes
10. Remove the baked butternut squash from heat and let i sit to cool.
11. Serve.

APPENDIX : RECIPES INDEX

Lamb Burger Spiced With Curry 92
Lamb Shanks, Smoke-braised 118
Leftover Brisket Tostadas With Beans & Cheese 25
Leftover Pulled Pork Hash With Eggs 66
Leftover Tri Tip Breakfast Sandwich 29
Lemon And Thyme Roasted With Bistro Chicken 96
Lemon Butter Mop For Seafood 127
Lemon Chicken, Broccoli & String Beans Foil Packs 18
Lemon Garlic Green Beans 90
Lemon Garlic Parmesan Chicken Wings 39
Lemon Pepper Chicken Wings 14
Lemon Smoked Salmon 77
Loaded Chicken Fries With Cheese And Bacon 49
Loaded chicken Nachos 45
Loaded Portobello Mushrooms 17
Lobster Butter 127
Low Carb Almond Flour Bread 116

M

Mango Bread 104
Mango Thai Shrimp 80
Maple Syrup Dipping Sauce 153
Margherita Pizza 15
Marinated Grilled Chicken Wings 39
Mexican Cornbread Casserole 12
Mexican Street Corn Salad 90
Mint Chocolate Chip Cookies 15
Monster Cookies 13
Monster Smoked Pork Chops 123
Mouthwatering Cauliflower 155
Mushroom With Fennel Dressed With Roasted Chicken 124
Mustard Crusted Prime Rib 26
Mutton Barbecued And Black Dip 121

N

Native Southern Cornbread 132
Nectarine And Nutella Sundae 131
New England Lobster Rolls 80
Next Level Smoked Porchetta 54
North American Pot Pie 109

O

Orange Chipotle Ribs 57

P

Pan Seared Ribeye Steak 25
Pancake Casserole 16
Pan-seared Lamb Chops 128
Pan-seared Lamb Loins With Horseradish Potato Gratin 132
Pan-seared Pork Tenderloin With Apple Mashed Potatoes 101
Pan-seared Ribeye Steak With Parsley Potatoes 113
Parmesan Crusted Smashed Potatoes 87

Peach Blueberry Cobbler 147
Peanut Butter And Jelly Chicken Wings 41
Pellet Grill Apple Crisp 155
Pellet Grill Chocolate Chip Cookies 149
Pellet Grill Funeral Potatoes 138
Pellet-grill Flatbread Pizza 99
Pepper And Onion Turkey Burger Sliders 82
Pepper Jack Bacon Burger 22
Peppercorn Grilled Pork Chops 67
Peppered Spicy Beef Jerky 37
Perfect Pulled Pork 58
Philly Cheese Steaks 31
Philly Cheesesteak Rolls With Puff Pastry 35
Pit Boss Apple Cake 99
Pit Boss Apple Crisp 143
Pit Boss Chicken Pot Pie 19
Pit Boss Marinated Chicken Kabobs 114
Pit Boss Smoked Italian Meatballs 155
Pit Boss Smoked Mac And Cheese 141
Pit Boss Smoked Sausage 135
Pit Boss Steak Kabobs 108
Pit Boss Stuffed Burgers 153
Pit Boss Stuffed Pork Tenderloin 71
Pit Boss beef Pot Pie 154
Pizza Bianca 129
Pizza Dough Roll 105
Polish Kielbasa 136
Poor Man's Burnt Ends 29
Pork And Portobello Burgers 130
Pork Belly Banh Mi 71
Pork Belly Burnt Ends 60
Pork Belly Chili Con Carne 72
Pork Butt With Sweet Chili Injection 54
Pork Carnitas 94
Pork Dry Rub 112
Pork Fennel Burger 152
Pork Rack Roasted With Romesco Sauce In Spanish-st 93
Potluck Favorite Baked Beans 135
Prime Rib Roast 33
Prosciutto-wrapped Melon 155
Pulled Chicken Corn Fritters 46
Pulled Chicken Jalapeno Sliders 46
Pulled Pork 56
Pulled Pork Carnitas 69
Pulled Pork Nachos 55
Pulled Pork Poutine 61
Pulled Pork Queso Dip By James Brown Of Grill Nation 73
Pulled Pork Sandwich With Pretzel Bun 75
Pulled Pork Stuffed Sweet Potatoes 62

Pulled Pork Taquitos 64

Quick And Easy Teriyaki Marinade 149

Ranch Burgers 141
Raspberry Chipotle Pork Kebabs 68
Raspberry Chipotle Pork Ribs 68
Raspberry Spiral Ham 63
Red Chile And Lime Shortbread Cookies 138
Red Wine Beef Stew 129
Red Wine Braised Short Ribs 131
Reverse Sear Tomahawk Chop With Peppercorn And
Thyme 29
Reverse Seared Ny Steak 37
Reverse Seared Picanha Steak 36
Reverse Seared T-bone Steak 32
Reverse-seared Tilapia 134
Rib Roast And Yorkshire Pudding With Bacon And
Rosemary Jus 119
Rib-eye Steaks With Herb Butter 26
Roast Bison Sirloin 128
Roast Chicken With Caramelized Shallots And Fingerling
Potatoes 125
Roasted Almonds 96
Roasted Buffalo Wings 145
Roasted Ham 145
Roasted Korean Short Ribs 122
Roasted Lamb 120
Roasted Mustard Steak 125
Roasted Pineapple Salsa 90
Roasted Pork With Strawberry 102
Roasted Steak 136
Roasted Tri-tip With Spanish Adobo Rub 128
Rosemary Braised Lamb Shank 154
Rosemary Cheese Bread 130
Rosemary Chicken Glazed With Balsamic With Bacon
Pearl Onions 110
Rosemary-garlic Lamb Seasoning 141
Rosemary-smoked Lamb Chops 92

Salmon Cakes And Homemade Tartar Sauce 79
Salt-seared Calf Liver And Beacon 152
Salt-seared Kobe Beef With Tarragon Shallot Butter 111
Salt-seared Prawn 94
Sandwich With Roasted Beef 144
Satisfying Veggie Casserole 108
Sausage Pepper Skewers 95
Savory Applesauce On The Grill 124
Scalloped Potatoes 90
Scalloped Potatoes With Ham, Corn & Bacon 63
Scallops Wrapped In Bacon 78

Scrambled Eggs 136
Seafaring Seafood Rub With Smoked Swordfish 137
Seafood On Skewers 153
Seared Ahi Tuna Steak 77
Seared Venison Chops With Marsala 92
Seasoned Potatoes On Smoker 135
Shepherd's Pie With Steak 142
Shrimp Scampi 79
Shrimp Tacos With Lime Crema 80
Simple Roasted Butternut Squash 157
Simplest Grilled Asparagus 106
Simply Bossin' Tortilla Chips 88
Skillet Shepherd's Pie 22
Slum Dunk Brisket 120
Smashed Cheeseburgers 36
Smoke Pork Side Ribs With Chives 111
Smoked & Braised Crispy Pork Belly 57
Smoked Apple Crepes 17
Smoked Bacon 120
Smoked Bananas Foster Bread Pudding 134
Smoked Beef Back Ribs 29
Smoked Beef Caldereta Stew 33
Smoked Beef Ribs 135
Smoked Beef Short Ribs 30
Smoked Beef Stew 156
Smoked Beef Tenderloin 111
Smoked Beer Cheese Dip 13
Smoked Bologna 102
Smoked Bone-in Pork Chops 72
Smoked Boneless Chicken Thighs With Teriyaki Glaze 52
Smoked Bourbon Pecan Pie 15
Smoked Brats 138
Smoked Bratwurst 69
Smoked Brisket 108
Smoked Brisket Chili 28
Smoked Brisket Pie 129
Smoked Brisket With Sweet Heat Rub 22
Smoked Burgers 126
Smoked Cheddar Cheese 115
Smoked Cheese Dip 94
Smoked Cherry Bbq Sauce 125
Smoked Chicken Drumsticks 48
Smoked Chicken Legs With Spicy Cola Bbq Sauce 51
Smoked Chicken Lo Mein 49
Smoked Chicken Quesadilla Ring 52
Smoked Chicken With Perfect Poultry Rub 121
Smoked Christmas Crown Roast Of Lamb 133
Smoked Chuck Roast 107
Smoked Corn On The Cob 127
Smoked Cranberry Sauce 107
Smoked Deviled Eggs 119

Smoked Dr. Pepper Ribs 67
Smoked Garlic Sauce 117
Smoked Garlic White Sauce 103
Smoked Ground Pork Burgers 66
Smoked Homemade Breakfast Sausage Links 61
Smoked Hot Paprika Pork Tenderloin 133
Smoked Irish Bacon 157
Smoked Kielbasa Dogs 36
Smoked Lasagna With Cold Smoked Mozzarella 74
Smoked Lemon Sweet Tea 12
Smoked Mac And Cheese 131
Smoked Mac And Cheese Quesadillas 68
Smoked Meatloaf 25
Smoked Mushroom Sauce 104
Smoked Mushrooms 143
Smoked Peach Parfait 155
Smoked Pheasant 111
Smoked Pork And Green Chili Tamales 73
Smoked Pork Belly 59
Smoked Pork Chops Marinated With Tarragon 105
Smoked Pork Cutlets In Citrus-herb Marinade 148
Smoked Pork Cutlets With Caraway And Dill 151
Smoked Pork Loin In Sweet-beer Marinade 147
Smoked Pork Ribs With Fresh Herbs 148
Smoked Pork Shoulder 126
Smoked Pork Tenderloin With Mexican Pineapple Sauce 103
Smoked Porterhouse Steak 104
Smoked Pot Roast 109
Smoked Potatoes 116
Smoked Pumpkin Pie 146
Smoked Queso Dip With Pulled Chicken 47
Smoked Rack Of Lamb 123
Smoked Rack Of Pork With Sweet Potato, Fennel & Mustard Gravy 64
Smoked Rib Eye With Bourbon Butter 99
Smoked Ribs 144
Smoked Salmon Dip With Grilled Artichoke And Cheese 78
Smoked Sausage & Potatoes 138
Smoked Scalloped Potatoes 91
Smoked Soy Sauce 117
Smoked Spicy Pork Medallions 103
Smoked Sriracha Sauce 130
Smoked St. Louis Style Ribs With Tequila Bbq 56
Smoked Teriyaki Tuna 115
Smoked Tomato Cream Sauce 123
Smoked Tri Tip With Java Chophouse 23
Smoked Tuna 126
Smoked Turketta (bacon Wrapped Turkey Breast) 85
Smoked Turkey 122

Smoked Turkey Legs 83
Smoked Turkey Tamale Pie 82
Smoked Up Salmon And Dungeness Crab Chowder 11
Smoked Vegetables 131
Smoking Burgers 110
Smoky Caramelized Onions On The Pellet Grill 135
Smoky Skillet Pimento Cheese Cornbread 20
Southern Fried Chicken Sliders 40
Southern Green Beans 89
Soy Dipping Sauce 110
Spatchcocked Quail With Smoked Fruit 113
Special Mac And Cheese 100
Spiced Cherry Pie 14
Spiced Nuts 149
Spicy Chopped Brisket Sandwich With Sauce And Jalapeno 30
Spicy Tofu Marinade 152
Spinach Artichoke Chicken Grilled Cheese 48
Standing Rib Roast 24
Steak Sauce 141
Strawberry Rhubarb Pie 17
Strip Steak Smoked And Seared 133
Stuffed Pork Shoulder 55
Succulent Lamb Chops 127
Summer Treat Corn 94
Super-addicting Mushrooms 150
Sweet And Sour Chicken Drumsticks 40
Sweet And Spicy Baked Beans 16
Sweet And Spicy Cinnamon Rub 127
Sweet Brown Sugar Rub 150
Sweet Heat Cajun Spatchcock Turkey 86
Sweet Potato Medley 88
Sweet Potato Spiced Fries 152
Sweet Sensation Pork Meat 120
Sweet Tooth Carving Rhubarb Crunch 139
Sweetbread Skewers With Lemon 98

T

Take And Bake Pepperoni Pizza 125
Tea Injectable 109
Texas Barbeque Rub 108
Texas Chuck Roast Chili 26
Texas Smoked Ribs 54
Texas Style Smoked Brisket 32
Texas Style Turkey 83
Texas Styled Smoked Flounder 109
Texas Twinkies 22
Texas-style Brisket Rub 112
Thai Dipping Sauce 104
Thanksgiving Smoked Turkey 15
Thanksgiving Turkey Brine 149
The Boss Burger 34

CPSIA information can be obtained
at www.ICGtesting.com
Printed in the USA
BVHW011813290721
613018BV00041B/573